THE ALGERIAN CIVIL WAR 1990-1998

The CERI Series in Comparative Politics and International Studies
Series editors: JEAN-FRANÇOIS BAYART AND CHRISTOPHE JAFFRELOT

This series consists of translations of noteworthy publications in the social sciences emanating from the foremost French research centre in international studies, the Paris-based Centre d'Etudes et de Recherches Internationales (CERI), part of Sciences Po and associated with the CNRS (Centre National de la Recherche Scientifique).

The focus of the series is the transformation of politics and society by transnational and domestic factors — globalisation, migration, and the post-bipolar balance of power on the one hand, and ethnicity and religion on the other. States are more permeable to external influence than ever before and this phenomenon is accelerating processes of social and political change the world over. In seeking to understand and interpret these transformations, this series give priority to social trends from below as much as the interventions of state and non-state actors.

Founded in 1952, CERI has forty full-time fellows drawn from different disciplines conducting research on comparative political analysis, international relations, regionalism, transnational flows, political sociology, political economy and on individual states.

Cover picture Voting in the December 1990 elections, in which the FIS was deprived of its victory. (Photo: *Africa Events*)

LUIS MARTINEZ

The Algerian
Civil War
1990-1998

WITH A PREFACE BY
JOHN P. ENTELIS

TRANSLATED FROM THE FRENCH BY
JONATHAN DERRICK

Columbia University Press
New York

in association with the
Centre d'Etudes et de Recherches Internationales, Paris

Columbia University Press
New York

First published as *La guerre civile en Algérie* by Karthala, Paris, 1998
English translation and updating © C. Hurst & Co. (Publishers) Ltd, 2000

Printed in Malaysia

Library of Congress Cataloging-in-Publication Data

Martinez, Luis, 1965–
[Guerre civile en Algérie, 1990–1998. English]
The Algerian Civil War, 1990–1998 / by Luis Martinez.
   p. cm. — (The CERI series in comparative politics and international studies)
Translation of: La guerre civile en Algérie, 1990–1998.
Includes bibliographical references and index.
ISBN 0–231–11996–8 (cloth) — ISBN 0–231–11997–6 (paper)
   1. Algeria—Politics and government—1990– 2. Islam and politics—Algeria. I. Title. II.
Series.

DT295.6 .M3713 2000
965.05'4—dc21   99–043326

C 10 9 8 7 6 5 4 3 2 1

ACKNOWLEDGEMENTS

I wish to thank the Centre d'Etudes et de Recherches Internationales of the French Fondation Nationale des Sciences Politiques, and especially its Director Jean-François Bayart who gave this project his unceasing backing and encouragement. This book is based on my doctoral thesis, supervised by Gilles Kepel, to whom I am grateful for his criticisms and his exacting standards; the thesis was in turn derived from a DEA (Diplôme d'Etudes Approfondies) dissertation for the Institut d'Etudes Politiques (IEP). It benefited from the teaching of Rémy Leveau and Jean Leca under the IEP's Analyse du Monde Arabe Contemporain (AMAC) programme. I also owe a great deal to my two 'accomplices' in the 'African Economies and Societies' seminar, Béatrice Hibou and Richard Banegas. Pierre Conesa constantly made conditions easier for my work. Madame Thieck, in memory of her son Jean-Pierre, showed determination to back me. I thank Jonathan Derrick for his translation. I have a debt of gratitude also to Rachel Bouyssou and Hélène Arnaud for the text's progress from thesis to book, and to Eric Goldstein for his comments on the translation. Lastly my thanks go to all those in Algeria who trusted me and gave me such a generous welcome.

Paris, Spring 2000   LUIS MARTINEZ

CONTENTS

vii

PREFACE

by John P. Entelis

Algeria has suffered over 100,000 deaths and thousands more wounded in one of modern history's most savage and incomprehensible civil wars touched off by the military *coup d'état* of January 1992, which put a sudden halt to the country's incipient democratic process. While the scope of the conflict has been somewhat reduced in recent years, its brutality remains undiminished as does the search for its causes. Despite scores of informed and opinionated writings that have been produced in an effort to give reason to the irrational, none has been remotely successful – not until now.

This translation of a French-language book originally published in 1998 (*La guerre civile en Algérie, 1990-1998*) by a young French-Algerian scholar writing under the pseudonym of Luis Martinez provides the best analytical interpretation of the rise and evolution of the civil war in Algeria during the 1990s. It is packed with primary data and sources gathered over several years of in-country field work, including fascinating personal accounts of participants in the struggle at the level of the masses.

Martinez writes with authority and conviction without, however, losing his scholarly objectivity. The detailed empirical analysis is contained within a broader context of social science theory; in this case, a rational calculation of choices made by self-interested parties using violence, war, and savagery to achieve clearly-defined goals – economic wealth and political power. Rejecting culturalist explanations as too simplistic, the author concentrates on actors who act deliberately to maximise their advantage. Analysis begins at the level of the individual and culminates in questions about collective actions, choices, and institutions. Within this framework, Martinez argues that there are few differences between incumbents (state élites) and insurgents (Islamist militants) in their efforts to consolidate their control over resources in a manner little different from their historical predecessors in the precolonial Ottoman beylik, the anticolonial nationalist struggle, and the postcolonial military state.

Martinez's defence of his thesis is comprehensive and compelling. Unlike others who have treated the subject, he is the first to bring together a unified theory of warlike behaviour in the context of both institutional-historical and rational choice paradigms substantiated by an impressive array of solid empirical data gathered directly from the field. Those who are uncertain whether analytic comparative political

ix

theory and single country expertise can find scholarly expression when applied to the Middle East and North Africa will be happily rewarded with the appearance of this book.

In short, this is an original and provocative study of war and violence in Algeria from the competing yet overlapping viewpoints of incumbents and insurgents. It assembles a wide range of primary and secondary sources reflecting a broad appreciation and understanding of key theoretical arguments supported by detailed empirical data. Given the enormous difficulty and danger of trying to obtain this kind of information under current conditions, Martinez's study will remain the definitive account for years to come. It will also serve as the premier scholarly interpretation of a difficult and complex subject that has perplexed and, by the depths of its brutality, outraged the international community. Yet Algeria's importance as a major actor in the international political economy and as a potential model for democratic transformation in the Arab world requires the kind of theoretical insight and empirical depth that Martinez provides.

For an English-speaking audience, a certain knowledge of the historical background and political context is required with which the books French speaking audience was doubtless already familiar. So in the following the focus is on the nature of state-society relations that provides the framework for understanding the detailed analysis of warlike behaviour presented by Martinez.

State-Society Relations in Algeria: the Dialectics of Contested Rule

Algeria's current crisis can only be understood in the context of ongoing state-society relations which themselves have been, and continue to be, affected by a combination of historical circumstances – especially the colonial era, the war of national liberation, the search for national identity and integrity, the conflict among political élites, and the efforts at state-building that ample hydrocarbon reserves seemed capable of facilitating if not substantially achieving.

The legacy of 130 years of French colonial rule and nearly eight years of bloody war, resulting in Algeria's political independence in 1962, has profoundly affected virtually every aspect of state-society relations in contemporary Algeria. The war of national liberation was itself a contested experience resulting in a superficial but pragmatic assemblage of diverse political tendencies whose sole objective was the ouster of the French occupier. The National Liberation Front (FLN) served the useful function of providing an umbrella organisation that could speak with one voice. Yet when independence was achieved Algeria was left prostrate with its economy a shambles, its society disassembled, its culture disfigured, and its political institutions virtually non-existent. How these challenges were met by the new political order and its successive leaders helps explains the nature of state-society relations today and the impact this has had on the prospects for political legitimization, democracy, and development.

Six postindependence periods can be identified in the evolution of state-society relations:

(1) 1962-5. Ahmed Ben Bella's leadership represented a period of great drift and uncertainty as inflated ideological rhetoric substituted for pragmatic solutions to pressing problems in state and society.

(2) 1965-78. Houari Boumedienne's assumption of power following his military *coup d'état* of 19 June, 1965, represented a significant shift towards political institutionalisation and away from the 'politics of personality' associated with Ben Bella's brief tenure. The flood of petrodollars made possible by the 1973 OPEC oil price increases accelerated Algeria's efforts at state-led development through a policy of 'industrialising industries' intended to project Algeria on to the regional and world stages as a model of socialist self-sufficiency and revolutionary aspirations. A kind of 'social contract' was imposed by the expansive state in which civil society would submerge its associational wants and demands for the sake of national unity and in return would be guaranteed a broad range of welfare benefits including free education, subsidised health care, housing, and key foodstuffs, among others. This 'contract' was ensconced within an ideological program of revolutionary socialism which found its political focus in the FLN but which was eventually expanded into an array of state-led institutions including national, regional, and local assemblies. The process of 'institutionalizing the revolution' (Entelis 1986) according to a formula of state-led top-down nation-building was greatly facilitated by the political unanimity of the army-led governing class, the rise of an instrumentalist technocratic elite, and the economic bonanza that increased hydrocarbon revenues made possible.

(3) 1979-88. Chadli Bendjedid's assumption to the presidency in early 1979, following the unexpected death of Boumedienne from a rare blood disease in December 1978, represented the beginning of the end of the socialist state as it had evolved in the previous decade. Several factors influenced the shift away from state-led development strategies. Principal among them was the sharp decline in oil and gas revenues as global prices for these commodities began to weaken and then collapse in the early and mid-1980s. The so-called social contract could no longer be honored as the welfare state's financial health significantly declined with mounting debts to foreign creditors forcing shifts in social spending. This became particularly acute at a time when the results of many of the previous regime's social policies began to be felt, among them an uncontrollable birthrate that created one of the world's youngest

populations, overpopulation in the cities fostering a condition of over-urbanisation but under-urbanism, inadequate and overcrowded housing, over-enrolled primary and secondary schools in which students attended classes in rotating shifts of two hours a day, expanding numbers of university graduates looking for employment in the now contracting public sector, declining health services as medical personnel looked elsewhere for more profitable financial and professional opportunities, crumbling infrastructure including inadequate water supplies to cities and towns, and the pauperisation of the countryside as years of neglect of agriculture in favor of heavy industry eventually made Algeria into one of the most food-dependent countries in the world.

These social and economic challenges forced a serious reappraisal of past socialist policies and the introduction of a kind of Algerian 'perestroika' (Entelis 1988) or economic reform program involving the gradual withdrawal of state intervention into the economy in favor of private sector participation and the encouragement of foreign investment. However, Chadli's liberalisation policies, similar to those of Gorbachev in the former Soviet Union, were too little and too late to prevent the outburst of deep social and economic discontent which found its most violent expression in the deadly nationwide riots of October 1988.

(4) 1988-91. The violent demonstrations and riots which took place in early October 1988 left hundreds dead and wounded as thousands of students, youth, unemployed street people, and others expressed their rage against the authorities by targeting in their attack all symbols of state power including FLN offices, national companies, government buildings, and such like. Neither the police nor local authorities were able to stop the rioting which affected Algiers, Oran, and other major cities and towns. When the army was finally called in, it viciously suppressed the demonstrators and, in the process, fundamentally compromised its standing among its once admiring mass public. For his part, Chadli used the occasion to push forward political reforms commensurate with the economic reforms already promoted. The main distinguishing characteristic of this phase was the formal withdrawal of the army from political power and the implementation of a democratic system of rule via a new constitution which guaranteed, among other things, a multi-party democracy including basic freedoms of association, expression, and organization.

As a consequence, civil society emerged with incredible vigor in which a multitude of associational groups were formed to give expression to the long-suppressed populist demands of feminists, Berberists, union workers, students, Islamists, journalists, farmers, and many others. The state was now clearly on the defensive as it began to retreat on many fronts although the apex of power remained in the hands of Chadli and his associates, however tentatively. Chadli believed like Gorbachev that he could contain and manage this democratic outburst, and his regime permitted the first-ever free, fair, and multiparty elections to take place in June 1990 which saw the overwhelming victory of the Islamic Salvation Front (FLS) and the humiliating defeat of the FLN, the party of the state and the army. At this point virtually all previous ideological assumptions and political arrangements which had defined state-society relations in Algeria for the preceding three decades were brought into question. For its part, the army remained cautiously in the background fearing that to do otherwise would rekindle the deep animosities among ordinary Algerians that had resulted from the army's brutal killings of its own citizens in 1988. Yet, the scope of the FIS victory and the uncertain nature of what would follow should events be allowed to take their 'natural' course, led the army to return in June 1991 as they imposed martial law following FIS-led demonstrations in May directed against the regime's effort to manipulate the forthcoming parliamentary elections. With the imprisoning of the FIS leadership, it could be said that this was the beginning of the end of Algeria's brief democratic experiment. When elections were ultimately rescheduled for December 1991 and the FIS was once again on the verge of a achieving a decisive electoral victory, the army generals staged a *coup d'état*, sacked Chadli from the presidency, and closed down the whole democratic experiment.

(5) 1992-9. The army's assumption of authority following the coup of 11 January 1992 marked the return of state power over civil society in Algeria. Once again *le pouvoir* had exhibited its enduring dominance as it recaptured the instruments of authority through direct control of the state's coercive, economic, and bureaucratic centres of power. This initial action was subsequently followed by an effort to re-institutionalise authority through a series of tightly controlled electoral exercises including a presidential election in 1995 (won by General Liamine Zeroual), an amended constitution in 1996, and parliamentary voting in 1997. This overall exercise, however, failed in its ultimate objective of re-legitimising a deeply discredited regime which was viewed as having done little to prevent the mass killings that resulted from the virtual civil war that had broken out following the coup, while doing a great deal to protect and promote the state's hydrocarbon sector from which it extracted the necessary resources to maintain its power aided by the willing collaboration of multinational oil companies.

(6) 1999 and beyond. The uncontested election of the army-supported Abdelaziz Bouteflika to the Algerian presidency in April 1999 represents the latest phase in the ongoing struggle between competing and calculating actors in state and society to maximise their advantage. Despite efforts to broker a ceasefire with the FIS's armed unit, the Islamic Salvation Army (AIS), as a prelude to a broader national reconciliation, the

most violent of the insurgents, the Armed Islamic Group (GIA) remains unbowed as it pursues its policy of armed insurrection directed simultaneously at military personnel and innocent civilians. Just as disturbing is the continued presence of the army high command within the civilian political process. There is nothing to date to give one hope that the army is the appropriate agency for the introduction of democratic reforms. As a result, one remains pessimistic about the return of civil society to the stage it had reached in the late 1980s without which, however, it seems unlikely that the violence, discontent, and broad social malaise that affects so many strata of Algerian society will be alleviated or reduced anytime soon.

ABBREVIATIONS

AIS	Armée Islamique du Salut
ALN	Armée de Libération Nationale
ANP	Armée National Populaire
APC	Assemblée Populaire Communale
DEC	Délégation Exécutive Communale
ENP	Entreprise Nationale Publique
FFS	Front des Forces Socialistes
FIDA	Front Islamique du Djihâd Armé
FIS	Front Islamique du Salut
FLN	Front de Libération Nationale
GDP	Gross domestic product
GIA	Groupement Islamique Armé
HCS	Haut Conseil de Sécurité
IEFE	Instance Exécutive du FIS à l'Etranger.
IMF	International Monetary Fund
LIDD	Ligue Islamique de la Da'awa et du Djihâd
MBC	Middle East Broadcasting Centre
MEI	Mouvement pour l'Etat Islamique
MIA	Mouvement Islamique Armé
MNA	Mouvement National Algérien
MSI	Mouvement pour la Société Islamique
MSP	Mouvement de la Société pour la Paix
MTLD	Mouvement pour le Triomphe des Libertés Démocratiques
OAS	Organisation de l'Armée Secrète
OS	Organisation Secrète
PAGS	Parti de l'Avant-Garde Socialiste
PCA	Parti Communiste Algérien
RCD	Rassemblement pour la Culture et la Démocratie
RND	Rassemblement National Démocratique
RPG	Rocket-propelled grenade
SAP	Structural Adjustment Programme
UGTA	Union Générale des Travailleurs Algériens

Currency

The exchange rate for the Algerian Dinar in December 1999 was US $1.00 = 68 d. and GB £1.00 = 110.34 d. (*Source*: MEED)

CHRONOLOGY

1962

18 March Signing of the Evian agreements.

1 July Referendum in Algeria; approval of the agreements granting independence to Algeria.

3 July Proclamation of the independence of Algeria. Arrival in Algiers of the GPRA headed by Benyoussef Ben Khedda.

9 September The ALN commanded by Houari Boumedienne enters Algiers.

20 September Election of a Constituent Assembly.

27 September Mohammed Boudiaf founds the Parti de la Révolution Socialiste.

1963

29 March Ahmed Ben Bella issues decree on Self-Management.

14 August Ferhat Abbas resigns as President of the National Assembly.

8 September Referendum on the Constitution. One-party state installed.

29 September Guerrilla force formed in Kabylia against President Ben Bella's regime, by Hocine Aït Ahmed. Formation of the Front des Forces Socialistes (FFS).

1964

17 October Aït Ahmed arrested in Kabylia.

1965

19 June Houari Boumedienne deposes Ahmed Ben Bella as President.

1967

15 December President Houari Boumedienne sacks Colonel Tahar Zbiri, Chief of Staff, in rebellion against the government, and assumes command of the army himself.

1971

24 February Nationalisation of pipelines, natural gas, and 51 per cent of the assets of French oil companies.

8 November Proclamation of Ordinance and Charter on the Agrarian Revolution.

1976

27 June Referendum on the National Charter.

1978

27 December Death of Houari Boumedienne.

1979

7 February Colonel Chadli Bendjedid is appointed President of the Republic.

1980

20 April Riots at Tizi Ouzou.

1982

20 November Violent incidents between Islamist and progressive students at the Ben Aknoun university halls of residence

1984

16 November Islamist demonstration at Kouba during the funeral of Sheikh Soltani.
9 June Adoption of the Family Code, restricting women's rights.

1986

16 January Adoption of the new National Charter by referendum.
8-12 November Riots at Constantine and Sétif.

1987

24 June Following the arrest and attendant death of Moustapha Bouyali, 'Emir' of the MIA, 202 Islamists appeared before the Médéa security court.

1988

4-10 October Riots in Algiers.
3 November Referendum on constitutional amendment; multi-party system installed.
22 December Re-election of Chadli Bendjedid as President.

1989

14 September Legalisation of the FIS.
15 December Return of Hocine Aït Ahmed from exile.

1990

12 June FIS victory in the municipal elections.

1991

17 January Start of the Gulf War.
5 June State of Siege. Sid' Ahmed Ghozali appointed Prime Minister.
15 June Abassi Madani calls for a general strike.
30 June Abassi Madani and Ali Benhadj arrested.
26 December The FIS wins the first round of the parliamentary elections.

1992

11 January Chadli Bendjedid announces his resignation.
14 January Haut Conseil d'Etat set up by the Haut Conseil de Sécurité.
16 January Return of Mohammed Boudiaf after 28 years of exile; he becomes Chairman of the HCE.
9 February State of Emergency declared for 12 months
4 March FIS dissolved by the Algiers Administrative Court.
11 April Dissolution of 485 People's Assemblies (Assemblées Populaires) at Commune and Wilaya level with FIS majorities; Délégations Exécutives Communales (DEC) appointed in their place.
22 April Conseil Consultatif National (CCN) installed; Redha Malek elected its Chairman.
29 June Assassination of Mohammed Boudiaf at Annaba.
1 July Ali Kafi, secretary-general of the Anciens Moudjahidin organisation, appointed Chairman of the HCE.
8 July Sid' Ahmed Ghozali replaced by Belaïd Abdesselam as Prime Minister.
15 July Abassi Madani and Ali Benhadj sentenced to 12 years' imprisonment by the Blida military tribunal.
26 August Bomb explosion at Algiers airport (11 dead and 128 injured).

26 September Formation of a special section responsible for coordination of anti-terrorist action, under General Mohamed Lamari.

30 September Decree-Law on the 'struggle against terrorism and subversion', setting the age of criminal responsibility for offences related to terrorism at 16 instead of 18.

30 November Curfew instituted in the Wilayas of Algiers, Blida, Boumerdès, Tipasa, Bouira, Médéa and Aïn Defla.

22 December All places of worship made subject to official approval.

1993

7 February Extension of the State of Emergency.

27 March Diplomatic relations severed with Iran and Sudan.

29 May Extension of the curfew in force since 5 December 1992 to the regions of Chlef, M'Sila and Djelfa.

10 June Abdelhak Layada, 'Emir' of the GIA, arrested in Morocco.

July Appointment of Liamine Zéroual as Minister of Defence.

21 August Redha Malek, the Foreign Minister, is appointed Prime Minister.

17 September Formation of a FIS overseas executive (IEFE), headed by Rabah Kébir.

1994

31 January Liamine Zéroual appointed by the HCE as head of state.

24 February Release of two senior officials of the former FIS, Ali Djeddi and Abdelkader Boukhamkham.

26 February Death of Djafaar el Afghani, 'Emir' of the GIA.

11 April Appointment of Mokdad Sifi as Prime Minister.

1 June Rescheduling of the foreign debt ($26 billion).

13 September Abassi Madani and Ali Benhadj transferred to house arrest, and their three fellow-prisoners N. Chigara, K. Guemmazi and A. Omar freed.

31 October Liamine Zéroual announces a presidential election before the end of 1995.

21 November Opening in Rome of a 'Colloquium on Algeria' under the auspices of the Community of Sant'Egidio, attended by the main opposition parties.

24 December Passengers on an Air France Airbus taken hostage at Algiers airport by an Islamist commando group.

26 December Storming of the Air France Airbus at Marseilles airport by France's Groupement d'Intervention de la Gendarmerie Nationale (GIGN), the four hijackers being killed.

27 December Murder of four White Fathers at Tizi Ouzou.

1995

13 January Draft 'National Contract' for a solution to the crisis published in Rome by the main opposition groups meeting in Rome.

26 January Announcement of a forthcoming presidential election by the President's office.

14 February Beginning of the 'dialogue' with political parties, on the subject of the presidential election.

4 April Four 'exclusion zones' set up around the oil fields.

11 July Imam Sahraoui, one of the founders of the FIS, murdered in Paris.

28 August The signatories of the 'National Contract' call for a boycott of the presidential election.

16 November Election of Liamine Zéroual as President of the Republic.

31 December End of Mokdad Sifi's government; Ahmed Ouyahia appointed prime minister.

1996

18 January Boualem Benhamouda replaces Abdelhamid Mehri at the head of the FLN.

26 January MSI-Hamas enters the new government.

18 February The partial curfew imposed since December 1992 is lifted.

13 March Algeria attends the anti-terrorist summit at Sharm el Sheikh in Egypt.

27 March Kidnapping of seven monks, the GIA claiming responsibility. They are found dead on 30 May.

5 May President Liamine Zéroual announces that parliamentary and municipal elections will be held before the end of the year.

28 November Referendum on revision of the Constitution.

1997

28 May The IEFE headed by Rabah Kébir publishes its 'strategy for resolving the crisis in Algeria'.

5 June The RND, with 155 seats, officially wins the parliamentary elections. The MSP wins 69 seats, the FLN 64, En Nahda 34, the FFS 19, the RCD 19.

10 July Mediterranean Forum in Algiers.

15 July Conditional release of Abassi Madani.

28-29 August Massacres of villagers at Raïs (100-300 victims).

1 September Abassi Madani freed, but later returned to house arrest, following an 'appeal to halt the bloodshed'.

5 September Massacre at Béni Messous in the Algiers hills: at least 120 people killed.

21 September The AIS calls for a truce.

23 October The RND officially wins the municipal elections, with 55 per cent of seats.

27 October Opposition demonstration in Algiers to denounce 'massive fraud'.

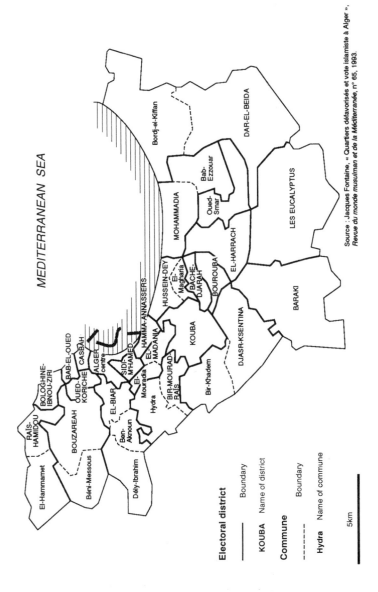

MEDITERRANEAN SEA

Bordj-el-Kiffan

DAR-EL-BEIDA

Bab-Ezzouar

Oued-Smar

MOHAMMADIA

LES EUCALYPTUS

HUSSEIN-DEY

El-Maghania

BACHE-DJARAH

EL-HARRACH

BOUROUBA

HAMMA-ANNASSERS

ALGER centre

CASBAH

BAB-EL-OUED

OUED-KORICHE

BOLOGHINE-IBNOU-ZIRI

RAIS-HAMIDOU

El-Mouradia

SIDI-M'HAMED

EL-MADANIA

Hydra

BIR-MOURAD-RAIS

KOUBA

BARAKI

Bir-Khadem

DJASR-KSENTINA

EL-BIAR

Ben-Aknoun

BOUZAREAH

El-Hammamet

Béni-Messous

Dély-Ibrahim

Electoral district

—— Boundary

KOUBA Name of district

Commune

----- Boundary

Hydra Name of commune

5km

Source : Jacques Fontaine, « Quartiers défavorisés et vote islamiste à Alger »,
Revue du monde musulman et de la Méditerranée, n° 65, 1993.

GREATER ALGIERS

xxi

1

INTRODUCTION

On 15 April 1999 Abdelaziz Bouteflika was elected President of Algeria. During his election campaign he promised to reconcile Algerians in order to 'put an end to the bloodletting'. Indeed Algeria has been sunk in civil war since the army interrupted the electoral process in January 1992, following the victory of the Front Islamique du Salut (FIS) in the parliamentary elections of December 1991. The massacres of civilians during the summer of 1997 in small places in the Mitidja focused the world community's attention for the first time on the secret tragedy going on in Algeria since the outbreak of the conflict between the Islamists and the military regime. 'How did things reach this pass?', G. Grandguillaume asked, and answered: 'One explanation is now present in all minds: it is Islamism that has led Algeria into the state of decay in which we see it today.'[1] From that viewpoint Islamism seems to be the product of two factors: the economic and social crisis and the failure of the imported state. This book is an analysis of the origins and development of the civil war. To help understand it, we need to explain that a certain number of received ideas on the collapse of the Algerian state do not stand up to analysis. Very few factors made it possible for anyone to imagine how the Algerian state would drift into civil war; the arguments used to explain it have been based on factors present since independence (poverty, corruption, authoritarianism etc.).

This book demonstrates that the political crisis arising from the interruption of the elections in January 1992 produced a dynamic of violence whose roots are to be sought in a war-oriented *imaginaire*[*] in which violence is a form of accumulation of wealth and prestige. Briefly, the civil war destroyed political machinery that ensured social control, and thus opened new ways for social progress through violence.

After the riots of October 1988 in Algiers, President Chadli Bendjedid organised a referendum on a Constitution which opened the way to multiparty politics in Algeria. In municipal elections in June 1989 the FIS won control of more than half the town halls and became the main political force. The Islamist party's ambition was to set up an Islamic state in Algeria; its programme worried a section of society and the military leaders who were afraid of becoming expiatory victims of an Islamic regime based

---

[1] G. Grandguillaume, 'Comment a-t-on pu en arriver là?' *Esprit*, January 1995, p. 12.

[*] There is no adequate equivalent in English of the French noun *imaginaire*, which roughly means 'world view' or *'Weltanschauung'*. It is left in French in this translation.

on righteousness. So when the FIS won the first round of the parliamentary elections in December 1991, the army halted the process, deposed President Chadli Bendjedid and banned the FIS, in the name of 'safeguarding democracy'. Those events set off an armed confrontation.

The rise of Algerian Islamism is to be explained, according to one received idea, by the growth in social inequality during the 1980s. It is suggested, briefly, that the Islamists are a fruit of the failure of the Socialist development model followed by the Houari Boumedienne regime (1965-78). Before developing our own hypotheses on the origins of the civil war, we would like to emphasise the weakness of that explanation.

The myth of the 'Black Decade' (1979-91): the economic and social 'crisis'

One of the factors supposed to account both for the success of Islamist mobilisation in 1990 and 1991 and for the civil war is an increase in social inequality under the presidency of Chadli Bendjedid (1979-92). This, it is suggested, was a contrast to the period of 'development' and 'progress' characterising the regime of Houari Boumedienne (1965-78) – or, indeed, it destroyed the legacy of the Boumedienne regime.

Marc Cote has written: 'The big growth period corresponds strikingly with the regime of H. Boumedienne. It continued under the regime of C. Bendjedid until about 1986...at the end of the 1970s, the country was one vast construction site. Everywhere roads, factories and schools were being built. Unemployment figures were going down, the standard of living was improving, diets now included meat every day. GDP per inhabitant was twice as much as in Morocco or Tunisia.' After that growth phase, from 1965 to 1986, came a phase of regression: 'GDP per inhabitant, which had grown by 4.2 per cent per year, fell to 0.7 per cent annual growth between 1980 and 1992.'[2] Thus a period of growth and hope was followed by a period of frustration inherent in the growth in social inequality. Cote goes on: 'This worsening of social disparities in a country that had seen itself as an egalitarian one for fifteen years lay behind the riots in 1986 in Constantine, in 1988 in Algiers and other cities, and the rise of the Islamist movement.'[3] According to this view the civil war resulted from the failure of economic development, leading to social and political protest. Such an explanation recalls in some ways the theory of J.C. Davies, that 'revolution is most likely to take place when a prolonged period of rising expectations and rising gratification is followed by a short period of reversal during which the gap between expectations quickly widens until it becomes intolerable.'[4]

[2] M. Cote, *L'Algérie*, Paris: Masson, 1996, p. 120.

[3] Ibid., p. 123.

[4] J.C. Davies, 'The J-Curve of Rising and Declining Satisfactions as a Cause of Some

But does the explanation based on the failure of economic and social development stand up to historical analysis? In short, did the presidency of Chadli Bendjedid, marked by the emergence of Islamist movements on the political scene, really see an increase in inequality? The historian André Nouschi comments: 'Sociologically speaking, at the time of Boumedienne's death there were several groups in Algeria: in the cities and in the countryside, out of eight million people able to work, scarcely 2,300,000 had an occupation or a job. Housebound women accounted for three million in all while the jobless numbered one and a half million...Above that huge mass there was the sub-middle class with its big rural land owners, its salaried workers, its small traders and craftsmen, subordinate apparatchiks, etc., in all 600,000 to 800,000 people.'[5] This observation of a profoundly inegalitarian society at the end of Houari Boumedienne's presidency is shared by R. Escalier who notes that in 1977 the population of the cities of Algeria consisted of '83 per cent of the deprived classes (including 20.3 per cent marginal people and 62 per cent poor and half-poor), 11 per cent of the "middle classes" and 6 per cent of the "upper classes".'[6] These figures show how illusory is the vision of the 1970s as a period of 'progress' and 'development'.

So, under Boumedienne, despite a regular rate of growth,[7] profound inequality persisted. This challenges the idea of the Chadli Bendjedid decade as the period of creation of inequality *par excellence*. In fact many of the criticisms of corruption, growing inequality, etc. during the 1980s were already present during the 1960s. 'On the social side', wrote G. Chaliand and J. Minces at the very beginning of the 1970s, 'a sharpening of inequality was noticed. This was reflected in the strengthening and enrichment of some urban classes, especially the administrative bourgeoisie (civilian and military), which derived its power and privileges from sharing in state power, and the non-state bourgeoisie (trading, industrial and business), often linked to leading circles of the army and the administration. At the other extreme of the social scale the great mass of the population, consisting of landless peasants, poor peasants and the urban sub-proletariat, saw its standard of living stagnate or deteriorate and become dependent on money remitted by emigrant workers in Europe.'[8]

Great Revolution and a Contained Rebellion' in H.D. Graham and T.R. Gurr (eds.), *Violence in America*, Washington, DC: US Government Printing Office, 1969, p. 415.

[5] A. Nouschi, *L'Algérie amère, 1914-1994*, Paris: Ed. de la MSH, 1996, p. 267.

[6] Quoted in Nouschi, op. cit., p. 303.

[7] On the economy during this period see M. Ecrement, *Indépendance politique et libération économique. Un quart de siècle de développement de l'Algérie, 1965-1985*, Grenoble: PUG, 1986.

[8] G. Chaliand and J. Minces, *l'Algérie indépendante. Bilan d'une révolution nationale*, Paris: Maspéro, 1972, p. 153.

Corruption, unemployment and poverty were present in the Algeria of the 1960s and 1970s. They were not a feature of Chadli Bendjedid's presidency alone. The theory of a sudden halt to a development phase, after the fall in oil prices in 1986, to explain the emergence of Islamist contestation is not confirmed. So is the explanation to be found in changes linked to the country's demographic structure? Did the persistence of social inequality in independent Algeria, whose population reached 28 million in 1990 compared with 11 million in 1962,[9] perhaps become unendurable to the new generations? Philippe Fargues states that demography alone is not an incitement to violence: 'Demography is rather a contributor to violence than a determining cause of it, the relationship does not seem to have been demonstrated either generally or in any particular case.'[10] The demographic crisis, like the economic crisis, was thus no more than a favourable opportunity for contestation against the Algerian government.

While economic and social inequality does not create violence, those two variables are not unconnected. The correlation between the permanence of acute inequality and the development of violence can be illustrated by the 'tunnel effect' analysed by Hirschman. Jean Luca suggests that 'relative frustration' could explain the Islamist mobilisation. 'Imagine two trains travelling in the same direction, coming to a halt on parallel tracks in a tunnel; if the passengers in the train that is not (yet) moving see the other start moving in the right direction, they will expect that something is happening and that their own situation too will change for the better...That is in a sense what happened in Algeria after the colonialist "tribe" left the scene, in that progress by those were already benefiting by independence gave others the feeling that their train too would move. But the Algerian experience reveals the need for other conditions: that some movement must be seen in the second train also; that the first does not pick up excessive speed; and lastly and most important, that once on the move, the second train does not stop or slow down, and takes on an increasing number of "passengers" in the economic and administrative compartments'. He added: 'One cannot imagine a people agreeing to leave under the second scenario in reverse, except if the train is under mortar bombardment, that is, if the state and its army turn against society...'[11] Such a theory makes it possible to consider the civil war not as the breakdown of the political system but as an economic

[9] D. Sari, 'l'indispensable maîtrise de la croissance démographique en Algérie', *Maghreb-Machrek*, no. 129, 1990.

[10] Ph. Fargues, 'Violence politique et démographie en Egypte', *Dossiers du CEDEJ*, Cairo, 1994, p. 223. See also 'Explosion démographique ou rupture sociale?' in G. Salamé (ed.), *Démocraties sans démocrates*, Paris: Fayard, 1994, pp. 163-97.

[11] J. Leca, 'Etat et société en Algérie' in Basma Kodmani-Darwish (ed.), *Maghreb. Les années de transition*, Paris: Masson, 1990, pp. 37 and 48.

and political resource: in that case the political crisis started by the interruption of the electoral process in January 1992 can seem like an alibi for the army turning 'against society'. Such an approach allows us to put the cultural explanations of the collapse of the Algerian state in perspective; it recalls that violence is a political instrument which the army, better than any other protagonist, is able to exploit.

Besides the political and economic factors that can help explain the civil war, there is the historical factor. The civil war, it is suggested, shows that the Algerian state's historical foundations are artificial, because only the French colonial presence (1830-1962) provided Algeria with a political order that did not exist before. From this point of view, the inability of the Algerian state to 'imitate' European states, and hence its drift towards civil war, are seen as a historical regression.

The failure of the 'imitation state'

To account for the failure of the 'imitation state',[12] the historian André Nouschi turns to precolonial political structures: 'Algeria was split up into several *beyliks* more or less independent of the *dey* of Algiers (who changed in accordance with the mood of the soldiers). This means that the Algerian state, imitating foreign ones and taken over by the FLN, has no roots.'[13] The civil war, according to this view, is due not to the impossibility of creating a state but to local incapacity to produce a political sphere of activity. Such a conclusion recalls in some ways the harsh analysis by the historian E.F. Gautier: 'There lies the problem which has dominated all the history of the Maghreb, and which is found at every page. In the history of our European nations, the central idea is always the same: through what stages the state, the nation have been constituted. In the Maghreb, in contrast, the central idea is a different one: through what chain of particular fiascos the total fiasco has been affirmed.'[14]

The collapse of the 'FLN-state', it is therefore suggested, is explained by the inability of the FLN to create ideal sorts of conditions for a modern state – to overcome what President Houari Boumedienne called in one of his speeches 'the archaic idea of the beylicate in people's minds; use of cunning to rob the state seems to have become the rule, as if the

---

[12] On the theme of transplants of the state, see the debate between Bertrand Badie, *l'Etat importé*, Paris, Fayard, 1992, and Jean-François Bayart, 'L'historicité de l'Etat importé', *Les Cahiers du CERI*, no. 15, 1996. On its application to the Maghreb see Michel Camau, 'Politique dans le passé, politique aujourd'hui au Maghreb', in J.-F. Bayart (ed.), *La Greffe de l'Etat*, Paris: Karthala, 1996, pp. 63-96.

[13] A. Nouschi, op. cit., p. 331.

[14] E.-F. Gautier, *L'islamisation de l'Afrique du Nord. Les siècles obscurs du Maghreb*, Paris, 1927, quoted in L. Valensi, *Le Maghreb avant la prise d'Alger*, Paris: Flammarion, 1969, p. 115.

state was a foreign state.'[15] Against the theory of the failure of the 'imitation state' one should mention, following the works of Charles Tilly, the role of violence and war in state formation: 'War makes State', he wrote.[16] In the same way, and on the same lines, Karen Barkey has shown how, under the Ottoman Empire in the sixteenth century, consolidation of banditry favoured a process of state centralisation,[17] and how continued contestation of the state was accompanied by the 'construction' of it. The distinction made by John Lonsdale and Bruce Berman between 'state-building' and 'state-formation' makes it possible for us to cope with that paradox; 'state-building' is defined as 'a conscious effort at creating an apparatus of control', and 'state-formation' as 'an historical process...of conflicts, negotiations and compromises between diverse groups...'[18]

On the basis of that distinction the Algerian civil war can be analysed as a situation-related phenomenon in which actors compete for control of the state. This means that the civil war has not been accompanied by a collapse of the state; military, administrative and educational institutions continue to operate, more or less. The national territory of Algeria that emerged from the Ottoman Empire and was given institutional form under colonial rule (1832-1954)[19] is not challenged by any of the warring parties, even the most radical.[20]

Comprehensive explanations predicated on the nature of the state or on poverty do not suffice to account for either the emergence or the consolidation of the civil war. The war must thus be understood in its entirety. Islamist contestation in Algeria has, as J.-C. Vatin's analysis has shown, favoured the 'construction' of the state: 'Whatever the circumstances were, [Islamic] resistance was never able to turn into the majority, and

---

[15] *Révolution africaine*, 28 Sept-4 Oct. 1977.

[16] C. Tilly, 'War Making and State Making as Organized Crime' in P.B. Evans, D. Rueschmeyer and T. Skocpol (eds), *Bringing the State Back in*, Cambridge University Press, 1984, p. 170.

[17] Karen Barkey, *Bandits and Bureaucrats, The Ottoman Route to State Centralization*, Ithaca, NY: Cornell University Press, 1994, 282 pp

[18] J. Lonsdale and B. Berman, *Unhappy Valley: Conflict in Kenya and Africa*, London: James Currey, 1992, Book T, p. 5; for a discussion of these concepts, see B. Hibou, *L'Afrique estelle protectionniste?* Paris: Karthala, 1996, p. 93, and J. F. Bayart, 'L'historicité de l'Etat importé'.

[19] C.A. Julien has written: 'The influence of the Turks, accustomed by their relations with Europeans to political ideas unknown to the Maghrebian dynasties, had important consequences for the establishment of the Barbary States. By bringing in the idea of precise borders instead of borderlands which had satisfied everyone before their time, they were the main creators of the distinction which operated in the sixteenth century between Algeria and Tunisia (whose names date only from the July monarchy) and Morocco', *Histoire de l'Afrique du Nord. Des origines à 1830*, Paris: Payot, 1994 edition, p. 644; on this theme of the emergence of the state see M. Camau, 'Politique dans le passé, politique aujourd'hui au Maghreb' in J.-F. Bayart (ed.), *La greffe de l'Etat*, pp. 63-96.

[20] Chapter 9 analyses the declarations and ideology of the Islamist guerrillas.

the Turkish, colonial and national states always succeeded in restraining or destroying them or even taking them over. In this confrontation over a century and a half, it is the state which seems to have triumphed.'[21] Cultural explanations of the collapse of the state leave out the part played by violence and conflict in state 'formation' and hence in the behaviour of actors involved. So this work seeks, on the basis of analysis of the warring parties' strategies, to take account of the functioning mechanisms of the civil war. For that purpose it derives inspiration from Yvon Le Bot's approach; in his view, while the combination of 'social and political blocs' and the 'economic crisis' created conditions favourable for Guatemala's slide into war, it is necessary, in order to 'take account of this phenomenon...to analyse the actors' behaviour, their strategies and their objectives, and above all the breaches, the gaps and the hiatuses between strategies, reality and *imaginaire*.'[22] That approach, according to the author, makes it possible to understand why certain Amerindian societies slipped into war and why some other societies were spared it.

Such an approach can explain why on the one hand Algeria descended into war after the halt to the elections followed by the dissolution of the FIS in 1992, while on the other hand Tunisia did not do so after the government's refusal to recognise the MTI (Mouvement de la Tendance Islamique) as a political party under the name of Parti de la Renaissance (En Nahda), which prevented that party from contesting the parliamentary elections of April 1989;[23] and Syria did not do so either, after the repression directed against the Muslim Brotherhood in 1982. Explanations on the basis of the economic crisis or the failure of the 'imitation state' cannot take account of the diversity of actors' strategies. The central hypothesis of this work is that a war-oriented *imaginaire* is common to the warring parties in Algeria and contributes towards making violence a method of accumulation of wealth and prestige.

Our hypothesis: a war-oriented imaginaire

To judge from analysis of the terminology used by the two camps, one would suppose that the civil war was like a religious war between enemies with unreconcilable sets of values. One would think that the determination to set up an Islamic state, governed by the principles of the *shari'a*, was opposed by a military regime that sees Islam only as

[21] J.-C. Vatin, 'Puissance d'Etat et résistance islamique en Algérie. Approche mécanique, XIX-XXe siècles' in *Islam et Politique au Maghreb*, Paris: Ed. du CNRS, 1981, p. 267.

[22] Y. Le Bot, *Violence de la modernité en Amérique latine*, Paris: Karthala, 1994, p.191.

[23] See G. Krämer, 'L'intégration des intégristes: une étude comparative de l'Egypte, de la Jordanie et de la Tunisie' in G. Salamé (ed.), *Démocraties sans démocrates*, p. 301. See also C. Jolly, 'Du MTI à la Nahda', *Les Cahiers de l'Orient*, 2nd quarter 1995, pp. 11-40.

the official state religion. The Islamists in the guerrilla campaign regularly denounce such a regime as 'impious' and its leaders as 'apostates'; in reply the regime denounces the guerrilla fighters as 'heretics' influenced by foreign ideologies.[24] Considering this sort of denunciation, it is tempting to see the civil war as one of the numerous discords (*fitna*) which have punctuated the history of the 'Muslim states' since the 'Great Discord',[25] or even as the resurgence of a movement like the Kharijites.[26] From this viewpoint the war against the government is seen as arising from the question of the latter's legitimacy, and the struggle for the institution of the *shari'a* is seen as one reappearing identically and chronically in 'Muslim societies'. Bernard Lewis writes, 'The principle of war against the apostate...opened up the possibility of legitimate, even obligatory, war against an enemy at home, which in modern times has been developed into a doctrine of insurgency and revolutionary war as a religious duty and a form of *jihad*. This too has its roots deep in the Islamic past.'[27]

According to this view the violence of the Islamist fighters is supposed to be justified by reference to a 'Islamic *imaginaire*' which incorporates all situations of civil war and violence in the states of the Arab and Muslim world. Mohamed Arkoun writes, 'It is right to speak of an *imaginaire* again here, because since the experience at Medina, the ardent longing for the City of Virtue, wholly conceived and guided according to the precepts already applied by the Prophet, was strengthened in the course of continual disappointments in the real history of the Caliphate and then the Sultanate. The opposition between the call for an ideal government, in conformity with the demands of the *shari'a*, and the regimes that were imposed by force everywhere has a new topicality in our modern age. The Islamist movements derive their strength and efficiency from an *imaginaire* fuelled for centuries by appeals to legitimacy and the constant refusal of leaders to apply "lawful policy" (*siyâsa shar'iyya*).'[28] So, it is suggested, Islamist mobilisation has succeeded, in Algeria for example, because its agents have been able to adapt to modern times an *imaginaire* that can arouse fervour in varying ways according to varying political and social contexts: 'Charismatic leaders, Mahdis, spiritual heads of

---

[24] In one his speeches Prime Minister Mokdad Sifi exclaimed: 'You, the young members of the security services, are the living symbol of the Algeria which has the will to win and will win – which will defeat *bida'a* [heresy] and *fitna* [disorder], will defeat ignorance, will defeat conspiracies.' *El Moudhajid*, 11 Jan.1995. Chapter 3 of Part II studies 'Islamism' in the army's expressions of its outlook.

[25] See H. Djaït, *La grande discorde: religion et politique dans l'Islam des origines*, Paris: Gallimard, 1989, 421 pp.

[26] M. Chekroun, 'Islamisme, messianisme et utopie au Maghreb', *Archives de sciences sociales des religions*, 1991, no. 75, pp. 127-52.

[27] B. Lewis, *The Political Language of Islam*, University of Chicago Press, 1988, p. 90.

[28] M. Arkoun, *L'Islam, morale et politique*, Paris: Desclée de Brouwer, 1986, p. 121.

brotherhoods, saints, *marabouts*, and more recently Imams have found motivation in the Model', says Mohamed Arkoun.[29] From this aspect opposed ideas of the state are seen as the cause of the Algerian civil war. The violence committed by the parties is explained by tension fomented by the authorities' refusal to apply the *shari'a* and the Islamist fighters' 'duty' to take up arms in the name of Islam.

However, the idea that an Islamic *imaginaire* explains the motives and references of the Islamist movements comes up against the historically defined character of 'Muslim societies',[30] as Arkoun admits: 'From the viewpoint of political anthropology, a new variable needs to be introduced to understand correctly the relationships between Islam and the state: namely the traditional solidarities (*asabiyya*) existing prior to the "Islamic" slogans and still active in the process of conquest and exercise of all power. The elementary structures of blood relationship, strategies of alliance among families, clans and tribes, and ambitions to control the state apparatus have always counted for more than "Islamic" slogans which merely cover with a more or less thick sacred veil archaic forces and mechanisms, still recurrent, of conquest of power.'[31] Thus the Algerian civil war cannot be understood on the basis of the 'Islamic *imaginaire*', especially since, as J.-F. Bayart emphasises, 'there would then be a big risk of seeing in that *imaginaire* virtues that have just been denied for culture, and conferring on it the capacity to be the main determinant of political behaviour. In fact the concept of an *imaginaire*, understood in this way, is only a pedantic revival of the notion of culture. In reality, in any given society, we only encounter processes in an *imaginaire* that give rise to more or less strong, more or less widely shared and more or less stable figures.'[32]

It is rather through analysis of a war-oriented *imaginaire* or world view that the present situation in Algeria seems comprehensible to us. That *imaginaire* is made up of historical figures which, through the use of violence, have enhanced their symbolic and material resources. An *imaginaire*, J.-F. Bayart writes, 'has to be operational if one wants it to survive, to reassure, to entice, and that depends, at least in part, on its relationship with given material facts.'[33] Our theory is that war is a method of accumulating wealth and prestige and is, for that reason, constantly being readapted by the participants in the conflict. 'Violence', Omar Carlier has written, 'is built up and then built up again in imagination and in deed...in

---

[29] Ibid., p. 57.

[30] For a criticism of this expression, and a proposal for the alternative of 'Maghrebian society', see J.N. Ferrié, 'Vers une anthropologie déconstructiviste des sociétés musulmanes du Maghreb', *Peuples méditerranéens*, 54-55, Jan.-Feb. 1991, pp. 229-46.

[31] M. Arkoun, op. cit., p. 55.

[32] J.-F. Bayart, 'L'historicité de l'Etat importé', p. 36.

[33] J.-F. Bayart, *L'illusion identitaire*, Paris: Fayard, 1996, p. 185.

the interaction of an ancestral culture confronted with colonial history and national history reinvented in the tradition of *jihad*.'[34] But, contrary to what the concept of war culture might suggest, the theory of a war-oriented *imaginaire* does not mean that it is exclusive. Rather, one should examine the concrete historical situation of the civil war to look for a combination of elements inherited from history, according to processes which we cannot analyse exhaustively, but which seem to have proved their symbolic and material efficacy in the eyes of contemporary actors in the conflict.

Corsairs, Caïds, 'Colonels' and 'Emirs': the changing face of the political bandit

From this definition of the *imaginaire*, our hypothesis is that the 'Emirs' – the leaders of the armed Islamic groups – prefer to define themselves, more or less consciously, in relation to certain historical models that have achieved distinction, at different periods, by social advancement through war. Denounced as outlaws, bandits or 'mercenaries' in their own time, the corsair under the Ottoman Empire, the Caïd (native official) under colonial rule and the 'Colonel' (officer of the ALN) during the liberation war followed paths that led to political leadership positions. This process of advancement placed violence in a 'cultural code of social improvement'[35] where the dominant figure is that of the political bandit.

In the current civil war, belief in the virtues of violence as a means of accumulating resources and prestige is characteristic of individuals following strategies of social advancement. It influences both the military and the Islamist guerrillas, both prominent people[36] and criminals – people very varied in their political allegiances, but closely akin in their life histories and their following of common role models. Each of them claims a monopoly of power, whether local, regional or national. Each uses violence and cunning to achieve that aim. However, there is no question of seeing war as the only means of accumulation, or assuming that every individual has a strategy for accumulating wealth. Contrary to the idea of a war culture, we do not assume *a priori* that Algerian society is imbued with a certain form of political behaviour, that is, warlike behaviour.[37] In speaking of a war-oriented *imaginaire* we suggest rather a code in which the use

---

[34] O. Carlier, *Entre Nation et Jihad,* Paris: Presses de Sciences Po, 1995, p. 393.

[35] An expression borrowed from J.-F. Bayart, S. Ellis and B. Hibou, *La criminalisation de l'Etat en Afrique*, Brussels: Complexe, 1997, p. 58.

[36] M. Harbi writes: 'As a form of personal power, linked to rural society, the prominent people – whatever their origin, whether they are from distinguished families or parvenus – are men whose influence is supported by three pillars: an inheritance, a system of personal relations and violence': *1954, la guerre commence en Algérie*, Brussels: Complexe, 1984, p. 131.

[37] This idea of a warlike Algerian 'personality' is found in sayings such as 'The Algerian is a warrior, the Moroccan a shepherd and the Tunisian a woman'.

of violence is respected as a means of social advancement. Just as the need for political activity is not something universally shared ('It seems that political apathy is a natural state among the majority of men; it would be no less unreasonable to expect every individual to show keen interest in politics than to ask him to feel passionately about chamber music'[38]), belief in violence as a means of accumulation of wealth, prestige and power is not a common trait of all Algerians.

Our theory is that this belief is derived from the individual life histories of men of power throughout history. The conviction shared by the warring parties, of violence being a means of accumulation, is in our view a powerful factor for perpetuation of war, as the history of war and violence in contemporary Algeria is well able to illustrate. As Carlier notes, 'Here more than elsewhere, history is violence and extends over a long period. Algeria has had two wars of independence, exceptionally drawn out and destructive, at the beginning and end of colonial domination, and two world wars in which it was heavily involved. It has also known a range of forms of war: "revolutionary" war in the liberation from colonial rule, and two "civil wars", if one includes the bloodstained conflict between the FLN and MNA and the present terror.'[39] These wars have nonetheless been experienced and perceived in different ways by different individuals; the collective memory of this contemporary history of violence retains more than the most tragic effects and events.

In fact the colonial and liberation wars precipitated social and political changes which, in particular, allowed the emergence of leading families and reinforced the virtues of violence. For in spite of the human dramas that they produced, they became instruments of social advancement for some groups in society that sought to draw advantage from them. This strengthens the conviction that war is the crucible of equality, that it offers an opportunity to improve one's social situation: a belief shared by all the protagonists in the civil war, as we show in this work, for they remain influenced by the life stories of the 'big names' of modern Algeria. The colonisation of Algeria during the nineteenth century and the liberation war were both periods of opportunity for the most deprived, and of emergence of new elites.

In 1850, according to statistics recorded by the historian Jacques Frémeaux, 'out of 160 Caïds (66 per cent of the total number, which was then 241), 40 per cent were considered of aristocratic origin ("the warrior nobility of the *djouads*"). Out of 241 names there were only three individuals of humble origin.'[40] The long phase of military colonisation later

---

[38] According to H. MacClosky, quoted in P. Birbaum and F. Chazel, *Textes de sociologie politique*, Paris: A. Colin, 1971, vol. 2, p. 223.

[39] O. Carlier, op. cit., p. 399.

[40] J. Frémeaux, *Les bureaux arabes de l'Algérie de la Conquête*, Paris: Denoël, 1993, p. 89.

offered opportunities for Algerian social groups of humble origin (Chaouch Turks and Kouloughlis)[41] to join the colonial forces and establish themselves as new local elites. Thanks to colonial rule they experienced real social advancement, to the detriment of the local 'warrior nobility',[42] and supplanted the latter in appointments as Caïds. 'French officers', wrote Colette Establet, 'always hesitated between two sorts of appointment: entrusting the post of Caïd to an outsider (Chaouch or Kouloughli) or to a man of the tribe. With the triumph of the Chaouchs in the twentieth century, it was the first solution that prevailed.'[43]

The war of colonial occupation produced new economic relationships, it redistributed wealth. By joining the colonial forces the new Caïds, of humble origin, obtained the best chances of acquiring wealth and prestige, which took the form of heritable property. Colette Establet argued: 'Why be a Caïd? The Caïd hoped for promotion...he hoped to pass power on to his children', emphasising that power was shown by acquisition of land, symbols of power. 'No official text mentions the existence of land given to Caïds as a privilege of office. It was by the accident of conflicts among Caïds that the existence of such land was belatedly revealed to us.'[44] In collective memory the colonisation of Algeria is a cruel experience of war, but it also appears like a time when new elites emerged, weakening the power and prestige of the 'warrior aristocracy'. Mostefa Lacheraf unhesitatingly described the new leading families as 'mercenary and dynastic feudal lordships'.[45]

Those families, although denounced by the nationalists during the war of liberation, served in their turn as models for the guerrillas, soldiers of the Armée de Libération Nationale. As Mohamed Harbi noted, 'Beyond the clash of individual interests and passions, beyond their manoeuvres and plots, the leaders of the FLN all had in common their total participation in the war of independence and their patriotism. But should that stop us from seeing at the same time that inside these victims of and rebels against colonialism masters were slumbering, whose model was not the official, nor the settler, but the Caïd and the leading rural citizen, symbols of power that had its roots in national tradition?'[46] Like the Chaouchs and

---

[41] The Kouloughlis were children of Turks and native women, whom the Janissaries, according to R. Mantran, 'strove with perseverance to exclude from power'. See R. Mantram (ed.), *Histoire de l'Empire ottoman*, Paris: Fayard, 1989, p. 354.

[42] On the decline of the 'warrior nobility' in Algeria see A. Berque, 'Esquisse d'une histoire de la seigneurie algérienne', *Les Annales*, April-June 1951, pp. 277-9; see also the review by F. Braudel of that article, 'Faillite de l'aristocratie indigène en Algérie (1830-1900)', in *Autour de la Méditerranée*, Paris: De Fallois, 1996, pp. 151-4.

[43] Colette Establet, *Etre Caïd dans l'Algérie coloniale*, Paris: Ed. du CNRS, 1991, p. 46.

[44] Ibid., p. 254.

[45] Mostefa Lacheraf, *L'Algérie, nation et société*, Paris: Maspéro, 1965, p. 24.

[46] M. Harbi, *Le FLN, mirage et réalité*, Paris: Jeune Afrique, 1980, p. 8.

Kouloughlis, promoted to be new elites (Caïds) at the expense of the 'warrior nobility' through the war of conquest, the 'Colonels' took advantage of the war of liberation to put an end to the domination of the Caïds. Ferhat Abbas, one of the political victims of the 'Colonels' in 1962, did not hesitate to write, 'Abane[47] detected in the Colonels a tendency to exercise absolute power: "They are all murderers", he told me."They are carrying out a political policy contrary to the unity of the nation." '[48]

Caïds and 'Colonels' lived as feared and respected local community leaders, whose wealth and prestige were derived directly from their participation in the wars of conquest and liberation. Those historical experiences were not without effect on the current civil war; each of the two sides draws some of its motivation from them. The social advancement of the Chaouchs and Kouloughlis in the nineteenth century and that of the 'Colonels' in the twentieth showed them that violence is a particularly good way of accumulating wealth. The war-oriented *imaginaire* is strengthened by success stories of individuals starting from humble backgrounds. So, we suggest, the 'Emirs' (leaders of armed groups) of the Islamist guerrillas follow in a line of continuity from those historical figures.The emergence of the 'Emirs' in the civil war of the 1990s, far from constituting a breach with the past or even a revolution in Algeria, forms part of the image of war as the special way of getting access to wealth and prestige.

Such a belief cannot be attributed solely to the processes of colonisation and decolonisation.[49] Certainly those historical periods emphasised the element of aggressiveness in the 'emotional economy' analysed by Norbert Elias.[50] However, the belief in the practice of violence as a way to improve one's social position was already present in Ottoman Algeria. The Algerian historian Mahfoud Kaddache emphasises that, under the Regency of Algiers in the sixteenth century, posts of provincial governor (*Beylerbey*) were very often given to former corsairs: 'Most of the *Beylerbey* and *Khelifa* were *Raïs*, men of war who owed their appointments to their courage and their feats of arms.'[51] It was through piracy in the Mediterranean that corsairs accumulated the resources needed to acquire governorships, for the

[47] Ramdane Abane was considered as the theoretician of the Revolution (1954-62) and the brains behind the Soummam Congress which, in 1956, sought to strengthen the armed struggle and give it a national direction. The congress laid down the primacy of political over military power and internal over external forces. On 27 December 1957 Ramdane Abane was murdered in Morocco by 'his own people'. See Khalfa Mamerie, *Abane Ramdane*, Paris: L'Harmattan, 1988.

[48] F. Abbas, *Autopsie d'une guerre*, Paris, Garnier, 1980, p. 211.

[49] Alexis de Tocqueville said on the subject of the colonisation of Algeria, 'We have made Muslim society more destitute, more disordered, more ignorant and more barbarous than it was before knowing us', *De la colonie en Algérie*, Brussels: Complexe, 1988, p. 16.

[50] N. Elias, *La civilisation des moeurs*, Paris: Calmann-Lévy, 1973, chapter 'Les modifications de l'agressivité', pp. 279-97.

[51] M. Kaddache, *L'Algérie durant la période ottomane*, Paris: OPU, 1992, p. 49.

rise of Algiers was due to piracy. Braudel wrote of 'Algiers' fortune' in the sixteenth century: 'With Leghorn, Smyrna and Marseilles, it was one of the young powers of the sea...piracy, a major industry, gave coherence to the city, made it united in defence and exploitation of the sea and the hinterland... There followed rapid, abnormal growth for the city, with changes in its appearance and its social realities.'[52] Like the war of colonial occupation and the war of liberation, piracy produced new economic and political ties. It favoured the emergence of new elites, often coming from humble social backgrounds and varied geographical origins.[53] The figures of the Raïs, the Caïd and the 'Colonel' are role models on which values are based. Their life histories showed that the practise of violence and cunning is capable of elevating people to positions of honour. And if the historic mosques of Algiers[54] are due to the pious munificence of the corsairs, do the mosques of independent Algeria not owe their construction to the generosity of the 'rebels' of the liberation war, promoted to be 'Colonels'?

The maquis as the school of power

'When colonisation triumphed, France had no more need of warriors, the aristocracy of the sword in the East [*djouad*],' J.-C. Vatin has written.[55] Honour and prestige were acquired through joining the colonial forces; the Caïds, those 'new local petty lords', replaced the 'aristocracy of the sword'. The prestige of the warrior's occupation did not however disappear, for the structures of Algerian society 'resisted': 'Algerian society did not break up immediately. It even maintained its own network beneath the network of European institutions, and its own game beneath the game of Western criteria and references. Traditional social and mental structures thus continued to survive.'[56] The issue here is not emphasising the permanence of 'traditional' structures, but rather showing how 'tradition' (the experience of the maquis) has been subjected to permanent reinvention by Caïds, 'Colonels' and then 'Emirs'.

The experience of the maquis was one that produced an identity, that of the Moudjahid: in the war of liberation as in the current civil war, recognition of the status of guerrilla came through exile from the city to the countryside. Besides proving the genuineness of the fighter's faith by calling

---

[52] F. Braudel, *La Méditerranée et le monde méditerranéen à l'époque de Philippe II*, Paris: A. Colin, 1990 edn, vol. II, p. 636.

[53] Godfrey Fisher, *Barbary Legend: War, Trade and Piracy in North Africa (1415-1830)*, Oxford University Press, 1957.

[54] The Ali Bitchin mosque in Algiers, dating from 1622, 'was built by a Venetian renegade who was none other than Admiral Piccini'. See M. Gaïd, *L'Algérie sous les Turcs*, Algiers Mimouni, 1991, p. 233.

[55] J.-C. Vatin, *L'Algérie politique, histoire et société*, Paris: Presses de la FNSP, 1983, p. 151.

[56] Ibid., p. 148.

on him to break with his environment, the maquis carried out a process of selection among candidates for prosecuting the war. By giving prime importance to warlike values (courage, endurance, foresight and cunning), it turned the social hierarchy upside down, favouring newcomers without educational qualifications over the 'educated' and 'holders of qualifications' favoured before; thus the maquis became the preferred arena for political brigands.

While the experience of the maquis during the liberation war was a school of power for the leading citizens of independent Algeria, the maquis still remains, in the current military leaders' outlook, an instrument of social advancement. General Khaled Nezzar has written:

> While in better times there were innumerable candidacies for ministerial posts and other public offices, especially at the level of municipalities, during the *bourrasque* [the present civil war], only the most sincerely devoted men agreed to be considered. Their commitment is all the more praiseworthy in that it was given in awareness of the dangers involved, by people also warned of the lack of consideration which, alas, had often been shown to their predecessors. For some – and it is greatly to their honour – accepting an official post in these circumstances was 'taking to the maquis a second time'.[57]

Civil war as an economic and political choice?

The existence of a war-oriented *imaginaire* influencing behaviour in Algeria does not mean that one can speak of a warlike society. It is convenient to see in the current civil war traces of the 'warlike fanaticism' recorded by the Arab Bureaux in the colonial era[58] or the indication of the presence of a 'death-dealing' ideology in Islamism.[59] The choice of war, made both by some senior military officers and by Islamist militants, is in response to a purpose in mind and fits into a particular context. Certainly the dynamics of war and the practise of violence cannot be understood solely on the basis of rational behaviour by those involved, as Jean Leca has stressed.[60] One can adopt the theory of Geffray, who notes in his study of the civil war in

---

[57] Interview with General K. Nezzar, *El Watan*, 15 May 1996.

[58] At the beginning of the colonial era in Algeria, writes J.-C. Vatin, the Arab Bureaux were 'only a minor organ for translation attached to the chief of staff of the occupation forces. It developed into executive agencies multiplied in the military territories and their distant descendants, the S.A.S., *Sections Administratives Spécialisées*.' P. Lucas and J.-C. Vatin, *L'Algérie des anthropologues*, Paris: F. Maspéro, 1982, p. 115.

[59] F. Khosrokhavar writes, 'The death-dealing aspect is the consequence of the disintegration of the old world at a time when the new one is not yet visible in its intrinsic potential...The failure of the Shi'a utopia leads to a form of religiosity where the incomplete individual emerging from modernisation is tempted by the prospect of his own annihilation': *L'islamisme et la mort*, Paris: L'Harmattan, 1995, p. 27.

[60] J. Leca, 'The phenomenon of political violence', *Les Dossiers du CEDEJ*, Cairo, 1994, pp. 17-42.

Mozambique that war can be waged with 'joy'. He writes: 'It was with joy that young people recruited then as *m'jiba* went off to fight,' and asks: 'How can one interpret this murderous joy and creativity?' In the Mozambican civil war, as in the Algerian, 'murderous creativity'[61] or a 'desire for dissidence' are factors that help to explain a good deal of behaviour.

However, it has to be recognised that the choice of civil war made by the military leadership in January 1992 was also a political response to an unfavourable situation. War, seen as a destructive phenomenon, dramatic in human terms and economically unproductive, can turn out to be a profitable activity: 'War', says Jean-François Bayart, can thus in theory be subjected to 'capital accounting'.[62] Besides being an 'instrument of policy' according to Clausewitz,[63] it remains an activity with an 'economic orientation' according to Max Weber's definition.[64] By its dynamics it is capable of modifying both political behaviour and economic relations. André Nouschi recalls that the Algerian war of 1954-62, despite the human dramas, was a period of intense economic activity: 'From the statistics one can tell that the war and investment made possible a spectacular development of the building and public works sector: until 1960 Algeria was one vast construction site, first and above all in the cities. Major projects were carried out in Algiers, Oran, Tlemcen, Sidi-bel-Abbès and Constantine. The metallurgical industry made it possible to supply metal casings and tubing of all sizes for the oil industry, and copper wiring for electricity. The needs of the army (500,000 men) explain the expansion of food industries, while an influx of Europeans and Muslim Algerians set off a boom in construction, a fever of property speculation and a rise in building prices.'[65]

In many respects the Algerian civil war presents a paradox: an intense degree of violence has been accompanied by job creation (especially in the profession of arms), by considerable investment in the oil and gas sector, and by lively activity in the commercial sector, based on the creation of import-export companies. This in a way recalls Braudel's comment, 'Wars are thus, more often than we may think, economic incentives'.[66] This paradox helps explain the long duration of some civil wars; if analysed as economic enterprises, they emphasise the part played by violence as an instrument, and by the maintenance of violence.[67]

[61]   C. Geffray, *La cause des armes en Mozambique*, Paris: Karthala, 1990, p. 78.

[62]   J.-F. Bayart, 'L'invention paradoxale de la modernité économique', p. 39 ff., in J.-F. Bayart (ed.), *La réinvention du capitalisme*.

[63]   See R. Aron, *Sur Clausewitz*, Brussels: Complexe, 1987, p. 63.

[64]   'Every sort of activity, even violent, can have an economic orientation', M. Weber, *Economie et société*, Paris: Plon, 1995 edn, vol. 1, p. 102.

[65]   A. Nouschi, op. cit., p. 208.

[66]   F. Braudel, op. cit., p. 121.

[67]   A. Mbembe, 'Pouvoir, violence et accumulation', *Politique africaine*, no. 39, 1990, pp. 7-24.

The outbreak of the civil war can thus be seen as a socio-economic operation aimed at encouraging accumulation of wealth. As we show in this study, far from being the symptom of a local 'war culture' or the product of dislocated identity, it has on the contrary favoured conditions for a 'plunder economy'[68] from which warring elites and leading personalities profit. Weber emphasised that in ancient Greece 'chronic war was...the normal situation for the full Greek citizen, and a demagogue like Cleon knew perfectly well why he urged war: it enriched the city, while periods of lasting peace were not endured by the citizen class. Anyone who sought peaceful gains was among those who did not have access to the possibilities offered by citizenship.'[69]

Of course the Algerian civil war is different from the ancient Greek cities' wars of conquest. Even so, the consolidation of the civil war has not been without economic consequences: it has enriched the warring parties, brought them heritable property and favoured the allocation of symbolic wealth. Because it has breached the state's 'legitimate monopoly of violence', the civil war has been accompanied by a privatisation of violence which has led to the private accumulation of economic goods. G. Simmel suggested that 'besides giving, theft is the most natural form of transfer of property'.[70] Our conclusion is that the civil war cannot be explained only by a single factor: its mainsprings are numerous and the explanation needs to be sought in a combination of factors in which the actors' strategies and their *imaginaire* have a central place.

The search for the causes of the war, analysis of its progress and understanding of its actors are the subject matter of this book. Besides those aims there is another, consideration of the final outcome of the war. Is a return to civil peace possible? After seven years of conflict, the presidential election campaign raised for the first time the possibility of national reconciliation. Can the election of Abdelaziz Bouteflika by default – following the withdrawal of the other six candidates – really set a dynamic of reconciliation going? The new president's shortage of legitimacy suggests it cannot, and it must be feared that violence will continue to rage. Yet the presidential election campaign made it possible to assess the expectations of a part of the population. Battered by seven years of violence, it is expressing its need for a return to civil peace. The reactions of the FIS and the AIS immediately after the presidential election made it clear that the conditions in which Abdelaziz Bouteflika was elected do not constitute a handicap for the pursuit of direct negotiations with FIS and AIS representatives.

---

[68] An expression borrowed from J.-F. Bayart, S. Ellis and B. Hibou, *La criminalisation de l'etat en Afrique*, p. 45.

[69] M. Weber, *Histoire économique*, Paris: Gallimard, 1991, p. 350.

[70] G. Simmel, *Le conflit*, Strasbourg: CIRCE, 1992, p. 17.

On 21 September 1997 Madani Mezrak, national 'Emir' of the Armée Islamique du Salut (AIS), issued a communiqué in which he '[ordered] all commanders of companies fighting under his command to cease combat operations as from 1 October and [called on] other groups devoted to the cause of religion and the nation to respond to this call.' Two months earlier, on 8 July, Abdelkader Hachani, the Front Islamique du Salut (FIS) Number Three who had been in preventive detention since 22 January 1992, had been released, as was Abassi Madani – one of the two top leaders of the FIS – on 16 July. The President's office started direct negotiations with the national 'Emir' of the AIS, with a view to 'completing the setting up of state institutions' and closing the FIS question. The aim was to have a cease-fire called before the municipal elections due on 23 October 1997; this, it was hoped, would be a political and military turning point. Those local elections were to restore elected representation to replace the Délégations Exécutives Communales (DEC) that had been appointed after the dissolution of municipal councils – under majority FIS control – in 1992. Through the new elections the Presidency was emphasising the return to political life at the local level; while a truce was supposed to show that violence was now truly just 'residual terrorism'.

General Boughaba, then commanding the 5th Military Region (the Constantine area), had approached AIS leaders in May 1996 with a view to starting negotiations. The Presidency seems to have persuaded the AIS of the disadvantages for both sides of continuing the armed struggle, which could only strengthen the 'eradicators on both sides', leading inevitably to chaos. The national 'Emir' justified the decision in favour of negotiation in this way: 'The AIS is attempting, through these contacts, to make the enemies of yesterday and today face their responsibilities, to warn the faint-hearted of the harmful consequences of their cowardly behaviour, to encourage sincere sons of Algeria who love their country to take the initiative to work together for the return of peace and stability, to bring the country out of its crisis...to foil the plans of those who are waiting for an opportunity to harm Algeria and the Algerians...and to unmask the enemy lurking behind the abominable massacres and isolate the residual criminals of the GIA and those hiding behind them.' After three years of war against the regime the AIS admitted its inability to achieve through violence the objectives set out on its formation in July 1994 – the rehabilitation of the FIS and the creation of an Islamic state. Forced by the army to flee into the Ouarsenis mountains, the AIS could not influence the course of the conflict as its rival the GIA, established in the Mitidja and the residential suburbs of greater Algiers, was able to do.

However, although the truce was a major event in the conflict, its immediate effect was limited by the GIA's refusal to respect it. Moreover, by giving up the armed struggle the AIS increased the GIA's chances of assuming a monopoly over the *jihad*, and hence over the revenues from the war economy, such as collection of the revolutionary tax. In addition the truce was criticised by some FIS leaders in exile, such as Ahmed Zaoui who even spoke of 'treason'. Indeed, as Madani Mezrak recognised, the truce could turn into a 'trap' if the AIS failed to back up its claim, i.e. to show that it was the main protagonist of the Islamic guerrilla campaign. Thus the AIS was obliged, on pain of being completely marginalised, to fight and overcome the 'perverse extremists of the GIA'.

The massacres of villagers that accompanied the release of the historic leaders of the FIS and the appeal for a cessation of hostilities were a stark reminder of the limited immediate impact of the truce. But the fact remained that after six years of civil war, the government succeeded in turning a conflict between Islamist guerrillas and the security forces into a pitiless struggle between the GIA and the AIS. In parallel with the 'total war' against the armed Islamist groups there was a gradual absorption of the guerrillas into society. A victory of the AIS over the GIA, helped by the backing of a section of the army, would surely hasten this process, and would confirm one of the theories put forward in this book – that violence is seen as a virtue in Algerians' political world view. For by refusing to make the FIS a partner in power in 1991 despite its success in the elections, by declaring in December 1997 that 'the file on the dissolved party has been definitively closed', and then giving a privileged role to the AIS, the Presidency showed that the way to power is not through the ballot box but through armed resistance.

The truce is a step towards resolution of the civil war and it can be conjectured that if it succeeds, it will certainly extend to the other Islamist factions still in the maquis, such as the FIDA (Front Islamique du Djihâd Armé) and the LIDD (Ligue Islamique de la Da'awa et du Djihâd). In fact, since the truce was proclaimed the AIS has stated that '3,000 fighters have been able to join the truce camp while retaining their autonomy.'[71] The government took three years to persuade the AIS to lay down its arms, at the risk of arousing criticisms of its strategy. How much time will it devote to dealing with the GIA, the most radical guerrilla faction? In the absence of real democracy there is reason to fear, for the Algerian population, an equally long and painful process before a conclusion is reached.

[71] *El Ribat,* October 1998.

Part I

THE SHAPING OF THE CIVIL WAR

In June 1990 Algeria celebrated the start of multi-party politics with the holding of its first free elections – local elections. The existence of more than fifty political parties[1] and the free tone of the press seemed to be tying the country firmly to a plural system.[2] Eighteen months later parliamentary elections were interrupted after the first round was won by the FIS. Leaders of political parties and associations, journalists and university teachers gradually fled the country, victims of the emerging civil war.

This first part analyses the attitudes adopted by those who had voted for the FIS after the ban on that party in 1992; it seeks to call into question the relationship between political mobilisation and the recourse to violence. For that purpose it draws inspiration from the analytical framework of Tilly's sociology of conflict, and aims, on the basis of observed micro-mobilisations, to achieve 'a description of the transition between phases and a presentation of the reciprocal actions of the opposed or allied parties.'[3] To take account of the processes of mobilisation, analysis of the context in which Islamist voters have developed is very important; so is analysis of their personal itineraries. Understanding the mobilisation behind the FIS has shed light on the relative failure of the armed Islamic groups, analysed in Part II. For the factors that ensured the success of the FIS in a particular political context did not necessarily operate in a war context; voting for the FIS did not necessarily lead to a commitment to violence against the regime.

Analysis of the FIS' mobilisation of support in the municipal elections of June 1990 and the parliamentary elections[4] of December 1991 in four municipal districts (communes) in the south-eastern suburbs of Algiers[5]

---

[1] See A. Djeghloul, 'Le multipartisme à l'algérienne', *Maghreb-Machrek*, no. 127, 1990, pp. 194-211.

[2] Even homosexuals, despite having to dissemble, saw things in much the same way: 'The years 1990 and 1991 were the best in my life, 1990 especially: we flirted openly, before everyone's eyes', 'Anis, un homosexuel algérien à Paris', *Le Monde*, 22 June 1996.

[3] C. Tilly, 'Action collective et mobilisation individuelle' in P. Birbaum and J. Leca (eds), *Sur l'individualisme*, Paris: Presses de la FNSP, 1991, p. 232.

[4] In the municipal elections the FIS won control of 55 per cent of the communes, 853 town halls out of 1,539, and it won the first round of the parliamentary elections with 47.27 per cent of votes cast (24.59 per cent of registered voters). See J. Fontaine, 'Les élections législatives algériennes', *Maghreb-Machrek*, no. 135, Jan.-March 1992, p. 155.

[5] FIS candidates were elected in the first round of the parliamentary elections with scores

and in a small town in the Hauts-Plateaux shows the contradictions in the political commitment of FIS voters. While petty traders voted FIS because they favoured a 'minimum state' guaranteeing freedom of trade, militant Muslims – many of whom were Arabic-speaking students and unemployed graduates – expected that victory for their party would be a prelude to the institution of an Islamic state, in which the Arabic language (rather than French) would be a criterion for selection on the job market. On its side Algeria's unemployed youth, not very politicised, saw the success of the FIS as an act of revenge against the 'FLN-state' responsible for the blood-stained repression of the riots of October 1988 in Algiers.[6] The FIS, then, embodied for our sample divergent and even contradictory religious, political, social and economic aspirations. We shall be looking into those contradictions themselves to find the causes of the party's failure when put to the test of civil war.

In 1992, after the interruption of the elections, armed militant organisations which had been founded earlier – such as the small group Al Takfir wa-l Hijra[7] and the Mouvement Islamique Armé (MIA) – emerged publicly. These organisations did not originate from the interruption of the parliamentary elections of December 1991. Before then there had already been rivalry between their leaders and the FIS elected representatives over the direction of the struggle against the regime. So they saw in the dissolution of that party and the imprisonment, exile or murder of its officials an exceptional opportunity to represent the Islamist electorate. They found in the communes recently supporting the FIS a fund of sympathy which made it possible to launch guerrilla operations against the security forces in 1992 and 1993. During the latter year they seemed to be in conquered territory; those who had voted for the former FIS thought then that victory was near and saw their communes as 'liberated areas'. The FIS electorate was regarded by the armed militants as a war chest, consisting of traders

---

of 74 per cent in Les Eucalyptus, 62 per cent in El Harrach and 70 per cent in Baraki and Chararba. See J. Fontaine, 'Quartiers défavorisés et vote islamiste à Alger', *Revue du monde musulman et de la Méditerranée*, no. 65, 1993, p. 159; *Journal Officiel de la République Algérienne* (JORA), no. 1, 1992.

[6] In October 1988 riots broke out in Algiers and its suburbs. Symbols of the FLN were targeted by groups of young people, which led to the intervention of the army. The number of dead among the rioters is estimated at 500. See Hocine Benkheira, 'Un désir d'absolu: les émeutes d'octobre 88 en Algérie', *Peuples méditerranéens*, 'Algérie: vers l'Etat islamique?' nos 52-53, July-Dec. 1990, pp. 7-18.

[7] That small group included 'Afghans' (Algerians said to have fought against the Soviets in Afghanistan), and its ideological affiliation was of Egyptian origin. Al Takfir wa-l Hijra (Excommunication and Hijra) is an organisation that emerged in Egypt in 1977. Its members practice *takfir* (excommunication) against a society considered as in an impious state. See G. Kepel, *Le Prophète et Pharaon. Aux sources des mouvements islamistes*, Paris: Seuil, 1993 edition, p. 73.

able to finance the guerrilla campaign and a reservoir of young men available to replace its fighters.

Faced with a situation that was getting steadily out of its control, the regime embarked from April 1993 on a policy of military reconquest of the Islamist communes of Greater Algiers. The army instituted a strategy of isolation: special units made up of soldiers, gendarmes and police were entrusted with dislodging the fighters. In a parallel action it implemented a policy of terror against the people to dissuade them from supporting the armed struggle groups. The practice of torture, humiliations and deadly reprisals carried out by the security forces provoked an outburst of violence in the communes. However, the military objective was attained: the fighters were forced to retreat into the surrounding maquis, where they became a focus of armed resistance.

There, however, they encountered a different environment, where the hostility of 'veterans' of the liberation war was an obstacle to their taking root. Among those veterans the regime's political determination from 1993 to wage war without respite against the Islamist guerrillas found a favourable echo. They saw the energetic policy of the chief of staff of the armed forces, General Lamari, as inheriting the mantle of President Boumedienne's authoritarianism, and were convinced that the defeat of the Islamist militants was near.

2

SOCIAL AND POLITICAL CHANGES

This chapter analyses the successful mobilisation of support for the FIS, seeking to show that its electoral victories were due to an opportunistic coalition of four social groups with contradictory demands: the military entrepreneur, the petty trader, the *'hittiste'* and the devout Muslim activist. Our hypothesis is that the mobilisation of FIS support in 1990 and 1991 cannot be simply attributed to factors relating to identity and culture alone, nor to an essentialist interpretation of Islam which sees it, as Maxime Rodinson put it, as a 'closed totality in which only Islamic phenomena are invoked to explain other Islamic phenomena'.[8] We would on the contrary prefer to stress, on the basis of a study of FIS voters' life stories, the variety of political, economic and social choices and issues at stake, all providing motives to vote for that party.

The FIS's economic partners in local government (1990-91)

Analysis of the management of municipal councils by the FIS elected representatives makes it possible to discern the political practices of that party's local leaders, and to understand the voters' expectations and demands. Although the government had passed a law ending state subsidies to municipal authorities, so as to deprive Islamist elected representatives of any capacity for action, those representatives were able to respond to various expectations on the part of the local people. The political practices of the FIS councillors in the communes studied (El Harrach, Les Eucalyptus, Chararba, Baraki) reveal the Islamist leaders' ability to extract financial resources from their strongholds (which did not exclude some external financing).[9] So, as we shall see, the Algerian Islamists, in their political, economic and social environment, reveal their ties with various actors; this makes it impossible to see them as a distinct social group.[10] While, on the political level, this convergence of views is obvious, it is also found on the

---

[8] M. Rodinson, *L'Islam: Politique et croyance*, Paris: Fayard, 1993, p. 231.

[9] Prince Sultan Ibn Abdulaziz, Saudi Arabia's Minister of Defence, in a statement published in *Al Sharq al Awsat* on 26 March 1991 revealed that his country had financed the Islamist movements in Algeria and Tunisia.

[10] A. Roussillon has written: 'Maybe it is necessary to stop seeing in Islamism a coherent collection of attitudes and values attributable to actors socially identifiable in terms of socio-professional categories. Or else, maybe we should stop seeing Islamism as anything but an "analyser" of socio-political and economic changes' in 'Entre el Djihâd et el Rayyan. Phénoménologie de l'islamisme égyptien', *Maghreb-Machrek*, no. 127, 1990, p. 50.

economic level; the 'petty' traders, some military entrepreneurs, and many agents of informal commercial activity were generous with donations to the movement, though they did not share the FIS's Islamisation objectives. The actors linked with the FIS (military entrepreneurs, licensed wholesalers, 'petty' traders, local community leaders) oscillated between pursuit of a partnership with the FLN and massive investment in the FIS during the elections process (1990-1).

The FIS victory in the June 1990 municipal elections brought to the fore, in the municipalities where it won control, a social group hitherto confined to discreet but nonetheless lucrative activities: private traders. The abolition of state subsidies to the new councils prompted the FIS to seek funds from individuals or economic partners supporting the Islamist alternative for Algeria. In the communes of the greater suburban area of Algiers, three social groups represented the main owners of wealth: managers of state enterprises (for example shoe and refridgerator manufacturing units), military entrepreneurs, and 'petty' traders. The first-named group, targets of criticism from Islamist activists (alleging embezzlement, incompetence etc.), were opposed to the FIS local councillors, from whom they expected nothing good. With the military entrepreneurs[11] (former ALN officers who had turned to business), it was different. They had been established in those communes in some cases since independence, in others since the early 1980s, and in recognition of their services during the war of liberation they obtained 'vacant property' (settlers' villages, agricultural enterprises, estates etc.)[12] in the Mitidja area. Having land at their disposal in the outskirts of Algiers, they sold parts of it to family members or people from the same *douar* (rural community), and thus they rebuilt their native *douar*s, with all those villages' restraints linked to the prevailing social hierarchy. However, there was a dispute over the legality of resale of those portions of land – which had been state property after independence – between the new owners and, on the other hand, families claiming property titles from

---

[11] The Algerian military entrepreneurs are comparable to what J. Bahout calls 'the new class' in Syria: 'Les entrepreneurs syriens. Economie, affaires et politiques', CERMOC, no. 7, 1994, p. 50.

[12] M. Raffinot and P. Jacquemont record: 'In the years 1961-62 nearly 900,000 people left Algeria, almost all Europeans. As a result 2,000 industrial and commercial enterprises, 200,000 homes, 20,000 square metres of office space and thousands of shops changed owners between 1961 and 1963. The laws and decrees relating to empty property notably allowed clients of the new state power to occupy them in force, boosting extravagant appetites and sordid settling of scores. The legal apparatus...allowed the dispossession of former owners, thrown out of the complex game of alliances and clans developed during the war, and the transmission of confiscated property to new categories, sometimes also suspect, who applied to succeed to the ownership. The precise results obtained by the implementation of these texts is not however known; published mention of confiscations only rarely appeared in the *Journal Officiel*.' *Le capitalisme d'Etat algérien*, Paris: Maspéro, 1977, p. 55.

before the nationalisation of land.[13] Those families contested the resale of those plots of land by military entrepreneurs to immigrants from the interior who were attracted by the capital's economic dynamism and anxious to escape from the authority of interior warlords, the Caïds of post-colonial Algeria.

The military entrepreneurs were few in number in these places, but their power was measured by the great diversity of their activities, on which a large proportion of the population depended. The various Islamist movements realised that the military entrepreneur – head of a crafts enterprise, owner of food stalls or *hammams* or commercial vehicles or hotels and restaurants in France – was an economic actor who could not be bypassed.[14] This was especially true because some young Islamist sympathisers were '*trabendistes*'[15] working for those economic actors – who were the only people able in those places to provide foreign currency needed to purchase consumer goods in Europe, the required administrative permits for importing the goods, and distribution networks for their sale (shops, stalls, market space etc.) with the guarantee of working without hindrance. However, the income from the informal economy did not go directly to the FIS, because the party did not control the commercial networks that were in the hands of senior civil servants and military entrepreneurs. The autonomy of the informal economy in relation to state power is in fact an illusion, since the latter is so much controlled by the former.[16] In Les Eucalyptus Hadj Sadok is an example of this type of actor, and his relations with the FIS elected representatives during the electoral process throw light both on that movement's implantation strategy and on the ability of such economic actors to adapt to political change.

---

[13] On 22 March 1989 former landowners held a demonstration in front of the People's National Assembly building, calling for the return of their land which, on 19 May 1988, had been recognised by an interministerial circular to be the property of military entrepreneurs who had been allocated it after the nationalisation of land in 1963 and the Agrarian Revolution in 1971. See A. Rouadjia, *Grandeur et décadence de l'Etat algérien*, Paris: Karthala, 1994, p. 337, and 'D'anciens propriétaires réclament la restitution de leurs terres', *Le Monde*, 25 March 1989.

[14] In 1990 there were no fewer than 15 political formations of Islamist persuasion. Nine of them were set up after the FIS' success in the June 1990 local elections. See Névine Mos'ad, 'Violence politique et mouvements socio-religieux, le FIS en Algérie', *Les Dossiers du CEDEJ*, Cairo, 1994, pp. 155-65.

[15] '*Trabendistes*' are individuals living off informal trade (*trabendo*). They hawk consumer goods bought in the big cities of Europe and resell them on markets that developed during the 1980s in Algeria.

[16] A. Henni has shown that informal trade was originally an economic activity controlled by leading figures in the state. However, he stresses, the development of informal trade has been accompanied by autonomy of that sector, to the point where it has become 'parallel' to the national economy. *Essai sur l'économie parallèle. Cas de l'Algérie*, Algiers: ENAG, 1991; 'Qui a légalisé quel *trabendo*?', *Peuples méditerranéens*, no. 52-53, 1991.

Hadj Sadok, suburban military entrepreneur

Hadj Sadok, who comes from a small village on the border of Lesser Kabylia and the Babors Massif, comes from a trading family and took part in the liberation war as a guerrilla fighter. After independence he and his brothers set up a small plant producing wafers in their home village and then, some years later, acquired land in the Les Eucalyptus commune, then uninhabited, where they set up a 'villa-warehouse'. Above all Hadj Sadok restored an enterprise in the Mitidja, the abandoned and partly damaged former property of a settler, where he started a business of storing domestic gas cylinders. This gradually became the central part of his business, and he handed the management of the wafer enterprise over to his children to concentrate on working with state enterprises in domestic gas marketing. During the 1980s he modernised older facilities with the help of the local authorities and then became a central figure in the commune.

As a regular pilgrim to Mecca Hadj Sadok was highly respected in the local community, on account of his personal career as well as the fear aroused by his numerous contacts. Like other rich entrepreneurs he helped fund the building of mosques, attractively finished, which are a contrast to the still half-finished urban landscape around them. This public generosity is based in his view on the obligation to pay back 10 per cent of the profits that he derived from the Mecca Pilgrimage through buying gold every year in Saudi Arabia for resale at considerable profit in Algeria. Father of numerous sons who support the Islamist cause – following both the FIS and Hamas-MSI – he had no difficulty in meeting the new elected representatives in charge of running the municipalities, in contrast to several other heads of families. His social standing even brought him several visits from Abassi Madani, Chairman of the FIS, which aroused the wonder of the young sympathisers and voters of the neighbourhood:

'Every month Madani's Mercedes arrived at his house. At the mosque the Imam said that Hadji Sadok had given the FIS, for the building of an Islamic state, a million dinars; that is why, when they arrested A. Madani, he left here, because everyone knew he was a friend of the Sheikh.' (A sympathiser of the former FIS, suburbs of Algiers, 1994)

This example shows that before the arrest of Ali Benhadj and Abassi Madani on 30 June 1991, some of the funds paid into the FIS treasury came from rich military entrepreneurs, not necessarily supporters of the Islamist cause.[17] Their financial independence, derived from special relations

---

[17] Névine Mos'ad has written: 'In fact the question of the Front's financial resources is a matter of controversy. In some people's view the Front does not have significant resources, as many of its supporters are unemployed. Others believe that the Front has a considerable financial margin for manoeuvre. Its expenditure on propaganda, during the elections of 1990 and 1991, and the publication of a number of newspapers of which *Al-Inqâdh* was the most important (220,000 copies) indicates it is suggested, that the Front is well off.' Névine Mos'ad, op. cit., p. 159.

with the military due to their service in the war of independence, made it possible for them to invest in these new parties, which were financially weak and thus dependent on social groups such as theirs, at the meeting point of various interests. The diversity of Hadj Sadok's activities offered him opportunities for big profits, and the investment he made in the FIS was aimed at ensuring him the same advantages if that party took power.

The partnership between the FIS and military entrepreneurs shows how the symbol of wealth was given value and legitimacy by the FIS councillors. They were quick to point out how, in the Koran, trade is encouraged and poverty denigrated.[18] Hadj Sadok was respected because his wealth did not make him arrogant but, on the contrary, generous towards his district, as proven by his part in building a mosque at Les Eucalyptus. So, despite his wealth, he did not arouse resentment among deprived young people; quite the contrary, everyone admired this man who knew how to do good works. The way he finished his home showed the extent of his contacts, for while local people struggled to obtain cement and iron needed to build their houses,[19] never completed, in contrast Sadok's 'Dallas-style' villa and the mosque were examples of highly finished architecture, which lacked nothing.

It was in the organisation of informal trade that his contacts were shown most clearly, for with the help of his eldest son, Hadj Sadok set up a network of *trabendistes*, children of the neighbourhood (*awlad houch*), who have gone around Europe since the mid-1980s to bring back consumer goods to be resold at great profit in Algeria. These hawkers benefit from Hadj Sadok's logistic facilities (foreign currency, administrative permits, protection, etc.) which help ensure success for their business without difficulty. Besides profits this brings Hadj Sadok the esteem of those who, thanks to him, have succeeded in getting some money together. *Trabendo* is the main activity of young people in some communes,[20] and is carried

[18] M. Rodinson wrote: 'Economic activity, the search for profit, trade and, therefore, production for the market are regarded with as much favour by tradition as by the Koran. One finds extravagant wording about merchants there. It was said that the Prophet declared, "the sincere and trustworthy merchant will (on the Day of Judgment) be among the prophets, the just and the martyrs". According to holy Tradition, trade is a specially favoured way of earning one's living. 'If you derive profit from what is lawful, your action is a *Jihad*, and if you use it for your family and those close to you, it will be a *çadaqa* (that is, a pious work of charity)...The Koran, as a contemporary Muslim apologist sums it up, does not only say that the worldly sphere must not be neglected, it also says that one can validly combine worship and material existence, trade even during the Pilgrimage; it goes so far as calling commercial profits "God's grace".' *Islam et capitalisme*, Paris: Seuil, 1966, p. 31.

[19] At Les Eucalyptus, since a large number of homes have been built without permits, their dwellers do not have access to official supplies of building materials and are obliged to seek supplies on the parallel market.

[20] J. Charmes estimates that 25 per cent of jobs are in the informal sector. 'Visible et invisible: le secteur informel dans l'économie urbaine du monde arabe', paper delivered at seminar on 'Urban Society in the Arab World: Changes, Issues and Prospects', G. Agnelli Foundation, Turin, 12-13 Dec. 1994, 16 pp.

on by numerous qualified but unemployed people who, under the protection of a 'boss', readily travel to unknown cities. However, it is mainly less qualified people who are involved in resale of the products in Algeria, in various informal markets. Through his varied contacts with the military, *trabendistes* and FIS councillors, and his economic and social activities (as an entrepreneur, manager of informal trading networks and public benefactor), the well-connected Hadj Sadok is highly valued in his commune by the FIS elected representatives. Although rich, he does not embody the symbol of injustice in the eyes of the local Islamists. On the contrary, his position is considered to be 'in the public interest', as it generates goods and services. Local militants distinguish very clearly, among the rich, between the 'parasites' and the hard workers, for it is not wealth that is condemned so much as ways of acquiring it.[21]

'Petty' traders and the FIS. Although he is the principal economic actor in the commune, the military entrepreneur could not on his own provide backing for the FIS councillors. So these turned quite naturally to petty traders[22] – butchers, bakers, grocers, hardware merchants and above all jewellers, who gave the Islamist activists political and financial backing. Support for the FIS, which some petty traders even joined, is explained by the great opportunity presented for that social category – up against official discrimination since independence – by the arrival of new political office holders. In such localities petty traders represent family businesses whose daily activity is centred around the search for the staples of their trade.

Unlike families of regular or daily-paid workers living in low-cost housing estates built in the early 1980s, these traders have private homes that they have built illegally on local government land. Their multi-storey houses are also places of work as the ground floor is arranged for business use. These buildings, erected in haste, are built on land whose local government ownership title is contested by former owners claiming rights over land nationalised against their will by the Ben Bella government in 1963. During the 1970s some of the Mitidja land was resold by military entrepreneurs to individuals who quickly built houses without permission. In a parallel process military entrepreneurs with contacts with local councillors sold commune-owned land, wholly illegally. For example, the 'hay Hidouci' district in Les Eucalyptus was erected on land belonging to a leading figure in the village of Mérouana, in Batna Wilaya. The result was unregulated

---

[21] S. Makhloufi, editorial writer in the former FIS newspaper *El Mounqidh* between 1989 and 1991, later the 'Emir' of the MEI (Mouvement pour l'Etat Islamique), wrote: 'Puritan morality demanded personal investment. When societies lose contact with what has made them, thinking, work and culture no longer have any direction, and thus the system collapses. Enjoyment and pleasure become ways of life...': 'Vision islamique de la crise économique', *El Mounqidh*, no. 1, 1989.

[22] Petty traders are represented at the national level by a professional association, which claims 300,000 members.

building which, however, followed a certain logic: families migrated from the interior of the country and bought plots of land in the suburbs of Algiers. Communes like Les Eucalyptus were thus populated partly by people originating from the east of Algeria, who bought their land from one owner. Throughout the 1980s clashes occurred in those suburbs between the authorities and the local people, because of problems in implementing the Greater Algiers urban improvement programme (building motorways and a new airport etc.). The people acquired arms – the fathers of families covered by our interviews, for example, were armed with hunting rifles, to defend their homes by violence if necessary. After the interruption of the election process in January 1992 they were used, with their barrels sawn off (*mahchoucha*), by the Islamists in their campaign.

Besides this ongoing dispute over illegal housing, petty traders felt badly treated by the behaviour of senior officials who, in the allocation of raw materials, favoured entrepreneurs like Hadj Sadok to their disadvantage. To keep their businesses going they were obliged every day to beg for 'left-overs' from the state enterprises: bags of flour for the butcher, tinned food for the grocer, etc.; this turned each day into a Marathon:

'At the depot I had sometimes to wait for hours for nothing. They said there was no flour, and when there was flour, they said, "There is no yeast". In fact they hoarded goods for their friends or for wholesalers who resold the goods retail, without declaring it, as the wholesalers paid more and the employees pocketed the difference. Sometimes I had to go to the port to find yeast. But with the FIS, I swear to you, I had my yeast and my flour every day, without having to wait. They were ashamed to say there was no more flour when I saw stocks in front of me.' (Trader, Les Eucalyptus, 1993)

State control of imports and distribution of goods and products gave employees at warehouses a significant role and means of making money. In accordance with the amounts offered they chose whether or not to supply customers regularly. In that market petty traders were the losers, for if they bought goods at the prices stated on the invoices, to take possession of the goods they had to make an additional, unrecorded payment (*archoua*) to the staff, without being able to recoup that sum from the retail price, because of the strictness of the price control officials.[23] For military entrepreneurs and large-scale traders, this problem was less acute, to the extent that the diversity of their businesses made up for losses due to corruption – especially as price control offices were rarely mobilised to move against those businesses, even the most illegal ones like *trabendo*.

[23] This was in spite of the law of July 1989 providing for liberalisation of price control. It is true that that law related only to industrial products at that stage. Regarding petty traders S. Goumeziane, Minister of Trade between 1989 and 1991, noted that at that time that 'in parallel with the provisions of the law, extremely strict control measures were enforced on petty traders'; he also said: 'The price control officials are readier to punish petty traders than to take serious action against speculation networks.' *Le mal algérien*, Paris: Fayard, 1994, p. 193.

Petty traders' support for the FIS was based on the hope of reversing this unequal treatment, which the FIS elected representatives could not deliver because of their partnership with the military entrepreneurs, the main beneficiaries of the *status quo*. That is to say that the coalition of interests backing the FIS had its contradictions. However, its victory in the municipal elections of June 1990 provoked a change of attitude towards their customers among the warehouse employees. Petty traders, whose sons and daughters then joined the ranks of the FIS in large numbers, suddenly emerged as customers to be treated with care, because of their new contacts in the APC (Assemblées Populaires Communales). Local activists, particularly aroused against senior officials, no longer hesitated to lecture them, voicing resentment at the numerous vexations endured by their parents. The victory of their party, and conviction of its certain coming to power, altered the internal rules of operation for those officials:

'When there was the FIS, it worked well, there was no more corruption. At the beginning people tried to continue practicing *archoua*, but that did not work. Afterwards people felt shame, they no longer dared to try that, but now corruption has comeback and in addition it has made up for lost time.' (Petty trader, Chararba, 1993)

In this context, the collusion of interests between petty traders and FIS leaders was also based on common experience. Since independence these two social groups had been forced by the nature of the regime into informal activities. When, at the beginning of the 1970s, petty traders were struggling to build the walls of their houses hastily at night without building permission, small Islamist groups were being subjected to the repressive fury of Houari Boumedienne's regime. All were establishing arrangements for survival based on family and social mutual aid. Petty traders compensated for their eviction from the state banking system with the help of 'informal private banks' in which families' funds were placed, lending at strict rates and on strict conditions.[24] The Islamist militants developed networks for distribution of books and pamphlets, to make up for the difficulty of getting published by state agencies.[25] Their literature circulated clandestinely among the faithful, until 1989 when, once the Islamist movements had been legalised, real Islamist book markets emerged in the capital. These parallel experiences based on concealment and mutual aid, characteristic of two social groups

---

[24] Djilali Liabes explains that, among the 10,000 family micro-enterprises (with up to four wage-earners) enumerated in 1980, insufficient contact with the state banking system was compensated by an informal banking system 'with strict rules', capital being placed in common in the name of ties of blood. *Capital privé et patrons d'industrie en Algérie, 1962-1980*, Algiers: CREA, 1984.

[25] This did not exclude efforts by the regime to nationalise the expressions of Islamist thinking by having them published in the magazine *Al Asâla*. See J.L. Deheuvels, *L'islam dans la pensée contemporaine en Algérie, la revue Al-Asâla (1971-1981)*, Paris: Ed. du CNRS, 1991, 307 pp.

of varied social and geographical origins, may explain how they share a common outlook fashioned in clandestine activities and fed by the violence of the state's assertion of power.

Those two groups swelled in numbers during the 1980s. Petty traders in the private sector, victims of official discrimination in favour of the state sector, nonetheless seemed privileged in the eyes of the deprived population. The status of wage-earners, whose income was devalued by inflation and above all by the profits from *trabendo*, lost its prestige among young jobseekers,[26] who were more interested in joining the trading petty 'bourgeoisie' in question. The latter was certainly confined to the outskirts of Algiers[27] and was always subject to official harassment,[28] but it felt sure of itself. The effectiveness of the petty traders' informal and secret survival arrangements is based on their 'ethic' as economic actors. Respect for the pledged word, maximum exploitation of local resources and the 'cult' of the family make up an ethos, one that is also found in the rhetoric of the Islamists, with their determination to fight profligacy[29] and restore a code of honour in social relationships, damaged by *khechna*.[30]

Ahmed the hardware merchant: trade and individualism. The itinerary of Ahmed the hardware merchant illustrates the hidden process which led him to hope for a victory for the FIS in the municipal and parliamentary elections. Even so, he defines himself only as an Islamist sympathiser and did not in fact vote. His shop at Les Eucalyptus was a family business which he managed jointly with his elder brother. Their father, a worker in France, invested his income in this business in Algeria, which allowed his family

---

[26] See G. Duvignaud, 'L'économie clandestine au péril du contrat social en Algérie' in C. Bernard (ed.), *Nouvelles logiques marchandes au Maghreb*, Paris: Ed. du CNRS, pp. 181-201.

[27] This geographical marginalisation of the petty traders to the outskirts of Algiers recalls in some ways the merchants' experience of discrimination in the Middle Ages in Europe. For that comparison see A. Henni, 'Economie parallèle ou société parallèle', *Politique Africaine*, no. 60, Dec. 1995, pp. 153-62.

[28] M'Hamed Boukhobza has written: 'Despite the political condemnation of this sector and the halt in concessions during the 1970s, it must be admitted that it showed particularly vigorous progress: scarcely 900 traders with employees in 1954, 8,000 in 1966, about 22,000 in 1980.' 'Etat de la crise et crise de l'Etat', *El Watan*, 27 June 1994.

[29] Ali Benhadj, in a sermon in October 1989, exclaimed: 'Dear brothers, I know houses, I know empty houses! Houses which are occupied only on Thursdays and Fridays to practice depravity and sin! Villas! Palaces! Empty...Have you seen the zoo? Day and night electricity is wasted there! And what is to be found there? Believers praying, fasting, fearing God and calling on His name in the various prayer positions? Not at all! Rather there are people who jig about, play around and wallow in sin, while we, the people, do not know where to live! How can such places be built? Where are Algeria's finances? Where is this people's money?'

[30] The word *khechna*, in the dictionary of Algerian Arabic, describes behaviour consisting of 'rudeness, lack of education and roughness'. See Y. Nacib, 'Anthropologie de la violence', *Confluences Méditerranée*, no. 11, summer 1994, p. 71.

to live comfortably in his absence. For the two sons who ran the business the father's foreign currency gave them access to certain special privileges from local officials looking for francs for their 'holidays' in France. Convinced that his success owed nothing to the regime, Ahmed cursed the obstacles that the authorities put in the way of the development of his business. Coming from the Jijel region, he is from a pious family but, in 1993, did not practice as a Muslim much, although his financial and verbal support went to the FIS representatives:

'I did not vote, but I am with the Muslims, we are all Muslims. I prefer to see Muslims in charge, but first of all I prefer to be left alone, one must be left to work in peace...and we must have stadiums. As you have seen, people play football in the street like Africans, we have nothing; how do you expect us to get to America for the World Cup?' (Hardware merchant, Algiers suburbs, 1993)

His individualism shelters him from political and religious passions, so that he can concentrate on improving his business. Fascinated by the wealth of the military entrepreneurs who own luxury villas, he is convinced that despite the bad state of the national economy, it is still possible to get rich. Although macro-economic data and statistics on the health of the economy show a decline setting in from 1984, because of the sudden fall in the oil price,[31] in his opinion that economic crisis only affects those who depend on the state.

The draining of the state's financial resources and the bankruptcy of the state sector have led to a rush of people to start small businesses. Abdelkrim, Ahmed's friend, worked as a warehouseman in a state company for household electrical goods. He explains how the collapse of his enterprise led him set up his own small business:

'We sold everything – TVs, fridges, cookers. The problem was the waiting time for customers – one year, two or three years, depending on the customers. But I worked there for seven years, not for the pay – a cigarette seller earned more than I did. Thanks to that job I supplied equipment for all the families of my neighbourhood, they paid a bit more, and I bought myself a small shop which, *hamdou lilallah*, provided me with work. Because at one time people could get their products quicker with *trabendo*, and most of all, we had fewer and fewer things to sell. Sometimes there were more warehouse staff than items for sale, so I began to stop going to work, I stayed in my shop. Managers sold on the black market products that we should have sold, so there was nothing more to be done.' (Petty trader, Baraki, 1994)

Jobs in the public sector lost their attraction, and determination to have one's own business, legal or illegal, became the norm. It was based on the desire

---

[31] According to A. Benachenhou the price of oil per barrel fell from $40 in 1981 to $14.8 in 1986, export earnings from $13 billion to $8 billion, while inflation, from 6 per cent in 1983, reached 13 per cent in 1986 and jobs created declined from 150,000 in 1983 to 60,000 in 1988. 'Inflation et chômage en Algérie', *Maghreb-Machrek*, no. 139, Jan.-Mar. 1993, p. 31.

to be like the local military entrepreneur, a product of the national liberation war. However, before the outbreak of the civil war in 1992, only *trabendo* and petty trade could provide an opportunity similar to that provided by the war for the military entrepreneurs. They require, for those starting from the bottom, determination and above all cunning. Nobody during the electoral process in 1990-1 imagined that a civil war would come and would open up opportunities for social advancement.

New players on the political stage

The FIS victory in the municipal elections of June 1990 brought new political players onto the local stage, emerging from among the three million people whom the FIS claimed, through the voice of Abassi Madani, to have behind it.[32] At Les Eucalyptus, as at Chararba and Baraki, the local councillors were people of their communes, who had been born there; their fathers and mothers, however, were very often originally from the interior. The political commitment of these new urban dwellers is seen as the invention of a new identity, since by it they broke free from their former allegiances, family or regional – though that did not stop voters from regarding them as 'Sétif people', 'Kabyles' or 'Chaouis', on the basis of their regional origins.

An Islamist local councillor, the mayor of Les Eucalyptus. Toumert, elected Mayor of Les Eucalyptus, is a teacher[33] with a reputation for mildness and generosity, highly regarded by numerous families that he knows personally. Like other councillors, Toumert aimed to take up the challenge of running the commune, which for the Islamists of the FIS meant bringing in a new spirit favourable to 'development'. As the FIS press organ put it, 'How are we to make headway against the problems of housing shortage and unemployment, educational problems, lax management in industry and agriculture, etc.? For the FIS, what is essentially needed is to make the spiritual and temporal conditions prevail that are necessary for harmonious, all-round development. In other words, it is a matter of breaking the chains that imprison the mind and the body and so encouraging the outpouring of the national genius...For that, it is necessary to interest the citizen in the problems of the commune, make him participate in the search for solutions and their application for resolving of problems...To achieve that, communication must be restored at the heart of the whole municipal system, and it is

---

[32] *Jeune Afrique*, 12 Feb. 1990.

[33] Ignace Leverrier stresses that teachers played a major role in the mobilisation of the Islamists: 'The teaching profession provided the FIS with a vast and solid base for indoctrination and social pressure'. 'Le FIS entre la hâte et la patience' in G. Kepel (ed.), *Les politiques de Dieu*, Paris: Seuil, 1993, p. 52.

becoming urgent to set up an information system involving intensive use of the commune's network of mosques.'[34]

Toumert, who was elected with 70 per cent of the vote, had the support of the Imams of the commune's state-owned and private mosques,[35] which have continually extolled his virtues. His election aroused no fears in the commune, even among those who did not support him, because his generous spirit made him a bastion against his party's hegemonic tendencies. Funded by petty traders (while the military entrepreneurs financed the national organs of the party directly), the candidate campaigned on the issue of regularisation of land used for unauthorised dwellings; he promised if elected to ensure a title deed for everyone.

The themes of establishment of an Islamic state and application of the *shari'a* were left to the party's national representatives, to 'stars' of Islamism such as Ali Benhadj and Abassi Madani. Toumert, for his part, felt obliged to respond to other concerns, such as insecurity: petty traders were complaining about the behaviour of certain local residents. One low-cost housing estate built hastily during the 1980s houses families originally from the Casbah, moved because of the dilapidated state of that district of Algiers, which threatened to collapse on its inhabitants' heads. Those families, which had made a living in the Casbah through drug dealing,[36] found themselves at Les Eucalyptus (20 km. from the city centre) without resources, and tried to resume some of their previous criminal activity. As the police and gendarmes no longer responded to the people's requests, after his election the Mayor set up an informal police force, made up of activists and unemployed young people, who were assigned responsibilities by the new local government officers.

Although the Mayor could not respond to every call for help (over housing, jobs, insecurity etc.), FIS voters and others started to attend the mosque regularly. It was a new centre of power now that the APC (Assemblée Populaire Communale) had had its state subsidies withdrawn by the government. Demands were expressed within the mosque, which attracted more and more practicing Muslims. That created an illusion of unanimous feeling which, after the dissolution of the FIS in March 1992, was to appear in retrospect, to activists of that party, as lies and hypocrisy:

---

[34] 'Election campaign and management of the communes', *El Mounqidh* no. 19, 1990 (Thursday 21 Dhi al-kaada 1410 h).

[35] State-owned mosques have Imams who are state employees, unlike the private mosques–not appproved by the local authorities because of being 'under construction'–where Islamist' self-proclaimed Imams' preach. In order to preserve a mosque's 'private' state, the Islamists have left their places of worship incompletely built so as to escape the control of the state authorities. See Ahmed Rouadjia, *Les Frères et la mosquée*, Paris: Karthala, 1990, p. 92, and A. Moussaoui, 'La mosquée au péril de la commune', *Peuples méditerranéens*, July-Dec. 1990, pp. 81-9.

[36] See M. Vergès, 'La Casbah d'Alger, chronique de survie dans un quartier en sursis', in G. Kepel (ed.), *Exils et royaumes*, Paris: Presses de la FNSP, 1994, pp. 69-88.

'You know that there were those who never went to the mosque before the FIS. When it won the municipal elections, every Friday they filled up the mosques, they thought it was there that the Mayor would distribute housing, jobs, land, water, electricity, just anything. Those people were real *munafiq* [hypocrites], they came purely out of self-interest, but now we see clearly, we see who is on which side.' (Student, Algiers suburbs, 1994)

What did voters want: an Islamic state.or a 'minimum state'? There was common consent among FIS voters that the party offered a credible alternative to the FLN-State. They saw its programme as aimed at dismantling the dead weight of administration at the local and national levels. A lively determination to get rich existed as much among voters for the FIS as among the Front's opponents. Among the young FIS voters was emerging a will to change the rules of the game, to democratise the opportunities to acquire wealth. Explanations of the social situation as due to the economic crisis, which the regime put forward, were questioned because the military entrepreneurs and *trabendo* showed that ways to ostentatious enrichment remained. The Islamists' criticism was not based on the inequality of the international economic system, responsible for the fall in oil prices, but on the predatory behaviour of the political leaders:

'In this country there are too many, really too many thieves. For anyone who enters the government, it is as if he is seizing a slice of the cake. Nobody thinks of the country, of the people, or anything – it's their stomachs first, then their families, and you just watch them at it.' (Djamel, delivery man, Algiers suburbs, 1993)

The public good does not exist and the state is not an instrument for regulating inequalities – that was what the Islamist voters concluded. State control over the economy was in their eyes not a way to increase the wealth of the nation, but a political instrument used to stop the emergence of private economic and political entrepreneurs.[37] They saw proof in the fact the government had not hesitated to machine-gun the rioters of October 1988 in Algiers, causing more than 500 deaths; this showed them that the national leaders were only pursuing their own interests and were ready to use violence to preserve them. Those leaders, described as 'thieves', were seen as cunning characters, greedy for wealth, who had quietly taken control over the state. Their violence was explained by their social and regional origin: coming from the peasantry, they followed customs prevailing in the *douars*. Krim readily made an on-the-spot sociological study of the Algerian decision

---

[37] This processes can be explained, in L. Addi's view, by 'the neo-patrimonial form of the state' in which 'the economy is perceived in neo-patrimonial practice as a political resource, and is placed under state control not to make up for deficiency of private capital, but to stop formation of civil society independent of political society and able to demand, over time, a public space in which contradictory private interests would coexist'. 'Forme néo-patrimoniale de l'Etat et secteur public en Algérie'in Habib el Malki and J.-C. Santucci (eds.), *Etat et développement dans le monde arabe,* Paris: Ed. du CNRS, 1990, p. 79.

makers; he saw in them the distinguishing marks of formerly poor people overwhelmed by so much wealth and frightened at the thought of being deprived of it by the ambitions of people as 'hungry' as they formerly were. Krim, son of a worker, holder of a technology institute diploma, was convinced that the fear aroused in the regime by the FIS came from the complexes of 'illiterate' leaders who sought only to perpetuate a political system in which they felt at ease:

'The whole system is rotten, from study to work. In France you study to acquire a skill, here it is to get a qualification without any value. You work to draw pay, without producing anything. But the worst of it is that they do not like qualified people, for thirty years it is peasants who have governed us, they have not done any studies and they are proud of it, because they say that after all they are rich. For them you are worth nothing when you have studied, and if in addition you want to explain them anything, they tell you, "What have you done to give lectures?" What they want is asses like themselves, that way they remain on top.' (Unemployed college graduate, Algiers suburbs, 1994)

What Krim expected from the FIS was a reversal of that trend: the establishment of a competitive job market based on the idea of merit. So, as a qualified man without a job,[38] he was waiting for the establishment of an Islamic state to lead to complete Arabisation of the educational system and the economic sectors, which would give him a chance of a job.

Similarly, the motivation of some petty traders in the suburbs and villages came from their hope of breaking free from local restrictions, so as to acquire rights on the same terms as the military entrepreneurs; this implied some problems for the FIS councillors, who were in partnership with both groups as we have seen. Little passion was to be seen among the traders, for whom the FIS victory in the local elections was a step towards the 'minimum state' which they wanted. They were anxious to see the regime concern itself only with controlling the borders and exploiting natural resources, thinking the state should leave the rest to the citizens. For them the Islamic state was a state which placed no obstacles in the way of the outpouring of individual energy. The demands made by Djamel, a sympathiser with the former FIS in a small Hauts-Plateaux village, were an example of such expectations:

'What we need is for them to let us work quietly, freely. I tell you that if they let us work freely it would be better than America here. You know, it was not for nothing that the French did not want to leave. The state deals with oil and gas, but let it leave the rest to the people. If I want to import 100 cars to sell here I can't, because I don't know the right people, that is not right, one should be able to work according to

---

[38] According to the National Planning Council there were, in 1992, 74,000 unemployed people holding the baccalauréat or a higher education diploma; of these 23,000 had studied for five years after the baccalauréat. See A. Benachenhou, 'Inflation et chômage en Algérie', *Maghreb-Machrek*, no. 139, Jan.-Mar. 1993, p.34.

one's ability. They block our way, so that we pay import duties, on just any goods. In that way we are always bowing and scraping before them to get import licenses; even if you have money, you have to bow before them.' (Trader, village in the Hauts-Plateaux, 1993)

The petty traders were ceasing to accept their economic subordination. It was becoming intolerable to them that despite their success, they were not recognised for what they now were, effective entrepreneurs in a country that was sliding down into pauperisation. Because the administrative system was slow to recognise this fact they wanted to see the system disappear completely. Having survived the 'FLN-state', they derived strength and prestige from having done well without state aid, while the state enterprises collapsed into bankruptcy. This attitude did not make them insensitive to the general interest: the failure of Algeria's development, and its loss of influence in the region, hurt them deeply. They were in fact nationalists, and the FIS policies did not seem to them to be in contradiction with that feeling, as the party aimed so much to represent the nation. However, they wanted their own careers to be a model for economic development, and wanted an end to all obstacles to trade and the will to produce.

The logic of their ideas did not involve impoverishment of the state or its servants; the military who ran the state had, through exploitation of natural resources, the means of acquiring wealth without having to fear competition from others. While the unemployed college graduate Krim thought that the national leaders slapped down people with ability so as to restrain ambitions to govern, traders such as Djamel and Nadjim considered that the obstacles placed by the state in the way of individual self-enrichment were due to the leaders' fear of being 'overtaken in wealth'; this led to failure to exploit the country's potential, which in a paradoxical way guaranteed the stability of a regime afraid of dynamism:

'We have oil and gas in Algeria. It is a rich country, in the desert there is gold and silver, there is unexploited wealth. That is Algeria for you – unexploited wealth. If they let us work, it will be like California here.' (Nadjim, grocer, village in the Hauts-Plateaux, 1993)

The activists and local councillors of the FIS understood remarkably well this need for recognition felt both by unemployed qualified people and by petty traders. But were they in a position to meet such demands? The Mayor of Les Eucalyptus, like those of other municipal councils run by FIS representatives, was in quite a difficult position in the face of so many hopes and so few resources – especially as the devout activists' expectations diverged from those of ordinary voters.

The devout activists' agenda

The faithful who were activists of the FIS were distinct from the party's financial partners and from ordinary voters backing it: they were ideologically devoted to the religious cause that the FIS aimed to defend. Coming to a great extent from the university world, they took the Islamist programme to heart. Neither the traders nor the junior officials who voted FIS had the ardour of the students convinced that the future of Algeria, and their own, lay in the creation of an Islamic state. The problems of housing, water and electricity, although they knew them, were not objects for discussion; only the Islamic state and application of the *shari'a* aroused debate.[39]

The work of the devout activists. At Les Eucalyptus, as in other communes of Algiers, the devout activists embarked on an in-depth social and cultural programme which started with the removal of satellite dishes receiving Euro-sat, to favour the use of Arab-sat dishes. Those satellite dishes, owned by a number of households in the residential districts, allowed people to receive television broadcasts from European and particularly French channels. They were nicknamed '*paradiaboliques*'* by the Muslim faithful, who also called the French TV channel Canal Plus 'Canal Blis' (Iblis being one of the names of Satan in Arabic); they were a major symbolic issue for the militants' activity. For them the FIS was not about 'water and housing', it stood for the expression of nationalist feeling, in which the religious element was fundamental. Accordingly French television programmes brought into people's homes were seen as cultural aggression. The globalisation of cultural exchange inherent in that of the world economy did not spare the commune of Les Eucalyptus. In the devout activists' view to watch those programmes, especially those on French channels, was to accept a form of neo-colonialism, in addition a decadent form because of the numerous erotic scenes. To fight against that situation which was declared sinful, they suggested to their families and to the inhabitants of the districts, if they did not want to be reduced to watching Algeria's state TV channel, the alternative of satellite dishes able to receive Arab-sat satellite television; this was seen by devout activists as an opportunity to 'put an end to the French presence in Algeria'. In the space of one year (1990-1) numerous families redirected their satellite dishes under activists' pressure. The MBC (Middle East Broadcasting Centre)[40] channel, dubbed the Arab world's CNN[41], accounted for a good deal of this success,

---

[39] The leadership of the FIS brought together varying political, ideological, even religious tendencies. These divergences are illustrated by the opposition between the *'Djazaaristes'* who called for the practice of nationalist Islam and the *'Salafistes'* such as Ali Benhadj who supported international Muslim solidarity. See A. Ayyachi, *Al islamiyyun al djaz'iriyyun bayn al sulta wa al rusas* (The Algerian Islamists between power and arms), Algiers, no publisher, 1992; and S. Labat, 'Islamismes et islamistes en Algérie' in G. Kepel (ed.), *Exils et royaumes* (note 36), pp. 41-67.

* This is a play on the French term for a satellite dish, *antenne parabolique*, and the word *diabolique*.

[40] On that channel see doctorate thesis by M. El Oifi, 'La réception de MBC au Maroc', Paris: IEP, 1995.

[41] *Le Monde*, 7 Aug. 1993.

as it was able to win over a public of Arabic-cultured students who saw in it a window on the Arab world. Only the fathers of families in our sample in the southern suburbs were against this choice. Deprived of news in French, they turned to the children to understand television news in standard Arabic, which they often understood very little. They suffered above all from seeing their children prefer Saudi, Moroccan, Turkish or Tunisian channels to the Algerian one!

The work of the devout activists of the FIS at the local level, after their victory in the municipal elections, was directed not only at the 'eradication' of satellite dishes but also at social works and at maintaining the organisation of the party. Their activity sought to keep up the enthusiasm aroused by the election victory. The political dynamics arising from it, owing to the prospect of parliamentary elections, had to be kept from being weighed down by the voters' social demands (the right to housing and work, abolition of corruption). They changed the issues at stake in the FIS victory from the socio-economic field to that of culture and religion. The victory which was experienced by the voters as a punishment of the 'FLN state' became, for the militants, a counter-attack against history and a challenge for the future. The fear that it aroused in France was a guarantee of the movement's sincerity, for it was worrying the former colonial power and 'international Zionism':[42]

'Algeria is a Muslim country, it is normal that people should vote FIS. The FIS wants our good, it wants us to live according to the straight path of Islam, for France did everything to separate us from the Muslims, but we remained Muslims. The FIS, all Algeria wants it.' (Wahab, militant of the ex-FIS and petty trader, Algiers suburbs, 1993)

The FIS was a channel for resentment and hope, feelings of revenge and challenging of the former colonial power. Wahab, although converted to Islamism only in 1989, adopted as his own the revision of history in which France is the enemy of the Muslims in Algeria. He felt a real enthusiasm for the FIS, which recalled the 'partisan passion' and the 'faith of the convert' of football fans studied by Christian Bromberger.[43]

The Islamist passion

The invention of difference. The FIS, founded in 1982 and legally authorised in 1989,[44] invented a new way of dressing, physical appearance and

---

[42] M. Slimani wrote in *El Mounqidh*, 'It is those who know true Islam who are afraid of it, and they are known to all, both at home and abroad, because, as we said above, it threatens their illegitimate gains and the world order based on the exploitation of peoples by the powers of high finance dominated by international Zionism.' 'Islam, Islamism and Politics', *El Mounqidh*, Thursday 10 Ramadan 1410 AH (no. 14, 1990).

[43] C. Bromberger, *Le match de football, ethnologie d'une passion partisane à Marseille, Naples et Turin*, Paris: Ed. de la MSH, 1995, p. 78.

[44] On the history of the party see A. Khelladi, *Les islamistes face au pouvoir*, Algiers, Alfa, 1992; and S. Labat, *Les islamistes algériens: entre les urnes et le maquis*, Paris: Seuil, 1995.

discourse – 'the FIS is the people', 'Islam is the solution' – which became
the central features of a new identity in, for example, the commune of Les
Eucalyptus. Distinguished by wearing of beards and the *kamis* (the long
flowing shirt, inspired by the Prophet's clothing), the local FIS activists
discovered the passion of politics, and their faith in the party drew strength
from the novelty it brought.

Les Eucalyptus, Baraki, Chararba and many other places were submerged
by the new 'look', which initially aroused irony and mockery within families,
among those who did not join the trend. For the first time young people who
were born in those communes, but whose parents originally came from
the interior of the country and retained the 'culture' of their home areas,
defined themselves in this way as people of Algiers. The FIS favoured the
invention of a new way of life for citizens, and the inhabitants of the commune of Les Eucalyptus sought to reinvent cordial relations, mutual aid and
equality among 'brothers', on which so much has been written in Muslim
tradition.[45] A consistent conviction spread that living like a pious Muslim
is the solution for all problems. That experience, although limited (June
1990-December 1991), remained for many a special moment, the start of
a new order. Once the civil war began that time took on the retrospective
appearance of a 'golden age'.[46] Lahcen, a delivery man, worked in Bab el
Oued and previously complained of the repeated thefts of which he had
been victim during his numerous delivery stops. With the coming of the
FIS and social control by the devout activists, there was a complete change:

'After 1988 the country was magnificent, I assure you; you could go out, nobody would
make trouble for you, nothing like that. With the FIS, I assure you, nobody dared to
steal any more, or get in a fight – nothing. The young people here, they were afraid of
the rod, for when someone stole, the "bearded ones", if they caught him, made him
regret his stealing.' (Delivery man, south-eastern suburbs of Algiers, 1993)

In the Islamist passion there was longing for order and for authenticity, a
protest against the disorder supposed to have started under the presidency
of Chadli Bendjedid. In this the devout activists, influenced by an *imaginaire*
in which order and security were valued and crime and disrespect for the
pledged word condemned, more or less voiced the desires of traders an-
gered by unemployed youths who stole and and flouted social norms. So
one can understand why the passion of the devout activists was directed

---

[45] L. Gardet wrote, 'In Islam, the first foundation is bound to be the very strong and constant
feeling of absolute equality of rights among all members of the Muslim community. All
believers are equal before the Law, because they are brothers'. See the chapter 'Théocratie
égalitaire' in *La Cité musulmane. Vie sociale et politique*, Paris: Librairie Philosophique
J. Vrin, 1976, p. 51.

[46] The 'golden age' was the term used for the period from 632 to 661, that of the 'Righly
Guided Caliphs' (*Rashidun*) who succeeded each other after the death of the Prophet–a
period that became a myth among the Islamists. See A. Rouadjia, 'Le mythe de l'âge d'or
islamique', *Peuples méditerranéens*, no. 56-57, 1990, pp. 267-83.

against a single enemy: the thief (*saraq*). Whether a thief hung around a residential district or strutted around at the top level of the state, he was the embodiment of the evil to be fought. While his eradication was very quickly achieved at the local level, at the top level it came up against the impossibility of throwing out the other thieves, the political leaders. For Omar, in 1993 a student of Islamic civilisation, the abundance of thieves in Algeria was due to 'bad' upbringing, 'too far removed from Islam'. In his view applying the *shari'a* would change nothing because people were not trained in the principles of Islam, but in the principles of swindling, thieving and lying. When contacted by the activists of the Mohammadia commune in Greater Algiers about standing as a candidate in the parliamentary elections of December 1991, Omar refused, arguing that the Algerians were not capable of living under an Islamic state. That was why, to channel the passion of the faithful, he practiced as an Imam, the only activity, in his view, that could start building of an Islamic state on secure foundations.

In his view the disorder prevailing in Algerian society, the cult of money and the taste for prestige, were due to the usurping of power by 'thieves' just after independence in 1962. He believed the evil set in then. The 'thieves' spread their immoral practices and 'vices' and corrupted society; they turned Algerians away from the ideals for which they had sacrificed themselves. Here the violence of passion for the FIS is equal to the affront suffered:

'It is not the Moudjahidin[47] who have been governing us, it is only thieves, they stole the Moudjahid's credentials, in reality they are Communists. Because one should not think that the FLN is the FLN of former days. All they are after is living well here on earth. The real Moudjahidin, those who kicked France out, they got nothing, they were never in power.' (Omar, student, southern suburbs of Algiers, 1993)

The need for an enemy. The violence of the devout Muslims' passion came from their discovery that 'Communists' had spread bad behaviour: the decay of the state and the moral lawlessness of individuals' lives were due to the hold established by 'Communists' over the country since independence. This image of the enemy,[48] even if false, had very real consequences and took on very many characteristics. Robbery was seen as the enemy's way of operating, and he was seen as belonging culturally to the 'French-speaking group'. Criticisms were focused on an 'atheist enemy', still tied to the former colonial power by his use of the French language. The key to the actions of the enemy was, in Omar's view, centred on that edifice which, thirty years after independence, still stood in Algeria:

[47] The term Moudjahidin (fighters for the Faith) is used in Algeria for those who fought in the war of liberation (1954-62).

[48] M. Grawitz stresses, on the subject of the image of the enemy, that 'Even when false, the mere fact that it exists in people's minds makes its consequences real.' 'Psychologie et politique', in M. Grawitz and J. Leca (ed.), *Traité de science politique*, vol. 3, Paris: Presses Universitaires de France (hereafter PUF), 1985, p. 93.

'Over the whole world Communist regimes are collapsing, but ours do not want to go. It is Communists who govern us, it is the PAGS.[49] You know it is Communists, French-speakers – thirty years after independence, it is French-speakers who govern us.' (Student, Algiers suburbs, 1993)

After the fall of the Berlin Wall and the coming to power of democratic regimes in the former Communist states, the devout activists saw the Algerian regime as Communists standing against the 'direction of History'. They used the words of Ali Benhadj who, in a sermon in October 1989, said that Algeria 'still had a Communist Party'.[50] The devout activists later thought Communist control of the machinery of state was proved by invitation to the PAGS, the former PCA which later became At Tahaddi, to join the High Council of State set up in January 1992 after the interruption of the elections.[51] All personalities and organisations backing the government after that date were called 'Communists' or 'French-speakers'. The illegitimacy of the regime led the devout activists to detect every day proofs of their political depiction of the enemy. In a TV report in 1993, during the 8 p.m. news programme, Redha Malek[52] (then Foreign Minister), on a visit to Mali, spoke in French with his Malian counterpart. To Omar that report showed once more that the government was 'French-speaking'!

To flesh out the picture they drew of their enemy, the devout activists adapted to their purposes the myth of 'the people' monopolised by the

[49] The PAGS (Parti de l'Avant-Garde Socialiste) was founded in 1966, but approved only in September 1990. It then changed its name and was called At Tahaddi ('the Challenge'). Historically, the PAGS arose from the Organisation de la Résistance Populaire (ORP) which was formed soon after the coup d'état of 19 June 1965 and combined the left wing of the FLN and former members of the Parti Communiste Algérien (PCA). The ORP was changed into the PAGS in the 1970s, now including only former activists of the PCA.

[50] 'In the Communist countries, now, Communism has collapsed; it has now collapsed. But here, in Algeria, we still have a Communist Party! The father is dead, but the son is still living!' Sermon by Ali Benhadj, October 1989.

[51] Following the resignation of President Chadli Bendjedid, the High Security Council (Haut Conseil de Sécurité, HCS) formed on 14 January 1992 a High Council of State (Haut Conseil d'Etat, HCE) to exercise the powers of the President. The Chairman of the five-member HCE was Mohammed Boudiaf until his assassination (16 January-29 June 1992), then Ali Kafi (3 July 1992-31 January 1994). On the legal imbroglio arising from the resignation/overthrow of President Chadli Bendjedid, see J.J. Lavenue, 'L'armée algérienne et les institutions: de la Constitution du 23 février 1989 à la mort de M. Boudiaf le 29 juin 1992', *Revue du Droit Public et de la Science Politique en France et à l'Etranger*, 1992, p. 121.

[52] Redha Malek replaced Lakhdar Brahimi at the Foreign Ministry in February 1993, and in August became Prime Minister, until 1994. A spokesman for the FLN at the Evian negotiations that ended the Algerian war (1954-62), he was opposed to negotiations with the FIS, which explains the enmity of FIS voters towards him. He said in an interview, 'The state has a form, that of the Republic, it is unthinkable to alter it. No question of turning Algeria into any sort of Emirate or Sultanate. To be able to make progress, it is necessary to condemn terrorism. Those people of the FIS do not accept that yet.' *Humanité Dimanche*, Paris, no. 295, 9-15 Nov. 1995.

FLN from the start of the revolution in 1954 ('revolution by the people and for the people'). Emphasising that Algeria still remained under the influence of France, they wanted to demolish the legitimacy of the leaders founded on the acquisition of independence in 1962, and in that way altered the stakes of their struggle. From a struggle against the dissolution of the FIS in March 1992, it became a war for the complete and real 'liberation' of Algeria. At the symbolic level they focused on the object of destroying 'Houbal'[53] (the Islamists' name for the Martyrs' Monument and shopping malls built in 1986), as an embodiment of inequality and idolatry.

The shopping malls (*galeries marchandes*), frequently a target of foiled armed attacks, contain a number of businesses grouped together in a luxurious centre, where brand products, because of their cost, are reserved for a well-off clientele – consisting, says Omar, of the 'thieves' in power. The commercial centre, with its cafés, restaurants and discothèques, is considered to be like a place of debauchery where 'Communists' and 'French-speakers' go to relax with their children, called 'Tchi-Tchi';[54] it illustrates the accumulation of Algeria's wealth in the hands of the 'thieves' who, behind closed doors, enjoy their fill of the good things of this world. The activists, in contrast, emphasise the poverty of leisure facilities in their commune, although it is inhabited by a population of hard-working but never rewarded petty traders. The shopping centre symbolises the legalisation of inequality and the consecration of the new rich whose accumulation of funds is thought to be based on 'embezzlement'.[55]

'The FIS is the People': ambition for hegemony. The devout Muslims' partisan passion, and their identity strategy based on invention of difference derived from 'culture imagined as authentic', had a hegemonic tendency and thus was always 'potentially totalitarian', according to J.-F. Bayart's expression.[56] The FIS, 'all Algeria wants it', one heard. The FLN was seen as definitely defeated – it had failed in its mission and the people had turned away from

---

[53] Houbal was the name of a god in the Mecca Arabs' pantheon in the pre-Islamic period.

[54] 'Tchi-Tchi' is the expression used in popular parlance to describe children of the 'Nomenklatura', and especially girls dressed in Western style.

[55] M. Cote has written about Chadli Bendjedid's presidency: 'The class in power, which existed before, enriched itself considerably during this period. Having remained discreet until then, now it displayed its wealth in its luxury cars and villas....The new government opened the doors wide to imports...Every transaction with other countries was an opportunity for major bribes, embezzlement, rapid enrichment.' M. Cote, *L'Algérie*, Paris: Masson, 1996, p. 123.

[56] 'Such regressive definitions of modernity make identity strategies potentially totalitarian. First of all because the culture imagined as authentic is defined as opposed to neighbouring cultures that are seen as radically different, and because this assumption of "other"-ness is equivalent to a principle of exclusion whose conclusion quickly becomes an ethnic cleansing operation: cultural exchange is then felt as alienation, loss of substance, even pollution.' J.-F. Bayart, *L'illusion identitaire*, Paris: Fayard, 1996, p. 185.

it. As for other political groups, they appeared insignificant. Many FIS militants were convinced that their party obtained more votes in the parliamentary elections than the official poll results declared.[57] The joy of winning the elections was mingled with disappointment at the realisation that the cause of the Islamic state was not mobilising all Algeria; in their attitude there was a failure to comprehend the varied choices by the voters. All the Islamists with whom we spoke were convinced that the FIS would succeed the FLN, and would thus have a monopoly of representation of the people.[58] The loss of a million votes for the FIS between the municipal elections of June 1990 and the legislative elections of December 1991 was explained not as a sign of loss of enthusiasm among the electorate, but as the consequence of a change in the law to ban fathers of families from voting on behalf of their wives: many husbands were said to have refused to let their wives go out to vote. The conviction that the FIS was the future of Algeria was reflected in denial of the political difficulties the party was encountering.

Among the fifteen Islamist groups that contested the parliamentary elections in December 1991 two, apart from the FIS, had a real sociological base. The others were creations of the government or of individuals, without any economic or political foundations. Mahfoudh Nahnah's Hamas-MSI[59] and Abdallah Djaballah's An Nahda[60] were political parties that interfered with the strategy of the FIS leaders;[61] their Islamist message, devoid of the radical rhetoric characteristic of the FIS, was aimed at an electorate of civil servants and traders, worried about the FIS' hegemonic ambition. Forced to distinguish themselves from their rivals, some FIS candidates, with an eye on the December 1991 parliamentary elections where more than fifty political parties would be contesting, emphasised the general theme of

---

[57] The FIS estimated that it obtained 82.5 per cent of votes cast in 1990. See the results published in *El Mounqidh* in a special issue, 28 dhou al qi'da, 1410 AH.

[58] Lahouari Addi stresses that this political attitude forms part of 'a permanent presence of populism in Algeria'. 'De la permanence du populisme algérien', *Peuples méditerranéens*, July-Dec. 1990, pp. 37-47.

[59] Mahfoudh Nahnah was born in 1938 at Blida. A grassroots militant during the war of liberation, he was condemned in 1976 to 15 years' imprisonment for an attempted Islamist uprising, but pardoned in 1981 by Chadli Bendjedid. He played a part in the Ligue de la Da'wa, and in 1988 founded the Association Al Irchâd wa al Islâh (Orientation of Life and Reform). In December 1990 he turned his association into a political party, Hamas (Mouvement de la Société Islamique), officially approved in April 1991.

[60] The Mouvement de la Nahda (=Renaissance, 'rebirth') Islamique, MNI, was founded in 1988 and legalised in 1990. An Nahda, wrote Abdellatif Lamchichi, 'supports the aims of creating an Islamic state and application of the Shari'a, but within the framework of democracy and pluralism. It desires dialogue, exchange and collaboration among the different tendencies in Islamism, and is against the monopoly of the political scene, even of preaching, exercised by the FIS.' *L'Islamisme en Algérie*, Paris: L'Harmattan, 1992, p. 106.

[61] A. Kapil, 'Les partis islamistes en Algérie: éléments de présentation', *Maghreb-Machrek*, no. 133, July-Aug. 1991, pp. 103-11.

challenging the regime and rejecting democracy,[62] though that caused some unease within the party.

Flushed with their victory in the first round of the parliamentary elections in December 1991, devout activists such as Omar saw the interruption of the elections, followed by the ban on their party, as a seminal fault of the regime. As the party of the 'people', the FIS was in the activists' view a matter of necessity. They saw the acts of terrorism attributed to the party as the work of the security services, concerned to deprive the FIS of legitimacy:

'It was not the FIS that planted the bomb at the airport.[63] They say it was the FIS, but that is false. Not one policeman was killed at the airport, do you find that logical in an airport filled with police? When the bomb went off all the police were away from the scene. It is 'they' who are firing on the people. The FIS does not do that, kill civilians. Today, as they have lost, they want to achieve victory by force. They will lose again, for Islam is what the Algerian people want and call for; you can't go against the people.' (Omar, student, Algiers suburbs, 1993)

'The people' was turned into something real, and homogeneous, in Omar's mind. In his eyes the FIS was simply the people on the march against the regime and towards the establishment of a revolutionary vanguard in the Arab world. 'Algeria', he said, 'will be an example for the Arab and Muslim countries as a whole. Already the Egyptians have understood that only force can overcome the Communists in power in the Arab countries.'

The Islamists of the FIS followed the nationalists in appropriating the idea of '*shaab*' (people), making themselves heirs to the PPA (Parti du Peuple Algérien) on which the historian Omar Carlier has written, 'From 1936 that word became their watchword, they made it their emblem in the same way as the anthem and the flag. It set them apart, it distinguished them from the political class. The Shaab was them, and them alone...Two slogans fed the *imaginaire* of action and defined its meaning: "The word of the people" and "What was taken by force will be taken back by force".'[64]

---

[62] A. Difraoui emphasises how the FIS leaders used language critical of democracy, to distinguish themselves from other Islamist groups which accepted the framework of political pluralism, but also to avoid being seen as 'traitors' to Islamism by foreign Islamist movements. That author wrote: 'By its participation in the elections, the FIS was open to accusations of betraying Islamic ideals.', 'La critique démocratique par le FIS' in G. Kepel (ed.), *Exils et Royaumes* (note 36), p. 119.

[63] On 26 August 1992 a bomb outrage at Algiers airport left eleven dead and about 100 injured. On 28 August an underground FIS communiqué condemned it and assured everyone that 'the accusing finger must be pointed at those who are exploiting the event politically to discredit the image of the fighters and the objectives of the *jihad*'. *Le Monde*, 30 Aug. 1992.

[64] The comparison between the PPA and the FIS is not without interest, especially regarding the social groups composing them. O. Carlier notes: 'No [other party besides the PPA] consisted, in its top positions and at the middle levels, of such a high number of petty traders and craftsmen, taxi drivers and more or less qualified workers rising from the ranks.' *Entre nation et djihâd: histoire sociale des radicalismes algériens*, Paris: Presses de Sciences Po, 1995, pp. 218, 228.

From that point of view the FIS was what Olivier Roy calls an 'Islamo-Nationalist' movement.[65] And the contempt in which it was held by the political leadership, which went so far as to call it the 'beggars' party', increased its popularity among all those who, whether abstentionists or not, identified that movement with the defence of the deprived.

While it was backed by some of the most dynamic sectors of Algerian society (the military entrepreneurs, the petty traders, the *trabendistes*), the FIS leadership also sought to represent the '*hittistes*' ('those who prop up the wall').[66] They, however, had a way of life at the opposite extreme from that of the party leaders: passionately fond of Raï music,[67] football, girl-chasing and living by fiddles, they readily scoffed at the new 'look' (beards, *kamis*) of their childhood mates. The FIS appealed to them first of all because of the threat it posed to the regime, with which they had a score to settle three years after the repression of the 1988 riots. Farid, an unemployed man who was traumatised by that episode[68] in which he took part, saw in the FIS a turning of the tables. The street was in the hands of the discontented again. The hatred he had borne against the regime since 1988 made him a sympathiser with all movements ready to fight against it. He was certain that the regime dreaded its own people: 'They [the political leaders] say that out of 26 million Algerians, only six million have the right to exist.'

Leaving aside their resentment against the government, the *hittistes* have developed a way of life that in many respects runs counter to the ideal of the devout militants of the FIS. 'Propping up the wall', living in the street and from the street, doing casual work, far from all family or regional constraints, seem to be typical of that social group which was a pivotal one after the outbreak of civil war in 1992. Such a life is accompanied by boredom and disillusion, and the experience of emptiness as a daily routine[69] is

[65] According to Olivier Roy, 'Whatever references it makes to the Muslim Umma, the FIS is an Algerian nationalist movement as much as an Islamist one, from now on one should speak of Islamo-Nationalists'. *L'échec de l'islam politique*, Paris: Seuil, 1992, p. 165.

[66] The '*hittistes*' are jobless youths who spend their time 'propping up the wall' (*hit* means 'wall' in Arabic).

[67] Raï music, originating from Oran, became during the 1980s the preferred musical style of Algerian youth. Its songs express taboo themes such as love, alcohol and boredom. See Marc Poulsen, 'Essai d'analyse d'une chanson raï', *Annuaire de l'Afrique du Nord*, Paris: Ed. du CNRS, no. 30, 1991, pp. 259-81.

[68] Testimony collected from the local press brings out the trauma experienced by some of the rioters: 'The paratroopers came in waves to beat people up. At night torture recommenced. There were two rooms, one including a tub and rags. The tub was in fact a saucepan full of liquid waste and vomit in which people were drenched. There was a room where people (young people especially) were sodomised with stakes and bottles. Some were directly raped by the paratroopers. Toenails were torn off with bayonets.' Quoted by *Algérie-Actualité*, no. 1204, 1988, p. 16.

[69] The anti-hero of the film by Merzak Allouache, *Omar Gatlato*, is an example of that sort of life.

reflected in frenzied consumption of *zombreto*, a local drink made from methylated spirit and other ingredients. Farid had very good reasons to rebel against his situation; however, he did not react to the halting of the elections in December 1991, nor to the banning of the FIS in March 1992. Should one conclude that the prospect of an Islamic state aroused no hope in him? L.A. Coser has written, 'It is only when hopes have been displayed before them that people who suffer from privations react with revolutionary energy against a regime that seems to be opposed to the achievement of their new hopes.'[70] And what could he hope for from an Islamic state? The moral discipline preached by the devout activists certainly helped petty traders in their business, because it protected the honour of families by the respect imposed on girls in the street, and above all created a powerful hope that an Islamic state would be an employer-state for all the unemployed college graduates and students. But for Farid, apart from the end of the 'FLN-state', few issues were able to arouse him; does that explain the apathy of the 'disinherited' immediately after the interruption of the elections? Only the repressive policy carried out from 1993 was to arouse among the *hittistes* a profound feeling of indignation, leading to violence.

The FIS election victories in 1990 and 1991, then, cannot be explained by identity or cultural issues at stake; but a part of the explanation, in the urban districts analysed, lies in social changes in post-colonial Algeria. The increased strength of the petty traders, fascination for the military entrepreneur *nouveaux riches*, experience of *trabendo* for some of the youth (especially the better educated), and the craze for money and notoriety (as achieved by stars – Raï singers, footballers and Islamist popular leaders) aroused new demands which the FIS took on board. The FIS leaders, champions of a market economy, became the heralds of these demands to which they added social work of mutual aid and solidarity, able to help the worst-off. The political dynamics started by the FIS had some effects; economic actors and social groups supporting the party detected in their daily lives the changes taking place in the Islamist urban districts. Following the example of Houari Boumedienne and his modernising programme, the FIS planned to turn 'Algeria into California'. The excitement of the devout activists, spurred on by determination for revenge against France and against Algeria's post-colonial state, inspired a sense of duty to succeed, as that alone could restore 'respect' for Algeria, lost during the years of 'decline' in the 'Chadli decade'.

[70] L.A. Coser, *Les fonctions du conflit social*, Paris: PUF, 1982, p. 120.

3

A REVOLUTIONARY SITUATION

The municipal experience of the FIS councillors aroused new hopes which were supposed to be fulfilled with the creation of an Islamic state. The interruption of the elections in December 1991 was followed by the proclamation of a state of emergency, initially for twelve months, in February 1992, and then the dissolution of the FIS in March and of the municipal and Department authorities run by its representatives in April. Those events did not provoke an uprising by those who had voted for the party. On the other hand they created conditions for the emergence of small groups that had remained marginal until then, and which now sought to capitalise on the disarray of the ex-FIS electorate and legitimise *jihad*.[1] However, those small groups were, during the year 1992, 'neutralised' by the security forces which considered then that a repressive policy was capable of bringing about the Islamists' submission. The perverse effects of that strategy began to appear from 1993: a number of FIS voters, who had been adopting a wait-and-see atiitude until then, now became, under the impact of repression, sympathisers of or participants in violence against the regime. There arose a revolutionary situation[2] with an uncertain outcome, characterised by the emergence of 'multiple sovereignties' and the conviction, among some devout militants of the FIS, that there would be a rapid victory.

Conditions favouring Islamist dissidence

The interruption of the elections in January 1992, followed by the dissolution of the FIS in March, put an end to any legitimacy for the regime in the eyes of those who had voted for the party. The arrest of militants and operations to intimidate young sympathisers increased the numbers ready

[1] Etymologically, the word *jihâd* means 'concentrated effort towards a determined aim'. However, as A. Morabia notes, the word has undergone gradual changes according to Muslim societies' preferences. He wrote: 'We shall translate the word gihâd, in conformity with Muslim scholars' practice, as "holy war" or "fighting for the Triumph of the Faith".' *Le Gihâd dans l'Islam médiéval. Le combat sacré des origines au 12e siècle,* Paris: Albin Michel, 1993, p. 120; see also R. Peters on varying interpretations of the word *jihad*: *Islam and Colonialism: The Doctrine of Djihâd in Modern History,* The Hague: Mouton, 1974.

[2] C. Tilly defines a revolutionary situation as comprising '(1) The appearance of contenders, or coalitions of contenders, advancing exclusive alternative claims to the control over the government which is currently exerted by the members of the polity; (2) Commitment to those aims by a significant segment of the subject population... (3) Incapacity or unwillingness of the agents of the government to suppress the alternative coalition and/or the commitment to its claims.' *From Mobilization to Revolution,* Reading, MA: Addison-Wesley, 1978, p. 200.

to listen to the 'supporters of *jihad*', until then confined to underground activity. For the third time in its history, the Algerian regime faced armed resistance, following the 'Kabyle uprising' led by Aït Ahmed and Colonel Mohand[3] in response to the constitutional referendum in September 1963 and Moustapha Bouyali's '*jihad*' between 1982 and 1987.[4] (There had been other attempts at resistance, like that by Mahfoudh Nahnah who planned to form an armed group in 1976,[5] but that attempt had no effect on the regime's stability.) None of those earlier uprisings found an environment and conditions so favourable as those encountered by the 'supporters of *jihad*' in 1992. The uprising in 1963 by the FFS guerrillas, whose criticisms of Ben Bella's regime (1962-5) closely resembled FIS criticisms of the FLN in 1989, were doomed to failure because of the weariness of the population after seven years of war.[6] And the call for a *jihad* launched by Moustapha Bouyali in 1980 against a regime already denounced as 'impious' found little echo in a country still generally ignorant of the teachings of revolutionary Islamism. The re-Islamisation of expressions of discontent had not started in the early 1980s.

Islamisation of expressions of discontent. The work of the devout activists of the FIS, during the 18 months of local government power, extended the spread of the Islamist model and its language. The interruption of the elections hastened the process. Kader, a student in the 1980s, a voter for the FIS in 1990 and 1991, explained how the halt to the parliamentary elections in 1992 proved the validity of Islamist arguments. By that act the regime revealed its apostasy: if not, why oppose the creation of an Islamic state? Moustapha Bouyali's past action appeared to him then as having shown profound acumen, accompanied by a sense of sacrifice:

[3] After the setting up of a National Constituent Assembly in September 1962, Ahmed Ben Bella's regime organised a referendum on the Constitution (September 1963), which, according to R. Redjala, 'institutionalised the single party', because 'the first popular consultation that took place in independent Algeria was a mere show of democracy, no challenge to the government being allowed'. He explains that a third of the future deputies chosen in August were arbitrarily excluded for being 'opposed to the Political Bureau appointed by Ahmed Ben Bella'. The referendum on the Constitution aroused opposition, notably from Aït Ahmed who set up the Front des Forces Socialistes on 29 September 1963 and took to the maquis. A. Redjala, *L'opposition en Algérie depuis 1962*, Paris: Harmattan, vol. 1, pp. 55, 139.

[4] F. Burgat has written: 'M. Bouyali, a former guerrilla, father of seven children, a good worker with the Société Nationale d'Electricité, former parliamentary candidate, went underground in April 1982, after the murder of one of his brothers by the police...From 1982 to the month of February 1987 – probably with the help of part of the population of his home region (Larbaa, near Algiers) – Bouyali successfully defied the forces of order...M. Bouyali fell on 3 February 1987 in an ambush, with three of those close to him...': *L'islamisme au Maghreb,* Paris: Payot, 1993 ed, p. 167.

[5] See A. Ayyachi, *Al islamiyyun al jaza-iriyyun bayn al sulta wa-l-rusas* [The Algerian Islamists between government and arms], Algiers: Alfa, 1992, p. 206.

[6] Chapter 10 develops this comparison.

'What is happening, he had already foretold it, but we did not see it here. We did not understand that he had launched the *jihad* because he had understood who was governing us. It is now that we understand what he did, but we were not ready for the *jihad*. While he was fighting, we were going to Houbal.'[7] (Kader, unemployed college graduate, Algiers suburbs, 1994)

Convinced with others that General Khaled Nezzar and General Mohamed Lamari are the 'enemies of Islam', Kader has since 1991 used the Islamist set of values in his denunciation of the regime. A student during the 1980s, he was not very politically committed then; he dreamed of opening a private medical practice in France, even of marrying a *beurette*. He discovered the mosque in 1991, under pressure from his neighbourhood which was largely converted to the Islamists' cause, and joined the movement. However, he was not to go so far as to wear the *kamis* and the beard. As an 'Islamist at heart', which is how he defined himself, he came through that experience to see the emptiness of the plans he had made as a student. Why open a medical practice in France and not in Algeria? He feared that like many penniless young doctors, he would at the end of his studies be posted to the south of Algeria. But as a native of Algiers he rejected any move of that sort, at least until the victory of the FIS. His desire to leave for France after his studies was due to his 'disgust' with the system, which, in his view, was based on patronage and incompetence.

However, what was rejected shortly beforehand was accepted after an FIS victory: if, under an Islamic state, he was asked to go, he would go to the south. The idea of living in France was banished, he considered that marriage to a *beurette** 'was a mad idea...one might as well marry a prostitute'. 'Why study in Algeria and treat French people?' 'And what is the use of independence if it is to leave Algeria without doctors?' The emergence of the FIS and the hopes placed in it aroused all these questions in him. In 1991, while he was waiting for a posting after qualifying, there was a profound change in his way of thinking. His attitude to social realities was transformed, and, above all, a way out appeared. To work for 6,000 dinars (about 600 francs) seemed, before the emergence of the FIS, like social regression. What could you do with 6,000 dinars in Algiers? – especially when petty trade offered more for less investment. With the FIS there was an inversion of values; people with educational qualifications felt valued and recognised as representing the future of a country that had been 'on the way to destitution' before the coming of the FIS. Kader felt he was ready with the FIS for collective sacrifice if his country would benefit.[8] He, a doctor in an insecure position, became

[7] Houbal is the nickname given by the Islamists to the War Memorial adjoining the Shopping Gallery (Riad el Fateh).

* A *'beurette'* is a girl from among the *Beurs*, as the French-born younger generations of North Africans in France are called.

[8] O. Carré emphasised how this sense of sacrifice is able to influence the 'modernisation of states'. He wrote: 'With Islamic approval, the same modernising action will have in

through the Islamists' 'revolutionary ideology'[9] a valued person, necessary for Algeria. During the ten-year rule of Chadli Bendjedid, it was common to hear people in the residential areas of Algiers say, 'To get married, you need to be a footballer, a singer or a *trabendiste*'; a student who got a qualification, even if he was bilingual, was not a good catch for a girl's family. To such qualified people the FIS offered a feeling of coming into their own.

The Islamic state: an employer-state? Kader's personal itinerary ending in the Islamist movement illustrates the enthusiasm that the emergence of the FIS was able to arouse among better educated people, despised by a society valuing material success, in which they felt deprived. In fact they were left standing by the *hittistes, trabendistes* and criminals who prospered and proclaimed a code of success ethics based on fending for oneself, swindling and violence. The educated people mobilised behind the FIS appeared to be quite outside the Algerian economy, which made little use of skilled workers. Yet Kader was, to a jobless youth like Farid, a 'bourgeois' (though one without capital) who despised the fiddles and tricks that helped people survive. The gap between those two FIS voters was not religious, it was between two worlds with different sets of values: a frenzied individualism in which each person's chances lay in the most complete opportunism, and a solidarity-oriented patronage system in which one could develop under the protection of a political network.

In addition, the FIS aroused hope among qualified people in insecure positions because of expectations that contradictions in the educational system could be put right. For example, suggesting the teaching of English as second language instead of French was, in the minds of many Islamists, a way to end privileges of the French-speaking networks adapted to the economic system.[10] In addition, Arabisation of primary and secondary education led to a contradiction with important consequences for the university

---

return the necessary authority and thus a sufficient mobilising force. Max Weber has well described the economic role which a religious movement can make at times of "big changes", especially an Islamic movement of the "Mahdist" type, comparable, he says, to radical Calvinism': *L'islam laïque ou le retour à la Grande Tradition*, Paris: A. Colin, 1993, p. 103.

[9] P. Ansart emphasises that 'a revolutionary ideology redistributes periods of history, redefines what is glorious and what is insignificant, re-categorises major historical players, fixes the moments which must be considered the most significant in the indefinite temporal continuity', *Les idéologies politiques*, Paris: PUF, 1974, p. 16.

[10] G. Grandguillaume wrote: 'The key sectors of industry and the administration, the specialised branches of education, use French exclusively, which contributes to making knowledge of that language an important factor in social success'. He noted that when 'M. Rahal, Algeria's Minister of Higher Education, received Algerians with Arabic educational qualifications and heard them complain about not finding career opportunities, he said, "It is not Algeria's fault if the economic sector does not operate in Arabic...Algeria cannot bear on its own the burden of Arabisation and the responsibility for this gap".' *Arabisation et politique au Maghreb*, Paris: Maisonneuve et Larose, 1983, pp. 19 and 20; see also K.T. Ibrahimi, 'Algérie: l'arabisation, lieu de conflits multiples', *Maghreb-Machrek*, no. 150, Oct.-Dec. 1995, pp. 57-73.

system. Youssef, a Physics student, a sympathiser with the former FIS, blamed the 'French-speakers' over the failure of higher education. His criticisms related not to the use of the French language but to the privileges French-speakers had on the job market:

'I studied in Arabic up to the baccalauréat, with four hours' French a week. When I had the *bac* and registered at the university to read physics, the whole programme was in French. The lectures were in French, nobody understood anything. So at the university I learned more French than Physics. Why are there no Physics courses in Arabic as in Saudi Arabia and Iraq? In Algeria there are lecturers able to give them, but everything is done to make them go away, because those who have the posts are French-speakers. It is they who hold power. The result for us is catastrophic, you lose a year or two years because of the use of French.' (Physics student, Algiers suburbs, 1994)

For him, as for Kader, an Islamic state meant first of all a state adapted to their training. Fascinated by Saddam Hussein's Iraq, a country able to 'keep its scientists', he was angry at the Algerian regime for provoking emigration by select groups.[11] When many students dreamed of leaving Algeria for Canada, the United States or even Australia, this was seen as the result of political calculation by the leadership: the emigration of that budding elite saved the regime from the risk of seeing it contest a system which, in Kader's view, was deliberately unequal. The FIS' aim to Arabise the school and university system completely responded to one of the many expectations of qualified people of the new generation. For that generation the idea that modernisation and Arabisation did not fit together was no longer acceptable. The Gulf War was a powerful revelation of the error of that view, because of the model of Iraq. Information relayed by the media on a military-scientific complex that was competent and Arab seemed like a miracle: the marriage of the Arabic language and modernity was in the realm of the possible. The craze for the Iraqi cause was equalled only by the 'disgust' for the Algerian regime, seen as incompetent, touchy and corrupt.[12] The Islamist utopia assumed a nationalist guise, the Iraqi model recalling that of Houari Boumedienne.

[11] More than 90,000 qualified people live abroad, according to the daily *El Watan* (4 May 1994).

[12] Franck Fregosi has written: 'That episode of the Gulf War made it possible to measure how much the Islamist and Algerian movements in particular are in line with the Arab national movement. It showed through that very fact the ability of the FIS, as a movement of contestation based in the first instance on Islamist ideology, to divert to its advantage the nationalist feeling of the Algerian masses. The commitment by the FIS to support of Iraq, under pressure from the street, thus made it possible for the Islamists to add to their struggle in the name of Islam and their anti-Western rhetoric the nationalist dimension which could not be ignored, as in spite of the circumstances and the obvious failure of various regimes claiming to follow it, nationalism still continued to arouse many passions.' 'Fondamentalisme islamique et relations internationales: le cas du FIS', *Trimestre du Monde*, no. 25, 1994, p. 36.

The FIS and the myth of the strong state (latest version). The Islamists' local government experience, although short-lived, was nonetheless very revealing. It showed how the FIS utopia was coloured, among the voters and sympathisers, with nostalgia for the Boumedienne era. This is definitely paradoxical: how, for example, could private sector traders, thrust down by the authorities, long for the return of a 'Socialist' regime?[13] The answer to that question lies perhaps in the changes that occurred in the civil service, which was all-powerful under Boumedienne's presidency, but whose staff grew poorer under Chadli Bendjedid.[14] The resources spent on the civil service, considerable after the nationalisation of oil in 1971, encouraged vocations to public service careers, but the trend was reversed after the oil crisis following the fall in world prices in 1986. So one can suggest that the growing poverty of officials in the 1980s led traders who had become *nouveaux riches* to expect that their money would enable them to secure from officials any services they needed for their business activity. Did they hope to find in the Islamist administrative authorities what they had been unable to obtain from those following a 'Socialist' direction?

Convinced that they had sufficient funds, petty traders hoped to be privileged negotiators with the new administrative authorities. Their expectations from the new local FIS elected representatives (regularisation of land used for building, water and electricity supply, etc.) were extended to include other requests (access to foreign currency, import licenses) which touched on the central government's responsibility. The Islamist utopia did not correspond, for them, with an insubstantial theocratic 'city', it meant recruiting of staff close to their concerns and thus sensitive to their requests. The language used by local Islamist leaders was rarely unconnected with local concerns; that contributed to their success.

The fear of an Islamic state in Algeria felt among the non-Islamist electorate and abroad – a fear kept going and amplified by the media, according to the Islamists[15] – proved that their party was on the right track. Such a fear

[13] B. Cubertafond defined the Boumedienne regime as 'a combination where borrowings from Socialism, Islam and nationalism could be seen'; preaching egalitarianism, it saw in the 'bourgeoisie of the big cities' resistance to its policy based on a spirit of social and political unanimity. *La République algérienne démocratique et populaire*, Grenoble: PUF, 1979, p. 103.

[14] Z. Daoud has written: 'Speculators and *nouveaux riches* display the external signs of their recent fortune, while the number of poor people increases, Islamism is spreading and the middle classes see their standard of living decline.' 'La frustration des classes moyennes au Maghreb', *Le Monde diplomatique*, Nov. 1996, p. 6.

[15] Besides dramatisation of the Islamist phenomenon, the media were criticised for failure to criticise social inequality. Ali Benhadj, in a sermon in October 1989, said: 'At Berragui it is the same thing; people are sleeping in tents; they have gone on hunger strike. But in spite of that, Gathering of Muslims, what do we see? We see that others eat, drink,, receive heads of state, receive ministers as if there was nothing like that going on! And journalists come, they keep quiet about all that, they hide that from the people! By God, journalists' responsibility is great before God!'

could only be based on the challenging of an order unfavourable to Algeria. To express that theme the FIS revived memories of the Boumedienne era:

'Before, when an Algerian was killed in France, Boumedienne would say on television the same evening that Algeria protected its nationals, and warned France against racism. But with Chadli that was finished, Algeria was no longer worth anything in the world. Chadli worked on building castles and left people to their own devices.' (Wahab, young trader, Algiers suburbs, 1993)

For Wahab the FIS was not the vanguard Islamist political party, but a party aiming to restore 'dignity to the Algerian people'. The myth of the Boumedienne era was a reference point and became a model. F. Khosrokhavar has written: 'Myth-making activity is all the more intense when the political field is non-existent or dislocated and unable to convince the public about social demands and their representativity. The collective *imaginaire* goes wild, it takes refuge in myth to make up for suspicion of the political structure.'[16] In the case of the FIS sympathisers and voters, the myth flourishes because the political field has dried up. Houari Boumedienne, like the FIS leaders, was not sparing in criticisms of France, which, even if they had no effect, kept up a feeling of competition, as the example of football illustrates. For Youssef, a drinks vendor, there was a better standard of football under Boumedienne than today.[17] He described an event that occurred during the Mediterranean Games of 1976:

'The French were leading at half-time; Boumedienne went to see the players in the changing rooms and said to them, "If you don't win, you will join the million and a half martyrs!"[18] The Algerians won the match by equalising and gaining the advantage in the second half.' (Algiers suburbs, 1993)

If Boumedienne represented, in the FIS sympathisers' and voters' *imaginaire*, the man through whom Algeria recovered its dignity trampled upon by colonialism, the sermons of the Islamist militants and elected representatives on international questions drew on the same set of values, even kept up the same stereotypes. Algeria was celebrated, its people worshipped as sacred, its destiny seen as inescapably glorious. There was only one thing to spoil the picture: today 'French-speakers' and 'Communists' were an obstacle to Algeria's realisation of its potential, whereas yesterday, under

[16]   F. Khosrokhavar, 'Le mythe du guide de la Révolution Iranienne', *Peuples méditerranéens*, no. 56-57, July-Dec. 1991, p. 255.

[17]   On the instrumentalisation of football, see Y. Fates, 'Jeunesse: sport et politique', *Peuples méditerranéens*, July-Dec. 1990, pp. 55-72.

[18]   According to B. Stora, 'The conflict, according to the most probable approximations, caused somewhere near 500,000 dead', but 'the FLN, at its Tripoli Congress of June 1962, gave an estimate which was to have the force of law: "A million martyrs fell for the cause of Algeria's independence".' *Histoire de la guerre d'Algérie (1954-1962)*, Paris: La Découverte, 1993, p. 91.

Boumedienne, the 'bourgeoisie'[19] presented an obstacle to the greatness of the Algerian state. For the leaders and local councillors of the FIS, running the communes was a prelude to running the state; their efforts to involve voters in the problems of their localities aimed precisely to restore the link, supposed to have become overstretched, between a 'people' and its 'state'. In retrospect, that challenge appeared like a success in the minds of the faithful and a certain number of FIS voters, who saw the party as the representative of the 'people'[20] and the 'Muslims'.

The interruption of the elections and the policy of repression which put an end to that experiment filled them with indignation. The proclamation of the state of emergency in February 1992, and then the dissolution of the Assemblées Populaires Communales in April 1992, encouraged the spread of the 'desire for dissidence'. Gradually individuals confronted the regime and its agents in arms, fuelled those opponents' violence with their own, and resented the regime as 'foreign' and illegitimate.[21]

Indignation

At Les Eucalyptus, the transition to violence was derived from a feeling of indignation aroused by the flagrant injustice of the interruption of the elections process and the repression that followed. The Western silence about, even approval of the government's action against the Islamists produced 'implacable' indignation, wrote L. Boltanski; this feeling 'expressed itself by seeking backing from a demand for justice offended by the scandal displayed before the world, and committed itself to violence through emotions aroused by the impossibility of uttering denunciation in a way understandable by others, getting it recognised and shared.'[22] The war started by the regime against the Islamists surprised more than one FIS voter, because few envisaged such a possibility. The mass arrests[23] following

[19] B. Cubertafond has written: 'For the [Boumedienne] government, the class struggle revolution was over, since the European exploiters had left, and there was not really any exploiting bourgeoisie in Algeria. However, in a period of crisis, it is in fact the bourgeoisie that is advised to keep calm; the bourgeois making up the "French party" were denounced during the oil crisis of 1970-1; the bourgeois not exploiting their land directly were called upon not to spread malicious false rumours and not to impede the agrarian revolution.' Op. cit. (note 13), p. 121.

[20] Abassi Madani took over the theme of defence of emigrant Algerians: 'We are not among those who trade in their children. The emigrants are victims...They are our countrymen wherever they are, and we shall see that they are respected everywhere.' *Jeune Afrique*, no. 1543, 25 July 1990.

[21] R. Girardet defined a crisis of legitimacy as 'the moment when the government, the principles on which it is based, the practices that it implements, the men who run it and embody it come to be resented as "other" and are seen as enemies or foreigners'. *Mythes et mythologies politiques*, Paris: Seuil, 1990, p. 88.

[22] L. Boltanski, *L'amour et la justice comme compétences*, Paris: Ed. Metailié, 1990, p. 122.

[23] According to the Minister of the Interior 6,786 people (14,000 according to the FIS) were interned in 1992 in seven detention centres in the south of the country: Reggane, El Homr,

the interruption of the elections, and the policy of intimidation, provoked the beginnings of resistance among the people of the commune.

Symbolic resistance of the Islamist faithful. The bearded postman of Les Eucalyptus, a well known sympathiser with the FIS, continued in spite of threats to wear his beard. By that act he emphasised his allegiance to the FIS despite its dissolution and the risks faced by its activists. Many refused to shave off their beards and said, like Omar: 'It is the *Sunna* that requires it.'[24] In fact that symbolic resistance to the regime's violence made the transition to physical violence easier, a transition for which there is abundant evidence. In 1992-3 the municipality of Les Eucalyptus endured the presence of the security forces rather than fighting them, and no uprising or explosion of violence took place. The FIS invented a new identity in the commune, based on a dress code; then the violence produced another identity, that of the martyr and victim. The 'young' Islamist humiliated by the security forces became bit by bit a 'hero', the 'witness' to the illegitimacy of the regime. Abdellah, a newsagent, a sympathiser with the FIS and friend of the Mayor, had proof that the regime had renounced Islam. One of his friends was subjected to harassment because he wore the beard and the *kamis*; he was arrested by the security forces who cut his robe down to a 'miniskirt' and shaved off one side of his beard:

'I tell you, they don't like Muslims. How do you expect that man not to blow them all up now? He's a man, you don't do that to a man. You turn him into a woman and throw him into the street in front of everyone in a miniskirt! They told him, "You come back tomorrow to get your papers, and shave off the other side." He came to my house, he was crying, he was crying in a nervous state, he was ready to explode. They did worse to other young men, they burned their beards – the Prophet, peace be upon him, wore a beard, but they, they burn our beards. It's to young people they do that. If people are Muslims they can't do things like that, I can't believe that Muslims are capable of doing that.' (Abdellah, newsagent, suburbs of Algiers, 1993)

The reaction of the security forces was the result of the constant tensions during 1991. The arrest of the FIS leaders, Abassi Madani and Ali Benhadj, was followed by a campaign of civil disobedience.[25] As in 1988, the forces

---

Tsabit, Ain M'guel, In Salah, Ouargla and Bordj Omar Driss, *Le Matin* (Algiers), 13-14 March 1992. Those arrests were justified by a presidential decree (no. 92-44 of 9 February) enforcing a state of emergency. Article 5 of that decree laid down: 'The Minister of the Interior and local communities can order the placing in a centre of safety, in a fixed place, of any adult person whose activity is seen to be dangerous to public order, public security or the proper functioning of the public services.' *Journal Officiel de la République Algérienne* (10), 9 Feb. 1992.

[24] The *Sunna* sets out the deeds and words of the Prophet as reported by his Companions, put into writing in the Traditions (Hadith), the second source of the *Shari'a* after the Koran.

[25] In May 1991 Abassi Madani announced an indefinite strike in protest against the demarcation of constituencies. There followed bloodstained clashes between FIS militants and

of order no longer aroused the fear necessary for their security. The gendarmerie deployed its forces in the residential districts in 1992 and arrested, humiliated, even tortured people to discourage any uprising by the Islamist sympathisers. But those sympathisers waited to see what would happen; the end of the Islamist communal councils was seen as the end of the utopia.

The absence of an Islamist uprising. Convinced of their ability to influence the actions of the three million voter-sympathisers, the FIS leaders, during the electoral process, threatened to overthrow the regime by force if it interfered with the smooth running of the parliamentary elections. But the elections were halted and the FIS banned without any of the effects on which the party's leaders had been counting.[26] Why did the FIS sympathisers not react spontaneously to the dissolution of their party? For them the question was: should we fight for the creation of an Islamic state? Following Olson, we suggest that such an objective remained imprecise and, above all, that the expected achievements were vague for voter-sympathisers knowing little about Islamist teaching. In contrast, mobilisation in support of the FIS during the electoral process had required no effort – voting and going to meetings at the Stade du 5 Juillet[27] involved no risk – and the advantages gained were significant: priority in housing allocation, regularisation of titles to land used for illegal building, a symbolic victory over the people responsible for the repression of October 1988. Support for the FIS during the elections was in that sense comparable to support for trade union activity, arousing hopes of gain at the smallest cost. With the dissolution of the FIS in 1992, defending it involved staking all on a war that meant inevitable losses,[28] and that put FIS voters off.

---

the security forces. Before his arrest in June 1991 Madani drew up a statement calling for civil disobedience: he recommended that people should 'organise self-defence and the struggle in the districts...mount 24 hours a day patrols within the communes and districts...sabotage equipment of the police, gendarmerie and ANP [Armée Nationale Populaire] forces and destroy their buildings...train groups to specialise in operations against sensitive points whose destruction harms the enemy, or else escape into neighbouring Wilayas or take to the maquis, etc.' Quoted by A. Touati, *Les islamistes à l'assaut du pouvoir*, Paris: L'Harmattan, 1995, p. 263.

[26] In contrast to June 1991, when Ali Benhadj and Abassi Madani called for a *jihad* after the postponement of parliamentary elections initially planned for June 1991, no statement from this party called for violence against the regime or *jihad* in the immediate aftermath of the cancellation of the elections in January 1992.

[27] That 80,000-seat stadium in Algiers was used by the FIS in its election campaign; activists and sympathisers coming from most regions met there.

[28] M. Olson wrote: 'Collective bargaining, war and the civil service have this in common, that the "advantages" obtained by all three accrue to everyone in the respective groups, whether or not he has supported the trade union, served in the army or paid his taxes.' *Logique de l'action collective*, Paris: PUF, 1978, p. 117.

From the moment when the party was banned it was their lives that former FIS voters staked if they joined the *jihad* to set up an Islamic state. Many were not sure of seeing its achievement, even less of getting any benefit from investment in the *jihad*, so vast was the gap between the regime's resources and the guerrillas' destitute state. M'Hamed, a *trabendiste* by profession, not much of a practicing Muslim but a sympathiser of the FIS, hoped for military victory for the Islamists who were fighting the regime in the name of respect for democratic acceptance of changes of government. When confronted with the contradiction between his support for a party calling for Islamisation of society and his own feeble religious practice, he found no difficulty in justifying himself:

'I voted FIS for things to change, the FLN here does nothing for us, it prevents us from doing anything. We shall try out the FIS, if it's good, so much the better, but if it does nothing, we shall do what we did with France and now with the FLN, we'll chuck them out.' (M'Hamed, *trabendiste*, a small village in the Hauts-Plateaux, 1993)

M'Hamed's support was in words only: he understood the Islamists, because they had been robbed of their political success, and he hoped for their military victory without making any personal investment in their action. 'Trying out the FIS' cost nothing; but to make success possible for the guerrilla campaign meant sacrificing one's life for the benefit of numerous un coordinated armed groups.

The perverse effects of the repression policy. The only armed actions against the forces of order at that time were carried out by 'supporters of *jihad*', who had since 1990-91 opposed resort to the ballot-box as a way to an Islamic state. To prevent any link-up between those armed groups, still marginal then, and sympathisers of the ex-FIS, the forces of order applied, after the arrests of militants of the party in March 1992 and on into 1993, a policy of intimidation with formidable results:

'You see what they did to me [he showed multiple scratches on his body] – "they are Muslims", they said among themselves afterwards. As for me, I say that to do that to a Muslim, you have to be a Jew. It's Jews who do that to the Arabs. They said they knew me and that was just a warning. Now, they telephone me in the evening, they tell me, "This is *dark al watan* (the gendarmerie), we're watching you". They told me, "If ever there is another dead man at Les Eucalyptus, we'll kill you, it's you who are behind it". They think I know the Moudjahidin and work with them.' (Abdellah, newsagent, Algiers suburbs, 1993)

Known in his neighbourhood as an FIS sympathiser, Abdellah displayed his beard and *kamis*, and his words of hatred towards the regime arose from his disgust with the forces of order since the repression of the October 1988 riots. Despite his appearance he remained far from the political objectives of the Islamist militants and his preferred reading was sports newspapers. He was as ignorant of the Islamist press as of the press of all other political tendencies; he did not define himself as an 'Islamist' or a 'brother' but as a 'Muslim', his dress being rather derived from the fashion invading his neighbourhood. Wearing certain clothes and a beard was like a code, a sign of recognition or even of distinction and belonging which transcended limited regional and social sentiments. Above all it denoted clearly, through wearing of the *kamis*, a collective identity. Abdellah's violence remained verbal. There were many Islamist sympathisers tortured as he was, sometimes tortured to death, in an effort to break any inclination towards rebellion.[29]

The interruption of the elections was followed, during 1992, by the occupation of mosques by the security forces. As places of worship and cells of the party, the mosques had a wealth of information on the structures and local organisation of the FIS. Thus a large proportion of the mass arrests in some suburban districts of Algiers was facilitated by seizure of documents in mosques with the names of local militants and the party's economic partners. The reaction was immediate and the central police intelligence offices at El Harrach were attacked by Islamists who, in their turn, took possession of the names and addresses of civilian employees of the police.[30] As each side had lists of the names of opponents, targeted murders continually increased in number, leading to the first resignations of policemen who felt their security threatened.

In parallel with this specific campaign, a targeted and 'rational' one, there were an increasing number of 'mistakes', inherent in the precarious situation of policemen exposed to danger in the midst of the urban zones supporting the FIS between 1990 and 1991. Scared by an environment hostile to them, policemen picked up young passers-by arbitrarily and vented their resentment against them. In that way Youssef, a young drinks vendor at a street stall in Les Eucalyptus, was arrested and tortured because he was accompanying a 'young bearded man'. Practicing his religion very little, disillusioned with the political class including its Islamist part, Youssef had passions only for the cinema, preferably American, and sport. His arrest aroused in his neighbourhood indignation over the injustice of the act, corroborating what the Islamists were saying about the arbitrary behaviour of the regime:

'They tied my hands behind my back and all the policemen coming back to the station said, "Ah, you're a friend of the bearded ones, take that!" They kicked me and spat on me. For two days I had nothing to eat, I thought they wanted to kill me. I did not even know why. They told me nothing – to them, I was with the "bearded ones",

---

[29] See the list of victims drawn up by the Comité Algérien des Militants Libres de la Dignité Humaine et des Droits de l'Homme, which is in fact a grouping of ex-FIS militants in exile. *Le Livre Blanc sur la répression en Algérie*, vol. 1, Geneva: Ed. Hoggard, 1995, 221 pp.

[30] According to a policeman who had resigned after working in the suburbs of Algiers, whom we interviewed in 1994.

so they beat me. They broke my arch, I bled, they said to me, "We're going to kill you all." They released me when my family found me.' (Youssef, drinks vendor, 1993)

The torture of ordinary youths who were very little interested in politics gave credence to what the Islamists said about the government's loss of legitimacy, but without making those people Islamist militants. In fact it was later, in the neighbourhood armed bands which were formed from 1993 onwards and which many of them joined, that their search for revenge came near to acts of *jihad*. Meanwhile, they placed their hopes of revenge in the 'Moudjahidin' of the MIA (Mouvement Islamique Armé) led by the 'lion of the mountains', Abdelkader Chébouti, 'Emir' of the first Islamist faction struggling against the regime.

Waiting for the avenger

The interruption of the elections in January 1992 and the policy of repression that followed developed among the FIS voters and sympathisers a feeling of sympathy for the 'supporters of the *jihad*', then led by the MIA. In the eyes of the devout activists the regime was displaying its apostasy, while for the FIS sympathisers, it was just preserving its privileges by force. Fearing an uprising by the communes supporting the FIS, the regime embarked on a strategy of occupation and control of those districts by the security forces. The fighters of the MIA, then settled in places adjoining the Blida Atlas where their maquis was operating, were momentarily paralysed in their movements. The 'Carrefour des Quatre Saisons' at Les Eucalyptus, which marks the border of the Algiers and Blida Wilayas and remained the necessary route to take towards Larbaa – home village of Abdelkader Chébouti, 'Emir' of the MIA in 1992-93 – became, because of its strategic position, a place of daily clashes.

Breach with legality. In 1992, as there was no general uprising by Islamist sympathisers, the regime hoped for an easy victory.[31] The arrests of militants and the dissolution of the party in March 'decapitated' the Islamist movement which, however, at its grass roots waited to see what would happen. But regular murders of policemen obliged the police to make their presence felt. Insecurity and suspicion became general, political allegiances broke down under assault from local loyalties. The young people of those places were initially subjected to arbitrary arrests, and suspected the presence of informers *(biyar)* among them. One of the first publicised killings of women occurred at Les Eucalyptus in April 1993. The woman, named Karima and working as a secretary at the social work and sports department of the

---

[31] See the interview given by a senior military officer in exile to the newspaper *Le Monde* (16 Sept. 1994), where he said, 'At the beginning, we thought we could win'.

General Directorate of National Security, was killed in front of her home,[32] because she had been accused by the Islamist sympathisers of reporting people to the authorities. Her murder crystallised two attitudes in the district, which summed up the opposed outlooks of two generations. For parents, the killing of a woman was something inconceivable, inexcusable, totally illegitimate. The views expressed by the young were quite the opposite: woman or man, every threat must be eliminated:

'What! They wanted us to cry for her? To hear them, Karima was perfect. At the mosque they said she worked for Military Security and gave information about the Moudjahidin.' (Mourad, unemployed college graduate, Algiers suburbs, 1993)

That murder caused a real division among the inhabitants of the district. The parents of the people we interviewed recalled that Karima had fed her family from her pay, and asked how could people call themselves 'Moudjahidin' and murder a young woman? Condemnation of that murder, constantly re-broadcast on television, followed a code of ethics in which any attack on women, whether symbolic or physical, was unacceptable. Some parents concluded that 'the young understand nothing about life, they believe anything, while on television Karima's parents were seen saying their daughter was innocent.' When the newscaster on the 8 p.m. news programme announced that murder and broadcast reports on the reactions of the victim's family, 'old' people were stunned. As for Mourad, a sympathiser with the former FIS, sure of his sources he laughed at and mocked the 'old' people who felt distress over a girl and forgot the government's violence against the Islamists and young people suspected of sympathy towards them.

This example showed that, for the Islamist sympathisers in 1993, the cause of the 'supporters of *jihad*' was just. After a year of repressive policies a breach with legality appeared, though it did not yet take the form of a revolutionary programme. Young unemployed men, the main victims of reprisals by the security forces, continued to wait for a 'saviour'. Arrested and maltreated, paradoxically they hoped, like Youssef and Abdellah, to leave Algeria for France; but rumours went around the commune and young men of Les Eucalyptus thought there were files on them and no visa would be granted to them: 'You can't go to France any more', said one of Youssef's friends, 'you're condemned to stay here now.' Another said: 'No, it's not that, if you've been arrested there is a file on you, you can't have a visa for France any more. They work together, France and Algeria. You, Youssef, you've been arrested, you can say goodbye to France.' Aware that they were prisoners of the civil war now setting in, they turned to waiting for an avenger.

The political field narrowed and thus new actors, for whom violence was the only language, emerged. The generation of parents who had known the

---

[32] *El Watan*, 8 April 1993.

liberation war knew what that would lead to. Where the 'old people' talked of young people killing for money, or out of jealousy or madness, the younger generation saw only fighters with sincere commitment. Fed from different sources of information, the '54 Generation'[33] solidly supported the official line, stopped going to 'political mosques' and saw the 'supporters of *jihad*' as simple terrorists. People in their twenties, for the sake of honour and loyalty, went to mosques even though the security forces had won the 'battle of the mosques' in 1992. The mosques remained centres of information where the 'Moudjahid' was seen as a hero. As for the adolescents, they became used to the language of war, developed skill at dodging fighting, kept company with the bitter experience of brothers and friends subjected to deadly reprisals. In place of the 'Moudjahid' idealised by their elder brothers, they placed the figure of the 'Emir', the local armed gang leader who, from the end of 1993, was to express their resentment through violence.

Fear of a 'war worse than the war against France'. Before the emergence of the 'Emirs' of armed gangs, who reduced the extent of violence to a strictly defined local territory, the Moudjahidin's actions were presented in the minds of their sympathisers in a national, political and religious way. The Moudjahid represented all Muslims, the 'Emir' only his own men. Thus, in 1993, Mourad thought that the MIA Moudjahidin's action showed ambition to be defenders of the Muslims in Algeria:

'No, the Moudjahidin only kill those who are contrary to Islam. All those who have spoken against Islam, they kill. At a big compulsory demonstration[34] [so called because of the draconian conditions imposed by the state on companies, to ensure that their staff and workers, as well as schoolchildren, were released for the time allotted to the demonstration] journalists asked a man – no, an ass – "why are you here?" He answered, "We must fight the terrorists." You know where he is now? The Moudjahidin caught him and killed him. Why didn't he keep his mouth shut on television? They forced you to speak! Say it, instead of saying just anything.' (Mourad, qualified job-seeker, Algiers suburbs, 1993)

The Moudjahid fitted into two sets of ideas: for the *hittistes* ill-treated by the security forces he was an avenger, for the devout activists, the students and the jobless college graduates a defender of Islam. For the latter categories the Moudjahidin were fighting against an impious state headed by atheists – Communists who were in addition French-speaking. The meaning of the word 'Moudjahid' in young people's *imaginaire* was related to their culture as well as to their social group. For some the religious sense of the term

[33] The '54 Generation' represents people marked by the war of liberation. That period became the prism through which they looked at their environment.

[34] On 22 March 1993 a march 'against violence and terrorism' was organised in Algiers and regional capitals in response to a call from the UGTA and several organisations.

was obscured by the warlike actions, the Moudjahid's methods fascinated them more than his aim – the creation of an Islamic state. But for the parents' generation such attitudes were incomprehensible. To call the Algerian state impious was absurd; it was French-speaking no doubt, but, as the father of one of the young people we spoke with said, 'It is French-speaking like all the older generation, I too am French-speaking'. His wife thought that the current events, which she called 'Madani's revolution', were like a crisis of youth, a generation problem. In that conflict parents felt excluded and marginalised by the young whom they criticised for plunging the country into a war 'worse than the war against France'. The re-Islamisation of society by activists from culturally well-off backgrounds, brought up in and retaining Islamist ideas that the older generation found incomprehensible, left that generation helpless. They sensed in their 'children' who were FIS activists or sympathisers a 'desire for dissidence'[35] against the regime, whose violence deprived their arguments of legitimacy. The fear of civil war haunted the parents of our interviewees from 1993, because they saw that the development of the conflict between Moudjahidin and the regime would be an opportunity for a general settling of scores in a commune riven by economic and social conflicts. Drawing on lessons learned in the war of liberation, they knew that war can be a cover for a great number of crimes committed for other than political motives. But for their offspring the outside points of reference were to be found in the present day first, only afterwards in history.

Arguments based on outside events

Hama and the 'Occupied Territories'. In 1993, while the meaning attributed to the word 'Moudjahid' indicated the varying social groups to which FIS sympathisers belonged, the outside events which they used as reference provided a better indication of their political *imaginaire*. Their development of ideas about situations comparable to what they saw as their own was backed by descriptions in the media and in books. Direct experience of a violent situation was absent, except for the parents' generation for which the liberation war was a permanent point of reference and comparison. For young FIS sympathisers the violence experienced by their neighbourhood in Les Eucalyptus was comparable with that in the city of Hama in Syria,[36] which symbolised the martyrdom of the Islamist Cause at the hands of an 'impious' state power:

'They are going to crush us like that Jew Assad did at Hama. You know, at Hama, in that city, they killed all the Muslims with tanks, aeroplanes, helicopters. They rased

---

[35] A phrase used by C. Geffray, *Les causes des armes au Mozambique*, Paris: Karthala, 1990, p. 78.

[36] See M. Seurat, 'L'Etat de barbarie. Syrie, 1979-82' and 'Terrorisme d'Etat, terrorisme contre l'Etat', *Esprit*, November 1983 and October 1984.

the city to the ground, today you can see the ruins. They are going to something like that to us here one day.' (Farid, unemployed, Algiers suburbs, 1993)

Algerian air force helicopters flying over Les Eucalyptus on their way to the mountainous Massif of Meftah, stronghold of the MIA maquis in 1993, counted for something in this comparison with the Syrian city. People feared that repression would come from the 'sky' and fall indiscriminately on the commune. But the everyday comparison was made with television reports on the Occupied Territories of Palestine. Besides the curfew and the fear of being arrested at the mosque there was also the dynamiting of houses used as hideouts for Islamist commandos:

'This is Palestine, this is Palestine here, my friend. They have sealed off everything, we can't leave the district or enter it.' (Abdallah, vendor, Algiers suburbs, 1993)

After each murder the district was momentarily occupied by the security forces, who penetrated suspect houses and banned all movement. The Islamists added 'Jews' to 'Communists' and 'French-speakers' as enemies; the regime was compared with the Israeli government in its fight against the 'Arabs'. Such comparisons sought to drive home the loss of legitimacy by the government based on the interruption of the elections in 1992. For the Islamists the struggle against the Jewish state remained a legacy of the Arab nationalist message, and mobilisation around bellicose slogans against 'Tel Aviv' still aroused enthusiasm. Did the FIS leaders hope, after the interruption of the elections, to produce mobilisation comparable to that which occurred at the time of the Gulf War,[37] and to associate the Jewish state, the Syrian state and the Algerian state in the voters' and sympathisers' *imaginaire*, in the expectation that more general contestation against the Algerian state would follow? Anyway, that did not happen. Very soon another comparison was being made, between the Algerian government's methods and practices and the more classic example of colonial France.

Bringing back memories of French rule. Although none of the young people we interviewed had known the colonial period, it was constantly mentioned. Was this a legacy of school teaching, or more generally of the abundant criticisms of colonial France in conversation and the press? For the numerous television programmes on the Algerian war of 1954-62, filled with arrests, searches, battles and individual armed attacks, there were parallels in the present situation. The dynamiting of a place called 'La Montagne' at El Harrach, where six 'terrorists' had fled, was the starting point for the comparison with colonial France among our sample. It was expounded in 1993 by Mourad, an unemployed college graduate. Terrorised by the roar of armoured cars, then by the RPG fire from the security forces at the 'terrorists'' hideout, traders

[37] On 18 January 1991 there was a demonstration in Algiers, on the Islamists' initiative, by volunteers offering to fight with Iraq. See Franck Frégosi, op. cit. (note 12), p. 35.

and passers-by fled, taking care, however, to repack their goods. A young woman wearing a veil shouted after every rocket burst, 'Those are our lions over there', pointing to the Islamists entrenched in the house, and a man shouted repeatedly *'Allahou akbar'* amid the general panic. In 1993 the population was not used to such a degree of violence. Its behaviour was to be very different in 1994-5; with experience of dodging and escaping, it was then to show coolness and well learned survival reflexes.

For Mourad and his companions there was joy – such resistance in the heart of Algiers, it was something unimaginable. At Mourad's home he described how 'the Moudjahidin hung on to "la Montagne", stood up to the rockets'. He was impatient to see the 8 p.m. news programme to see if 'they will at least speak about this battle'. A news flash announced then that mixed army-police forces had neutralised three terrorists who had taken a woman and two children as hostages. To Mourad 'those hostages, it's propaganda', which meant that 'the soldiers had caused three deaths among civilians' and 'blamed it on the Moudjahidin'. Disappointed by the absence of pictures and the laconic commentary, Mourad decided, the next morning, to check on the situation. At El Harrach there was amazement, a crowd of passers-by was looking on from the so-called 'Briquetterie' bridge (there was a ruined brickworks nearby) at the spectacle of 'La Montagne'. The fighting was still going on, the district was sealed off, Mourad was overjoyed: 'See, I knew they were lying, they did not neutralise anything at all.' He asked his neighbour what was going on; the neighbour replied, 'The Moudjahidin are in a house, they are not succeeding in getting them to come out'. He was happy – a 24-hour battle! He blessed Heaven: 'It's incredible, with rockets, armoured cars, they can't succeed in beating them.' Full of joy, he returned to his neighbourhood and waited impatiently for the 8 p.m. news, with all his family. The news programme began in a deeply silent room. It was an immense disappointment, the newscaster's commentary was made against a background of pictures: a house was dynamited, the one where the 'terrorists' had sought refuge.

Insults against the regime, the army and the Jews flew from all members of the family, except the father. Angrily Mourad broke out:

'It's incredible, you have seen what they do, it's like the French now, they are doing like the French. It's incredible, they do that and then they say they are Muslims, that they respect human rights. The Minister, he has said, "Algeria respects human rights". It is said to be a country of human rights. They are doing to us like the French did; have a good look, Dad, see who the terrorists are.' (Mourad, unemployed college graduate, 1993)

The dynamiting of the 'terrorists'' hideout greatly shocked Mourad; that method recalled the portrayals of the Israeli security forces' practices and the images of the 'Battle of Algiers' in 1957. Mourad's angry reaction was also the end of a hope – the Moudjahidin were not the stronger side. Their resistance had aroused expectations dashed by the supremacy of the security forces. As the previous day, Mourad decided to go to the 'La Montagne' district, a work of mourning – he had to calm his inner revolt. Going together with one of his friends of the neighbourhood, he was stupefied; the security forces had completely disappeared, in their place there was a crowd of people around the ruins. They picked up and stored still usable objects so as to give them back to the family occupying the house, which had been dynamited because of the failure to dislodge the 'terrorists'. A collection was later organised for the family. In 1994 there were rumours that one of the 'Emirs' of El Harrach had generously compensated that family, close to the family of Ali Benhadj.

'Les Eucalyptus is like Chicago or Sicily'. Comparisons of the present situation with the Occupied Territories, or French colonial rule, or Hama were not the only ones made. Those were above all the comparisons expressing the outlook of Islamist sympathisers, which reflected their reading of the conflict. They showed, if not formal commitment to the Moudjahidin camp, at least approval of their methods. For others, who abstained during the elections (1990-1) and were not much interested in political activity, the most eloquent comparisons were those made with Sicily or Chicago,[38] arising from American television dramas about the Mafia and its methods. In comparisons of that sort the Moudjahidin and the security forces were considered together under the same heading, that of 'bandits'. The figure of the policeman corrupted by the Mafia in American films (*The Godfather* is an example) had its extension in Algeria and especially in those localities. From 1992-3 identification of the protagonists was ambiguous; insecurity came as much from 'thieves', 'bandits' and 'Islamists' as from 'policeman', all of those people prospering amid the terror:

'You don't know any more, you don't understand any more, there are thieves now, bandits too. They have found the opportunity to work undisturbed. The place is full of thieves in this district, I assure you; at work, if you leave something for just a minute, you come back and it's gone. There are no more policemen, there is nobody any more to deal with them, they have a free hand. Here it's become worse than Chicago now.' (Karim, building day-labourer, Algiers suburbs, 1993)

The policemen who, in 1992-3, were busy baiting traps were still there later, but no longer in uniform;[39] they were no longer entrusted with keeping

---

[38] The comparison with Chicago was already there at the time of the OAS in 1961: 'The weeks before the cease-fire strengthened the resemblance between Algiers and Chicago', wrote A.M. Duranton-Crabol in *Le temps de l'OAS* (Brussels: Complexe, 1995), p. 150.

[39] Policemen are sometimes used as bait by the GIS (Groupe d'Intervention et de Surveillance), a special unit in charge of the anti-terrorist struggle, called 'Ninjas' because their faces are covered with balaclavas. Policeman are posted in districts known for the presence of 'supporters of the *jihad*', while GIS men hiding nearby wait for those people to emerge by attacking the policemen on duty, and neutralise them.

order, but dealt more with intelligence ('*biyar*', informers). Political crimes, social violence, economic crimes became part of daily life in those areas. For 'supporters of peace and quiet', like Karim, all the warring parties were much the same, on the lines of an imagined Sicily where politicians, policemen, criminals and Mafiosi are found side by side and flourish in the same setting.

Incomprehension at the army's refusal to come to terms with the FIS. The involvement of the army in repression from 1993 aroused bitterness and sadness among sympathisers of the former FIS. They noted that the ANP (Armée Nationale Populaire) was refusing to come to terms with the FIS, in spite of its inability to suppress the Islamist violence. Their rejection of the Algerian political class did not, paradoxically, extend to that institution, although it had been running the country since independence.[40] Rarely did their discourse turn against military personnel. Such an attitude on the part of the Islamist leaders was a calculated one, aimed at keeping on good terms with the main player in the regime; but even among sympathisers who were not under any political constraint, and were used to expressing their thoughts freely, very few criticisms were directed against the ANP. The army, until 1993, was even seen still as a possible partner with the former FIS if the latter took power. The Islamist sympathisers' hatred was until then concentrated on the FLN, symbol of nepotism and '*hogra*' (contempt) towards them: with the Communist (Tahaddi) party it was seen as mainly responsible for the prevailing situation. Those sympathisers therefore expected that in view of the FIS' election success, the army would put an end to its partnership with the FLN and would run the country in cooperation with the political victors:

'It is disheartening, I swear to you, I don't understand why the army is defending the Communists. They should let them die or leave for France if they want to live like "*kuffar*" [infidels]. I don't understand why the army is not with the FIS. The FIS is the people, the army must be with the people. Even though it's true there are some soldiers on our side – but not all.' (Student, Algiers suburbs, 1993)

As in Ibn Khaldun's theory of cycles,[41] the Algerian Islamists were convinced that the FLN's time had passed, giving way to the time of the FIS. So the army should have noted that the 'people' were no longer identified

---

[40] See A. Yesfah, *Le processus de légitimation du pouvoir militaire et la constitution de l'-Etat en Algérie* (Paris: Anthropos, 1982), 201 pp., Chapter 'Constitution d'un groupe social hégémonique: l'armée'.

[41] 'The State, in Ibn Khaldun's theory of cycles, goes through a cycle of three phases: youth, when the groups constituting the elite share power equally; middle age, when one group gets rid of the others and, supported by its enfranchised clients, monopolises power, wealth and manpower; and old age when *asabiya* (group spirit) breaks down, when the original rigour gets lost amid luxury and refinement, when the state becomes the property of Praetorian Guards.' A. Laroui, *Islam et modernité*, Paris: La Découverte, 1986, p. 115.

with the former single party but rather with the FIS, and that accordingly its refusal to come to terms with the new political force was illogical. The army's involvement in repression changed the enemy's identity: the political class ceased to be the target of the Islamists' verbal attacks, and the army assumed that role. For the army, coming to terms with the FIS would have cost more than the policy of eradicating the Islamists, for reasons explained by J. Leca: 'If contending parties do not feel too vulnerable, they can accept a pact guaranteeing that nothing will happen to them. If one of them considers itself all-powerful, it will not think of a pact; on the other hand, if all sides feel entirely vulnerable, a pact is equally unlikely since mutual suspicion will be stronger than readiness to let the others have control of significant resources. In the first case, the low probability of a pact is due to the assumption that it will bring fewer gains than the temptation to suppress or destroy the enemy – insufficient profits, that is. In the second, people feel sure that compromise means in fact a very high probability of an intolerable result – that is, excessive costs.'[42] Conviction that an agreement with the FIS would lead to 'dictatorship'[43] made the army insensitive to risks. But the absence of an Islamist-military agreement against the other political formations (especially the FLN and FFS) increased support for the MIA guerrillas who had embarked on war with the security forces.

The maquis: centre of armed resistance

The time of jihad. Disappointed by the army's decision to fight the Islamists rather than govern with them, the sympathisers turned to Abdelkader Chébouti, 'Emir' of the MIA (Mouvement Islamique Armé). He was a hero to those who saw in him a defender or avenger motivated by 'hatred' of the authoritarian behaviour of the security forces. In the political *imaginaire* Chébouti, called '*liwa*' or General, was the perfect Moudjahid, the good 'general' compared with the 'bad' generals of the ANP; the fascination he aroused was in proportion to the despair felt by his admirers. Why Abdelkader Chébouti? The MIA 'Emir's' charisma counted for little in that respect; during the elections he was marginalised, his supporters did not remember any intervention by him except for his forecast that the parliamentary elections would be halted by the army if the FIS won. Seen as a visionary like Ali Benhadj, Abdelkader Chébouti assumed heroic proportions because of the repression that thrust people who had suffered ill-treatment, injury and humiliation at the hands of the forces of order into the orbit of his movement. Thus he attracted young people wanting to fight the regime

---

[42] J. Leca, 'La démocratisation dans le monde arabe: incertitude, vulnérabilité et légitimité', in G. Salamé (ed.), *Démocratie sans démocrates'* Paris: Fayard, 1994, p. 42.

[43] General Khaled Nezzar wrote in *El Moudjahid* of 15 March 1990, 'Democracy is not anarchy, freedom of expression cannot be synonymous with violence and intimidation, it would be intolerable if men coming to power through democracy led us to dictatorship'.

or to find in the maquis some protection against the arbitrary behaviour of the security forces:

'This is not going to last, Chébouti will come down from the mountains with his Moudjahidin, and I swear to you he will kill them all. One shouldn't believe what they say in France: "They are terrorists". They are repeating what our journalists say. Chébouti is a general, he has men, real soldiers, Moudjahidin, and there are more and more young men who want to go to the mountains.' (Abdellah, newsagent, Algiers suburbs, 1993)

Many of those young men were turned away by the maquis, because it had no room for them, as the movement's logistics had not been adapted. The MIA was nonetheless, in 1992-3, the only armed opposition organisation present in the Mitidja. Thus all murders, attacks and other guerrilla actions were attributed to it. The lion of the mountains' men seemed to have the gift of being everywhere.

In reality, after the dissolution of the FIS in March 1992 the organisational framework among FIS voters was very much weakened. Among the Algerian Islamists various armed groups were competing as from 1990-1. The small Takfir wa-l Hijra groups[44] linked to the 'Kabul' mosque at Belcourt in Algiers, the 'Jerusalem Brigades' (Kataeb el Qods) and the Algerian Hezbollah (formed in March 1990) were in direct competition with the MIA for a monopoly of the *jihad*. The MIA, while disapproving of the electoral process, stood ready for a *jihad* in case of army intervention to stop a victory for the FIS in the parliamentary elections. Those small groups which set out too early on the *jihad* path were the first to suffer from the repression. Their breakup was blamed by their admirers on the FIS political leaders, who were afraid that involvement in the armed struggle might harm the running of the elections process by providing a pretext for military intervention:

'Hachani[45] is a nitwit, he let himself be manipulated, it was because of him that the "Afghans" were arrested. All those who were against the elections but for the *jihad* were arrested or murdered because of him. When they arrested Madani and Benhadj [June 1991], the "Afghans" said, "We must wage a *jihad*." But he told them to wait. The army came straight away to the mosque and arrested or killed them all. Some

---

[44] The small Takfir wa-l Hijra group, called 'the Afghans', was responsible for the attack on the Guemmar frontier post on the Tunisian border in November 1991, an action which led the Prime Minister, Ahmed Ghozali, to say: 'Once he came to power Hitler burned the Reichstag. We have had the Guemmar events where Algerians have been killed, slaughtered.' Interview with *La Libre Belgique*, 21 Jan. 1992.

[45] Abdelkader Hachani, member of the FIS Council, was promoted after the arrest of Abassi Madani and Ali Benhadj to be head of the party's Political Affairs Commission. Following the Batna Congress of July 1991 he succeeded in increasing his influence over the leading positions in the party, which he persuaded to take part in the parliamentary elections fixed for December 1991. He was arrested in October 1991 and remained in custody without trial at Serkaji prison in Algiers. He was released in July 1997.

people, the ones who had joined the MIA, are still alive.' (Mourad, unemployed college graduate, Algiers suburbs, 1994)

The small groups that started the *jihad* early, such as Takfir wa-l Hijra, were neutralised in 1992 and 1993. With the FIS banned, its activists gaoled, its voters and sympathisers kept under watch, the government thought it only had to complete the dismantling of small groups devoted to violence that were known and on file. From then on the FIS voters and sympathisers were without any organisation; they were reduced to facing the problems of daily life without a political intermediary capable of easing them. In that context they saw in the MIA, which alone had escaped from the repression started in 1992, a well constructed and rational form of resistance – especially as the MIA, by setting up its maquis in mountainous areas close to Algiers (Chréa, the Blida Atlas), updated the map of resistance by the 'knights of the crests' in the colonial period.[46] The MIA was in 1992-3 the pole to which all discontented people ready for action could be attracted:

'That will end with their defeat. Do you know why they are going to lose? Why does the army fight? For cars, houses. But now they see they can't enjoy life undisturbed any longer. With Chébouti they understand that justice is coming, the hour has come to settle accounts. Because the young men, the Moudjahidin, they don't fight for cars, they fight for justice and because they have the Faith, they will win.' (Wahab, young trader, Algiers suburbs, 1993)

Chébouti's men were endowed with all the virtues and were seen as fighting against soldiers 'greedy for material possessions'. Convinced that the Moudjahidin were better motivated and more effective than the soldiers, many FIS sympathisers and voters thought victory was near at the end of 1993. Defending one's home, that is one's family and its property, seemed to count for little compared with religious zeal. Such an analysis, as we shall see later, had more to do with the fantasies of the FIS voters and sympathisers than with a realistic assessment of the situation. For those sympathisers the MIA had a glorious destiny before it. The military ability of the Moudjahidin was described in terms of high praise, rumour gave them innumerable qualities, the reports of foreign journalists were also quoted to back up those ideas:

'Chébouti with his 2,000 men in the mountains, he can never be caught. A German journalist went to meet him, the Moudjahidin were waiting for her at the airport and took her to the mountains. She said later that she had seen an army with tanks

---

[46] Abdelkader Djeghloul stressed how the figure of the 'resistance fighter' and that of the 'outlaw' overlap in Algeria; such a figure is called in poetry the 'knight of the crests': 'The theme of outlaws has an important place in the regional poetic repertories. The outlaw is above all he who has dared to rise up and to die, he who has responded to the affront to the community. He is the anti-state, but also the counter-state, the "Sultan", the "lion".' *Eléments d'histoire culturelle algérienne*, Algiers: Enal, 1984, p. 185.

and soldiers, that they were training like soldiers.' (Omar, student, Algiers suburbs, 1993)

Among that group of people there was complete certainty that the 'lion of the mountains' would win. This feeling made up for the failure of the FIS to manage its relations with the regime. To those sympathisers and voters it seemed inconceivable that a political party that had mobilised about three million voters could be banned without the government being severely shaken. They considered that the potential of Islamism in Algeria had been very badly used by the organisers of the movement; fascination for the military-Islamic organisations was strengthened by the idea that they would know much better how to use that potential:

Chébouti told them not to take part in the elections, first of all because in Islam there are no elections. We have our own system, a total system, Islam has no need for elections to represent power. Chébouti, he said to Madani and Benhadj, 'The elections are a trap'. He knew that government already, he was with Bouyali. They said: 'The Islamic state will be created by throwing out the Communists, with God's will'. Benhadj told him, 'We shall play the game of their democracy and show them that Islam always wins'. But Chébouti and the Moudjahidin did not vote, they knew it was a trap laid by the Communists. (Omar, student, Algiers suburbs, 1993)

The 'warriors of Islam' benefited from bias in their favour, and were described in the same terms extolling virtue as the 'FIS elected representatives' elected two years earlier. The MIA was the hero of the adolescents of the neighbourhood, who were witnesses to the security forces' violence. Bit by bit its fighters entered their *imaginaire*, created codes of honour in human relations, caused violence to be valued, and created a new identity, that of the Moudjahid. The socialisation started by the MIA was to have its effect, even after it had been driven from the *jihad* field, on the numerous armed groups created then by young men fascinated in their adolescent days by the 'Lion of the Mountains'.

4

DESCENT INTO WAR

In 1993 the regime was placed in check. The decapitation of the ex-FIS leadership and intimidation of the party's sympathisers were not succeeding in defeating the Islamists. Some communes of Greater Algiers slid into a pattern of urban guerrilla warfare, in which MIA commandos and local armed gangs were equally at home. Two new Islamist factions emerged, the GIA (Groupement Islamique Armé)[1] and the MEI (Mouvement pour l'Etat Islamique.). But in 1993 the MIA remained the most prestigious label among ex-FIS sympathisers, and its 'Emir', Chébouti, was still the 'Lion of the Mountains'. At Les Eucalyptus, Chararba, El Harrach and Baraki war was declared against the hated regime by young men, Islamists and others, who remained convinced that its collapse was within the realm of possibility.

As for the Islamist factions (the MIA, GIA and MEI in 1993), the failure of the 'people' to rise up against the regime convinced them that war cannot be prosecuted on the basis of the people's spontaneous feelings. So they established recruitment procedures to consolidate their military-Islamist organisation. Established close to the communes of Greater Algiers, in the maquis in the Blida Atlas, they turned the nearest places into battlefields, very often to their advantage. The people recognised the legitimacy of their struggle and gave them the necessary support. To cope with this situation the government, headed by a new team of senior military officers,[2] set about training a military corps specialising in counter-guerrilla warfare. It went into action in April 1993, and its 15,000 men invaded the Greater Algiers communes to dislodge the armed groups of various factions;[3] the regime embarked on a policy of winning back its territory and

[1] Abdelkader Chébouti's monopoly of leadership of the *jihad* was contested by leaders of the MIA like Abdelhak Layada, who set up the Groupement Islamique Armé (GIA) which distinguished itself at the end of 1993 with the taking of hostages at the French embassy. Saïd Makhloufi set up the Mouvement Islamique Armé (MEI) because of disagreements over the military strategy to be adopted against the regime. Part III, Chapter 2 studies the development of the guerrilla campaign and the changes it went through.

[2] In July 1993 General Liamine Zeroual became Minister of Defence, while General Mohamed Lamari succeeded Abdelmalek Guenaiza as Chief of Army Staff. The following were promoted to the rank of *général-major*: Mohamed Ghenim, Secretary-General of the Ministry of Defence; Mediene, head of the intelligence and security department; and Mohamed Touati and Taghit Abdelmajid, advisers to the Ministry of Defence. *Marchés Tropicaux et Méditerranéens,* 9 July 1993.

[3] Three divisions with a strength of about 15,000 men were to be stationed in the Algiers

the dissident population, expelling the Islamist fighters from the urban districts of the capital.

Control of the Islamist communes became a military and political stake in the conflict; their closeness to the centre of Algiers was a permanent threat for the regime, which feared that they would be a sanctuary for the Islamist factions. For those factions the communes were a military asset to be protected, and it was from among their inhabitants that they drew their fighters and their main economic resources. As they enjoyed a high level of sympathy because of the legitimacy of their struggle, they succeeded without great difficulty in establishing logistical networks for the guerrilla campaign. Faced with this unfavourable situation, the new military team chose a policy of isolating those communes. A new barracks was built in the south-eastern suburbs to back up the war effort. In the municipalities where armed Islamist groups lived, the regime 'abandoned' the local people to their fate; there thus developed a feeling of insecurity due to the presence of many actors using violence (thieves, criminals, armed Islamist groups, MIA commandos, informers etc.).

The Politics of Chaos

Increased crime. The communes of Les Eucalyptus and Chararba illustrate the regime's strategy. They went from euphoria under the FIS councillors to the 'hell' of civil war. Dissolution of the municipal councils controlled by the FIS also halted the Islamist activists' work of social control and crime prevention. The Islamist order ceased to reign there, and from 1993 petty traders complained about thefts again. To this problem were added protection rackets by soldiers stationed nearby. Believing that they were in enemy territory, the soldiers made the people pay for the risks they were facing, by direct extortion of goods:

'Every week an officer came with his men, he asked me for three, four or five kilos of meat. And watch out if you answer him back at all, he will take more. But I had a friend, an air force officer, I had told him by telephone that so-and-so was robbing me every week. One day he came and hid to one side; the others came and asked me for meat, I said, "No". The officer began to insult me, my friend came out and said, "Have you no shame?" and slapped him and told his men to take him away.' (Butcher, Algiers suburbs, 1993)

---

region. The security services had gone through the districts of Baraki, Chararba and Les Eucalyptus with a fine-toothed comb, and a gendarmerie communiqué said it had been a 'combined action by the forces of the gendarmerie, the army and the police, in accordance with new methods of struggle against terrorism'. 'The fact that that operation was launched from the "hideouts" of Baraki and Les Eucalyptus is indicative of the role played by those districts in subversive activity. It is in fact in Les Eucalyptus that the most murderous individual outrages have been committed,' wrote the newspaper *Liberté*, 27 April 1993. Chapter 7 analyses the establishment of these 'new methods of struggle against terrorism'.

The army's arrival in the commune was a burden on the local population which had to provide for its needs. But above all the victims of that extortion lived in terror of being seen at those moments by spies of the armed groups, because at that moment they appeared, like that butcher, to be accomplices of the security forces, giving them information as well as feeding them. The extortion of goods by soldiers was aimed at compromising the local economic actors who, by their trade, were also in contact with the armed groups and feeding them also. A visit by soldiers to a trader in broad daylight was a prelude to his murder by armed Islamist groups.

Besides the risk to life there were other ordeals such as the ubiquity of criminals. After the halt to the elections in January 1992 criminals became fully-fledged players on the urban guerrilla stage. Sometimes they were called police informers by Islamist sympathisers, while on other occasions they were condemned as the Islamists' allies by the other side. In fact they operated on their own account, collaborating in the Mitidja communes with the army or with the armed groups, according to the local balance of forces. However, the Islamist sympathisers' view of them changed after 1992, when they came to be viewed as a weapon used by the regime following the release of numerous common-law prisoners. That release was supposed to spread a feeling of insecurity among the people, so that they would see the need to back the security forces as the only ones capable of restoring order. By leaving criminals to act as they liked the regime hoped to encourage the people of the Islamist communes to start collaborating with it:

'Thieves are everywhere. You'll see, they steal in front of your eyes, nobody will come to tell them anything, it's normal now, there are no police any more, you've got to manage on your own; thieves are getting rich at this time, they can take any liberty, nothing is forbidden for them. The government has caused this deliberately, I tell you. It released 6,000 prisoners, thieves, bandits, all sorts, from the prisons, to make space for the Moudjahidin. Now all Algiers is filled with thieves, not only here. And if you see a policeman and say, "My car's been stolen, " he answers, "You wanted the bearded men (*sahb el ihya*), now you look after yourself!" (Mourad, jobseeker with Technology Institute diploma, Algiers suburbs, 1993)

This state of insecurity contrasted, for the sympathisers with the former FIS, with the period when their party had exercised social control over criminals. In their view insecurity came either from the security forces or from the criminals, while the Moudjahidin's actions were, in 1993, not seen as dangerous to them. The thieves, gangs of adolescents in the urban underworld, were seen as real parasites on daily life. A psychosis set in from 1993 in Algiers, linked to thefts of cars, hold-ups of traders, even burglaries of the homes of families suspected of being well disposed to the Islamists. The security forces, concentrating on the anti-guerrilla struggle, lost interest in common criminals, especially when the latter frightened people sympathising with the FIS. One effect of the general insecurity was the absence of solidarity against attack. Victims felt they had to count on themselves alone, because any urge to come to someone's help was restrained by uncertainty over an attacker's true identity – everyone feared that behind a criminal a security forces agent was lurking:

'Every day I come to make deliveries in the district. Not long ago I parked and began unloading the goods, when a group of young people arrived, beat me in front of everyone and wanted to steal my goods – while I fight with one of them the others do the stealing, that's their tactic. Well, I swear to you, nobody came to help me or even put some fear into the young people, nothing. Before onlookers they took my goods. You know, that's done on purpose, that's how people understand well that there are no more police and the thieves and bandits are free to do what they like.' (Lahcen, delivery man, 26 years old, Algiers suburbs, 1993)

Converting criminals to Islamism. The certainty that criminals were acting under the protection of the security forces inhibited any resistance to their attacks. In fact only the establishment of the armed Islamist bands in the urban districts in 1994[4] was able to stop crime, because they tolerated no interference in their territory. Led by an 'Emir', they declared war on the criminals, to the satisfaction of the local people and especially of the petty traders. Masters of the terrain, the 'Emirs' appeared to the local people first as a cure for the crime wave, and then as an instrument of revenge against the security forces' reprisal actions. The criminals were called upon to leave the area or to work with the Islamist bands; faced with this dilemma, they decided to convert to Islamism.[5] For the people, seeing former criminals parading with the Moudjahidin caused unease about the nature of those local Islamist armed bands claiming to fight in the name of the Groupement Islamique Armé (GIA).

The pitiless pursuit of criminals by the 'Emirs' led to some surprising conversions to the cause of the *jihad* among criminals. The transition from notorious criminal to 'true Moudjahid' following conversion to Islamism illustrates the complexity of the armed bands' operation; their dynamism encouraged a desire to enlist among people who were strangers to the 'just cause'. In fact it seems that criminals used the armed bands when those were in a powerful position and broke with them when the security forces regained dominance. The absence of Islamist bands from an urban area also favoured organised banditry. When the people were no longer protected either by the security forces or by 'Emirs' claiming to follow the GIA, criminals

---

[4] The local Islamist armed bands are studied in Chapter 5.

[5] A comparable example of rivalry between criminals and guerrilla groups is found in Sri Lanka. The JVP (Janata Vimukti Peramunas), in order to control its territory, started hunting down 'gangsters': 'Notorious gangsters hurriedly left their regions of origin, if not they were found hanged from a lamp-post in the morning,' wrote Rosel Jacob, 'La révolte des jeunes et l'érosion de l'Etat au Sri Lanka. La guerre d'une organisation secrète' in E. Roy and T. Von Totha (eds), *La Violence et L'Etat*, Paris: L'Harmattan, 1993, p. 223.

appeared as the principal actors on stage. When they were under the orders of an 'Emir' they could continue to practice extortion for the GIA's benefit. If the band was broken up, they continued the same activity for their own benefit, protected, so ex-FIS sympathisers said, by security forces acting on their own account;[6] or else those forces used the criminals as an instrument of terror to arouse support among the population for the regime's policy. But in either case the objective sought was not attained, because freedom of action for criminals did not encourage popular support for the security forces; it led rather to the emergence of Islamist armed groups, to protect families from the double threat of the army and banditry. But it was traders above all that were doubly penalised, because they were permanently being called upon to respond to demands by local actors – the GIA or groups of criminals. For the victims it always meant the same thing: an indefinite protection racket in the name of various causes, depending on the local balance of forces. In this civil war criminals have been among the main beneficiaries: whether it is the army or the armed GIA bands that control the situation, criminals place their skills at the disposal of the stronger.

The intoxication of violence

The feeling of insecurity. In parallel with the spread of criminal behaviour in the Islamist communes, the warring parties resorted to terror, instilling insecurity that aimed at 'a political division of the population, between friends and enemies'.[7] That was discernible among those people who had not defined themselves either as sympathisers with the regime or as Islamists, and therefore had more fear of being floating targets. The sense of vulnerability was diffused, varying according to place and time. At night, in the small towns of the Mitidja, families' anguish was at its height, as armed clashes and reprisals were most frequent then. Night time was chosen deliberately, for it allowed those who fought at night to avoid being recognised in daytime. Members of special night fighting units and Moudjahidin returned to anonymous activity at sunrise. The daytime *hittiste* could well be a night-time fighter, and the keen sportsman at a sports centre could belong to the special units. While the night was the time for fighting, the day was used by the security forces for locating possible suspects:

[6] See the testimony of 'Saïd, the policeman' in the newspaper *La Croix-l'Evénement*: 'We mount patrols every night, solely in the city centre. There terrorists are rare. The army has swept up everything. They are in the mountains, and there, it is the army which deals with them. We, our mission is simple, we have to keep order in the city. Currently there is in fact a revival of banditry. Gangsters and drug traffickers – most often young people – are taking advantage of the situation.' 7 July 1995, p. 5.

[7] S. Roche has written: 'The feeling of insecurity threatens social relations in two ways: as elaboration of rules which are presiding over division of the population in a political sense (between friends and enemies), and as inter-personal negotiation of everyday relations.' *Le sentiment d'insécurité*, Paris: PUF, 1995, p. 16.

'Going to work is dangerous, if the army checks us, they take us in directly. My brother and I are from Batna, we have no address here, so they will say that we are terrorists who come and kill and go. We have work when God wills, one day you have work, another you go to the worksite and they tell you there is nothing today. When you work, at the end of work it's night time. I am afraid then, after 7 p.m. taxis don't want to take you any more, they don't want to go to Les Eucalyptus. The driver tells you, "If I take you, I don't know if I'll get out of there". So it's serious now, what's happening in this country.' (Karim, building day-labourer, 28 years old, 1993)

While Karim and others like him felt insecurity when they moved around, with the fear of checks; others, especially unemployed youths, felt it in the district itself. From the interruption of the elections in January 1992 onwards the districts were visited during the day by strangers who were immediately suspected of working with the security forces. Fear of arrest kept people's movements to a strict minimum; going by bus to the centre of Algiers, 20 km. away, made people afraid. This was because contentious matters like a non-renewed military service deferment card or an expired identity card took on disproportionate importance; immediate regularisation was necessary, and that meant making contact with the military or civilian authorities. But from that moment the fear of entering a police station or barracks came into play; any suspicions aroused then could be fatal for the people concerned. Convinced that Military Security had its men everywhere, the people withdrew behind the walls of family or neighbourhood solidarity, for fear of informers:

'Before, you saw how everyone was here, they wore beards and *kamis*...Now that's all over, everyone is clean-shaven. The neighbourhood is filled with *biyar* [informers]. I see them coming to the shop, we never saw those people in the district before.' (Ahmed, trader, Algiers suburbs, 1993)

The supposed presence of security agents prevented any discussion of political events in public. The large number of 'new bearded men' in the district confused the outward signs of political affiliation; those policemen disguised as Islamists tried to make contact with the local people. Real and fake Islamists sowed confusion and increased suspicion, one concrete result being that fewer people went to cafés (supposed to be the favourite place for informers), preferring to get together in a someone's flat bedroom. The landmarks of the district crumbled; the café became much too dangerous, and young men reluctantly abandoned their favourite game, dominos, to sit in front of their television sets. It was as risky to leave Les Eucalyptus as to stay there. The isolation which the military strategists sought to achieve had its effects; the commune had its apprenticeship in daily terror. The imposition of a curfew on 30 November 1992 in seven Wilayas[8] worsened the climate of civil war. Ideas and expressions of view about the curfew restrictions varied according to locality and political allegiance. Changes in

---

[8] The Wilayas of Algiers, Blida, Boumerdès, Tipasa, Bouira, Médéa and Aïn Defla.

people's way of life due to the curfew hours (in 1993 9.30 p.m. to 5 a.m.; in 1994 10.30 p.m. to 5 a.m.; in 1995 midnight to 5 a.m.) had more effect, parado-xically, on young people who did not belong to the Islamist movement.

Those who lived in the residential districts, in small flats, were obliged to stay at home despite lack of space. Many families did not have enough beds.[9] Brothers and sisters used the same bed in turns (three eight-hour shifts in 24 hours) and so were out of doors for a part of the night, in the company of their friends with the same bad luck. Used to living in the street accord-ing to their own way of life, they suffered from the intrusion of the security forces into the only place where they felt at ease:

'They seal off the district, you can't go out any more, you must stay at home in front of the television. The café is dangerous, you don't know where to go any more. In the evening they make us go home like sheep or donkeys. Before you used to stay all night, you argued, you had nothing to do in the evening, you talked. In the sum-mer, what was one to do? Usually, at 10 in the evening, you'd only just left the beach, now I don't know how we're going to do. Back home at 9 p.m., it's hot, you can't even get out for fresh air.' (Lahcen, delivery man, Algiers suburbs, 1993)

In fact many people defied the curfew and stayed in stairwells or standing against the entrances of blocks of flats despite the risks. The curfew, which was lifted in 1996, affected young people whose daily lives were not structu-red around religious observance. Fond of Raï music, beer and gambling, they liked spending their evenings at the café. Forced to stay at home, they regularly broke the curfew regulations and so faced reprisals by the secu-rity forces, who saw them as spies for the armed groups or as 'terrorists'[10] in action. It was among them that the GIA found its reservoir of fighters from 1993. Exasperated by their pointless way of life, they re-established them-selves through the armed bands; deprived of leisure activity, they resorted to urban guerrilla warfare against the security forces, a 'game' in which everyone identified with a hero. They enabled the Islamist maquis (MIA, GIA, MEI) to keep up a high level of violence against the security forces without being present in the cities. From then on the feeling of insecurity continually increased, and people had to choose sides. Terrorist actions from the end of 1993 continued the strategy aimed at forcing the popula-tion to take sides.

[9] In 1992, according to an investigation by the Ministry of Health and Population, there were 3.2 people per bedroom and 2.7 per room: Office National des Statistiques and Arab League, *L'enquête algérienne sur la santé de la mère et de l'enfant*, Algiers/Cairo, 1994, 402 pp.; see review in *Problèmes et sociétés*, no. 307, November 1995.

[10] See the testimony of a policeman in exile in Paris, in *Le Monde* (7 March 1995): 'He said nothing', wrote the journalist, 'when his superiors ordered him from then on to fire without warning on outlines of figures seen in the night; "However", the police-man testified, "I knew that in the housing estates youths often slept in turns, leaving the bed to a younger brother so that he could sleep for three hours". Meanwhile they smoked a joint by the staircase.'

A strategy of terror. Besides the control of an area (a district or maquis), the Islamist guerrillas sought to ensure constant replenishment of their ranks. To that end they implemented a 'strategy of terror' in the Islamist communes, which 'sought to break the feeling of security steadily, removing all barriers which seemed to protect this or that category of people'. The response to this was a 'logic of generalised insecurity'.[11] Young men reaching the age of national service were a particular object of those strategies. Half of the strength of the Algerian army (ANP) consisted of national servicemen, and the Islamists calculated that the army would be considerably weakened if new intakes of conscripts dried up. So leaflets posted in the mosques urged young men called up for service to escape it by joining the maquis, threatening any who disobeyed this call with death. In response the regime initially launched a policy of regularising the military service situation of young men involved in some disagreement with the military authorities, to stop them joining the maquis out of fear; every individual was told to regularise his situation on pain of being considered as a deserter and hence as a 'terrorist'. The army's threat was thus added to the Islamist one for young men of the communes of Les Eucalyptus and Baraki. Being in an irregular situation, they could not leave the district any longer, for fear of checks at a military checkpoint; but if they regularised their situation, they risked being found fit for service and thus obliged to choose between the maquis and the barracks.

To back up their threats the warring parties were soon carrying out a number of violent acts against national servicemen. There were more and more murders, causing panic in families because the young men were becoming a stake in the war:

'The street was filled with dead people, when people went out and saw that they wanted to die also, they banged their heads against the wall, women shouted and wept. It was terrible to see that, there were only young men on the ground covered with blood, they were like dogs that died in the street. They were killed because they were national servicemen, they were in barracks in the south of the country, they wanted to go home for the Aïd es Seghir [the end of Ramadan feast], not to desert as the army said. They had requested leave but it had been refused because they were from here. That same evening the army came to look for them to kill them.' (Worker employed by a state enterprise set on fire by GIA armed bands, 32 years old, 1994)

The authors of these massacres were not often identified explicitly. The Islamists' sympathisers had no doubt that the authors were paramilitary groups. Others thought they were GIA Moudjahidin – whose reputation was beginning to grow – showing their determination in that manner. Those crimes, whoever ordered them, aimed at polarising allegiances and choices as the civil war began. They forced national servicemen to make a commitment for their future. The army could now motivate the troops by underlining the

---

[11] P. Braud, 'La violence politique: repères et problèmes', *Cultures et Conflits,* no. 9/10, 1993, p. 26.

enemy's 'barbarity'. Because of those crimes the national servicemen responded more readily to invitations by the army, at the end of their service, to enlist for a limited period as 'contract men';[12] they were afraid to return to their families, especially when they lived in districts where the Islamists' cause was considered legitimate. The crimes strengthened the troops' solidarity and forced the national servicemen to stay in the army, as the only protection available against GIA reprisals.

Because of these threats families 'placed' their sons among the various protagonists: when one brother was called up, it was not uncommon for another to be close to the Islamist factions. Thus the young gave each other mutual protection, and each one could bring to his 'brother' the vital information that could allow him either to escape police arrest or, if he was a soldier, to avoid being killed when he went on home leave to see his parents. The result, as we shall emphasise later, was the development of the profession of arms among young men. As stakes in the fight between the army and the Islamist guerrillas, they made their own personal investment in the various war machines (security forces, Islamist factions, groups of criminals, private protection and security agencies) to protect themselves and above all to protect their people. Enlistment was thus due more to compulsion than to any political motivation, which helps to explain why, within the same family, brothers made totally different choices, from Islamist fighter to policeman.

Mocking and despising danger: from hittiste *to* shahid. The beginnings of dissidence on the part of the *hittistes* (the people propping up the wall) took the form of 'derision'; reciting of some guerrilla actions underlined the aspect of comedy hidden in the drama of the first Moudjahidin. At Les Eucalyptus a story expressed derision at the forces of order, which was common at the beginning of the civil war, so vulnerable did the regime seem. It was common to make jokes about the behaviour of the gendarmes, soldiers and policemen, seen as scared, bent, etc. Islamist dissidents described the terror which froze their faces when they patrolled the streets of their districts. They joked about the gendarmerie armoured car driver who was not supposed to have his driving license, about the child of a *douar* (village community) who arrived in Algiers for the first time thanks to that military vehicle. In that context the story of two youths of fifteen with a Mobylette, armed with sawn-off rifles, illustrated how those new fighters went over to action. Riding around one district the two boys encountered a patrol; they fired on the vehicle and then escaped. Curious to know the result of their action, they returned to the scene and came upon the patrol dealing with the wounded. Then they opened fire again, firing at random, and escaped

[12] From 1993 the ANP offered national servicemen fixed-term contracts (of one or two years, renewable) for enlistment in its ranks.

unharmed into the alleyways of Les Eucalyptus, to recount their feat of arms; that was how Les Eucalyptus joined the *jihad* in the spring of 1993.

At that time the security forces aroused only contempt. To reassure themselves, Islamist sympathisers convinced themselves that those forces could not be effective against the Moudjahidin, who had all the human qualities with the faults of the security forces were contrasted:

'They think they make us afraid, but they are the ones who are really scared, they never dare to face the Moudjahidin. Once, in Les Eucalyptus, three Moudjahidin massacred a patrol. The soldiers heard the sound of the "*klasch*" (kalashnikov), then they came with the tank, men, etc. The Moudjahidin stayed opposite them and began to fire, the soldiers retreated, they didn't dare to fight against them, because the Moudjahidin know why they are going to die.' (Unemployed Islamist sympathiser, 1994)

When the soldiers withdrew to avoid losing men in an attack on the Moudjahidin, or to allow the special units (the 'Ninjas') to move in, this interviewee saw that only as proof of their cowardice, which he contrasted with the courage and nobility of the Islamist fighters who did not hesitate to die for the 'cause'. Some sympathisers in 1994 thought it was an honourable conclusion of the Islamist passion to be a martyr (*shahid*), demonstrating sincerity and Faith. With such determination, the Moudjahidin of the district inspired in their admirers confidence in final victory.

The generalisation of violence reversed roles. Those who, during the elections process, acted as local intermediaries (Islamist activists and elected representatives) were thrust aside by the invasion of these adolescent Moudjahidin, operating in armed bands at the end of 1993. Unknown to the various intelligence services, not mentioned in files kept on Islamist suspects, unknown to the mosque officials, the young neighbourhood 'Moudjahidin' were the product of repression and poverty. Having witnessed the mass arrests of FIS militants, the elimination of the small groups of 'supporters of the *jihad*' (Takfir wa Hijra, Kataeb el Qods, Hezbollah, etc.), they waited in an uncertain state until they heard tales of the battles led by Chébouti's men. Their *jihad* was not to be waged in the maquis but in their home districts, where they developed their activity with more assurance. Knowing perfectly all the streets, alleyways, roads, empty houses, unfinished tunnels and abandoned warehouses, they made the best use of the geography of their environment in their struggle. The security forces, unable to cope with the emergence of these new fighters grouped in armed bands in the suburbs of Algiers, seemed to be beaten. For the Islamist guerrilla movement, then organised behind the MIA, victory seemed near; its communiqués, according to people we interviewed, no longer hesitated to speak of 'liberated areas'. Here, as on the other side of the Mediterranean, the creation of an Islamic state in Algeria seemed inevitable; a French minister even told the press, 'The fundamentalists are on the point of taking over power in Algeria'.[13]

---

[13] François Léotard, then France's Minister of Defence, speaking to the Saudi daily *Al*

Liberated areas

The illusion of Islamist victory. In 1993 and 1994 the Islamist communes
were very like 'liberated areas': armed groups of the MIA rubbed shoulders with local fighters, the young adolescents turned Moudjahidin. The
people lived under the orders of the Islamists, without feeling subjected
to them. The adolescent Moudjahidin[14] paraded in arms and the Islamist
guerrillas ensured enforcement of their ideology – the French-language
press and satellite dishes were banned, and, above all, wearing of the veil
enforced. For sympathisers with the ex-FIS, victory seemed near and the
very violence of the regime prevented any turning back:

'Now we shall go on to the end; in the beginning we might perhaps have been able
to negotiate, but now the communiqués say all Communists must be killed, to the last
one. It is total war, with no turning back. I give you one year and Algeria will become
an Islamic state, if God wills.' (Student, Algiers suburbs, spring 1993)

Convinced that the young men coming from the FIS communes were favourable to the Islamist guerrillas and therefore ready to sacrifice their lives for
the Cause, the militants of the former FIS thought time was on their side.
Cities like Blida, Lakhdaria and Boufarik were regularly described in the
local press as occupied by the Moudjahidin. The sympathisers were convinced that the guerrillas were in the process of taking over the cities of
Algeria one by one. Everyone pretended not to see that the districts were
swarming with plain-clothes government agents, that military reinforcements were stationed around the Islamist communes and that arbitrary
arrests were more and more frequent – among the signs that the regime was
not on the brink of collapse as admirers of the MIA suggested. However,
the forces of order remained stupefied to see that in spite of the arrests of
elected representatives, organisers and activists of the ex-FIS, and the neutrali-
sation of the small armed Islamist groups that they already had files on, the
Islamist communes had in their midst so many young men ready to fight
the government forces. While the security forces concentrated on the FIS
activists on whom the DGSN (Direction Générale de la Sûreté Nationale)
had files, there came district Moudjahidin riding Mobylettes to attack
gendarmerie patrols, or young men happy to slake their thirst for revenge
against the security forces that had ruthlessly crushed the October 1988
rioters. The 'Emirs' of armed bands who gave a structure to the violence
and channelled it against the security forces emerged as new leaders, and
their enemy was embodied in the figure of the 'inspector' – a despised figure
in spite of the success of the television series *Tahar l'Inspecteur*, a comic
film whose hero is a friendly police officer.

Sharq al Awsat, quoted by *Le Monde,* 13 Oct. 1994.

[14] Those young men who formed armed bands described themselves as Moudjahidin,
like the MIA, GIA and MEI guerrillas.

Settling of scores. The accounts of murders of inspectors by ex-FIS sympathisers, living in districts where the memory of violence was inherent in the hostile relations between police and *hittistes*, are instructive. At El Harrach, in 1993, one anecdote described how men wearing suits and dark glasses, arriving in a Volkswagen Golf, parked close to a police station. They got inside the building without arousing attention and headed for the inspector's office, seized him and, threatening him with a revolver, told him to follow them. Faced with the reaction of the other policemen, the two men stated that a friend was waiting for them at the exit and that if he did not see them come out in a very short time, the Commissioner's daughter, who had been kidnapped meanwhile, would be killed. The Commissioner, informed of these facts, let the young men leave with the inspector, and the latter was found a short time later, dead, in an alleyway in El Harrach. For the person telling the story, it proved that the 'enemies of Islam' could not feel safe anywhere.

In fact the murders of inspectors, policemen or secretaries at police stations seemed to be doubly effective. It gave young men converted to the *jihad* an opportunity to fight enemies on their local level; a *hittiste* tortured in 1988 felt more hatred against the local police station than against the 'Communists' and 'French-speakers',[15] the targets which some militant Islamists preferred to aim at. On the other hand, such a crime constituted an initiation rite: after someone had carried out a murder without disguise he was obliged inexorably to join the ranks of the guerrillas, protected by the maquis. By choosing that type of target and method[16] the guerrilla instructors, advising the 'Emirs' to attack local policemen first, regularly got new recruits. Killing a policeman in 1993 also satisfied a longing on the part of those converts to the *jihad* by providing a guarantee of the genuineness of their turning to dissidence. That sort of action deprived them above all of the possibility of returning to civilian life like the Renamo fighters in Mozambique.

Another account set in Les Eucalyptus in 1993 illustrates well how the place of a killing was vital. For the new disciple of the *jihad* it was a decisive moment which, thanks to witnesses of his action, would ensure a

---

[15] One armed group, the FIDA (Front Islamique du Djihad Armé), even specialised in the killing of intellectuals in 1992-3. It was headed by Mohamed Brahimi alias 'Moh Lunettes', a physicist trained at the University of Bab Ezzouar in the suburbs of Algiers and editor in 1990-1 of a newspaper, *Al Tadhkir*, which was the mouthpiece of the Anouar Haddam tendency. The FIDA was active in Greater Algiers until 1994, when it was neutralised. It returned to the scene in 1995 and claimed responsibility for a considerable number of the attacks carried out during 1996 in Greater Algiers: *Algérie Confidentiel*, 5 June 1996.

[16] That method had been used by the FLN during the war of liberation. Alastair Horne wrote: 'At an early stage in the revolution it became a customary initiation ritual for a new recruit to be made to kill a designated "traitor", *mouchard* (police spy or informer), French gendarme officer or colonialist...' A. Horne, *A Savage War of Peace,* Harmondsworth: Penguin, 1977, p. 134.

reputation for him, a reputation that he would have to maintain. Three young men in a car, ordinarily dressed, parked close to a café where there were two policemen. One of the two was 'known for his hatred of the Muslims'. Approaching close, the attackers took out their weapons, asked one of the policemen to get away, aimed at the other, proclaimed '*Allah Akbar*' and machine-gunned him before eye-witnesses. They left and escaped. This account, apart from fascinating those who told it – by the coolness of the Moudjahidin, the selection among the victims (taking time to let one move aside, so as to kill the other) and the way the action proceeded – resembled a scene from a police film. In the 'liberated areas' the local Moudjahidin were avengers, their enemy was embodied in the policemen and inspectors, and the mutual hatred came from the similarity of their social backgrounds. Sometimes coming from the same background, the police and their attackers knew each other intimately and went on relentlessly hunting each other down.

The Moudjahidin were in a position of strength between 1993 and 1994 in the communes of the wider suburban area, and considered themselves the vanguard of the Islamist guerrilla campaign. But from 1994 they were confronted with the problems of 'managing' the municipalities under their control. The local population, especially the Islamist sympathisers subject to the 'Emirs', became aware that the 'liberated areas' were just a delusion, that they were more like areas deliberately 'abandoned' by the security forces, who sought to turn them into inaccessible and unbearable Islamist 'ghettoes'.

The suburban jihad *seen from the countryside*

In contrast to the urban and suburban zones, the rural areas were a bastion of support for the regime. The countryside, for example, benefited from public investment during the 1970s, which meant that many small villages have a better infrastructure than the suburbs of Algiers. The influential pre-sence of veterans of 1954-62 and prominent local citizens probably had much to do with this attention paid by the authorities.[17] So in the rural areas the Islamists, when they went over to dissidence, came up against the opposition of war veterans who assumed the task of establishing social control over the villages.

[17] M. Cote has written: 'In 30 years the effort to develop the countryside was remarkable. Symbolically, it began in 1962 with the building of rural schools, in the villages but also in open country...Electrification also reached rural areas very widely...The effort to install drinking water supply was more difficult, because developing that resource was more delicate. Everywhere wells, watercourses, or underground supplies were mobilised, water towers built, water supplies connected in the form of public fountains or running water in homes...Development of means of transport made it possible for people to stay in the country while benefiting from the town's services, even from its jobs.': *L'Algérie*, Paris: Masson, 1996, p. 78.

Older Moudjahidin against new ones. As in the districts of greater Algiers, from 1993 onwards violent acts that spread in the small villages and *douars* of the interior of the country followed the lines of numerous disputes and litigation that characterised local social relations. The Islamists' violence targeted clearly identified political and economic actors. The potential victims were well aware of it, especially the liberation war veterans who embodied the grievances of the Islamist sympathisers and activists. The former fighters or Moudjahidin of the liberation war belonging to the ONM (Organisation Nationale des Moudjahidin)[18] were convinced that they were the 'chiefs of Algeria', the 'sheikhs'; from the moment the elections were interrupted in January 1992 they were one of the few social groups to remain unshakably loyal to the government. Men of the land, they defined themselves as guarantors and servants of national sovereignty, in spite of their distance from centres of decision-making.[19] Former guerrillas of the ALN (Armée de Libération Nationale), they did not conceal their dissatisfaction with the way in which the Islamist phenomenon was handled by the political and military leadership. Only the appointment of General Lamari and the application of an ultra-repressive policy found approval in their eyes. In their view Islamism was an ideology imported from the Middle East, foreign to Algerian society; the regime had a duty to make that understood by the young people attracted to Islamism.

Between 1992 and 1994 the 'ex-combatants' tried to establish social control over the suspect population in the villages. They were among the first to form militias,[20] from the moment when the increasing strength of the maquis in the interior regions threatened them directly. To the FIS voters and sympathisers of the small communes of the interior, from 1992-3 the old men (*shuyukh*) became suspect:

'The old men, they should be treated with suspicion, they enter a café silently, they look at nobody, they pretend to listen to nothing, but in reality they listen to everything. Afterwards they go and tell the police all that they have heard, everything you've said. If they see a stranger in the village, they go and report that to the gendarmerie as well. The man they burned at M'Sila,[21] it was because of that. It was a warning to the old ones.' (M'Hamed, *trabendiste*, village in the Hauts-Plateaux, 1993)

---

[18] That organisation, of which Ali Kafi was elected Secretary General on 11 November 1994, represented the interests of the so-called 54 generation. However, scandals regularly break about the authenticity of its members' war service records: 'More than 68,000 people are said to be paid from the budget of the Ministry for Moudjahidin as "ex-combatants", without having proved their effective participation in the war of liberation,' wrote the weekly *El Haq*, 19-25 Dec. 1996.

[19] J. Leca has written, 'The rural world is where the government's legitimacy is, but not where power is.' 'Etat et société en Algérie' in B. Kodmani-Darwish (ed.), *Maghreb: Les années de transition*, Paris: Masson, 1990, p. 37.

[20] Chapter 7 studies the regime's security policy further .

[21] In April 1993, at M'Sila, a warehouse guard who was an ex-combatant was doused

In the rural Islamist sympathisers' *imaginaire*, the ex-combatants filled the role of the '*biyars*' in the Algiers suburbs. They were accused without distinction of collaboration with the regime. In truth these accusations were often a cover for prejudice and a strong resentment against a generation seen as privileged. And it is true that they have had various fairly trifling advantages such as reduced charges for cinema tickets (extremely rare) but also free travel on public transport and, until 1993, the possibility of importing a vehicle without paying customs duty; all that looked exorbitant to people who said they had no privileges at all. But those grievances are not enough to explain their physical elimination by the new Moudjahidin. In fact, besides the role played by the older generation in the civil war, the deliberate elimination of 'ex-combatants' had to do with a determination to remove representatives of the legitimacy of Algeria's independence. For while the guerrilla fighters found no difficulty in getting their sympathisers to believe in the idea that the regime's leaders were 'usurpers' of the ideals of 1954, it was more difficult for them to justify opposition to the 'ex-combatants', heroes of the liberation war.

In short the 'ex-combatants' were a 'weak link in the chain' for the Islamist ideology; their opposition to an Islamic state posed problems for the guerrillas who thought that the real objective of the fighters in 1954 had been precisely that.[22] Méziane, a veteran of the war of liberation, is an example of that attitude, characterised by total condemnation of the Islamist guerrillas and the expectation of a return to a 'strong state'.

Méziane, ex-combatant. A former soldier of the ALN during the war of liberation (1954-62), Méziane approved the interruption of the December 1991-January 1992 elections and, with other former guerrilla fighters, constantly called for a much more energetic policy against the Islamist maquis. The 'laxity' of the military authorities until 1993, when General Lamari launched the army into repression, was in their view the reason for consolidation of the Islamists' position. In Méziane's opinion Chadli Bendjedid's regime used the FIS to marginalise the FLN:

'If the government had asked the Moudjahidin [of 1954-62] to help it, there would soon have been an end to that little revolution. But there is no state capable of doing

---

with petrol by four 'Moudjahidin' and burned alive. He had been accused of collaboration with the security forces.

[22] See the letter of the AIS to the 'former Moudjahidin': 'We are not against you as the media – in the pay of the government, inspired and driven by Communists, sons of Harkis and Caïds – would have you believe. Our Islamic duty of giving counsel obliges us to open your eyes to the vast plot which is being hatched against you, because you are the symbol of a blessed revolution which still represents an example for those who revolt against oppression and arrogance...Our *jihad* is the logical sequel to yours. Our blood which flows is an extension of yours.' In *Mots de vérité*, collection of AIS/FIS texts, April 1995, p. 9.

its job. If, from the outset, the army had said no to the FIS, and had continued to work with the FLN, the problems we have now would never have occurred.' (Méziane, former ALN soldier, Hauts-Plateaux village, 1993)

Méziane continually referred to a golden age under Boumedienne, when the FLN-state exerted social control producing an attitude of proclaimed unanimity. The 'ex-combatants' and their local war chiefs, having been at centre-stage during the liberation war, were later associated with the Boumedienne regime, if not in practice, at least in the high status accorded to the 'Moudjahid' – despite their weakened position after the victory of the army of the borders over the guerrillas of the interior at independence.[23] Many of them, like Méziane, emigrated to France soon after independence for a short time, and came back once the Boumedienne regime was consolidated to live in Algeria, commonly in their *douars* of origin.[24] Today Méziane is proud to show his land, his house with a small pond, especially his tennis court 'for the children'. While in France he worked as a labourer, than as a builder, finally starting a business of laying tennis courts. With three workers he carried on this business for some years; then he bought two hotels which today bring in a considerable income in foreign currency. Returning to his village in Algeria, he bought the land of his 'ancestors' and settled down to life as a small landholder.

Méziane's story typifies that of the guerrillas, officers and men, who in the aftermath of independence were forced by the scarcity of resources or by the climate of civil war – already then providing an opportunity for settling of scores – to leave Algeria for a time. The emergence of last-minute Moudjahidin,[25] related to local administrative officials' determination to weaken the social group of 'ex-combatants', forced the latter to watch from the sidelines the accumulation of wealth by behind-the-scenes actors. Paradoxically it was in France that some, like Méziane, found the means of acquiring the necessary capital for returning to Algeria.

The formation of the maquis in 1993 in the mountainous regions close to their villages did not look like a real challenge to the 'ex-combatants'.

---

[23] On this theme see J. Leca and J.-C. Vatin, *Algérie politique. Institution et régime*, Paris: Presses de la FNSP, 1975, chapter on the army, p. 382.

[24] Apart from exile, some went into dissidence. A. Yesfah has written: 'The internal guerrillas, discontented [with the regime of Ahmed Ben Bella] were to stage rebellions here and there against the central government (the Draa maquis, the El Mizan maquis...). *Le processus de légitimation du pouvoir militaire et la constitution de l'Etat en Algérie* (Paris: Anthropos, 1982), p. 85.

[25] M. Lacheraf has written: 'At the time of the cease-fire and even later, certain officers of the maquis, the army in general, opposing groups, clans involved in the takeover of power, the Party, etc. worked hard at lining their pockets with the help of all sorts of figures, shady or at best newly redeemed or turned political: inflating the forces at their disposal and thus their clients immoderately, as if independence (which had in fact been achieved) was more important than the revolution to be carried out.' *L'Algérie: nation et société*, Paris: Maspéro, 1976, p. 30.

They had acquired national legitimacy by risking their lives in the independence struggle. While the political and military leaders sat in Algiers, up in the mountains they alone, so they thought, were capable of winning victory over the Islamists. Their ideas were not free of exaggeration, but they insisted on their own indispensability. The civil war meant for them a form of recognition, after their expulsion from local and national centres of decision-making when Chadli Bendjedid became President. The inability of the military authorities, until 1993, to crush the Islamists' armed resistance made the 'ex-combatants' precious allies in the eyes of the regime's leaders. They waited expectantly for the state to call publicly for their support, which the government of Liamine Zeroual did not hesitate to do.[26] That confirmed to them that implicitly they were the real 'chiefs' of Algeria:

'Here, the mountains are ours, they (the Islamists) cannot hide there because we would find them straight away. We know every hideout, I spent six years in these mountains, there were days when I ate leaves. Our Revolution, it was not like today, their Revolution, what is it? They've got everything now, you've seen the water, it reaches the *douar* now. We made the Revolution because we were dying of hunger before. Where you see sheep sleeping now, that was our home before.' (Méziane, former independence war Moudjahid, landlord today, 1993)

The 'Islamist revolution' of the guerrillas of 1993 had no basis; Méziane explained their dissidence as based on their desire for power. That was why they took the well worn path of war, the only way to achieve social progress and accumulate prestige and wealth. The *jihad* of these new fighters was thus like a war for '*kursi*' (power) because – according to Méziane, who was ignorant of the modern Islamist revolutionaries' theories – waging *jihad* in a Muslim country was an absurdity.

A war for kursi. Until 1993 much of the interior of the country was spared the violence which raged principally in the Algiers region. However, some communes voted for the FIS, both in the local elections of June 1990 and in the parliamentary elections of December 1991. But although the FIS local councils were dissolved, the voters did not spontaneously identify with the struggle carried on by the armed groups establishing themselves in the Blida Atlas. The Islamists' warlike rhetoric seemed ineffective, because it came up against the familiarity between the local people and members of the security forces – police, gendarmes and soldiers. Because of that leaflets issued by the Islamist guerrillas calling those people 'enemies of Islam' failed to produce effects. In a small village where everyone knew everyone else, calling a policeman, who was often father of a family and a practicing Muslim, an 'apostate' made no sense. Similarly, the soldiers

---

[26] There was all the more reason to expect a public appeal to the ex-combatants by the government because Ali Kafi, Secretary-General of the ONM, was appointed chairman of the High Council of State (Haut Conseil d'Etat, HCE) in July 1992.

stationed in the nearby barracks but in daily contact with the village population posed a problem for the local Islamists, who had difficulty justifying their murder. The contrary was also true: eradication of armed groups described as 'foreign to Algeria' meant in practice the killing of adolescents and young men – known to the village because they sometimes came from big families – who had been hiding in the neighbouring mountainous region. So it was not uncommon to see Islamist sympathisers warning the local policeman, or a soldier coming from the village, of a threat against him:

'People told him: don't go to the mosque on Friday, they are going to kill you. But he told us: "I've been praying since I was nine years old, why should I stop, the mosque isn't anyone's property". We knew him, it struck us in the heart that he was going to be killed. The Moudjahidin said that he was a policeman and went to the mosque to spy on people. One Friday, as he left the mosque, they cut his throat (in 1994), he had refused to listen, *Allah rahmou* [may he rest in peace].' (A friend of the victim, interviewed in 1996 in France)

The intimate ties between victims, killers and witnesses led to a pragmatic attitude and a reasoned interpretation of the conflict in the villages. Among young people, *hittistes* or *trabendistes*, memories of violence were not tinged with the same resentment as among their counterparts in the suburbs of greater Algiers. In the villages the traumatic effects of the repression of the October 1988 riots were absent; their attitude towards the Algiers area was that of villagers scared by a sprawling metropolis of more than four million inhabitants where murders were committed every day. Their resentment turned towards other targets: the privileges of the 'ex-combatants' and the prominent local citizens, and the unequal social relationships created by them. They found it hard to understand the Algiers suburban dwellers' enthusiasm for the *jihad*. The regime and its agents did not seem like usurpers of the ideals of 1954; rather, both they and those seeking to overthrow them were seen as people hungry for wealth and privileges:

'Over there (in the Algiers area), they are fighting for *kursi* (power), that is why they are killing each other today, only for power. Islam has nothing to do with it. The government is not yet sufficiently well fed (*ma-sbarsh*), and the others are hungry too, so they kill each other, that's how it is.' (Aziz, unemployed, small town in the Hauts-Plateaux, end of 1993)

So the armed actions against the regime by the MIA between 1991 and 1993, and then by the GIA and MEI, were seen as a means to seize power. To those rural people the ideological justifications put forward by the armed Islamist organisations were just arguments to be used as occasion arose, like those invoked by the government. In their villages their view of the civil war was based on a vivid collective memory, of a time when access to high positions was – during the liberation war and after independence – premised on the use of violence. However, although critical towards the warring parties, they still felt understanding for the Islamist guerrillas, and thought their violence was the result of the humiliation the regime had caused them.

Determination to get rich. Aziz's indifference to the issues at stake between the warring parties was also linked to the rise of individualistic behaviour highly suspicious of political organisations. In some ex-FIS sympathisers' view personal development did not depend on the establishment of an Islamic state. That alternative, even if it attracted them as was proved by their rallying behind the FIS during its legal existence, was a vision of something that could be used. It was expected to be a 'minimum state' guaranteeing the borders and national honour, but leaving the economic field to individual initiative. For Nadjim, a young trader, only the FIS was able to bring out the creative potential of the young. The social and economic difficulties of some of the population were due, according to him, to the constraints of a deliberately inegalitarian political system. And yet, in spite of the social barriers inherent in the networks of wealth accumulation, like Nadjim many people had 'made it':

'Do you know a country where young people of 16 become millionaires on their own, without stealing, just by *trabendo*? The young people here have the ability to do many things, they are resourceful, outside you see them as poor, but some have bank accounts in Oran and warehouses, they are capable of making it if they are allowed to.' (Nadjim, grocer, 25 years old, Hauts-Plateaux village, 1993)

His imagined Islamic state had nothing to do with any theocratic ideas; it was like an anti-FLN state, not interfering in economic affairs. However, this view of things was intimately linked to his social progress, which was much influenced by a determination to succeed in his business. The son of a trader, he took over from his father after failing the baccaulauréat examination. An ambitious man, he tried many times to extend the business of his father's small grocery shop, to start a food store on a larger scale. He came up against the local way in which a balance of favours was managed, and saw his applications to the administration for local government-owned land rejected several times. The state authorities in his village were under the influence of prominent local citizens with little desire to see rivals emerge.

Nadjim supported the FIS during the electoral process because he hoped to see the rules of the game altered. But the management of the commune by the FIS elected representatives, after their local election victory in June 1990, did not fundamentally disrupt the balance of forces. Deprived of all financial support from the government, the FIS commune councillors were dependent on donations from all those who, out of calculation or political allegiance, desired the success of the Islamist communes. In the Algiers suburbs and the small villages alike, the FIS elected representatives did not have the financial means to implement their policies. The prominent local people and entrepreneurs proved to be indispensable in the sums they donated, which ensured continuation of their privileges. For the FIS voters, like Nadjim, the expected change did not happen, because the FIS elected representatives lacked effective authority; only a FIS victory in the parliamentary elections of December 1991 would have been able to alter the balance of forces by giving the local councillors the financial backing of an Islamist government.

The interruption of those elections and the campaign by Abdelkader Chébouti did not produce a commitment to violence by the rural sympathisers of the former FIS. As in the case of Nadjim, the voter's reasoning was not that of the devout activist. For the ordinary voter, Muslim but not convinced of the relevance of the *jihad*, any sacrifice for a cause which would bring him no benefit was ruled out – especially as one could reasonably expect that changes in the balance of forces could come without him making any effort himself. Trade liberalisation measures from 1994 onward proved after the event that the FIS voter (both the petty trader and the unemployed college graduate) had been right not to join the guerrilla campaign.

In contrast to what happened in the war of liberation, the rural population was not a reservoir of fighters against the regime.[27] In 1993 the Islamist dissidence was limited to the suburbs of Algiers and the Mitidja plain. In the interior, except in the universities, violence against the regime was hardly perceptible; no curfew was decreed either in the east or in the west of Algeria, although many big cities had been under FIS local government in 1990-1. The regime found even in those regions backing among social groups such as the 'ex-combatants', marginalised by successive governments until then. However, interior regions spared the violence until 1993 were to experience war from 1994 onwards. The establishment of GIA, MIA and MEI maquis in mountainous regions of the interior, and the creation in July 1994 of a new faction, the Armée Islamique du Salut (AIS), was to turn certain regions into battlefields like the south-eastern suburbs of Algiers, at the mercy of local Islamist armed bands since 1993.

---

[27] M. Harbi has written, 'The importance of rural people's participation in the armed struggle contributed to the desire to make the peasantry a revolutionary class *par excellence*. Praise for the vitality of rural dwellers and their warlike qualities is a traditional theme of popular culture. From 1957 to 1959 new phenomena were witnessed: the FLN was driven out of the cities, the Wilayas were exhausted...At the same time there was reinforcement of the ALN on the borders, the formation of an army with a peasant base, with officers from the villages and towns. That army drew its recruits from among the refugees (numbering 200,000 in Tunisia).' *1954, la guerre commence en Algérie*, Brussels: Complexe, 1984, p. 166

Part II

THE MAINSPRINGS OF CIVIL WAR

From December 1993 the warring parties ceased to hope for a rapid victory, because neither the army nor the Islamists were succeeding in winning the war. Neither the mass arrests of FIS activists nor the ban on that party put an end to the Islamist alternative. On the other hand the launching of the *jihad* did not arouse among the three million FIS voters the enthusiasm on which the Islamist leaders had counted. Those leaders and the regime then devised policies aimed at augmenting the resources needed for their war efforts. Settling down to 'total war', the two sides decided to use all varieties of strategic attack to weaken each other's position, in the absence of victory in a frontal battle. From that point not only fighters but also economic assets and networks of support – financial and political, national and international – were declared as targets.

The two sides adopted policies designed to finance this war strategy, one based on the destruction of the enemy's resources and environment. The regime, which had halted debt servicing in 1993,[1] put an end to the economic policy followed by Belaïd Abdesselam[2] for settling the problem of the debt, estimated on his taking office in 1992 at $26 billion. He called on Algerians to 'rely on themselves first of all' and suggested that they should 'tighten their belts' to honour debt servicing, which amounted to $8 billion per year compared with revenue of $12 billion.[3] But the decline in revenue to $9 billion in 1993 brought the regime to financial bankruptcy. So the authorities, in 1993 and 1994, negotiated with the IMF on rescheduling of the debt and launching of a Structural Adjustment Programme (SAP) involving staged liberalisation of trade, the end of state subsidies on consumer goods, devaluation of the dinar and privatisation of state enterprises. Implementation of this economic programme was a precondition for obtaining loans and credits, which would alone be able to finance the regime's security-oriented policy. Rescheduling of the debt in 1994 thus released considerable resources: the ratio of debt service to exports of goods and services fell from 93 per cent in 1993 to 47 per cent in 1994 and

[1] See J. Ould Aoudia, 'La crise financière' in G. Ignasse and E. Wallon (eds), *Demain l'Algérie*, Paris: Syros, 1995, pp. 63-75.

[2] On 8 July 1992 Sid'Ahmed Ghozali was replaced as Prime Minister by Belaïd Abdesselam, former Minister of Industry under President Boumedienne.

[3] See Larbi Talha, 'Vers une économie de guerre', *Le Monde diplomatique,* August 1992, p. 10.

37 per cent in 1995 of export earnings, which amounted to $8.8 billion in 1994 and $10.2 billion in 1995.[4] From then on the regime's financial situation was considerably better than in 1993.

This financial windfall was a trump card in the government's war strategy against the Islamist armed groups. It made it possible to build up a repressive apparatus specialising in anti-terrorist operations, to expand its patronage network and to respond to demands from the private sector which had shown that it could be affected by the FIS message. Now refloated financially, the regime succeeded in containing the expansion of the Islamist armed groups, and thus confounded predictions of its rapid collapse. The institution of a market economy was therefore like a method of warfare. It worked in the regime's favour but at the same time, paradoxically, augmented the financial resources of its enemy, the GIA. For trade liberalisation also provided an opportunity for the budding war economy of the 'Emirs'; their involvement in the trading economy from 1994 onwards, through the creation of import-export companies, increased their funds and thus their capacity for fighting.

In Part II we aim to show how the warring parties took control to their own benefit of the 'transition' to a market economy. We shall also emphasise how the uncertainties of the civil war were involved in the international economic and financial situation. The Islamists of the former FIS, having been in a position to come to power at the beginning of the civil war on the strength of the assets they had – an electoral capital of three million voters and an enemy in a state of bankruptcy – did not succeed in exploiting those assets, and lost their relative advantage after three years of fighting. The following pages explore the economic and military processes leading to this reversal of the situation in the regime's favour.

[4] Source: Banque d'Algérie, *La Tribune*, 17 June 1996.

5

THE WAR LOGIC OF THE
ISLAMIST ARMED BANDS

From 1994 onwards the expansion of the Islamist armed bands[5] seemed irresistible, because they won the sympathy of the ex-FIS voters, who saw them as defenders of the Islamist cause. But the dynamics of the war, which ensured the supremacy of the 'Emirs' over the Islamist elected representatives, had effects on the structuring of the armed groups. The first generation of fighters, considered as heroes, protectors and avengers in their home areas, were succeeded by bands whose activities ran counter to the interests of the 'cause'. Forced to extract resources from their environment to remain in the field and consolidate, they were reduced, after the flight of the richer inhabitants, to extortion from petty traders. Masters of the communes that previously supported the FIS, the armed bands had to come to terms with contradictory interests in the running of their 'Emirates'. The flight of the military entrepreneurs led to disorganisation of the districts, aggravated further by the halting of *trabendo* due to Western countries' restrictive policy on issuing of visas.

The 'Emirs' were obliged, in order to live up to the standard they set, to embark on a policy capable of offering services similar to those offered by the military entrepreneurs. Consolidation of an armed group from then on depended on its 'Emir's' ability to protect the resources of his commune and increase the wealth accumulated in the urban guerrilla campaign. The time spent by the 'Emirs' on this task diverted them from their initial objective: the fight against the regime. The Islamist armed bands' concentration on taking power at the local level turned the Islamist communes into battlefields – which did not harm the regime, as the local people were so ill-disposed towards it.

The 'Emir' and the Model of the Military Entrepreneur

A local guerrilla war. While the FIS Islamist militants following the standard of the AIS (Armée Islamique du Salut)[6] saw the heroes of the war of

[5] The Islamist armed bands were groups of young people of the districts who came together 'spontaneously' and claimed to be acting in 1994 in the name of the GIA (Groupement Islamique Armé). In order to distinguish them clearly from that guerrilla faction, we call them simply armed 'groups' or 'bands'.

[6] In July 1994 the militants of the former FIS created the Armée Islamique du Salut. The AIS became the fourth faction, after the MIA, MEI and GIA, to embark on guerrilla war against the regime. Those armed organisations are analysed in Chapter 9.

liberation as their model to emulate, for the 'Emirs' of the autonomous armed groups of the Algiers region, who claimed to be fighting in the name of the GIA, the symbol of success and the model of the 'perfect fighter' was the military entrepreneur. However their activity is understood, the 'Emirs' of the armed bands were more interested in recasting the social relationships of their areas in their own favour than in fighting the regime with a view to replacing it by an Islamic state. Their war logic was in that respect opposed to that of the guerrillas of the maquis, whose personal histories and field of action led them to aim at erecting their structure at the national level. Analysis of the acts of war carried out by the armed bands shows, when placed in the local context, that they were far from wanting to destroy the regime, but rather aimed to take over the running of their local areas. Their methods disconcerted even sympathisers with the former FIS, who did not always understand their motives for killing agents of the state in the communes:

'The pity of it is this – why don't the Moudjahidin, instead of killing our policeman, the district policeman, get together and five hundred of them march on the Presidency and kill them all there? I don't understand why they don't do that. Isn't it possible to do that? Better that than everyday a skirmish here, another there, I assure you, that way they'll be gone faster.' (Kader, unemployed college graduate, Algiers suburbs, 1994)

Criticism of the armed bands' methods of fighting was related to their apparent inadequacy for the declared objective of overthrowing the regime. Those methods were to prove even more inadequate when turned against economic targets in areas of ex-FIS sympathy. Once enthusiasm for a rapid victory of the 'Islamists' in 1992-3 had passed, the sympathisers, who had fervently backed the MIA in 1993, grew tired of the neighbourhood Moudjahidin's guerrilla campaign from the end of 1994. The regime's resilience, linked to the increase in its financial resources, made daily murders of policemen seem pointless. And the policy of the 'Emirs', whose field of action was mainly in the communes previously run by the FIS, did not at all weaken the regime's ability to act – because, of course, the regime's economic and political resources were not located at Les Eucalyptus, Chararba, El Harrach, Baraki and little places in the Mitidja. So why should those places be turned into guerrilla terrain? The places where the symbolic seats of power were located – Hydra, El Biar, the Algiers city centre – were, by contrast, spared guerrilla violence, at least until June 1995, when the bomb attacks began.[7]

---

[7] According to a (not exhaustive) survey of the press, between January 1995 and February 1996 at least 16 car bombs exploded in the Algiers region, the bloodiest being that of 30 January 1995 at the Algiers central police station, leaving 42 dead and 286 injured. *El Watan*, 1 Feb. 1995.

This contradiction between the declared objectives (the overthrow of the regime and the creation of an Islamic state) and the methods of action (guerrilla attacks in underprivilegêd communes) was the result of the 'Emirs'' determination to take the place of the military entrepreneurs, the real holders of local power. That aim, not admitted but ardently pursued, was a reflection of their own social background, which kept their sights trained on the success that group had obtained through the liberation war. In contrast to the 'militants of Islam',[8] socialised in political struggle at the universities and mosques, the 'Emirs' were outside the religious arena until they joined the *jihad*. They were marginal people, workers, former *trabendistes*, and, in the image of a certain sort of active, cunning and resourceful young people, were free from family and inherited ties of all sorts. Their identity was developed not from political allegiance but from social background and living experience: the neighbourhood, the suburbs, sport and *trabendo*.[9] Paradoxically the 'Emirs' of the armed bands, in spite of appearances, were very far removed from the Islamic militants. The latter were fascinated by the Gulf states and felt contempt for the Western countries, although they had the means to travel there and many had studied there; in contrast to ordinary young people, who were fascinated by the West, they liked travelling in the Muslim countries.

Portrait of an 'Emir': Saïd the sheet-metal worker

These contradictions and paradoxes are illustrated by the example of an 'Emir' of Les Eucalyptus, Saïd the sheet-metal worker. At the head of 50 to 60 Moudjahidin coming from the residential districts of the commune in 1993-4, Saïd the sheet-metal worker reigned over his territory which he had known since his childhood. Until 1993 Saïd was a skilled worker with the merchant navy. Trained as a mechanic, on his shore leaves he did odd jobs in private homes: welding, water pump repairs, etc. Hence his local nickname of 'Saïd the sheet-metal worker'. At the time when the FIS was winning the municipal elections, in June 1990, Saïd had the reputation of a drunkard, his merchant navy job giving him easy access to liquor. But his elder brother, an FIS activist, was preaching the benefits of observing Islamic teaching in the district. He called for patience towards his younger brother and told the activists of an earlier hour that 'when he succeeded in bringing his brother back to Islam, then it would be easy to bring all Algeria back'.

[8] For that form of Islamism, see Gilles Kepel and Yann Richard (eds), *Intellectuels et militants de l'islam contemporain*, Paris: Seuil, 1990, 285 pp.

[9] The ties of solidarity uniting the Emirs with their districts recalled in some ways the 'urban asabiyyât' analysed by C. Cahen among the *shabâb* (young people) in Muslim society in the Middle Ages: 'Mouvements populaires et autonomisme urbain dans l'Asie musulmane du Moyen Age', *Arabica*, VI, 1, 1959, p. 51. However, that comparison does not lead us to conclude that there was a specific form of contestation in the 'Muslim city'.

In 1993 Saïd the sheet-metal worker, home on leave, heard that his elder brother had not escaped the round-up of organisers and activists of the FIS. From that moment onwards the inhabitants of the district saw him no longer, except for a few moments' glimpse of him shouldering a Kalashnikov. In the space of a year he became the 'Emir' of several districts, his authority was uncontested, and the fury with which he attacked patrols aroused the fervour of younger people:

'One day the soldiers entered the mosque with their shoes on, they said they were looking for a terrorist. They had not had time to leave when a J5 van rushed towards them, the rear door opened and Saïd the sheet-metal worker with his Moudjahidin got out with the *klach* [Kalashnikov]. They slaughtered them. How could they dare to enter the mosque with their shoes on?' (13-year-old schoolboy, 1994)

The 'Emir', in the urban setting, appeared like a protector and avenger for those who were trapped in the logic of breach with legality and felt they were potential victims of the security forces. He and his comrades in arms moved in small groups of three or four people around a well defined space watched by spies who informed them about the coming and going of soldiers and civilians. Besides men in arms the group included people who were assigned other tasks. The secret war that they waged obliged them to keep and maintain as many hideouts as possible. The survival of an armed group depended a great deal on its relationship with its environment, especially on the possibility of getting food and accommodation from families without running risks.

The 'Emir's' social ascent gave him notoriety equal to that of the military entrepreneur, his model. In the south-eastern suburbs of Algiers the military entrepreneur, like Hadj Sadok whose career was described earlier (see Chapter 2), organised the economic and social transactions of the housing estates, employing *trabendistes*. After he fled in 1992 the *trabendistes* went over to the service of Saïd the sheet-metal worker. Besides his role of protector, the 'Emir' had a duty to maintain client networks, to get effective logistical support in his war effort; for the strength of the armed group did not lie in the number of its fighters but in the range of people serving it. So it was natural for the local *trabendistes* to go over to his service. Technically unemployed, because of the conjunction of two events – their employer's departure and France's restrictive visa policy – they found in Saïd's *jihad* an enterprise able to solve their difficulties.

The path followed by Saïd, whose enlistment in the armed struggle at the local level was the result of his brother's death, should not lead to any generalisation about the causes of enlistment. But the sociology of the local 'Emirs', while it cannot be properly studied in view of the difficulties of collecting information about their histories, makes it possible nevertheless to suggest some hypotheses on the basis of examples. For example, the awarding of the 'Emir' title aroused feelings of envy: there was no lack of envy and jealousy among those who did not get the title while they were convinced they had the necessary qualities. Even so, those who had the title were convinced that they were truly leading the *jihad*: their commitment was not due to simple rational economic considerations that could lead them to use the armed group's budget for their own personal purposes. However, those who were already using violence and cunning as a means of acquiring goods before the start of the civil war in 1992 found that they were well placed, through their experience of life, to compete successfully for the title of 'Emir'.

The extreme diversity of motivations of the 'Emirs' means that the idea of 'enemy of God' (*Adu Allah*) varied from one group to another, and this altered the targets to aim at. The 'Emirs' heading a group consisting of some students preferred to choose as targets people from cultured circles, considered as 'apostates', and concentrated on murdering intellectuals, teachers and journalists. Sometimes the enemies were professional rivals, and they killed or destroyed what they knew best, such as the school in their district. As for Saïd the sheet-metal worker's group, it was made up of *hittistes* who were mainly engaged in guerrilla war against the security forces. Journalists and academics living in Les Eucalyptus were able to stay there until 1995, not without fear it is true. At Batna in the Aurès mountains Ahmed la Crosse's group attacked 'ex-combatants' (numerous in that region) and women above all. Murderous madness could also guide the actions of some 'Emirs'. The Munchar ('the Saw') group, which specialised in cutting up victims taken off trains on the Algiers-Oran line, was another example of the diversity of the methods used by the 'Emirs', inherent in the ambiguity of their personal lives. The 'Moh Jetta' and 'Napoli'[10] groups in the Upper Casbah specialised in the kidnapping and murder of men of religion. In view of the purely local rational considerations that determined the targets and methods of the 'Emirs', the 'militant of Islam' who was motivated by the political conviction of the need for an Islamic state had no course left but to join the maquis – that being a war machine in the hands of Islamist revolutionaries whose political and military objectives went beyond the local objectives of the district warriors.

Fascination and respect for the 'emirs'

The ranks of Islamist armed groups and the 'Emirs' leading them have been constantly replenished because of the positive, respectful view of their activities in their social circles of origin. In spite of the murderous acts they committed, the 'Emirs' or their groups remained no less attractive. Their actions which those who condemned them saw as criminal or irrational

[10] According to the weekly newsletter *TTU Monde Arabe* (11 Oct. 1996) Amar Yacine, alias Napoli, has been accused of the murder of several French people, including the television journalist Olivier Quéméner, killed in 1994.

were, on the contrary, always justified and respected by their sympathisers. But in the spring of 1994 the petty traders, students and *trabendistes* distanced themselves from the cause of the 'Emirs', because of the opportunities offered by the regime. The armed groups, particularly in the urban setting, from then on found supporters only in a pool consisting essentially of people humiliated by the arbitrary behaviour of the security forces or made desperate by the high cost of living; such people found revenge – for a very short time – in the armed bands. The members of the armed groups, and the 'Emirs' in the first place, conferred value on their identity through the figure of the Moudjahid, and ensured an enviable standard of living for themselves through the work of redistribution implicit in the running of a group in an aggressive environment.

The 'Emir' of an armed group, autonomous or in a 'joint venture' with the guerrilla operations in the interior, embodied – alongside football stars, Raï stars and the popular leaders of the FIS (Ali Benhadj, Abassi Madani) – a new type of hero. The certain death that awaited him glorified his image and testified to his courage; the title of 'Emir', which had an international resonance, transformed the social progress of an anonymous individual into the career of a 'public enemy number one'. The local 'Emir', hunted down by the security forces, aroused pity even among those who condemned him, for everyone saw him not as 'God's madman', but as the living embodiment of a despair bringing forth destructive energy. The discovery at sunrise of an adolescent of 15 to 18, riddled with bullets, with 'more bombs in his pocket', made people forget the crimes he had committed the day before. For behind the title of 'Emir' could now be seen the child of the neighbourhood, brother or close relative of an activist, the delinquent only just released or an adolescent who had disappeared more than a year before, now ending up like a wreck in a suburban alleyway. The place he left vacant was immediately filled, as longing for revenge spurred on a member of the victim's family or a childhood friend of his.

In this short cycle the principles of Islamism did not have time to get assimilated. Here there was a contrast with the maquis where instructors, *jihad* professionals, provided all-round training for a 'Muslim fighter'. For the urban Moudjahidin, guerrilla reflexes were most important. With experience from the consolidation of the conflict, they had adequate bases for their war effort. However, the security forces also were continually refining their repressive apparatus. The respect accorded to the status of 'Emir' was, at the symbolic level, due to the political system's low output of 'stars', 'heroes' and other successors to the 'historic figures of the 1954 revolution'. Some social strata among the youth, as in other countries, identified with violent 'heroes', greatly popularised by the film industry. Before glorifying Abdelkader Chébouti the sympathisers of the armed bands were fans of Schwartzenegger, Bruce Lee, Rocky and other cinema stars.[11]

---

[11] The influence of cinema heroes on the conduct of young fighters is a phenomenon

However, that fascination would not have had any practical effect if the 'Emirs" enterprise had not also led to many very lucrative activities. That is why the economic context in which the armed bands developed is of key importance; it makes it clear how, following an ostensibly religious cause (the *jihad*), the struggle was a response to the social disorganisation of the districts and became a means of laying hands on money so as to provide for local people hard hit by unemployment and the high cost of living. In 1992-3 the groups broken up by the security forces were composed to a great extent of students, workers, even technically qualified people. From 1994 adolescents and criminals became predominant. The ideological motivations of the former faded away, to be replaced by mobilisation for social reasons (revenge-seeking and survival strategy) and economic ones (seeking to profit from resources redistributed by the 'Emirs'). Nonetheless, the conflict was not cast rigidly in the mould of a contest between 'Islamist delinquents' and security forces. Following the trade liberalisation begun in 1994 the armed bands were a way for the most deprived to accumulate funds that were instantly reinvested in trading, through the formation of import-export companies.

The way the armed groups developed underlines the permanent redirection of their activity in accordance with the environment. Depending on the period, the 'Emirs' offered the following services: social revenge in 1992-3, protection in 1993-4, accumulation of 'capital' from 1994. For these different services people of different social and economic backgrounds were mobilised: the predominant student element of 1992-3 was weakened (students joined the AIS maquis in the rural areas), giving way to marginalised groups (criminals, humiliated people). The way in which the armed bands developed from their emergence in 1992 was complex even so.

It is therefore simplistic to view this war enterprise as a fight against an 'impious' regime that interrupted the parliamentary elections of December 1991-January 1992 – especially as a guerrilla campaign in the interior took responsibility for that activity. The political and ideological objectives assigned to the armed struggle were adulterated by economic criminal activity and social revenge-seeking, which – much more than study of the ideologues of revolutionary Islamism – lay behind the armed dissident movements.

How the 'Emirates' were run

The local organisation of the armed bands. The spread of violence, linked to the emergence of the Islamist armed bands and intense repression, drove the richer inhabitants out of the suburbs of southeastern Algiers from 1994. The military entrepreneurs' families left behind 'Dallas style' villas and

---

observed in the civil wars in Liberia and Sierra Leone, as shown in the work of P. Richards, 'Rebellion in Liberia and Sierra Leone: a Crisis of Youth?' in O.W. Furley (ed.), *Conflict in Africa*, London: I.B. Tauris, 1995, pp. 134-70.

ware-houses emptied of their machines, to return to their *douars* of origin in the interior, especially in the east of Algeria. During this period those buildings were illegally occupied by the Moudjahidin, when they were not sold off to individuals at rock-bottom prices because of the collapse of the property market in those places. The 'Emirs' could not escape, any more than the military entrepreneurs, from the problems of disputes linked to landed property and illegally occupied land.

There had been a dispute related to effective ownership of some land in the Mitidja since independence. Some families exhibited property titles dating back to the nineteenth or early twentieth century, mentioning their rights over parcels of land bought or confiscated by French settlers. Soon after independence the land was nationalised, and it was only from 1986 onwards that property titles were given.[12] As was mentioned in Part I, land was sold to individuals by those families without legal authorisation. Many other parcels of land were awarded to former guerrillas of the war of liberation, as a reward for service, in the Mitidja but also in their *douars* of origin. The institution of a land registry in the other regions considerably reduced the number of disputes arising from the exact demarcation of everyone's property. But this did not happen in the Mitidja, and 'anarchic' building considerably reduced the room for manoeuvre for development policies. When the building of roads and even motorways was held up by the presence of illegal dwellings along the route, this illustrated not a management failure in housing policy, but the absence of a single authority responsible for allocation of sale and property rights. The contesting of local government property rights over certain plots of land by families holding pre-nationalisation (pre-1962) property rights led to a proliferation of lawsuits.

Those disputes intensified after 1992 because in certain places (Les Eucalyptus, Chararba) families of military entrepreneurs were in dispute with families discredited after independence because of collaboration by some of their members with the French authorities. Land belonging to families of Caïds was nationalised in 1963, but their descendants never stopped claiming ownership.[13] That phenomenon, probably a marginal one, was said by the regime, in its statements on the war, to be one of the reasons for the Islamists' violence. The Islamists thus appeared as if they were

---

[12] The process of 'acquisition of property in agricultural land' was begun in 1983, but only in 1986 was it speeded up with the privatisation of the DAS (Districts Agricoles Socialistes). See J.-C. Brûlé, 'Attentisme et spéculation dans les campagnes algériennes', *Maghreb-Machrek*, no. 139, 1993, pp. 42-52.

[13] H.A. Amara has emphasised that the privatisation of land from 1986 constituted 'a return to the situation prevailing before 1971 (the agrarian reform), to the land statutes and division of property inherited from the colonial period...The restoration of land to the big families of Caïds and Bachagas favoured by the colonial administration shows the extent of the reversal made by the political class...for all that the re-establishment of the situation before 1971, after twenty years, was not easy...' 'La terre et ses enjeux' in P.R. Baduel (ed.), *L'Algérie incertaine*, Paris: Edisud, 1994, p. 191.

manipulated by families trained by the colonial regime for intermediate positions (Caïd, Bachagha, Agha) and then, after independence, condemned to exile, death or silence.

The regime's denunciation of a collusion of interests between the 'terrorists' and the Harkis[14] – because young men from those families were to be found in some armed bands, even among the 'Emirs' – caused a shock on the other side of the Mediterranean; however, it made sense in some localities or regions where military entrepreneurs were confronted with rights that pre-dated their ownership. In this situation the *jihad* was denounced as the 'revenge' of yesterday's losers.[15] However, such denunciations are interesting in another way: they revealed the extent to which land ownership was intrinsically linked to a war situation. The Caïd families profited from the colonial regime in their struggle against neighbouring tribes in competition for management and obtaining of property.[16] After the defeat of the colonial regime, those families met the same fate as the tribes they had weakened, the beneficiaries being the military entrepreneurs. The civil war starting in 1992 reopened those wounds and showed that those weighty disputes had not yet been settled, because both sides used the war – and hence the armed bands – as much as they could in their confrontation strategy.

The flight of the military entrepreneurs probably aroused hope among all those who had been contesting their authority or even their legitimate presence in certain places. The occupation of land by the 'Emirs' and the collapse of the property market produced an economic 'boom' in those disadvantaged areas. However, it was to a great extent the petty traders who made the most of the situation. They bought up the pool of houses sold at low prices (emigrants' houses notably), using the same opportunity to place their money in a safe fixed asset to escape extortion. What new balance of forces is to follow in those areas? Will the 'Emirs' succeed in definitively taking the place of the military entrepreneurs? That will be one of the issues at stake in the post-civil war era.

Development of the economic order. The flight of the military entrepreneurs did not mean that they abandoned their landed or business property, as is

[14] For example, Djaffar el Afghani, GIA 'Emir' from September 1993 to February 1994, was a 'son of a Harki' who lived in Nice until 1977. A member of the Daawa wa Tabligh since 1982, he left for Afghanistan in 1989 and returned to Algeria in 1992. He was credited with 138 murders and 283 attacks on public property. The Emir of the West, Kada Benchiha, accused of the murder in September 1994 of two French surveyors, was 'also the son of a Harki' according to *El Watan* (1 March 1994).

[15] This recalls a comment by Julien Freund: 'In countries where the revolution has triumphed, violence is justified as the indispensable instrument to safeguard revolutionary gains and hold would-be counter-revolutionaries, reactionaries etc. pitilessly in check, *Utopie et violence*, Paris: M. Vivien, 1970, p. 128.

[16] C. Etablet, *Etre caïd dans l'Algérie coloniale 1835-1912*, Paris: Ed. du CNRS, 1991. 380 pp.

clear from the testimony of a former employee of Sheikh Lahcen, who has returned since 1993 to a village in the Constantine region:

'The Sheikh, when the *boulahya* (the bearded men) won the elections, began to send lorries to take the equipment away. The warehouses have stayed empty since then. My family and I live on the ground floor of the house, that way we keep an eye on it in case things change. But every month someone from the family comes to see if all is going well, because the Sheikh does not want to sell.' (Security guard, Algiers suburbs, 1994)

The private sector entrepreneurs, as well as the wholesalers, had no private protection staff until 1994; that was why a certain number abandoned their too exposed warehouses in places in the Mitidja, to move to the inner suburbs of Algiers or even their *douar*s of origin. The military entrepreneurs, owners of many 'villas plus warehouses', moved without too much difficulty. Sheikh Lahcen, living in the Mitidja with his large family, first moved to one of his numerous villas in the vicinity of Algiers in 1992, and then left the region in 1993. The purchase of land and construction of outsize villas was, during the 1980s, a common preference of that social group.

Sheikh Lahcen, who specialised in wholesale distribution of consumer goods, was a favoured customer of the state corporations that manufactured tinned tomatoes and fruit juice, and a favoured importer of foreign consumer goods. A well known wholesaler, he left his *douar* in the Hauts Plateaux at independence in 1962 to settle in one of the numerous houses abandoned by the 'settlers'. Like many of his generation with a considerable fortune to his name, he took part in the war of liberation, not as a combatant but as the person responsible for supplying certain maquis in the Aurès, although he was then less than 20 years old. Driving a van and later a lorry, throughout that period he travelled all over Algeria; this was with a view to establishing networks as varied and as geographically dispersed as possible. But, he said, it was 'with the Jewish community'[17] that he established the best relations. He was to keep up his links with some wholesalers whom he valued particularly, established in Marseilles and Tunis.

Coming from a region badly shaken by the repression after the Sétif uprising in 1945,[18] Sheikh Lahcen has retained from that time accounts of the deaths of some of his family. His youthful involvement in the war of liberation was the consequence of that memory of war. The contacts he made then, at great risk, were to establish almost fraternal links with a certain number of chiefs of the interior guerrilla campaign. Their children became like his own, and vice versa. But at independence he left his native region and did not dare to go back to see his home *ghourbi*. Algiers became his city; abandoned

[17] See the chapter 'La Révolution et les juifs algériens' in M. Lebjaoui, *Vérités sur la révolution algérienne,* Paris: Gallimard, 1970, pp. 110-24.

[18] On the events of 8 May 1945 see B. Mekhaled, *Chroniques d'un massacre: 8 mai 1945: Sétif, Guelma, Kherrata,* Paris: Syros, 1995.

in 1962 by its French inhabitants, it was invaded by all those who, like him, were fleeing their past in search of a new life. In Algiers he, the son of a peasant, became through his participation in the war the friend of senior dignitaries of the state, including one of Houari Boumedienne's ministers.

After independence he made profitable use of the maquis supply networks. The economic disruption that accompanied the ALN guerrillas' coming to power enabled all those who, like him, were in a position to provide supplies to the cities to acquire positions of influence.[19] Those private traders in the service of the independent state retained, throughout the Boumedienne period, a monopoly of private imports of consumer products. They were also partners in the distribution of locally produced goods over the national territory. In fact they never entered into competition with the state import and distribution networks; a sort of share-out of imported products was established, with those bringing in considerable profits (vehicles, electronic products, machine tools, pharmaceuticals) remaining in the hands of leaders of the regime. The private sector concentrated on products for everyday consumption, with low added value. The influence of those traders remained nonetheless considerable; they amassed colossal fortunes, at a time when the French franc was exchanged for one and a half dinars at the official rate. Sheikh Lahcen invested mainly in real estate and had about ten 'Dallas'-style houses built, a distinctive sign of wealth. However, those traders were quickly overtaken in fortune and influence by a new type of economic actor, a product of the period of Chadli Bendjedid's presidency: the speculator. In Sheikh Lahcen's view the speculators were none other than those of his comrades in arms who had chosen to join the state institutions.

The nationalisation of oil and gas in 1971 and the 'oil shocks' of 1973 and 1979 augmented the state's revenue; military officers and senior civil servants were in charge of managing the increase in the oil price. The unconvertibility of the dinar gave considerable power to political personnel who held foreign exchange and readily speculated on the informal foreign exchange market. Resale of foreign currency to individuals like Sheikh Lahcen, at a rate higher than the official one, created a parallel market which continually expanded. Using their control over the currency the speculators developed a policy of massive imports of consumer goods, which weakened the private traders, drowned in the variety of imported products. Only solid friendships at the top levels of the administration allowed certain traders to keep their market shares safe from the emergence of rivals. However, the traders of the '54 generation saw themselves relegated in fortune and influence to the position of 'rich traders', well behind the speculators. The latter were transformed by the overlapping of the public and

---

[19] M.E. Benissad estimated that between 1962 and 1965 Algiers, Oran and Constantine accounted for 90 per cent of the wholesale trade turnover. *Economie et développement de l'Algérie,* Paris: Economica, 1977.

private sectors and exchange control into *nouveaux riches,* in fact into 'millionaires' according to Sheikh Lahcen and public rumour.

Following the drying up of state revenue due to debt servicing,[20] the speculators invaded the private sector.[21] The abandonment of the state apparatus at the end of the 1980s was a result of the carving up carried out by the speculators. George Corm notes: 'On coming to power through the Hamrouche government, in the autumn of 1989, the reformers found foreign exchange reserves at a very low level, about $800 million.'[22] From 1992 onwards the government instituted a 'war economy' to respond to the challenge of Islamist violence; state imports became scarce, which allowed approved traders and agents to make new profit margins, especially in distribution. With the dwindling of the state's resources between 1991 and 1994 military officers established a monopoly over management of revenue, because of their involvement in the repression. Owing to their determination to reorganise and modernise the repressive apparatus, possibilities for embezzlement of public funds dried at their source. However, from 1994 the rescheduling of the debt and the introduction of a market economy gave the traders a new lease of life, thanks to the resumption of the policy of importing products. But 'competition' set in because private and public actors were obliged to accommodate the interests of the army and also those of the new economic actors, the armed bands. Those bands were, in addition, sought after by all the economic actors, with a view to reducing or diminishing their rivals' resources as much as possible, as we shall see in the next chapter.

Having suffered a decline in the 1980s, the renowned trader Sheikh Lahcen found new vigour in the civil war. The time when he and others monopolised imports had passed, but the war had the merit, in his eyes, of levelling inequalities. Speculators, traders and state enterprise managers were obliged, in order to survive, to show imagination in the face of the 'Emirs' and guerrillas who were ready to destroy or disrupt their activities. In that game Sheikh Lahcen had some winning cards. Besides the fund of sympathy which the private sector got from the Islamists, he had experience valued by the 'Emirs', his past was of the sort that they respected. His exile far from the suburbs was disastrous for his staff, who lost their jobs, and

[20] The total debt, which was $16 billion in 1984, rose to $26 billion in 1989. Debt servicing payments rose during that period from $5 billion to more than $7 billion in 1989, then $8 billion in 1990.

[21] A. Brahimi has written: 'The supplementary budget for 1990 adopted by the ANP [Assemblée Nationale Populaire] in July legalised *"trabendisme"* by authorising international hawking involving resale to the state, on the domestic market, of imported goods. That budget also authorised approved agents and wholesalers to import consumer goods, capital goods and goods for industrial use for resale to the state.' *Stratégies de développement pour l'Algérie,* Paris, Economica, 1991, p. 319.

[22] G. Corm, 'La réforme économique algérienne, une réforme mal aimée?', *Maghreb Machrek,* Jan.-March 1993, no. 139, p. 22.

it obliged the armed groups to try vainly to provide the services he had offered. From the beginning of the civil war Sheikh Lahcen had nothing to complain about, no crime was committed against his family, still less any act of sabotage against his property. His 'villa-warehouses', although uninhabited, were respected by successive 'Emirs' and the security forces avoided stationing troops nearby, as they could provoke a clash with the armed bands and lead to damage to the Sheikh's property.

These 'big men'[23] have been passing through the civil war without too many accidents. The armed groups, in spite of their ardour, do not seem in a position to supplant them. For that they would need to unleash terror sufficient to make the military entrepreneurs flee for good, just as the departure of the settlers in 1962 contributed to the accumulation of wealth by Sheikh Lahcen. So far only intellectuals, journalists and officials have been leaving Algerian territory, leaving positions which the 'Emirs' have not been planning to take.

Economic determinants of the GIA's consolidation

The groups calling themselves Islamist benefited in 1992 from the enormous pro-FIS electorate. But it has to be recognised that in failing to maintain that asset, they let it decay. That failure was due to the demarcation of the 'Emirs'' territory and the organisation of their kingdoms. For the young men of the communes run by the FIS in 1990-1 had, independently, been engaged in many forms of contestation since 1988. The 'Emirs' thus had a political legitimacy derived from the interruption of the elections process in December 1991-January 1992 and the policy of repression.

Overpopulation and poverty: handicaps to consolidation of the GIA. The carving up of the communes by the 'Emirs' and their bands was, however, altered during the conflict with the security forces. The residential districts inhabited by young men sympathetic to the FIS and MIA until 1993 were a reservoir of recruits for the '*djamaat*' (Islamist groups). However, the latter could not take root in localities that were too deeply impoverished, where economic resources were rare and communication routes had no strategic importance – especially since the halt in armed attacks on banks, due to the creation of private security firms,[24] stemmed major inflows of liquidity.[25] The scarcity of economic resources weakened the armed

---

[23] On the 'politician-entrepreneur or big man' see J.-F. Médard, 'L'Etat patrimonialiste', *Politique Africaine,* no. 39, 1990, p. 31.

[24] Executive decree 94/65 of 19 March 1994 authorised private companies to ensure the security of public or private agents.

[25] A gendarmerie report published on 16 Nov. 1993 mentioned that 191 armed robberies were estimated to have been committed during the first half of 1993, representing 41.6 million dinars: *El Watan,* 17 Nov. 1993.

groups, as they were obliged to meet some operating expenses: logistics, food, lodging, vehicles, arms, and charitable spending (allowances for families of martyrs, financial help for acquisition of property, 'purchase' of military service exemption cards).[26]

Prosperity of the communes and vitality of the armed bands. The permanent establishment of the armed bands in areas like Chararba, Baraki and Les Eucalyptus is explained not only by extreme ardour for waging the *jihad*, but also by the abundance of financial resources due to the high proportion of petty traders whose business was expanding. To that was added geography hospitable to guerrilla warfare, because of the absence of an urban development plan. The maze of streets, a handicap from the architectural point of view, became an asset for the local Moudjahidin, who knew the smallest corners of their territory backwards. Similarly, main roads filled with vehicles favoured protection rackets and explained the proliferation of 'fake checkpoints'. Those urban zones, bordering the Blida Wilaya, were in close contact with guerrilla groups established in the neighbouring mountain ranges (the Chréa and Meftah Massifs). The MIA instructors found no difficulty in training adolescents in urban guerrilla war between 1992 and 1993; their maquis, in the Meftah mountains, was only 40 km. away. That environment favouring consolidation of urban guerrilla war probably explains why those three municipalities produced a certain number of prominent Moudjahidin.[27]

The extreme difficulty faced by the 'Emirs' in consolidating their positions in the inner suburbs of Algiers (Mohammadia, Bach Djarah) is explained by the absence of those geographical, social and economic characteristics. Although overpopulated, those areas did not allow an Islamist group to extract sufficient resources for its activity, as the local people were much poorer. The armed bands consolidated their positions in the most economically dynamic zones; that dynamism might be derived from the informal economy or illicit dealings. While the inner suburbs were in the forefront in the riots of October 1988, the outer suburbs, much too remote, remained on the sidelines. Since 1991 the reverse has the case. The outer communes of Algiers have been favoured by the armed bands who have taken advantage – besides the features mentioned above – of the

[26] According to *Algérie Confidentiel*, no. 72, Thursday 26 April 1996, the charge was said to be 300,000 dinars (25,000 francs). The military administration was apparently not to be outdone in profiting from the civil war, for the charge before the war was 5,000 francs; thus the GIA's threats against national servicemen multiplied the price of exemption cards by five.

[27] The most famous being Abdallah Yahyia, member of the commando which hijacked the Air France Airbus on 24 December 1994. He originally came from Les Eucalyptus, just as Abou Khalil Mahfoud (Mahfoud Tadjine), a close companion of Mohammed Allal (second 'Emir' of the GIA), came from the Château Rouge district in Les Eucalyptus.

absence of effective military-police infrastructure in areas considered less dangerous because of their distance from the centres of power (the heights of Algiers, Hydra, El Biar). The Casbah and Bab el Oued remained high-risk places,[28] but the violence there was more like common-law crime. Groups of criminals, on which a strong security forces presence lives parasitically by managing the drugs and burglary markets, resumed their activities for the benefit of the Islamist guerrillas. The extreme difficulty faced by the guerrillas in conducting their operations without risk in the centre of Algiers obliged them to make contracts with groups of criminals who undertook, in return for generous payment, to carry out missions assigned to them (murder of a particular person, moving a vehicle filled with explosives, shadowing people etc.).

These differences among the Islamist communes mean that one cannot speak in a generalised way about the armed bands' territory. Only resource-rich zones far from the centre of Algiers became real enclaves where the 'Emirs' consolidated their positions, on the lines of the armed bands in Brazzaville such as the 'Sharks' and the 'Cobras'.[29] The armed groups represented and defended the interests of social groups whose political loyalties and social origins varied. For in contrast to the extreme difficulty of identifying the authors of crimes in 1992 and 1993, the emergence of the armed bands rationalised the violence. When a territory was forcibly taken over and run by the Moudjahidin the local people had something like a feeling that order had been restored. The Moudjahidin appeared in broad daylight until 1994, even until 1995 in some areas, impelled by the need to manage their 'kingdoms'. Control of the south-eastern Algiers communes by armed adolescents bearing the GIA standard created an imagined frontier dreaded by all those who did not live there.

Protection and predation. Demarcation of an armed group's territory followed economic considerations: the boundaries of the 'kingdom' were indicated by the petty traders subjected to protection rackets by members of a group in the name of the same 'Emir':

'I was sitting down reading the sports newspaper, I was listening to music when two young men entered the shop and said, "Turn off the radio!" I turned it off and as I got up, I saw the *klach* they were carrying, then I understood that they were Moudjahidin. They told me to have no fear because I was a good Muslim. They told me I must give help to fight Tâghout.[30] I said I had no money, what I earned was just enough to feed

---

[28] The Islamist group headed by the Emir named 'Flicha' (from the French *flèche*, arrow – because of his ability to escape from security forces' ambushes) is still active.

[29] Rémy Bazenguissa-Ganga, 'Milices politiques et bandes armées à Brazzaville. Enquête sur la violence politique et sociale des jeunes déclassés', *Les études du CERI*, no. 13, April 1996, 32 pp.

[30] Tâghout was the name given by the Islamists to the state; it was taken from the Koranic vocabulary applied to the Devil. It meant above all, in the lexicon of the Islamist movements,

my family; then they said, "You give what you can", and in two days someone would come to collect the money, and they left.' (Brahim, petty trader, 35 years old, Algiers suburbs, 1994)

Protection rackets became general in 1993 and 1994 and involved all the economic actors in some communes.The armed bands, who had a mono- poly of violence in 1993-4, used and abused that asset in parts of the wider suburban area of southeastern Algiers. This went so far that local counter- resistance emerged, through the formation of groups of 'patriots' and 'militiamen' in 1995. While the 'Emirs', in taking control of certain areas, partially put an end to the proliferation of groups of criminals (some of whom joined them), their economic organisation, which involved pressuring the local people, turned out to be much too heavy a burden to bear, in spite of the services rendered. After the flight of the military entrepreneurs and the sabotage of the few industrial production units the petty traders alone had to bear the burden of sustaining the armed groups.[31] From 1994 on- wards they stopped supplying them automatically, so as to invest in new markets. This refusal was to lead to many killings of bakers, grocers, hard- ware merchants and jewellers, and hence to a new exodus in those trades, following the exodus of the military entrepreneurs, back to the home vil- lages. The armed bands in this way lost the essential part of their financial resources; thus weakened, they plunged their districts into terror:

'They cut two young people's throats and placed their heads at the crossroads. That is no good, that. I think that if they go on doing that, people won't be with them any more. Let them kill the others, the thieves (criminals and political leaders), but they shouldn't cut people's throats... They cut you up into pieces as if you were a sheep. I tell you, people are going to turn against them if that continues.' (Petty trader, 40 years old, Algiers suburbs, 1994)

The imbalance between the activities of protection and predation led to a change in the attitude towards the 'Emirs' among the people, and especially on the part of the victims. The armed bands no longer seemed like spon- taneous groups for defence of the district but rather as Islamist businesses, made up of more and more dubious individuals. The empathy with the first 'Emirs' of the commune was gradually lost, to be replaced by a more pragmatic relationship; in place of the initial donations the Islamist bands introduced a war tax. Abdallah, a former FIS voter and a sympathiser with the MIA at the time it flourished (1992-3), recalled how the 'Emir' of Les Eucalyptus, Saïd the sheet-metal worker, enjoyed the local people's confidence at that time:

---

the Tyrant, the Oppressor, the 'false god' who is worshipped out of fear. The term be- came fashionable following the Iranian revolution, when 'Taghouti' meant the supporters of the old regime. On the effects of the Iranian revolution see Y. Richard, *L'islam chi'ite. Croyances et idéologies*, Paris: Fayard, 1991, p. 261.

[31] The burden was all the heavier because in 1993 an official property tax was added, to contribute to the support of victims of violence.

'Everyone gave, those who had some money gave plenty, others gave what they could, 100 dinars, 200 dinars, 500. When Saïd the sheet-metal worker's men passed people had no fear, even if they had a *klach* on their shoulders. Because everybody was with them.' (Abdallah, vendor, Algiers suburbs, 1994)

Not only were the first 'Emirs' known, they did not really need the local people's money, because they raised most of their resources by robbing banks. But from 1994 that became highly risky because of the security guards recruited on a massive scale in the banking sector. Above all, the 'Emirs' encountered competition from the formation of guerrilla organisations in the maquis, also looking for financial resources. From then on every Islamist group had to protect its territory, and especially the traders working in it, so as to shield them from the demands made by rival 'Emirs'. The donations from 'petty traders' stopped and, because of the proliferation of Islamist groups, the 'Emirs' were forced to go from door to door to show their presence.

The petty traders became the object of numerous 'visits', which were sometimes fatal for them when several 'Emirs' were active on their territory, for then they were called upon to pay for the upkeep of several groups. They preferred to see their local area guided by one single 'Emir' for as long as possible, which would allow them to pay up only once and to the same armed group. The services rendered by the people to their 'Emir' were also intended to spare them from the emergence of new 'Emirs' with bigger financial demands, or even the takeover of a commune by a guerrilla faction, which could turn the commune into a battlefield. The success of the armed group thus depended on its leader's ability to maintain local resources. To do that he had to protect those who were funding him from threats of extortion from other groups. But systematic decimation by the security forces led to the arrival of new groups who made new financial demands on the petty traders, arousing their exasperation, even terrorising them when they refused to pay. In addition the people did not know these new fighters, sometimes strangers to the commune, who were wanted by the security services for acts committed in other places. The southeastern suburbs of Algiers had a reputation for dissidence in 1992, and so they attracted young people waiting to leave for the maquis in the Meftah area. From then on its people were more and more involved in the conflict. Chemists and doctors were, because of the services that they could render, very much sought after, and this led to their flight:

'It does not give me pleasure to leave my work, but it's impossible to work now. One evening I had a visit from three individuals, they introduced themselves as Moudjahidin, one of them was injured and they wanted me to treat him. But if the army had seen those men in front of my house, they would dynamite it, kill me and throw my family into the street like dogs. I have nothing to do with their war, I'm not on one side or the other, that's why I left. That war does not concern me.' (Chemist, 1993-4, Algiers suburbs)

The steady exodus of those economic actors was the second of its sort: after the military entrepreneurs, the liberal professions. There then remained only those who, like the petty traders, made their living from their homes which served as places of business. The Islamist groups from then on focused on those economic actors and subjected them to a war tax which very quickly took the form of a protection racket.

Wasting the FIS electoral capital

One effect of the emergence and then consolidation of violence was a breach in the ranks of the FIS electorate. In our sample FIS voters and sympathisers more than 30 years old – skilled unemployed people, petty traders or workers – ceased from 1994 to identify with the actions of the armed groups in the cause of an Islamic state. Assailed by terror, like the proclaimed targets of the GIA (civil servants, policemen, etc.), they cast the *djamaat* out of the Islamist fold. They had voted for FIS candidates in the June 1990 municipal elections and the parliamentary elections of December 1991 mainly from determination to put an end to the FLN-state.

Dissension among Islamist voters on the policies of the 'Emirs'. The armed bands' war against the regime, far from harming it, brought poverty and terror to the FIS voters, except for the traders integrated into the enrichment network; they, after the flight of the military entrepreneurs, were for a moment the main group with capital available. As has been shown, they bought up villas being sold off cheap at that time, and improved their profit margins thanks to the end of price control. However, there was a reverse side to these advantages; those economic actors were the only ones capable of keeping the armed groups going. While the first generation of 'Emirs' in 1993 had the traders' sympathy, the new claimants in 1994, much younger, aroused suspicion and fear. This was for a very simple reason: the age difference between the armed bands and the former FIS voters fed mutual ignorance. Between a petty trader of thirty five and an 'Emir' of thirty, a certain amount of complicity was possible, because their backgrounds had much in common despite the differences. Between an 'Emir' of sixteen and a trader twice his age, very little connection could be made – which did not mean that, when a connection was made, it could not prove lasting.

The age difference between members of the armed groups and former FIS voters was related to differing political *imaginaires*. From 1992 onwards the war encouraged the creation of new heroes, 'martyrs' who had fallen in battle; the district 'Moudjahidin' produced a world of sensation in which violence, death and fear were the central features. No attention was paid to the political dynamic set in motion by the rise of the FIS between 1989 and 1991, or to the political 'stars' of that time. The political field, generally speaking, seemed surrealistic, the speeches by senior Islamist figures abroad were unknown, there was even sometimes complete ignorance about the historic figures of the FIS. Sofiane, younger brother of Abdallah – the newsagent arrested and tortured just after the halting of the elections – was for two years a passionate supporter of the cause of the Moudjahidin. He adopted the ideas of older people who considered the 'Islamists abroad' as 'false' fighters. He and his friends followed closely the dismantling of the FAF[32] and the arrest of its leaders; they had been surprised to learn that leaders of the GIA could live in Paris:

'The "Islamists" in France, they don't count for anything. The man who Pasqua [Charles Pasqua was the French Minister of the Interior at the time] said was the so-called chief in France, he's just nothing, here, he's worth nothing, perhaps it's Pasqua who gave him the job! But anyway, all those who ran away, they have nothing more to do with the Moudjahidin. Because abroad they talk, they talk, that's all. To create the Islamic state we need Moudjahidin here, not over there.' (Young man of 16, Algiers suburbs, 1994)

His ignorance was such that he admitted later that he knew nothing about the political action of Sheikh Sahraoui, one of the co-founders of the FIS. That gap between the former FIS voters' identification with the imprisoned leaders (Abassi Madani and Ali Benhadj) and the armed bands' identification with 'Emirs' killed in battle increased their mutual incomprehension. In addition, the increasing role of strangers among the Islamist bands in the communes previously supporting the FIS could eventually lead the former FIS voters, if not to fight against them, at least to inform against them. Because in fact the Islamist bands waged a real war against those who, like the FIS elected representatives and sympathisers, were in some ways representative of the Islamist cause. But it was mainly from the regime's side that FIS activists suffered the most severe reprisals; the armed bands only had to defeat the last local claimants.

Selim, convinced of the 'just cause'. However, not all the former FIS voters rejected the violence of the Moudjahidin. In the view of a certain number of them, close to the social background of the fighters in the armed bands, those fighters were not the bloodstained killers described by the press or by traders subjected to their extortion. Their actions were rather imbued with 'justice', because their victims were not 'infidels' but 'torturers'. Thus murders of policeman, soldiers or informers were very rarely condemned, quite the contrary; those former FIS voters who sympathised with the Islamist bands justified their support by speaking, in response to any mention of the violence of the 'Emirs', of the repression by the security forces.

---

[32] The Fédération Algérienne de France (FAF) was the organ of the FIS in France. Under the chairmanship of Dja'far El Houari, a student of Statistics, it distributed a bulletin, *Le Critère*, until it was banned by Charles Pasqua, French Minister of the Interior, in November 1993, when many of its sympathisers and militants were arrested. See G. Kepel, *A l'ouest d'Allah*, Paris: Seuil, 1994, p. 293.

For those who believed in the cause of the armed bands, the Moudjahidin were on the right path:

'They don't do any wrong against Muslims, what they say in the newpapers is not true. One day, a Moudjahid had to kill an inspector who lived in a housing estate; his accomplices described what the inspector was like and at what time he left home with his son each day. So he waited in the estate, but the inspector looked out of his window and saw that that young man was not from the area, he alerted his station; meanwhile a man with his son left the block where the inspector lived, the Moudjahid thought it was his target, he fired three bullets into his head and escaped quietly in front of bystanders. When he learned that he had made a mistake he went to the victim's widow, he went on his knees and wept, he told her, "We are fighting in the path of God, and if you do not forgive me, I shall go to hell. Ask me for anything you want and I shall give it to you." He wept like a child although he is a Moudjahid, because of his mistake, since he feared God.' (Selim, clothes dealer, 28, Algiers suburbs, 1994)

Like Selim some former FIS sympathisers remained convinced of the just cause of the 'Emirs'. They refused to see any objectivity in the national and international media, which they accused of bias and contradiction. In Selim's eyes the armed groups were only redressing the balance of forces; the inspectors, all-powerful just a short time before, were now an enticing target for the Moudjahidin who, through their actions against those police officers, were identified as 'avengers' by some adolescents and young men scarred by beatings in police stations. However, an additional factor explained the determination to eliminate policemen and inspectors. In contrast to the soldiers and gendarmes living in barracks, policemen lived in the same residential housing estates as the armed groups. The daily killings of policemen during the 1992-4 period were aimed at ridding the 'kingdom' of people standing in the way of the 'Emirs' – especially as the inspectors had networks of informers among many traders, even though those were former FIS voters. Knowing and supplying an inspector was for petty traders an asset for smooth operation of their business. By eliminating the police or forcing them to regroup in places at a distance and thus better protected, the armed bands deprived the local population of any possibility of collaborating with the police. As for the gendarmerie posts, like the barracks, their relationship with the local people was much too superficial to be effective.

The strategy of systematic elimination of policemen and inspectors from the 'kingdoms' of the 'Emirs' further exposed the gap between the latter and the better-off former FIS voters. While Selim thought their killing was justified because they refused to resign or join the Moudjahidin, his employer thought their strategy was absurd:

'Ah Hababek, what good does it do to kill the policeman at the crossroads? He's a poor chap with a pistol which perhaps doesn't even work! What has he done? They kill him not to fight the regime, but to take their place, that way they do police work themselves, that's the truth. They kill people of our district, that means the police know the others [the armed bands] well.' (Proprietor of a clothes shop, 1995, France)

The former FIS voters, like Selim's boss, thought the real targets were not the 'poor policemen' or the national servicemen, but the 'big shots', the 'high ranking people' – those were the people who had responsibility. According to him the armed groups did nothing or too little against them – that was why he did not support them but did, in spite of himself, pay the 'war tax' to the 'Emirs'. Other people who had voted enthusiastically for the FIS in the municipal elections of June 1990 and the parliamentary elections of December 1991 started, like Walid, to make a discreet but real exit from Islamism.

Walid: from Islamist passion to apathy. Disillusioned and disgusted – that is how Walid, a 39-year-old native of the southeastern suburbs of Algiers, appears. Member of a large family, son of the proprietor of a small car repair yard, he looked on the conflict tearing his country apart with disillusion, and notably held out no hope of political change. Having got his baccalauréat through *archoua* (corruption) and begun studies out of disgust with a mechanic's job, Walid embarked on studies of economics and accountancy during the 1980s. He wanted to settle in the United States or Canada after his studies, as he was convinced that the 'system' was unreformable. But then Walid was surprised by the extent of the riots of 1988 and fascinated by the emergence of the Islamist opposition in 1989. The formation of the FIS in March 1989 and its victory in the June 1990 municipal elections aroused in him an enthusiasm for Algeria, the country he was getting ready to leave. Having practiced little as a Muslim until then, he became an assiduous practicing Muslim and, while not wearing the *kamis*, wore a wisp of a beard as a distinguishing mark and a sign of belonging. The Islamic state heralded by the FIS vistory in the parliamentary elections in December 1991 was seen not as the restoration of an Islamic golden age but as the realisation of a longing: for the punishment of the regime.

The interruption of the parliamentary elections, the banning of the FIS in March and the unleashing of 'total war' decreed mutually by the warring parties aroused ambivalent feelings in Walid. In 1992-3 Walid remained convinced that an agreement between 'the army' and the FIS was being sorted out. Disappointed with the failure of that theory, like many ex-FIS sympathisers and militants who expected an army-FIS alliance to take over from the FLN-state, he supported the first armed actions conducted by the MIA; he saw its fighters as 'avengers' against the 'thieves' who had stolen the December 1991 election victory. During 1993 his close relations feared that he would join the ranks of Abdelkader Chébouti's fighters. His grievances against the regime and his 'disgust' at the attitude of so-called democratic countries led him to hope for a victory for the Islamists. The emergence of the armed groups in 1993 increased that hope. Paradoxically, it was during the year 1993-4 that he wore the *kamis* every Friday, during the collective prayers, despite the risks involved. Confronted with the radicalisation of military and warlike conduct on the part of the warring parties, Walid hardened his conduct and attitude in daily life, his family life included.

Even though he reached the conclusion that only by joining an armed group could he appease, channel and express his revolt, it was the opposite that happened in 1994. Endless murders and outrages in his commune drowned his fury in 'disgust' which made him lose his bearings in his thinking and environment. His joy in the 1989-91 period gave way to an atmosphere of madness and murder in which he was nearly carried away. According to one of his younger brothers Walid intended to join a maquis but, from fear of death or of reprisals against his family, he gave up the idea:

'When they halted the elections, that began to make everyone afraid, Walid talked only of the maquis. We were afraid he would go...but as he stayed, he made war at home: why does so-and-so not go to the mosque? Why do people watch the state television? Why this and that? As for girls, they were not to be mentioned any more. He spoke only of the Moudjahidin and the *jihad*, nothing else interested him. But thank God, one day he stopped talking about those things and told his mother he wanted to get married.' (Walid's brother, Algiers suburbs, 1994)

Walid's withdrawal into his private concerns was due to the absence of a rallying point for Islamist guerrilla war. In his desire to turn his feeling of revolt into action Walid found, between 1992 and 1994, only a collection of armed groups whose members were constantly replaced because of the repression. Besides the absence of a centralised national structure there were also extremely cruel acts of war against human targets, against whom the accusations of crimes were not always convincing. Walid's progress from joy to revolt and then disillusion explains why the Islamist guerrilla campaign was deprived of that type of man and was manned by very young people socialised not by the FIS but directly by the armed groups. The voters and sympathisers of that party, like Walid, seem – according to other research – to have been led into strictly private religious practice and a totally disillusioned view of the world.[33] Their political dream ended with the civil war and their avoidance of active participation in the conflict drew them further away from the newly emerging political-military actors, the Moudjahidin.

The organisation and management of the kingdoms of the 'Emirs' were accompanied by terror practices that were all the more unendurable when one did not share the Moudjahidin's political and military aims. To the feeling of insecurity present during the year 1992-3 was added a climate of terror arising not from violence, which was mastered and taken on board by the people, but from the ritual of death. The year 1994, and especially the month of Ramadan, plunged the people into daily mourning; everyone knew of the death of someone close. The cemeteries of Algiers were

[33] M. Vergès, 'Les héros n'ont pas de préoccupations de ce monde' in R. Leveau (ed.), *L'Algérie dans la guerre,* Brussels: Complexe, pp. 71-87.

continually the scene of speeches over the dead and expressions of sympathy. Until then the war had not been faced by the great majority, who expected that an agreement among the warring parties would free the local people from their perilous position as a stake in the fight for *kursi*. Now it settled down for a long stay.

The Ambiguity of 'Total War'

The security forces (army, police, gendarmerie) and the Islamist guerrillas succeeded, amid very obvious chaos, in consolidating their war machines. The strategy of 'total war' decreed by the GIA was being applied, and President Liamine Zéroual[34] responded, in his speech in October 1994, with the objective of 'total eradication' of the armed groups. All the pseudo-moves for negotiation and discussion, in which a certain number of observers believed, were only delusions serving to divert attention from the real civil war getting under way.[35] But such a determination for confrontation had some political sense, for in declaring 'total war' on either side, the warring parties took on the task of closing off the political field, already damaged since the interruption of the elections in January 1992. The GIA, and with it all the armed bands in the wider suburban area of Algiers, embarked on systematic elimination of the surviving activists and organisers of the FIS[36] and declared its determination to wipe out the Armée Islamique du Salut (AIS).[37] On the other side, when an opposition agreement claiming to put forward a credible alternative was reached in Rome, the regime responded

[34] Liamine Zéroual was born on 3 July 1941 in Batna, capital of the Aurès. He took part in the war of liberation in the ranks of the ALN. In 1975 he became Commandant of the Ecole d'Application des Armes de Combat at Batna, and in 1981 he took over command of the Académie Inter-Armes at Cherchell. Promoted general in 1988, he was appointed ambassador to Romania following disagreements with the Chief of Staff, General Nezzar, and President Chadli Bendjedid. Against all expectations, on 30 January 1994, the Haut Conseil de Sécurité (HCS) 'entrusted' him with the Presidency. *Le Nouvel Afrique Asie* no. 54, March 1994.

[35] A. Rouquié has commented that 'even more than the elections, the "dialogue", its promises and its uncertainties were an integral part of the war. In the political wars in South America, good use of talks – geared for effect but also popular – was indispensable for conducting an overall strategy.' *Guerre et paix en Amérique latine*, Paris: Seuil, 1982, p. 289.

[36] Kamar Eddine Kharbane, a founder member of the FIS in exile in London, said in an interview that the GIA was responsible for 'the murder of Azzedine Biaa, former head of the FIS bureau at Blida; Nacer Tétraoui, former head of the Ouargla bureau; the famous Sheikh Mohamed Saïd, former head of the FIS Provisional National Bureau; Abdel Hamid Bouchi, very well known in the Casbah district; and Nassr Eddine Tourkman, Chairman of the FIS bureau at Médéa.' *Al Hayat*, quoted in *Courrier International*, May 1996.

[37] 'As they have not put an end to their unhealthy state of mind and their corruption on earth, it is our duty to fight them...and to conclude we tell our brothers that our struggle against the AIS is a duty.' GIA communiqué, *Al Hayat*, 10 Jan. 1995.

by accusing its promoters of seeking to internationalise the crisis and of being the political accomplices of the armed groups.[38]

The effect of these overall strategies was to spread terror at the local level. 'Total war' waged by the armed groups and the security forces targeted the infrastructure and the environment. Priority was given to acts of sabotage and destruction of the enemy's potential. That was why, from 1994, frontal attacks on barracks and police stations declined, while killings of soldiers, national servicemen and members of soldiers' families continually multiplied. The armed groups aimed in this war not at the collapse of the army, but at its isolation. The idea was to turn the army into a 'bunker' cut off from its surroundings. With that aim national servicemen were hunted down, their leaves became useless because they could not take leave; how could one return to one's family without risk? The mass slaughter of young national servicemen and the security forces' reprisals against suspects during 1994 in Chararba and Baraki were among the consequences of 'total war':

'It's the desert here now, there are only children and old people out of doors now. The army did a clean-up job, people saw hell here. Since then everyone else has gone to the maquis, or just anywhere, anyway you don't see young people any more. Even the press has spoken about it.[39] Here the security forces, they go to your house, and if they find a young man, they arrest him straight away, they think all the young men around here are Moudjahidin.' (Hussein, worker at a state enterprise that was burned down, Algiers suburbs, 32 years old)

An effect of 'total war' was to extend the notion of the enemy well beyond the actual warring parties. In Baraki, Chararba and Les Eucalyptus direct clashes between armed groups and the security forces were much fewer in number than acts of sabotage, murders and reprisals. The security forces, condemned to a labour of Sisyphus, increasingly targeted the Moudjahidin's environment, because the Moudjahidin were able to survive only because of that environment which had remained friendly to them. The terror which set in was itself an instrument of war, because it aimed at encouraging people to enlist in the ranks of the warring parties; people joined one or other war machine out of fear of being a floating target, without protection; the terror encouraged the use of 'protective violence'.[40] The objective of

[38] Through its ambassador in Rome, Benali Benzaghou, the government denounced 'interference in internal Algerian affairs' and the 'plot' seeking to internationalise those affairs. *La Tribune*, 26 Nov. 1994.

[39] The weekly newspaper *El Alem es Siyassi* ('the political world'), in July 1994, published a major feature on the desert-like state to which some communes of Algiers had been reduced.

[40] Jean Leca has written, 'Violence can be thought of as being originally not the effect of the passion for domination or destruction, but the effect of fear of being dominated or destroyed.' 'La "rationalité" de la violence politique', *Les Cahiers du CEDEJ*, 1994, p. 19.

'total war' was to turn every individual into an enemy. Those who did not join the ranks of one or other of the adversaries felt the most helpless:

'When you go to work, on the way you are afraid of something happening to you – a stray bullet, bandits killing you or robbing you for nothing, you don't know what, but you're afraid. At work you're afraid for your family, there are people who enter homes and rape young women today, it's incredible what is happening to us, unthinkable. That's happened to several families, it's worse than death if that happens to you, you can't live any more. So when I'm out of doors I long to go back home and once I'm back, I live with anguish that something may happen, because what could I do?' (Ali, restaurant waiter, Algiers suburbs, 35 years old)

Ali, who voted FIS in the municipal elections in June 1990 and the parliamentary elections in December 1991, did not understand how Algeria could have tipped over 'from heaven into hell'. Today, he can see nothing left of that 1989-91 period, which he describes as a 'golden age'. A prisoner of the 'total war', he seeks above all to survive a conflict in which he feels no part. A practicing Muslim since his adolescence, he did not need any political party or armed group to tell him what Islam is or what its benefits are. Disgusted and disheartened by the FLN-state, previously he saw the FIS as the best 'revenge' against those who had diverted the 'people's revolution' to their own advantage. After being momentarily tempted by the idea of emigrating to Canada, where one of his brothers was studying, he preferred to stay in Algeria, not out of nationalist feeling, but because it fell to him to provide for his family. For him, as for many former FIS voters and sympathisers of his age, the violence of the armed bands claiming to fight in the name of the GIA was that of wartime adolescents 'fearing neither God nor man', not heeding the risks they ran. Those adolescent Moudjahidin, however, did not have the time to assess the consequences of their actions, as their life expectancy was so short.

6

NEW WAYS TO MAKE BIG MONEY

Since 1992 only sound and fury have been heard from Algeria. Murders of intellectuals, journalists, civilians and men of religion lead one to think that all the economic and political actors are suspended from duty. But while the dynamics of the *jihad* have affected the Islamist armed groups and aroused paradoxical logics of war against the regime, the same is true of the economic actors, who have been establishing strategies of survival and balance between the two warring sides. This is especially necessary as they have had to react to changes in the country since 1994: the creation of a market economy on IMF recommendations has disrupted their businesses, because new opportunities for highly lucrative business have emerged. The civil war has not been leading necessarily to the ruin of economic players from the public and private sectors; on the contrary, violence seems to be accelerating procedures for accumulating wealth. So in parallel with the confrontation between the security forces and the armed groups, an economic war is developing, involving prominent local citizens, entrepreneurs, petty traders, senior government officials, and newcomers such as the 'Emirs'.

The war and its protagonists, far from confining themselves to the armed conflict, are inextricably mixed up with economic and political developments. The privatisation policy adopted by the regime since 1994 was instantly taken over by the participants in the civil war to their own advantage; this has led to a 'plunder economy'[1] in which prominent local people, 'Emirs' and military personnel have been laying hands on new resources and maintaining the level of violence in that way.

The other side of privatisation: destruction of the state sector

The ambiguity of the GIA's policy of destruction. The activities of the GIA armed bands are not limited to the armed struggle against the security

---

[1] In Africa 'the plunder economy' is exposed in privatisation processes: 'Privatisation of the economy can be understood in a wider sense; it does not only involve transfer of state enterprises to private players; it can also involve the acquisition, creation and capture of markets by other means, on the part of players with connections to the government but operating privately. In that sense privatisation of the economy is on a massive scale today and is in reality the dominant way in which the plunder economy operates'. J.-F. Bayart, S. Ellis and B. Hibou, *La criminalisation de l'Etat en Afrique*, Brussels: Complexe, 1997, p. 58.

forces. In parallel with attacks on military patrols, informers, policemen and recalcitrant civilians, there has been another war unknown to the media. As a part of 'total war', the actions started by the GIA to sabotage and destroy the economic order are aimed at weakening 'Tâghout'.[2] The regime, described as 'impious', is associated with an 'economy in the hands of infidels',[3] whose destruction cannot be wrong. The economic damage caused by that violence is considered lawful because every company, business or public transport vehicle destroyed deprives Algeria of the pernicious presence of 'Jews, Christians and renegades'. The armed groups' *jihad*, to be complete, needs to eliminate not only 'infidels' and 'Communists' but also their economic assets. How do GIA sympathisers view this determination to wreck the national economy? Tayeb, son of an executive working for Sonatrach,[4] after seeking refuge in France in 1993-4 (before leaving for North America) expressed the view that the armed groups ought to concentrate all their action on one objective, a strategic one for the regime's survival – the oil industry:

'I hope, I swear it, that they will succeed in blowing it all up. Because the oil and gas, the people see nothing of them, "they" pocket everything. It's of no use having that wealth, because of it "they" don't leave us alone. As long as it hasn't been blown up, they will stay, because they are fighting the war just for oil and gas profits. They are birds of prey who govern us, not normal politicians. Really, I'm just waiting for that moment, when they blow up their oil.' (Tayeb, GIA sympathiser in exile, France, 1994)

The violence of Tayeb's language against illicit use of Algeria's main economic resource expressed a profound disillusionment about what ought to have made the country's development possible.[5] The financial resources of oil and gas have 'blocked the country's progress' and, Tayeb said, provided backing for a 'caste of Janissaries' who are the main beneficiaries of the industry. Such comparisons aim to convince people of the alien nature of the military institution running the country since independence in 1962. Oil income, far from being an asset for Algeria, has turned out on the contrary to be a considerable political handicap[6] because it has prevented any

[2] See Chapter 5, note 30.

[3] *El Ansar*, no. 46, May 1994.

[4] Sonatrach is the main national corporation responsible for exploration, production and marketing of oil and gas. As those represent 98 per cent of Algeria's exports, that corporation is at 'the heart of the Algerian economy'. See C. Ardouin, 'Economie algérienne: quelles perspectives?', *Maghreb-Machrek*, no. 149, July-Sept. 1995, p. 15; and A. Bouhafs, 'Stratégie de modernisation de Sonatrach', *Economies et sociétés*, no. 29 (9), Sept. 1994, pp. 49-61.

[5] Houari Boumedienne, according to M. Gadant, 'saw oil as a means of buying industrialisation and cutting short the time it took in Europe, by jumping feet together into the era of state of the art technology' 'Boumediène, le discours de l'Etat', *(Pétrole et société), Peuples méditerranéens*, no. 26, 1984, p. 118.

[6] See G. Luciani on the crisis of rentier states: 'Rente pétrolière, crise fiscale de l'Etat

alternative to the established power structure, in view of the financial interests at stake. That is why Tayeb hoped that if it could not succeed in overthrowing the regime, the GIA would, by the destruction of the oil industry, put an end to the army leaders' determination to retain power. Several times the 'Emirs' threatened death to people working in that sector of the economy[7] and destruction to the oil industries.

This, however, had to do with the impossibility of overthrowing the regime, because by the spring of 1994 the prospect of a military victory for the Islamists had retreated to the realm of theory. Tayeb's wishes were not realised; the acts of sabotage and destruction targeted not oil and gas installations but state enterprises, notably transport, pharmaceuticals and cement manufacturing enterprises. Those actions, aimed at weakening the regime, had the paradoxical effect of redistributing those former state monopolies for the benefit of the private sector. Those war tactics on the part of the armed groups – aimed at destroying not the major resources of the state (95 per cent of the state's revenue comes from the oil and gas sector) but state enterprises that were often highly indebted, loss-making[8] or obsolete – seem surprising to say the least.

Systematic destruction of state-owned vehicles[9] led to a proliferation of private transport companies, which in 1996 accounted for 60 per cent of that sector in greater Algiers.[10] Transport privatisation had been started in the 1980s, but it was greatly expanded with the destruction of state-owned capital by the GIA fighters, bringing fat profits to the 'new' operators. Freed from administrative shackles, the 'new' bosses in the transport sector took advantage of trade and price liberalisation to import second-hand buses, mostly from France, and charge unregulated fares, that is much higher ones, without improving the service's performance even so (the buses are still overcrowded and the waits just as long). These new practices aroused contrasting reactions, notably on the part of traders who were former FIS voters:

'Since they liberalised trade and imports, those who had controlled the public sector abandoned it for private business, that is more profitable today. In Algiers one former manager of a state enterprise has in the past year set up a public transport company.

---

et démocratisation', in G. Salamé (ed.), *Démocraties sans démocrates*, Paris: Fayard, 1994, pp. 129-233.

[7] In a communiqué published in *Al Hayat* (14 Feb. 1996) the GIA repeated its threats and advised foreign companies not to invest in Algeria.

[8] Addressing the National Transition Council, the head of government gave a figure of 128 billion dinars for bank overdrafts in March 1996, compared with 39 billion in March 1995. *El Watan*, 7 July 1996.

[9] According to Amine Touati, in 1993, in the Algiers region, '442 lorries, 114 buses, 16 minibuses, 116 heavy public works vehicles and 154 light vehicles were destroyed'. *Les islamistes à l'assaut du pouvoir*, Paris: L'Harmattan, 1995, p. 179.

[10] According to a survey by the Ministry of Transport, financed by the World Bank. *La Tribune,* 17 June 1996.

He has at least thirty buses, all second-hand, bought from France. Private transport is the most profitable today. The Moudjahidin burn state-run buses, so there are fewer and fewer of them. The problem for poor people is that the private buses are more expensive, two or three times more expensive than state bus service fares. In addition you run no risk of your bus being destroyed. The only problem is that to import buses, you need to know the right people.' (Trader, specialising in meat marketing, Algiers area, 1994)

This craze for the private sector in the Mitidja and other regions was inherent in the expansion of the Islamist armed groups, whose war logic was dictated by local considerations. That was why destruction of oil and gas installations has rarely been attempted because, besides the risks that it involves, it is of no interest to the armed groups; the weakening of the regime that would follow would bring more benefit to the professional Islamist guerrillas belonging to various factions on the other side (AIS, MIA, MEI, FIDA),[11] who have been proposing an alternative agenda. In contrast the destruction of state transport enterprises led to a proliferation of private companies; these were then subjected to protection rackets by the armed groups, who in certain areas became 'inspectors' of those private buses. The expansion of private ownership of urban transport was correlated with the predominance of the armed groups, which extorted money from a company but also ensured protection for its vehicles in a very uncertain environment.

Extension of the privatisation process. This process has gone far in inter-city transport. Attacks by Islamist guerrillas in the interior of the country – safe from military assault until 1994 – on state-run buses and trains led to expansion of private freight haulage companies and a bigger role for inter-city taxis. The fake checkpoints set up by the guerrillas along roads were thus intended not only to hamper movement of army or gendarmerie convoys, but also to regulate road traffic to their profit; for the systematic destruction of state-owned vehicles brought private companies into that highly profitable corner of the market. Food supplies for the small and medium-sized towns of the interior are brought by rail and by road. Imported goods are initially stored at Algiers harbour; from there they were previously taken to the *souk el fellah* ('peasants' markets', state warehouses). Although those warehouses were poorly stocked, goods sold there were cheaper because they were subsidised by the state.[12] Adversely affected during the 1980s by the development of *trabendo* and petty retail trade, the state warehouses offered a very limited variety of products, especially where food was concerned. With the constant attacks on state-run freight

[11] Described in Chapter 9.
[12] Since 1994 a high proportion of goods have ceased to be subsidised. The government's programme provided, in agreement with the IMF, that no product would be subsidised any longer by the end of 1996.

vehicles, part of the *souk el fellah* no longer received supplies, to the greater profit of private traders who could now monopolise distribution of consumer goods.

The armed groups' concentration on economic targets, initially supposed to weaken or even destroy the regime's resources, had the effect of speeding up privatisation of the worst-hit sectors, to the profit of economic actors emerging from the regime or from the private sector, which had been expanding considerably since the 1980s. Certainly the damage caused was great, amounting to a real loss for Algeria's GDP.[13] But the destruction of state enterprises did not affect the regime, which essentially lived off oil and gas rent.[14] And, paradoxically, that destruction even spared the regime the heavy cost of paying for outdated economic facilities that had been kept running for political and social reasons.[15] Despite the personal profits earned by senior executives who managed loss-making enterprises, management posts in state enterprises lost their appeal in comparison with running a private company; movement from one position to the other was part of the logic of the war. For the employees, filled with anxiety at the idea of privatisation of their company announced in 1994, it came to seem a lesser evil than the systematic destruction carried out by the armed groups.[16]

Political and military stakes in privatisation. In parallel with the forced privatisation of some of the economic sectors hardest hit by the armed groups, a controlled process of privatisation of state-run operations was begun. During the year 1995 the National Transition Council[17] voted for privatisation of 1,250 state enterprises, of which 1,200 were in the sectors of tourism, restaurants, hotels, public buildings and works, insurance, and seaport and airport services. As for industrial enterprises, fifty of them were affected; for the 300 major state enterprises, an investment fund set

[13] It is estimated at $2.5 billion for 1994, compared with GNP of $40.2 billion. *Marchés Tropicaux et Méditerranéens*, no. 2582, 5 May 1995.

[14] In 1994 earnings from sales of oil and gas amounted to $8.6 billion out of total exports of $8.8 billion (i.e. 98 per cent); in 1995 to $9.7 billion out of $10.2 billion (95 per cent). Banque d'Algérie, *La Tribune,* 17 June 1996.

[15] Despite commitments made to the IMF, industrial concerns continued to weigh heavily on the state budget: out of a budget of 749 billion dinars for the year 1996, the government poured 124 billion dinars into the fund for rehabilitation of state enterprises. *El Watan*, 2 July 1996.

[16] According to M. Benhamouda, the sabotage of hundreds of factories and economic facilities by the GIA led to loss of jobs for 43,000 wage-earning employees. *Marchés tropicaux et méditerranéens*, no. 2582, 5 May 1995.

[17] The Conseil National de Transition (CNT) was the body that replaced the Haut Conseil de l'Etat, set up in 1992 after the dissolution of the People's National Assembly. It had 200 seats, 143 allocated to various representatives of associations, and to 29 small parties; 30 were reserved to representatives of the state and 27 to national political organisations.

up as a holding company organised the transfer of state-run activities to the private sector.[18] Other state enterprises, numbering nine in 1995, signed 'performance contracts' aimed at restoring their financial situation so that they could become autonomous,[19] as a prelude to privatisation.

The debate on privatisation, started in 1981, resumed in 1986,[20] and intensified after the onset of civil war. It led to concrete results from 1994, in accordance with commitments made by the government to the IMF and the imperatives of the civil war. Although privatisation had been extended only to marginal economic activities by the end of 1996, it was none the less a political instrument of war for the regime, as were the elections we examine in Part III. One possible hypothesis is that the privatisation of state enterprises, rejected during the 1980s because of their deplorable financial situation but carried out in 1994 when that situation had not improved, was aimed at satisfying, within Algeria, the patronage networks that had supported the regime and still remained necessary allies; and, abroad, the country's economic partners.

The reluctance to privatise more state enterprises was probably due to the government's fear of clashing with the trade union leaders in that sector. Fear was expressed, notably by the press, of an industrial conflict with the UGTA, the central trade union body. Such a fear however seems to have been groundless, as the UGTA was so closely linked[21] with the regime[22] and seemed scarcely likely to obstruct its policy. Employees, far from passively submitting to the uncertainties of economic policy, have developed strategies for economic survival. They have since the 1980s been supplementing their regular income by working as petty craftsmen or traders from home. Material diverted from state enterprises has been used to equip numerous workshops for welders, carpenters, electricians etc.

Privatisation, while not following a logic of economic profitability, appears to be an adjustment to political and military necessities. It can plausibly be argued that, in intentions and objectives, there has been something like what happened at the time of independence in 1962. The civil war that broke out just after independence between the GPRA (Gouvernement Provisoire de la République Algérienne), the 'army of the borders' and the guerrillas in the interior was defused through economic openings for the

---

[18] Executive Decree no. 96-134 set out conditions for transfer of shares.

[19] By 1995 130 billion dinars had been provided by the Treasury since 1994 to enterprises that had become autonomous. *El Watan*, 5 Sept. 1995.

[20] See K. Pfeifer, 'Economic Liberalization in the 1980s: Algeria in Comparative Perspective' in J. Entelis and P. Neylor (eds), *State and Society in Algeria*, Boulder, CO: Westview Press, 1992, pp. 97-117; and J. Leca and N. Grimaud, 'Le secteur privé en Algérie', *Maghreb-Machrek*, no. 113, 1986, pp. 102-19.

[21] Amar Benamrouche, 'Etats, conflits sociaux et mouvement syndical en Algérie (1962-95)', *Maghreb-Machrek*, no. 148, April-June 1995, pp. 43-54.

[22] The UGTA had ten seats reserved to it in the CNT (National Transition Council).

main contestants in the power struggle that was won by the 'army of the borders'.[23] Some officials and political leaders of the GPRA received import licenses that made them Algeria's future businessmen and wholesalers. For the heads of the interior maquis, an astute administrative division of the territory ensured positions as prominent local citizens.[24] As for the army of the borders, transformed into the National Liberation Army (ALN) by Houari Boumedienne, the nationalisation of land in 1963 and of oil and gas from 1971 assured it of a considerable rent. This process was extended under Chadli Bendjedid's presidency, when the army was transformed into the Armée Nationale Populaire (ANP). Officers of the ALN who 'resigned' or started new careers (because of the professionalisation of the army) were to receive help for the purchase of hotels and restaurants in Europe, and jobs as managers of state enterprises.

This model was followed in the second civil war starting in 1992. Privatisation of certain sectors was not aimed at co-opting the Islamist leaders, but first of all at consolidating, indeed entrenching the interests of the new officers of the army, engaged daily in the fight against the Islamist armed groups. Thus defence of the regime became also the defence of their own interests, and this involved some contradictions. The privatised hotel and restaurant sectors, which had since 1992 been subjected to threats from the armed groups because of 'practices contrary to morals' in certain establishments, tried as best they could after privatisation to 'conform to the norms' laid down by the 'Emirs', even though the new owners were close to the regime. For example, at Sidi Frej, a seaside resort near Algiers, restaurant owners were subjected to threats from the Islamist groups. The privatisation of some tourist complexes on the coast profited shareholders close to the regime, but did not, even so, allow anyone to continue his business except for those who obeyed the orders of the Islamist groups:

[23] 'Since independence compromises have always been arranged on sharing of power, but also on a certain number of exemptions and immunities that were to place the personalities involved in the liberation war beyond the reach of political, economic and financial measures, and extend to their friends and close relations, as transferable rights, privileges that they considered unchangeable. How else can one explain that A. Boussouf, a former GPRA minister with supreme control over secret services during the war, became a shipbuilder and businessman in a country where the legislation on foreign trade did not, in principle, leave any opening for private initiative? One of his protégés, M. Zeghar, also followed the same "business" path, apparently on the fringes of laws and regulations on import-export.' C. El Hadi, *L'Algérie, l'Etat et le Droit*, Paris: Arcantère, 1989, p. 30.

[24] M. Harbi has written: 'How to reduce the political tensions in a country where the war of independence mobilised thousands of people? Repression alone would not be enough. So there was also to be distribution of state resources...': see chapter 'Régulation politique et prédation', *L'Algérie et son destin. Croyants ou citoyens?*, Paris: Arcantère, 1992, p. 13.

'Here [an Algiers area seaside resort], before, the terraces were full, you could drink beer, alcohol as much as you liked. The Moudjahidin warned them that if this continued, they would destroy the restaurant. Some stopped, others continued, they burned those. The same thing for hotels: those that continued to bring in girls were set on fire.' (Trader, 1995, France)

The privatisations had a double advantage: they encouraged the new owners to link defence of their own property with defence of the regime, and, on the other hand, they preserved the economic fabric from destruction by the armed groups. Two years after the experiment of tourism and hotel privatisation, it could be assumed that the understanding between the different warring parties to spare the private sector[25] was a prelude to extending that process to state enterprises in other sectors.

Thus the war waged by the GIA fighters against state enterprises has favoured the activities of the private sector and extended the process of privatisation in the worst-hit sectors. However, there was a limit to this phenomenon, especially in major state enterprises gone bankrupt; although they had to deal with acts of sabotage and destruction, their senior executives were induced to remain in the public sector by the financial rent they raked in. The three hundred public state enterprises (Entreprises Publiques d'Etat, EPE)[26] are political rather than economic instruments, and they risk a grim fate. It is to be feared that many industrial units may become inscribed on the armed groups' hit list, as there seems to be such strong resistance to making them eligible for privatisation, even though that would be the only way to remove them from the list.

The eminent citizen and the guerrillas

The market shares lost by the state in transport, tourism and construction were partially taken over by economic actors who are fairly precisely known.[27] Local eminent citizens[28] appeared, in this 'total war', to be among the main groups to benefit. Often coming from the FLN, while they had fought in the war of liberation they – unlike the 'ex-combatants' – did not suffer violence from the armed groups. They owned many vehicles, hotels and restaurants abroad, trading businesses in their towns and villages, and

[25] On condition that it submits to GIA protection rackets – as was illustrated by the dynamiting of the only hotel in Les Eucalyptus in 1994.

[26] On the state enterprises' situation, see N. Chevillard (ed.), 'Algérie. L'après-guerre civile', *Nord-Sud Export*, June 1995, p. 171.

[27] According to a survey by the Ministry of Transport, financed by the World Bank, private transport operators held market shares of 100 per cent in Annaba and Sétif, 98 per cent in Constantine, 86 per cent in Blida and 74 per cent in Oran: *La Tribune*, 17 June 1996.

[28] The local eminent citizens are distinct from the 'ex-combatants', even though they too fought in the war of liberation. The eminent citizens are accused by the Islamists of turning the war to their profit, while the ex-combatants are said to have sacrificed themselves for independence.

'villa-warehouses' in the Mitidja, and had since a short time before been monopolising freight transport and food products distribution networks in the interior of the country. Their growing role was one of the most obvious effects of the establishment of maquis in the mountainous regions and the maquis guerrillas' violence against the economic and state infrastructure. So, in spite of their deep-seated rejection of the Islamists whom they described as 'bandits', they aroused among those people a fascination linked to a common experience of war as a means of accumulating wealth and prestige. For the Islamist guerrillas the national liberation war made Algerian independence possible but also contributed to the enrichment of individuals, including the local eminent citizens who offered the ideal example of social success. At the same time those leading citizens saw the Islamist guerrillas as 'upstart Moudjahidin' trying through the *jihad* to acquire attributes of power and respectability in their circles, being unable to acquire immediate income. These common attitudes favoured tacit arrangements among ideologically opposed actors:[29] 'Emirs' and leading citizens understood each other without knowing each other. The general outlook which they expressed regarding the means of social progress led them to work together rather than kill each other. The example of Si Lakhdar illustrates this behaviour by a leading local personality in a conflict which he called 'the bastards' revolution' (*thawra aulad haram*), as opposed to the 'Revolution of 54'.

Si Lakhdar: from one war to another. To members of his family, and to people he is fond of, Si Lakhdar regularly distils advice on the right behaviour in cafés and at work, on subjects to avoid discussing and above all on dubious friendships. In his view the victims of violence in Algeria since 1992 were people who did not know how to 'hold their tongues'. The seriousness and attention with which people listen to him are not due solely to respect for his age, about sixty; they are due above all to his experience as a man of action during the civil war. Entrusted by the FLN, from the outbreak of the insurrection in November 1954, with eliminating 'Messalists'* and other opponents in France, Si Lakhdar carried out his task in the suburbs of Paris. From Bondy to Nanterre he worked with others, after nightfall, to establish the hegemony of the FLN[30] and its monopoly of extortion of money from the Algerian emigrant community. Having remained tight-lipped about those events for many years, after the

---

[29] Carl Schmidt has written: 'The political enemy will not necessarily be bad according to morals, or ugly according to aesthetics; he will not necessarily play the part of a competitor at the economic level; it may even appear, on occasion, advantageous to do business with him.' *Notion de politique*, Paris: Flammarion, 1992, p. 64.

* These were followers of Messali Hadj (1898-1974), a pioneer nationalist leader in the 1920s and 30s who later opposed the FLN in the war of independence

[30] See Ali Haroun, *La VIIe Wilaya. La guerre du FLN en France (1954-62),* Paris: Seuil, 1991, 522 pp.

launching of the struggle by various armed Islamist groups against the regime Si Lakhdar was more forthcoming with accounts of his past. Sometimes bitter about the absence of recognition for the missions he carried out, he is jealous of the title of Moudjahid conferred by the state on former soldiers of the ALN, calling it a 'diploma'.

Those murderous clashes[31] between rival organisations, covered up by official historiography, provided Si Lakhdar with an experience on which he drew in his view of the current conflict. While convinced that today's guerrillas had no aim other than to possess property and wealth that they had never had, he did not advocate any opposition to their practice of extortion:

'They called themselves "Moudjahid" but they are bandits, racists. All that they want is your money. They are a bunch of jealous, hungry people: they are hungry for everything they've never had. They can't even go to France any longer to learn civilisation; so here, they steal because they want cars, money, honour. There's no need to die for that, you should give to them and they will leave you alone.' (Lakhdar, eminent person in the east, 1994-5)

As for money, cars and possessions, Si Lakhdar had them. According to him the big difference between his past actions and those of the armed Islamists lay less in the extortion itself than in the absence of a political motive among the Islamists. He called them 'bandits' because they were driven only by the search for material possessions and not by a political ideal, and he preferred to satisfy them rather than die a pointless death. But he was aware that such behaviour might be harmful to his honour,[32] because it amounted to recognising the superiority of the Moudjahidin. Si Lakhdar replied ironically, to those accusations, that he had not got an ex-combatant's 'diploma' and, unlike those who had that, did not feel that he had a mission to protect the regime. However, he admired the courage of his 'ex-combatant' friends who refused to hand over their old hunting rifles and some sheep to the guerrillas. It was pride that drove those people, but above all fury at seeing their 'Moudjahid' title devalued by the Islamists. Si Lakhdar's recent readiness to talk about his past was due to his determination to show he was not a coward. But the present political regime did not deserve his sacrifice, he thought.

---

[31] B. Stora estimates the number of victims of this war between the FLN and the MNA (Mouvement National Algérien, founded by Messali Hadj), in France and Algeria from 1954 to 1962, at about 10,000 dead and 25,000 wounded. *Histoire de la guerre d'Algérie*, Paris: La Découverte, 1993, p. 26.

[32] Jean Leca and Yves Schemeil note that leading local personalities in the Arab world 'are known as those who have "face", prestige and honour, so that they have to adopt socially prescribed rules under pain of lowering themselves and losing their composure'. 'Clientélisme et patrimonialisme dans le monde arabe', *International Political Science Review*, 1983, no. 4, p. 10.

Owner of about ten lorries, boss of small businesses, he could not be bypassed by the guerrillas of the eastern region. In 1992, when 'Sheikh' Azzedine (aged 30), a militant of the ex-FIS, proclaimed himself 'Emir' and, with about ten fighters, fled into the Djemila Massif, Si Lakhdar, like many others, thought that the security forces would rapidly defeat those armed dissidents. At the same time, in the village as in the big towns of the country, ex-FIS militants were arrested, and sympathisers were ordered to report their movements to the police station every day on pain of being accused of murders or other 'attacks on state security'. The 'Emir' Sheikh Azzedine, as well as the sympathisers, was to be effectively neutralised by the security forces. During the year 1993 the villages of the region thus had relative peace. Although the gendarmerie increased their checks and roads began to empty at nightfall without any curfew being officially decreed, no policeman or gendarme was murdered. However, numerous armed groups were rumoured to be in the region, while commercial vehicle drivers told the owners that there were 'fake checkpoints' manned by the Islamists.

Si Lakhdar, a member of the FLN, a prominent local citizen, and a recent pilgrim to Mecca, saw the Islamists as representing a social group competing with the 'thieves of Algiers' (the political and military leadership) for the possession of *kursi*, power. Among the FIS leaders' ideas there were some that he readily shared, such as those laying down behaviour for women: 'A woman has only three reasons to go out of her house: once for her marriage, a second time for her father's death and a third time for her burial.' She should not work, and her mission was in the development of her family home. Si Lakhdar's opposition to the Islamists was due less to application of the *shar'ia* – on many points he would live with that – than to the use of violence among Algerians as a means of self-enrichment, which revived former practices, vainly covered up, of men of his generation.

The war being waged by the Islamists and security forces could not, he said, be explained otherwise than by a desire for personal enrichment. The proof of that – in his view – was that the word *jihad* was meaningless in the heart of a Muslim country. Ignorant of the leading contemporary Islamist thinkers,[33] he came to terms with the guerrillas for pragmatic reasons. For a year his lorries made their journeys without harm. The loss caused by diversion of goods was compensated by the monopoly situation which the decline of state distribution companies gave him.

Probably a bit ashamed of his informal dealings with the guerrillas, he justified himself by alleging that the political leadership also found a source of income in the violence, through the funds provided by the world community[34] in the form of loans and debt relief. Petty entrepreneurs like Si

[33] An ideologue like Sayyid Qutb, for example, was unknown to him despite his influence over some Islamist movements. See G. Kepel, *Le Prophète et Pharaon. Aux sources des mouvements islamistes,* Paris: Seuil, 1993 edition.

[34] Rémy Leveau estimated the economic and financial aid received by Algeria in 1994

Lakhdar showed great capacity for adaptation in coping with two changes in their activities. The first disruption was occasioned by the professionalising of the army, started under Chadli Bendjedid's regime with the aim of consolidating his authority; this led to redeployment of former ALN guerrillas into civilian life. A businessman like Si Lakhdar encountered, from the 1980s, big difficulties in getting access to imported products, because of the loss of his friendly connections in the customs service. In fact the recruitment of new officials wrecked the client networks built up during the war of liberation, to the advantage of new economic actors. Si Lakhdar found his salvation in the creation of a '*trabendiste*' organisation. Only bypassing of the state supply system could allow him to carry on his business activity.

As they could not get foreign currency from the state banks, several private entrepreneurs sought to obtain it on the unofficial foreign exchange market, supplied from the emigrant community. On their side those leading citizens helped with applications for property rights or supplied non-imported materials needed for building, notably cement and iron. They invested immediately in business activity in France (restaurants, hotels, warehouses etc.) to ensure regular inflow of foreign currency. This barter-based economy was to allow a number of emigrants to carry out their plan to 'return home' by becoming owners of villas. Thus provided with foreign currency, traders and private entrepreneurs like Si Lakhdar invested in purchases of second-hand transport vehicles and small factories producing consumer goods in Algeria. Thanks to the money they made, they cultivated new contacts in the civil service.

At the end of the 1980s Si Lakhdar's business activity included imports of fruit and vegetables from Morocco, furniture from Egypt, and clothing from Tunisia and Spain. All these imported goods were redistributed through small businesses leased to close or distant members of his family. The success of that informal economy overcame the resentment against favouritism practiced by officials in examination of applications for import licenses. In fact that success was due to various official bodies' tolerance regarding the ways in which those economic actors, the leading local citizens, made their money. By preventing an accumulation of their grievances against the administrative and political leaders who had grown rich from the oil and gas rent, the relative laxity at Algeria's customs frontiers acted as a safety valve. Because of the opportunities for enrichment that resulted, someone like Si Lakhdar had no desire to enter into dissidence against a regime that he could well have charged with ingratitude in view of his services during the liberation war. But not all the entrepreneurs had Si Lakhdar's skill and some did not manage to manoeuvre in this civil war, as the contrasting case of Brahim shows.

---

at 40 billion francs. 'Les pièges de l'aide internationale', *Politique internationale*, 1994, no. 65.

The 'Shari'a Express': when the way of God leads to the eminent citizens.
The 'Shari'a Express' was the term used by Brahim to describe the main
Algiers-Constantine road. As it had to pass through Lakhdaria, a region
where maquis were entrenched, this road became a real hell for his business' vehicles. About forty years old, Brahim owned about fifty commercial vehicles until 1994, when he was obliged to flee from Algeria. His
transport company, set up fifteen years earlier, then had only two lorries
bought secondhand. Only one was in use, the other was kept to provide
spares. Brahim was his own boss and carried mainly cement for a wholesaler of the Constantine region, a contractor who built villas for emigrants.
As one of his family was in the armed forces, he then made contact with
military circles and became gradually the transporter of goods for numerous retired officers who had gone into trade and the production of wafers,
ice cream and other products for everyday consumption.

During the 1980s, since the military entrepreneurs had established their
own transport networks, state enterprises became his main customers.
His vehicles then carried consumer goods and raw materials for the state
production units built in the industrial zones around medium-sized cities
in the interior of the country. Thanks to massive imports he was able, during this period, to increase his profits and diversify his operations. In 1992
he had fifty lorries at his disposal, to which were added private vehicles,
used when big orders came in. But the combined extortions by armed groups
and Islamist guerrillas were to increase so rapidly that all hope of breaking even would be lost:

'At the beginning I didn't believe it, trader friends talked of protection rackets, I
thought it was robbers who were doing that to make money. But when I saw Islamists demanding 500,000 dinars from me, with the threat of destroying one of my
vehicles every day, I had to pay up, after the complete destruction of two lorries and
the disappearance of a third. I thought I was rid of them, but no, new ones came to
demand double that sum, while my drivers passed on to me letters from Islamists in
the maquis demanding one third of all goods carried, threatening to seize my vehicles
otherwise. It was too much for me, my drivers were afraid. As I no longer knew who
to pay, I closed my company temporarily; they came to burn my vehicles and kill
two drivers. Then I started taking some orders again and tried to avoid the "Shari'a
Express". That worked for a time, then armed groups came to demand colossal sums
from me; so I closed everything down, I sold my lorries to private buyers and I left,
they didn't want my company to survive.' (Brahim, private transport operator, 1994)

In exile since 1994, Brahim has tried to understand why his company was
subjected to such unreasonable demands. In contrast to some of his com-
petitors, the armed groups did not leave him with any chance of survival.
He did not vote in the parliamentary elections of December 1991, because
he considered that the solutions proposed for the 'multi-dimensional' Algerian crisis were inadequate. Only the assumption of office as head of state
by Mohammed Boudiaf (assassinated in June 1992, a few months after

taking office) seemed to him likely to cure the country's ills. Any explanation of the persecution he endured on the basis of political motives was, in his view, to be rejected, because he had never been involved. With hindsight and the calmer view of the situation which he has now, he has no doubt that the armed groups were manipulated by rival transport operators. That theory also fits in with his own interpretation of the conflict. In parallel with the war between the Islamist guerrillas and the security forces, armed groups in the urban areas, on the outskirts of Algiers, operated – according to that view – either on their own account, going so far as to ruin business, or on behalf of hidden partners. However, their actions, under the cover of *jihad*, could in fact weaken the Islamist guerrillas in the maquis, as was illustrated by the case of Brahim, forced to flee even when he was ready to pay a portion of his profits to the guerrillas.

On the other hand, the establishment of the Islamist guerrilla campaign in regions where prominent people such as Si Lakhdar carried on their business activity was seen by economic actors in Algiers as proof that the armed bands were manipulated by 'bosses' of the interior. Brahim, like others, thought that the destruction of his company directly served the interests of transport companies in the interior which instantly filled the gap left in the market. Such statements, rather than being based on rational examination of the conflict, reveal the prejudices regarding some leading personalities and entrepreneurs of the interior who, because of their shady past in the liberation war, are described as local 'Caïds'. Their behaviour recalls the eminent personalities of Sicily confronting organised banditry in the nineteenth century.[35] The local Algerian eminent personalities adopted survival strategies that had the effect (a perverse one for the regime) of providing regular supplies to the Islamist guerrilla campaign. In a parallel process the destruction of the state economic base increased the power of private economic actors, especially eminent personalities of the east who were prominent in transport, marketing and production of everyday consumer goods.

The guerrillas' determination to weaken the state apparatus was tactical, as their aim was its destruction. But their motivation and the pleasure they felt were due not to feelings of jealousy and envy towards the beneficiaries of client networks, but to the closing of all avenues for social progress except for those approved by the political system. The leading citizens, traders and private entrepreneurs were envied and probably respected by the Islamist guerrillas because of their social success, which was clearly seen as having been achieved on the fringes of state-provided opportunities for enrichment. It was their capacity for initiative, endurance and craftiness that made them 'fit company' for the guerrillas. Hence it can be understood that the private sector economic actors' *imaginaire* was close to that of the

---

[35] G. Fiume, 'Bandits, violence and organization of power in Sicily in the early nineteenth century' in J.A. Davis and P. Ginsborg (eds), *Society and Politics in the Age of Risorgimento,* Cambridge University Press, 1991, pp. 77-84.

maquis groups. The absence of violence against them certainly had something to do with a tactical determination among the Islamists to conserve their major resources, but the leading local citizens also represented a model for success worthy of respect.

Lucrative new business opportunities

The forced privatisation process started by the government after the outbreak of civil war in 1992 was accompanied, in the sectors most affected, by modernisation of the economic base. Like the state transport companies, the national cement manufacturing enterprises were regular targets for the GIA fighters. Cement, like food products, remained until 1994 a scarce product, subjected to speculation, to the detriment of consumers (especially all those who, because they were building without permits, had no access to state-run markets). Demand never stopped growing throughout the 1980s: the low output of new housing (30,000 homes per year), combined with a high population growth rate, led to the building of illegal private dwellings in many of the communes of the Mitidja. However, getting cement – like getting flour for bakers or medicines for sick people – was an obstacle course with constant ordeals at every turn. The resentment that this caused was intensified by the paradoxical abundance of sacks of cement emerging from the national cement works scattered around the country. The people of the Mitidja thought that the Meftah cement works,[36] before it was sabotaged by the armed groups in 1994, ought to have supplied the region. But the state distribution networks responsible for sale to individuals were, as with other products, subject to the rules of patronage. As production by the cement works was irregular, military entrepreneurs, traders and others with capital bought up the output in advance, forcing 'small' customers to get their supplies on the informal market,[37] in other words – in practice – from them. Holding stocks of cement that could be sold in that way well out of sight of the local administration was one of the privileges of the local eminent citizens, and ensured that they had the economic means to rebuild, on the outskirts of the big cities, the networks of their native *douar*s.

However, double bypassing strategies were developed to get round both the state cement works and those monopolists. Those strategies, developed during the 1980s, came into their own after the outbreak of civil war as an alternative to the sabotage of cement works and the flight of the military entrepreneurs under pressure from the 'Emirs'. They also revealed a powerful determination to re-divide a geographical area, on the outskirts of

---

[36] One of the biggest, whose cost was estimated at $60 million. It was badly damaged in April 1994 by the armed groups.

[37] The price of a sack of cement varied from 50 to 70 dinars on the state-controlled market, but reached 130 to 150 dinars on the informal market.

Algiers in particular, for the benefit of new economic actors, as is illustrated by the case of Othman.

Othman, from carpenter to cement dealer: new actors emerging. Othman, about 40 years old, ran a wooden furniture making business in a small town in Greater Kabylia of which he was a native. Married to an 'Algiers girl' originally from the Constantine region, he had close business relations with his father-in-law. Besides his furniture making enterprise, Othman owned furniture shops in the outskirts of the big cities of Algeria, entrusted to members of his family. In the outskirts of Algiers it was his father-in-law who acted as manager. The shop, situated in an urban area inhabited by people coming from the east of Algeria, and belonging to an Algiers woman's husband, was saved by the father-in-law's presence from the commercial discrimination sometimes practiced against Kabyles. But when, at the beginning of the 1980s, Othman wanted to buy a plot of land to build business premises, he did not escape the 'racism' of the leading local personalities. His elder brother, a future air force officer, made it possible to carry out his scheme even so; better still, he fitted it into an embryonic cement import network. Othman continued throughout the decade to expand this activity by importing tons of cement illegally but regularly, constituting a parallel market separate from the state-controlled market. The intensive 'rural urbanisation' of the outskirts of Algiers ensured substantial gains for him, thanks to the profits from resale of sacks of cement 'on the black market'.

At the same time he continued his furniture-making business. The scarcity of his products[38] ensured profits that increased until the end of 1996, and would only be jeopardised by mass imports of furniture from Egypt, which he feared greatly. Established between Grande Kabylie and the outskirts of Algiers, Othman profited, after the onset of the civil war, from the social and economic decline of many areas. The emergence of the armed groups with their specific mode of operation led to the destruction or sabotage of the local cement works and the return of the military entrepreneurs to their *douar*s of origin. There followed a change in access to land and purchase of houses. Othman, enjoying the support and protection of his wife's brothers who followed the doctrines of the ex-FIS and the policy of the 'Emirs', had no cause for complaint. Certainly he, like other economic players, had to pay taxes collected at 'fake checkpoints' and the taxes levied by successive 'Emirs'. Even so, his losses were trifling compared with the profits which cornering the cement market brought him after the sabotage of cement works and, especially, the trade liberalisation which raised him – under the protection of his officer brother – to the status of an industrialist.

---

[38] A scarcity worsened by the destruction of forests by napalm because they were refuges for the Islamist guerrillas, which cut timber production. 230,000 hectares of forests are estimated to have been burned in 1994, according to *Al Hayat*, 20 Oct. 1994.

Indeed the growing demand for cement, inherent in urbanisation and the desire for home ownership, encountered an obstacle in the policy of sabotaging and destroying the cement works. In a parallel process new private cement manufacturing enterprises emerged. In the communes close to Greater Algiers such as Dellys Ibrahim, industrialists responded to demand without fear of attack from the GIA fighters who concentrated their attacks on 'the economy in the hands of unbelievers'. With imports from France (through import/export companies headed by Algerians with military backgrounds) of machinery or tools able to produce the required amounts regularly, the ways of becoming a home owner were transformed, and the government won assured backing in its policy of house building. For paradoxically, it was at the moment when economic infrastructure linked to house building was hit by economic terrorism that the government succeeded in building '180,000 housing units between 1994 and 1995'[39] – a record figure, in terms of the annual average. This led Mahfoudh Nahnah, chairman of the Hamas-MSI party, to wonder where the 'four billion dollars'[40] needed to carry out that building came from. Only the help of private actors made the success of the housing policy possible, especially in the cities of the east, which are considered pro-regime.[41]

So, because of competition from private industrialists, Othman left the outskirts of Algiers and went into partnership with very recently created property agencies to build private housing estates in the medium-sized cities of Algeria.[42] Brand new villas were erected in a different style from the 'Dallas' style of the 1980s. Omar, a town planner in a small commune in the east, and unofficial agent of one of those new private housing construction companies, gave this explanation of the transformation caused by the privatisation of sectors linked with cement production in house building:

'Our cities are ugly and "destroyed" because of the state monopoly. Someone who wanted to build his house before had first of all to find a plot of land which he bought illegally, then he had to store cement and quickly build the front; that way he could take refuge inside and could no longer be expelled. If he wanted material to improve his home, he found none, except at a very high price: timber, tiled floors, paint, etc. He had to fight again the battle he fought to get cement. Before, no private company

---

[39] According to the Minister of Housing: *Liberté*, 28 Dec. 1995.

[40] *El Massa*, 28 Dec. 1995.

[41] According to *El Moudjahid*, 27 Dec. 1995, Sétif Wilaya achieved the record figure of 12,290 housing units.

[42] Those markets were however closed to economic actors, however competitive, who were outside the networks. The Lorbeix company, based in France, which offered 'prefabricated houses at an unbeatable economic cost – 400,000 to 700,000 dinars maximum', had according to its Managing Director great difficulty in penetrating this market: 'Every time it is we who make that sort of offer, very attractive from the economic viewpoint, people are suspicious and barriers go up as if by magic'. Quoted by *La Nation*, no. 1550, 27 June 1995.

had the right to build villas, but that has changed since. Now, thanks to private enterprise, you can find houses resembling real villas: tiled roofs, wooden window frames, outside paint etc. People like that. But people can build all that thanks to the private sector which supplies all the materials, from cement to iron to timber. That alters everything, because the family which moves into those houses is not going to build a second floor, then a third, etc., as happened before. The '*douar*' with its houses is finished.' (Omar, town planner, France, 1995)

The way in which this new gap in the market – building of private housing estates – was filled was probably not so honest as those promoters suggested. However, it illustrated an underlying process – the ability of new economic actors to carry out a housing policy in the place of the state authorities, with all the social consequences flowing from that. Certainly that policy has so far been carried out in regions that are less densely populated than greater Algiers. Its aim is probably also to show to the state authorities the private sector's ability to participate in the project to build four new towns[43] – all the more so as national cement production capacity has been slightly reduced by the Islamist guerrilla campaign. The violence of that campaign against some economic targets (state transport, cement works, pharmaceutical enterprises etc.) was accompanied by privatisation of those sectors.[44] The result has been an increase in the financial and political resources of private sector economic actors, hitherto marginalised or stifled.

The Islamist groups' war against the regime favoured the enrichment of leading personalities and entrepreneurs who succeeded in finding a balance between the warring parties. They filled gaps in the market which, thanks to the policy of destruction and sabotage pursued by the 'Emirs', became lucrative. The regime, however, saw benefits in that violence which was all too readily described as blind by observers: the destruction of state enterprises, often indebted and unproductive, reduced the burden on the state budget. By not attacking the oil and gas sectors from which the regime has drawn the essential part of its resources, the local 'Emirs' have unwittingly helped the implementation of the Structural Adjustment Programme (SAP) that the regime promised the IMF to undertake. In destroying state

---

[43] A Ministry of Infrastructure plan of 1995 provided for the building of four new towns of 120,000 to 150,000 inhabitants in the Mitidja. See M. Cote, *L'Algérie,* Paris: Masson, 1996, p. 194.

[44] Even the Algiers city refuse collection was put in the hands of private companies, the refuse collection lorries having been sabotaged by the armed groups: 'The CPVA [Conseil Populaire de la Ville d'Alger], which had been responsible for refusal collection for the capital, at present handles it for the 15 communes of the Conseil Urbain de Coordination for the city centre, while assisting 13 other communes in the wider suburban area by mobilising 700 staff...There are now only three lorries in working order...the CPVA has been forced to resort to hiring private transport which costs it up to 3,000 dinars per day per vehicle. More than 1,000 lorries return every day to the Oued Smar rubbish dump.' *El Watan,* 25 July 1995.

enterprises the 'Emirs' directly put their employees on the dole! In that way they spared the regime the implementation of retrenchment measures provided for in the SAP, and spared the security forces the need to repress industrial action that could have been aroused by redundancies. However, the armed groups succeeded as much as the leading personalities and entrepreneurs in deriving advantage from the ongoing economic changes. Just as the corsairs (Raïs) of the Regency of Algiers in the sixteenth century were able to derive profit, through piracy, from the expansion of Mediterranean trade,[45] the 'Emirs' found a part of their livelihood in the trading economy.

The 'Emirs: 'Moudjahidin by trade'

Like the prominent local citizens and the private economic actors, the 'Emirs' benefited from the civil war situation which they perpetuated. Certainly the risks were much greater for them and the profits fairly uncertain. But, with no capital except the Faith in the struggle they were waging, they – or at least the more cunning among them – succeeded in climbing up the social ladder.

Bandit and Moudjahid. Just like the Algiers corsairs, the 'Emirs' have been described as bandits, murderers and outlaws. But both groups of people acted in the name of *jihad*: 'The Algerian Raïs were Moudjahidin fighting for the Faith against the threat from Spain', says the Algerian historian M. Kaddache.[46] Similarly today, the actions of the 'Emirs', although regarded as simple terrorism, are seen by those supporting them as fitting into the concept of *jihad*. In the alleyways of Les Eucalyptus the Moudjahidin actually wrote on the walls: 'If *jihad* is terrorism, then we are terrorists'. Besides this comparison between the corsairs and the armed groups, based on their use of questionable methods in the cause of Islam, there were also comparable life histories. Charles-André Julien has stressed, regarding the sociology of the Raïs, that 'most of its [the 'Taïfa' of the Raïs, the corsairs' guild] members were renegades from the poverty-stricken provinces of the Mediterranean, who practiced piracy as their brothers in Calabria, Sicily and Corsica practiced banditry.'[47] Is the conversion of the armed groups' fighters to Islamism not similar to that of the 'renegades' who, through that process, were able to practice piracy in the name of *jihad*? Perhaps one may, like the Benedictine monk Haedo who called those renegades 'Turks by trade', consider the fighters in the armed groups as 'Moudjahidin by trade'?

---

[45] F. Braudel wrote: 'The corsairs' piracy did not have the disastrous effects stated or suggested by so many testimonies or excessive complaints.. In fact piracy and economic activity were connected; when the latter expanded, the former profited from its growth.' *La Méditerranée et le monde méditerranéen à l'époque de Philippe II*, Paris: A. Colin, 1990 edn, vol. II, p. 639. See also G. Fisher, *Barbary Legend: War, Trade and Piracy in North Africa (1415-1830)*, Oxford University Press, 1957, 349 pp.

[46] M. Kaddache, *L'Algérie durant la période ottomane*, Algiers: OPU, 1992, p. 31.

[47] C.-A. Julien, *Histoire de l'Afrique du Nord*, Paris: Payot, 1994 edition, p. 638

The conversion of criminals to Islamism is an illustration of this phenomenon, mentioned in Part I of this book. The strategy of those who pass casually from the armed Islamist bands to the security forces in accordance with the local balance of forces makes it possible to study the element of calculation in the motivation of those fighters for Islam, while also showing their ability or lack of ability to respond to the problems of their environment. If one can only see the 'Emirs' as bandits or activists gone off the rails, one is forgetting that 'thanks to piracy, mosques, *marabouts* and pious foundations multiplied in Algiers'.[48] If those investments at that time served, among purposes, to launder stolen money, they were still lawful; those who made such gifts may well have had blood on their hands, but they honoured Algiers even so and continued to be seen in their environment, and among people dependent on piracy, as respectable people. Certainly the local 'Emirs' of the GIA were not in a position to build mosques; however, their activities, when they were successful, were able to provide services and honour the cause for which they waged *jihad*.

A war business. Like the former piracy, the armed groups' *jihad* was a lucrative business. It is that which explains the constant replacement of the fighters in spite of the losses suffered. Hatred and desire for revenge were also there as reasons for enlistment, but those feelings did a disservice to the 'Emirs'' enterprise when they were the only motivation behind it; several Islamist groups disappeared because of the exclusive murderous madness of their members. Those that managed to consolidate, in Les Eucalyptus and Chararba for example, owed their success to opportunities arising from activities that united the Moudjahidin. Those activities have changed; the *jihad* of 1992 was different from that of 1994, even more different from that of 1995. Only the prestige of the status of 'Emir' remained unchanged because of the constant dividends that successive 'Emirs' were able to procure, proving plenty of flexibility. The armed bands were able to respond better and quicker than the regime to the deplorable situation of people between 18 and 24 years old in Algeria,[49] confronted with a general feeling of 'pauperisation'.

Just as the FIS was able to mobilise students and unemployed college graduates, disappointed senior employees and civil servants facing pauperisation, so the 'Emirs' were responsive to the problems of the 'hard core' rejected by the other guerrilla organisations, such as the AIS and FIDA, who preferred to use former FIS networks in their struggle rather than those unemployed young men, seen as not very reliable. Only recruitment into

[48] Ibid., p. 658.

[49] According to a survey by the Ministry of Youth and Sport, among 18-24-year-olds only 14.6 per cent had vocational training while a 'hard core' estimated at 1,127,000 young people remained 'without solution', 60 per cent were without income and 70 per cent without qualifications. *Le Soir d'Algérie*, 22 Oct. 1995.

the security forces made it possible for those selected not to join the GIA armed bands. However, the difference between joining the security forces and conversion to the Islamism of the Moudjahidin lay in the possibility for the new recruit, if he followed the latter course, to achieve lightning progress. Enlistment in the armed bands offered, like the piracy of the old days,[50] the possibility of achievement which no policeman could dream of: the glory and prestige of being an 'Emir'. While the policeman worked anonymously for the survival of the state, the 'Emir' did not have to report to anyone except his client network, restricted to certain districts or a commune. What he earned he might be able to redistribute, gaining the sympathy of those around him in the process. The context was thus highly favourable to his activity. Unlike the policeman, he had empathy with the local population. Certain armed groups which provided the means for rapid social ascent resembled 'gangs' and small Mafioso groups inspired by an 'ethic' and a code valuing honour, the legitimate right of revenge and resentment against social inequality.[51] Such an ethic does not contradict that of the 'just warrior',[52] found in Islamic history and literature. The identity which the fighters in the armed bands built up for themselves derived some of its character from those two types: the 'Emir' saw himself as a just warrior, he was both bandit and Moudjahid.

From donations to protection rackets. The 'Emirs' active in the communes with abundant resources, thanks to the presence of petty traders and location on strategic main roads, succeeded in consolidating their groups, independently of backing from the local population. The gradual distancing of the 'Emirs' from their initial struggle against the regime, to concentrate on economic rather than military activity, was one of the major turning points in the urban guerrilla war. It was due in part to the successful recruitment of criminals into the armed groups and the increasing modernisation of the apparatus of repression, which little by little forced the Islamist groups to use the weapon of isolated attacks more. The steady elimination by the security forces of the first generation of district 'Emirs', who fitted well into their environment, brought to the fore new fighters attracted more by the profits of the enterprise than by the original objectives. Concern for making money was now stronger than concern for the struggle, and the people

[50] The careers of the Barbarossa brothers in the sixteenth century illustrates that social ascent. Originating from Rumelia, they became through piracy 'Kings of Algiers': 'The exploits of Aroudj were know to all the coastal cities', writes M. Gaïd, 'and were always celebrated loudly by the people of Algiers. His reputation made him the man of Providence, the instrument of salvation for the Muslims oppressed by the Spanish.' *L' Algérie sous les Turcs,* Algiers: Mimouni, 1991, p. 35.

[51] P. Arlacchi, *Mafia et compagnie ou l'éthique mafiosa et l'esprit du capitalisme,* Grenoble: PUF, 1986.

[52] See the type of the 'Muslim Fighter' in Islamic literature in J.P. Charnay, *L'islam et la guerre,* Paris: Fayard, 1986.

sympathising with the Islamists – both the FIS and the local 'Emirs' – from 1994 ceased to see in them protectors or even avengers. Donations from the faithful gave way to protection rackets, and those were not the only ways to bring in money – the 'Emirs' also carried out 'contracts' on behalf of the guerrilla fighters. This pursuit of cash revenue, during 1994, resulted from recruitment of criminals into the *jihad* combined with opportunities created by the liberalisation of trade since 1994.

Protection rackets and taxes. Between 1992 and 1994, much evidence confirms that the 'Emirs' received donations from the local population. The successful running of the 'Emirates' was partly based on empathy. The first 'Emirs' took care not to ruin their territories, and so they robbed banks, redistributing the loot generously to their clients who, when the time was ripe, became a network of support. But, as we noted in the previous chapter, the impoverishment of the communes put an end to the spontaneous gifts, and the difficulty of obtaining money by bank raids caused the Islamist groups' financial resources to dwindle. Those who managed to continue in action used plunder as a means of accumulating wealth, and practiced protection rackets to finance themselves: war taxes 'bloomed'[53] in the kingdoms of the 'Emirs'.

The general spread of protection rackets from 1994 onwards in the communes of the Algiers region did not mean that the local people had completely broken solidarity with the 'Emirs'; it meant, first and foremost, that they had steadily fewer means to subsidise the local Moudjahidin. Their 'executions' of agents of the regime were not necessarily condemned, and when they controlled a small town like Chararba, it was not so much their presence which bothered people as the obligation to supply them with their needs (money, food, petrol, lodging etc.). As new Caïds, the 'Emirs' pressured the people, imposed entry taxes on 'strangers' (notably emigrants on holiday, who when visiting their families had to pay 500 to 2,000 francs, varying according to the commune), and levied a 'tax' on traders whom they protected against other groups of predators. Protection rackets were in some communes the only way for the armed groups to accumulate funds; they were only practiced when the groups were in a position of strength, when the commune was 'abandoned'[54] by the security forces under their strategy of letting them rot. The Islamist groups were then like a private police force at the service of the petty traders enriched by the lifting of price controls recommended by the IMF; those traders were forced to pay up, but protected. In other communes nearer to the centre of Algiers, where security agents were more present, the armed groups led a more secret

---

[53] According to the expression used by F. Adelkhah, 'Quand les impôts fleurissent à Téhéran', *Les Cahiers du CERI*, no. 12, 1995.

[54] The following chapter analyses the security forces' 'tactics of leaving to rot' and their effects.

existence and lived off contracts which they made with guerrilla factions, with which they set up 'joint ventures'.

Temporary workers in crime. When Islamist communes were not abandoned by the security forces to the 'Emirs', the latter were obliged to alter their war tactics as well as their means of getting money. From El Harrach to Bach Charah the Islamist armed bands held on, despite the eradication policy, as anonymous fighters:

'Here [the suburbs of Algiers] there are no groups out of doors like in the towns in the Mitidja. Here they play dominos in the café or else stay leaning against the wall to talk. They are at work, you do not know someone is a "terrorist" as they say. It's in the evening that they work for others. They are still there. When the newspapers say that "terrorists" are dead etc., it is false, now they are in civilian clothes, like you or me. Only they know who they are.' (Trader, Morocco, 1995)

The guerrilla techniques used by those groups in some ways recalled the methods of the 'Old Man of the Mountain'.[55] Defeated by the security forces in their attempts to take over and control cities, the Moudjahidin waged an invisible war on the enemies of an Islamic state. That form of activity remained marginal because it involved groups of people on the edges of the guerrilla 'organisation chart'; they were a strike force, accurate, efficient, and costing the guerrillas less. In fact the armed bands in those communes turned into temporary workers in crime; they carried out 'contracts' for payment for various guerrilla factions, the jobs varying from killing of particular people to moving cars or lorries filled with explosives. The 'Emirs' of these 'temporary employment agencies' benefited in their work from the know-how of criminals converted to the 'cause', even though they were not protected against all forms of manipulation. It was mainly about the integrity of these 'invisible fighters' that the strongest doubts were expressed by the Islamist sympathisers. Rumours supported the idea that they were ready to carry out all sorts of missions and thus to respond not only to the needs of the guerrilla fighters, but also to those of the security services or even of influential private economic actors.

Islamist groups and illicit business. One possible hypothesis is that a certain number of armed groups 'gave up' the *jihad* against Tâghout because of the economic failure of management of 'their' territories, due to flight of the better-off to escape protection rackets, the growing poverty of other people, and more and more job offers from the security forces. But another is also possible – that of the consolidation of armed groups acquiring wealth from illicit business activity. Anticipating the consequences of the decline

[55] In the twelfth century the 'Old Man of the Mountain', Hassan Sabbah, reigned over a sect that practiced political assassination. See B. Lewis, *The Assassins: A Radical Sect in Islam,* London: Weidenfeld and Nicolson, 1967, and Oxford University Press, 1987.

into poverty of places most exposed to the guerrilla campaign and the flight of potential victims of protection rackets, they went beyond local sources of supply. In contrast to the armed groups active between 1992 and 1994, which 'managed' well demarcated territories, those who renewed operations after that acted differently, within networks. Defeated by the security forces in their attempt to set up 'liberated areas' in the cities, they started to move into clandestine money-making networks involving people of varying regional and political loyalties. This move by certain Islamist groups into illicit business activity explains the endless continuation of violence, for it allowed them to increase their purchasing power, especially in foreign currency, and thus to acquire more sophisticated weapons than their elders' famous *mahchoucha* (sawn-off rifle).

At Les Eucalyptus and Baraki, from the end of 1994, the time when the 'Emir' and his fighters did public relations work with the population was over. He and his men remained unknown to the people, only traces of their presence remained vivid: car bombs, gendarmes and policemen killed, etc. The ending of direct relations between the 'Emir', his group and the population was due in part to the ending of protection rackets directed at the poorest – the risk of being reported increased – and the targeting of economic actors instead. The sums extorted were considerable and the potential victims belonged to varying political tendencies, including Islamists. In Les Eucalyptus members of the family of the military entrepreneur Hadj Sadok, close to the FIS leaders, were no longer spared. The 'Emir' of an armed group, originally from Meftah, was said to have demanded from him, in 1995, a sum equivalent to what he had paid to the FIS elected representatives (1 million dinars).

The 'Emirs' were forced to extort from 'small' people who were increasingly impoverished or from 'big' people surrounded by security agents, or else to live off 'donations' from well-off traders for whom they tried to perform services in return: elimination of competing groups or criminals, or pressure on the administration to obtain facilities. However, some 'Emirs' did not hesitate to put profit-making aside in order to help destitute families unable to pay their rent.[56] But only the most dynamic and far-sighted 'Emirs' were able to avoid their armed group becoming just a gang or a private police force in the service of traders enriched by trade liberalisation and the spectacular rise in prices of consumer goods. In the suburbs of Algiers the change in the armed groups' activities began in 1994. It is true that the powerful presence of criminals in some communes made the reconversion of the armed groups easier. Being always on the move, young people had connections with various informal markets. And from the end of 1994 there was a new and lucrative market opportunity, in drugs.

---

[56] According to testimony gathered in France, landlords of flats in Baraki no longer dared to demand unpaid rent from their tenants after a 'visit' from the Emir.

The drug trafficking network seems to be connected with the much older one involving stolen cars, nicknamed 'Taiwan', that were resold in El Harrach. It operates in a triangular fashion: Islamist groups with foreign currency at their disposal buy *kif* (marijuana) in Morocco and deliver it in France to middlemen in exchange for stolen cars that have been altered and prepared for export. This barter trade has made it possible for the 'Emirs' to avoid the attention of the security services of the countries in question, because it does not require any banking transaction, but simply the connection of two sorts of network, one dealing in drugs, the other in stolen cars. Those networks have the advantage of not arousing suspicion, as they are so well protected by political and military leaders: drugs exports flourish under the aegis of the barons of the Rif in Morocco,[57] and the stolen car trade under that of some Algerian military personnel.[58] They have thus eluded the intelligence services, especially in Europe, looking out for 'Islamist networks'. The people involved in these circuits made use of established networks close to organised crime (the alteration of cars to go to Algeria was organised in France from cities such as Marseilles and Le Havre, and, increasingly, in Italian cities[59]). Besides being exported by sea, stolen cars could be taken by road, reaching Algeria via Morocco, under the protection of smugglers.

Profits from the stolen car trade turned the market at El Harrach into a considerable pole of attraction and development. The motor market, established on a site the size of a football stadium, displayed vehicles whose price was between 100,000 and 150,000 French francs (such prices were attractive because the buyer did not pay customs duty). From 1994 it was the scene of regular murders. Frequented by business operators coming from the armed forces or the private sector, it generally found customers among the children of the elite, nicknamed 'tchi-tchi', who were attracted by the latest models of Golfs, BMWs and other showy vehicles. One of

[57] See Béatrice Hibou, 'Les enjeux de l'ouverture au Maroc', *Les Etudes du CERI*, no. 15, April 1995.

[58] 'A network of trafficking in dodgy vehicles, called "Taiwan", has just been broken up by the security services. It involves a group of about thirty people, including military personnel.' *El Watan*, 5 July 1995.

[59] According to *Algérie Confidentiel*, 'In August 1996 imported Fiat Panda vehicles were held up at the ports until further notice by the Directorate of Counter-Espionage. Precise intelligence reports speak of the existence of an active arms traffic well organised in Switzerland and Italy. The arms dealers supplying the Islamist maquis used the mass of vehicles to convey their goods secretly...But despite the firmness of the order from the highest authorities holding up the goods, some Fiat Pandas were able to leave the harbours, Algiers harbour notably. The organisers of the trade, well organised and to all appearances with accomplices among the customs officers, changed the number plates of the detained vehicles.' *Algérie Confidentiel*, no. 97, 1996. In February 1997 the Algerian government halted imports of cars registered in Switzerland. *El Watan*, 1 March 1997.

the smart moves by the 'Emirs' working to adapt their groups to a new environment was to allow a 'customer' (if possible with high-up connections in the customs service) to 'order' a vehicle (absent from the El Harrach market) which was instantly loaded with arms and given false identity papers by the 'Emirs" external networks.[60] When the vehicle arrived at Algiers harbour the customer made arrangements for it to be allowed through (the higher his position, the less customs officers dared to check him). Once it was paid for, the vehicle was seized by the armed group. In fact it appears, after several cases of this sort, that the 'dealers' in the market became closer to the 'Emirs' than to their 'bosses' or customers. The extent of these criminal practices and the fear of successful establishment of the 'Emirs' in that trade led to staff changes in many government departments in 1995. Those new forms of making money (protection rackets, 'contracts' and illicit business) helped the 'Emirs' and their 'fighters' to leave the military field so as to invest in the trading economy. This disengagement from war activity seems to have been related to the growth, from 1994, in the number of import/export companies.

From armed groups to import/export companies

While the armed groups' territories became continually poorer under the combined impact of the flight of military entrepreneurs and people of the liberal professions and the reduction in opportunities for bank robberies, the trade liberalisation recommended by the IMF from 1994 unintentionally boosted the declining resources available to the armed groups. The 'Emirs' and the *trabendistes* around them injected financial profits acquired through the *jihad* into the trading economy and invested in import/export companies. New companies set up offices in communes unfavourably treated in the past;[61] in this way the armed groups redirected their activity. Since 1994 'nearly 11,000 trading companies have officially opened', and in the first six months of 1996 alone, 13,000 applications for official registration of traders were submitted – 60 per day.[62] The 'Emirs" enthusiasm for creation of these trading companies was due to the guarantees that activity offered, for nobody had to explain where the funds came from. Those trading companies could even legally become agents for international firms.

Could the administrative facilities given to the private sector following the agreements signed with the IMF, in April 1994, help the change of direction by the local Islamist armed bands? In short, will the trading

---

[60] Information gathered in France in 1995-6 from 'illegal immigrants' trying to get false papers.

[61] We have deliberately not specified the communes where these changes of direction have taken place, and are not mentioning testimony confirming that process.

[62] *El Watan*, 9 July 1996.

economy succeed where the 'eradicators' have failed? For the emergence of these young businessmen in the Algiers suburbs – new managers of commercial firms, abandoning the *kamis* and the beard for a 'golden boy' outfit – is a revolution in the civil war. Unthinkable just five years ago, this social progress through *jihad* and trade liberalisation holds out the prospect of one of the most honourable and profitable outcomes of war for some 'Emirs'.

At the local level, the emergence of this new class of economic actor represents a serious challenge both for the authorities and for the military entrepreneurs in temporary exile in their *douars*. Like them, the 'Emirs' turned managers of import/export companies succeeded in getting ahead socially through war. Former *trabendistes* working for their former 'bosses', the 'businessmen-Emirs' already look like the winners of the war. As new lords they have established relations with the commune police, some of whom were former *hittistes* from the same neighbourhood. Their contacts with members of the temporary employment agencies for crime, which are all over Algiers and work on contract, have assured them of a positive reply to all their claims on the authorities. Feeling cramped in their housing estates, they have bought villas (especially those of emigrants) or plots of land, helped by the fall in house prices in the Mitidja due to the insecurity. That is why the local authorities have assumed a right to vet private property transactions since 1995. This has not excluded the 'Emirs' from the state-owned landed property put up for sale by the local authorities to increase their budgetary revenue since 1995.[63]

The armed groups' switch to the trading economy does not mean that they no longer take part in the Islamist guerrilla campaign. By their personal histories the 'Emirs' who have become managers of import-export companies have retained their links to the Islamist guerrillas. The local 'Emirs', more or less autonomous since the beginning of the war, have shown by constantly adapting to economic and social change in their environment that they are well able to foresee the best opportunities.

However, although the trading economy is lucrative and brings in money, the 'Emirs'' import-export companies are nonetheless still attracted by the funds accumulated in the maquis, derived from the guerrillas' war economy.[64] In contrast to the district 'Emirs' and their men, the Islamist guerrillas have no choices, in their military action against the security forces,

[63] The letter from the Minister of the Interior and Local Authorities to the Walis (equivalent to Prefects in France) illustrates the cupidity that acquisition of landed property can arouse: 'It is public knowledge that the existence of these portions of land in the urban areas is arousing extreme cupidity among neighbours for a number of reasons, such as the lure of property speculation and enhanced value, passions aroused by individual acquisition of those pieces of land, competitive behaviour by claimants, and of course all the underhand approaches to which the local authorities are subjected.' *El Moudjahid*, 14 June 1995.

[64] The guerrillas' war economy is analysed in Chapter 9.

except to win, to die or to repent. The capital stored in the maquis (money, cars, lorries) can be invested in the suburban 'Emirs'' companies. From this viewpoint those companies play a money laundering role. The Islamist guerrillas benefit in this way from protection of their assets, and they collect, in the form of donations, a part of the earnings brought in by the import-export companies. As for the 'businessmen-Emirs', they augment their companies' capital without directly giving up criminal practices.

The combination of the Islamist guerrillas' war economy and the business activities of the 'Emirs' is one of the factors underlying the consolidation of violence. The geographical relocation of guerrilla zones from Greater Algiers to the interior of the country is explained by a redirection of looting operations. As we shall be emphasising later, the accumulation of wealth by the Islamist guerrillas relies essentially on the control of the main roads and understanding reached with prominent local citizens. Investment of this war booty in import/export companies shows that the return to civil peace in some parts of the wider suburban area of Algiers is compensated by violent acts, notably in the interior, to provide funds for those companies.

So, by fastening onto the trade economy, the Islamist armed groups have become independent of local economic contingencies. The impoverishment of their territories due to the flight of the richest and the increasing destitution of the majority have affected their activity less. Having found a place in Algeria's trade relations with foreign partners, they have made their organisation secure against financial problems. The trade liberalisation policy has favoured both the agents of the policy in Algeria and the Islamist groups fighting the regime. In short, Algeria's move into trade globalisation is proving a boost for all the parties fighting each other in the civil war. In 1994 the change to a market economy with economic reforms led to consolidation of the Islamist armed groups. It has helped development of a 'plunder economy' providing 'good luck for the Mafias';[65] 'Emirs', leading personalities and military personnel are exploiting the transition to a market economy as best their interests dictate.

[65] See Alain Roussillon, *L'Egypte et l'Algérie au péril de la libéralisation*, Cairo: Les Dossiers du CEDEJ, 1996, p. 107.

7

THE SECURITY POLICY

In January 1992, soon after the interruption of the elections, several dangers threatened the armed forces which had taken on the task of keeping the FIS far from the reins of power. The risk of an uprising by the three million people who had voted for that party was compounded by the risk of implosion of the machinery of repression. Once those two dangers had passed, from 1993 the army had to face guerrilla warfare waged by the maquis fighters and a large number of armed bands in the Algiers area. We have shown how those bands' war logic, avoiding attacks on oil and gas facilities, was not able to threaten the foundations of the regime. They wasted the ex-FIS electoral capital and were unable to mobilise the Islamist voters to back them in their struggle. Similarly, we have shown how the regime, through the policy of privatisation and liberalisation, was able to respond both to the demands of the petty bourgeoisie supporting the ex-FIS and to the interests of the army, by conferring ownership rights over privatised enterprises. In this chapter we analyse the regime's military policy more directly: is there a military strategy against the Islamist violence? What are the means at its disposal, and what are its aims?

Since the crisis of the summer of 1962, the army has been seen through the prism of clan rivalry;[1] many observers have foreseen its eventual breakup.[2] When attention is not focused on 'clans' or dark forces, cultural cleavages in the armed forces are highlighted.[3] The fact must be faced that after five years of civil war the armed forces have managed to overcome these divisions, giving support to the theory of its successful 'technicalisation'. So

---

[1] Immediately after independence different factions in the ALN-FLN struggled for power. The Armée Nationale Populaire (ANP), born – in J. Leca's phrase – 'from the ashes of the ALN', inherited a negative image from that period. But, as J. Leca and J.-C. Vatin have written: 'Between 1962 and 1967, the army made progress in the general direction of "technicalisation"...it absorbed the guerrilla spirit and entrapped former guerrilla officers promoted in the field, by imposing a new standard of reference on them...it brought numerous resistance fighters into its ranks in 1962-3, so many as to double its strength...The army's internal conflicts were no longer to be seen...The generation of new promotions from military academies, at Cherchell but also abroad, brought to the barracks and training grounds young officers and NCOs who had not been able to fight in the liberation war.' *L'Algérie politique. Institutions et régimes*, Paris: Presses de la FNSP, 1975, p. 392.

[2] See A. Yefsah, 'L'armée et le pouvoir en Algérie de 1962 et 1992' in P.R. Baduel (ed.), *L'Algérie incertaine*, Paris: Edisud, 1993, pp. 77-97.

[3] The lines of separation within the forces were said to originate from officers' initial training. The 'Arabic-speakers' represented the 'artillery group' because of their training

we shall try to answer the following questions, necessary for understanding of the army's relative victory: What are its resources? Who are its economic partners? For how much longer will those partners accept the cost of the civil war? Can the army depend on its patronage networks? It is partly in the response to those questions that the armed forces' relative success is to be found. As Theda Skocpol has commented, 'a state can remain fairly stable – and certainly invulnerable to domestic mass revolts – even after suffering a major loss of legitimacy, especially if the repressive apparatus retains its cohesion and efficiency.'[4]

This chapter sets out to emphasise the changes in the armed forces since the outbreak of the civil war in 1992, changes that have raised questions about the restructuring operations in the 1980s.[5] We submit that the outbreak of the civil war in 1992 produced a new form of legitimacy among the new leading organisers of repression, comparable with the 'revolutionary legitimacy' that the ALN 'colonels' acquired in the war of liberation. This process has owed a great deal to the debt rescheduling, which made it possible for the army, as for the Islamist armed groups and economic actors, to draw on financial resources available from 1994 onwards to maintain and modernise the repressive apparatus.

Creation of a special anti-guerrilla army corps

The anti-guerrilla struggle. Operations against guerrilla resistance developed in accordance with the financial resources at the army's disposal. Two periods can be distinguished. In 1992 and 1993 it was units of the regular

---

in Iraq, and the 'French-speakers' the *démissionnaires de l'armée française* (DAF) in view of their service in the French army before joining the ALN. R. Leveau has written, 'The presence in the ALN of a considerable number of those *démissionnaires de l'armée française* (DAF) officers and NCOs between 1958 and 1963 (more than two hundred) was one of the major factors in the organisation of that army...It was to be distinguished from other components such as the presence of former guerrillas or officers trained in Syrian, Egyptian or Iraqi military academies, which represented rival clans within the ALN.' *Le Sabre et le Turban. L'avenir du Maghreb,* Paris: F. Bourin, 1993, p. 211.

[4] T. Skocpol, *Etats et révolutions sociales,* Paris: Fayard, 1985, p. 58.

[5] Restructuring of the army was carried out under Chadli Bendjedid's presidency. To consolidate the regime professionalisation of the army was undertaken, aimed at absorbing a new generation of officers and reducing the influence of the ALN maquisards, favourable to Houari Boumedienne's regime. With the referendum on a new Constitution in 1988, the army's new status deprived it of a political role. A general staff was set up again (having been abolished in 1967 after the attempted coup d'état by Colonel Zbiri), with the military region commands coming under it. These changes made it a conventional army. In December 1988 most of the 21 ANP generals from the '54 Generation' were retired. On the army restructuring until 1988 see I.W. Zartman, 'The Military in the Politics of Succession: Algeria' in J.W. Harbeson (ed.), *The Military in African Politics,* New York: Praeger, 1987, pp. 21-47; John P. Entelis, 'Algeria: Technocratic Rule, Military Power' in I.W. Zartman and J.P. Entelis (eds), *Political Elites*

army, accompanied by the gendarmerie[6] and the National Security (Sûreté Nationale),[7] that were responsible for repression; no part of the army was prepared for counter-guerrilla operations. The army's 'enemy' was conceived only as an external one and only the gendarmerie, then headed by General Ben Abbès Ghézaïel, had a war machine suited for counter-guerrilla warfare; but it was quickly to find that the situation was too much for it. Algiers even saw units of the army stationed until then on the Moroccan border coming to take up positions at strategic crossroads in 1992 and 1993. Professional soldiers, men of the desert with the traditional *chehch* headgear, were posted around points of great sensitivity for the regime. Police and gendarmes tried in vain to neutralise the beginnings of the resistance by raids on the Islamist communes. It was only from 1993 onwards that a real army corps specialising in anti-guerrilla operations was created out of units from the army, gendarmerie and police. It had a strength of 15,000 and was commanded by General Lamari, who in July 1993 was promoted Chief of Staff of the armed forces. This corps, formed from elite units, became the pillar of the anti-guerrilla struggle. Its strength was constantly augmented, to reach 60,000 men in 1995; it was run by a Territorial Security Coordination Office (Coordination de la Sécurité du Territoire), set up in March 1995 and entrusted with centralised direction of activity by all services in the anti-terrorist struggle. Until 1994 the efforts of that army corps were concentrated on control of the cities – especially Algiers, which was encircled in 1993 – so as to remove the MIA fighters from them, uproot those fighters from their supportive environment and then drive them to the maquis of the interior.

The military authorities wanted at all costs to avoid politicisation of the population by Islamist activists who had taken to the armed struggle. By eliminating MIA guerrillas and ex-FIS activists systematically, they created conditions for the emergence of new actors, the Moudjahidin of the armed bands who became 'bosses' of the communes previously supporting the FIS. This strategy obliged the last leaders and activists of the ex-FIS to take refuge in the maquis, joining one of the various guerrilla factions, as the objectives of the armed bands seemed so different from their own. The military leaders thus won their first success against the guerrillas, leaving in the FIS municipalities only armed bands which did not fight

---

in *Arab North Africa,* New York: Longman, 1982, pp. 92-133. On the army since 1988 see J.J. Lavenue, *La démocratie interdite* (chapter 'L'armée algérienne et les institutions'), Paris: L'Harmattan, 1993, 279 pp.

[6] The strength of the Gendarmerie was estimated at 25,000 men in 1992; they were trained in techniques of keeping order, on the model of the French Gendarmerie, which until 1990 was in charge of the training of Algerian officers and NCOs. *L'Année Stratégique,* Paris: Dunod IRIS, 1995, p. 369.

[7] The Direction Générale de la Sûreté Nationale (DGSN) employs an estimated 20,000 men: *El Watan,* 2 July 1996.

in the name of that party, but waged *jihad* in the name of the GIA.[8] The next stage then consisted of 'abandoning' the suburbs to the district 'Emirs'.

Let-them-rot tactics: the creation of Islamist ghettoes. The progressive isolation of the Greater Algiers communes, besides leading to the flight of the richer people, transformed those areas into ghettoes for people staying behind. The Islamist armed bands reigned within the districts but could not leave them, for army units encircled them while not trying to dislodge the 'Emirs' prospering there. In that way, in the Mitidja (in Chararba and many other small villages) people lived under a 'double state of siege': encircled by the army stationed a few kilometres away and checking everyone entering or leaving, and under siege within by the armed bands loyal to the GIA, who did the same:

'It was incredible, the boys with Kalashnikovs on their shoulders, in all the streets. They checked people and kept an eye on who entered or left the city. You saw some of them with their backs against the wall, pistols in hand, arguing. They were perhaps not even 18 years old. People of the city no longer went out for walks. When you left the city, it was another encirclement that you found, by the soldiers. We were under a double state of siege.' (Inhabitant of a small commune in the Mitidja, 1995-6, France)

About 30 km. from Algeria, some areas thus remained under the control of the 'Emirs' who had a monopoly of violence there. The army deliberately decided to abandon the people to their control. That strategy of allowing areas to rot sought to avoid human losses for non-strategic zones, but also to lessen the demoralising effects of the 'dirty job'[9] on the troops, although it could mean providing the people with the means to organise their own defence when they were exasperated by the costs of providing for the 'Emirs'. The army thus created conditions favouring the organisation of militias, made up of civilians fed up with the 'Emirs'' policy, the militias' running costs being met by the government.

When the only active elements were the petty traders, and the armed bands had not succeeded in getting involved in the trading economy through formation of import-export companies, the alternative provided by the

[8] A guerrilla faction which, as we shall show in Chapter 9, is opposed to the FIS and its military wing the AIS.

[9] See interview with a military man in exile in *Le Monde,* 16 Sept. 1994: 'Secret liquidation was thus decided upon for a number of suspects. Then, when the terrorists began to cut the throats of young national servicemen, repression moved on to a higher stage. Out of fear of desertion the hierarchy decide to give an eye for an eye, and to implement the slogan, "Terrorise the terrorists". That was when atrocities became systematic: combing a district when an outrage was committed, summary executions of three, four or five young people chosen at random. I am not a killer. I had enlisted to defend a certain idea of a republic. But I am against the murder of innocents. Things went too far....'

creation of government-financed militias seemed like a windfall. Some traders readily used their influence to persuade young men to apply to the Wilaya authority for the necessary authorisation, at the same time urging 'fighters' to change sides and do the same job as before but under the protection of the army.[10] Enlistment in the local pro-government militia by converted Islamists was held up by the petty traders as an example to follow.

The militias: privatisation of violence. The tactics of 'letting them rot', a prelude to the emergence of militias, were not the only ones used. From the end of 1994 the militias[11] became active participants in the anti-guerrilla effort. In contrast to the Mitidja, the militias created in Kabylia, for example, resulted from a political choice. The leaders of the Rassemblement pour la Culture et la Démocratie and the Mouvement Culturel Berbère[12] called for arming of the local population from 1993, as the only way to fight against the Islamist groups. This request, initially rejected by the regime, was accepted after 1994. The debt rescheduling and the various forms of foreign aid to Algeria then made revenue available which was allocated to the security policy. Three types of militia appeared. In the first place there were 'self-defence groups'. Established mainly in Kabylia, they were the right arms of political parties and regional associations. Tolerated by the security forces, they were nonetheless not under their authority, and often grew up in response to real or supposed threats from the Islamists. The kidnapping of the singer Matoub Lounès, for example, gave justification and legitimacy to those militias, as it showed the insecurity in which the inhabitants of the villages lived.[13] The militias did the same

[10] In Khemis el Khechna, a town about 50 km. from Algiers, the inhabitants saw in 1995 local armed bands claiming to be fighting in the name of the GIA turning themselves into militias, according to accounts from witnesses.

[11] The word 'militia' is rejected by the government: 'Whatever certain politicians [a reference to Aït Ahmed] far from reality may say, there are no militias in Algeria, there are no mercenaries, there are only Algerians, former Moudjahidin, children of Moudjahidin, and patriots who have joined the security forces and the Commune Guards to defend the people against murder, robbery and rape.' This was said by Mokdad Sifi, then Prime Minister, quoted by *Liberté,* 9 May 1995. With regard to the 'militia phenomenon' – defined by E. Picard as 'taking of control of a part of the territory and its population by armed groups not belonging to the state' ('Guerre du Liban. Le triomphe de la culture milicienne', unpublished text presented to the CERI, 1996) – the militias in Algeria raise the question of privatisation of violence.

[12] From 1993 young people born in Algiers but with family origins in Kabylia returned to that region because of the prevailing insecurity in the capital; the MCB recruited them and made them its first self-defence 'brigades'. *La Nation,* no. 143, 16-22 April 1996.

[13] The Kabyle singer Matoub Lounès was kidnapped near Tizi-Ouzou by a 'GIA commando' during the night of 25 September 1994; he was released the following 18 October. Following that incident Saïd Sadi, General Secretary of the RCD, repeated his calls for the formation of self-defence militias in Kabylia (see interview with him in *Le Monde* of 27 Sept. 1994).

job of checking people as the Islamist armed bands did in the communes
of the Algiers area; militiamen were made responsible for checking people
entering and leaving their villages, and protecting them against the '*ghazias*'
of the Moudjahidin.[14]

Secondly, militias of the 'resistance' or 'patriot' type were combat units
working with the gendarmerie forces.[15] Equipped by the government, its
members became auxiliaries of the Ministry of the Interior. They were made
up of people threatened by the Islamists, or relatives of victims of the
Islamist groups. Those militiamen were approved by governmental
bodies such as the Organisation Nationale des Moudjahidin (ONM), who
guaranteed their integrity. They generally operated in the interior of the
country, close to towns and villages. They were accompanied by rural
policemen (in fact former fighters in the liberation war who had returned
to service) when they covered mountainous massifs where maquis where
hidden. The militiamen of the 'resistance' type were very often young country
dwellers, whose brother or uncle had had his throat cut by the Islamist
guerrillas, and were driven by a deep-seated desire for vengeance equalled
only by that of the suburban armed bands. Those militias are considered
responsible for many excesses and are credited with a certain military
efficiency:

'Before, it was the Moudjahidin who came down from the hills to attack; now it is
the militiamen who go up into the mountains to look for the 'terrorists', they go off
for a week and one morning you see severed heads placed along the road at the entry
to villages – they are the heads of Moudjahidin, militiamen have cut them off and
placed them by the road. Now things have changed, it's no longer the Moudjahidin
who cut off heads, it's the militiamen. If the militiamen go on long like that, in two or
three years they will have killed all the Moudjahidin. It is because of the militiamen
that Moudjahidin have surrendered, because the government says, "There will be
justice and *rahma* (clemency) for 'terrorists' who surrender", and on the other side
the generals say to the militiamen, "When you find them, cut their throats". Those who
went to the maquis out of fear prefer to give themselves up before the militiamen catch
them.' (Inhabitant of a small village; evidence recorded in France, 1996)

Lastly, a third type of militia with no particular name appeared during
1995 in the towns of the east.[16] It is a response to private interests; private

[14] From 1994 Islamist groups, consisting of about a hundred fighters, carried out reprisal operations against certain villagers accused of not supporting them; those attacks
were called by the people '*ghazias*'.

[15] These militias, although they only appeared in 1994, adopted the counter-guerrilla
tactics of General Ben Abbès Ghézaïel, head of the gendarmerie, who proposed the formation of mixed brigades of gendarmerie and police, as against General Mohamed Lamari's
plan to create elite counter-guerrilla units. See Nicole Chevillard, 'L'armée et les services' in *L'après guerre civile en Algérie*, Nord-Sud Export Conseil, Paris, June 1995.

[16] These militias recall those formed by some Caïds during the liberation war, who 'like
the Bachaga Boualem, dedicated to the cause of *Algérie française*...came forward to
form what were in effect yet more private armies'. A. Horne, *A Savage War of Peace:*

militiamen, financed by local eminent personalities, are entrusted with protection of those people's interests. Like the 'self-defence groups' in Kabylia, those militias are tolerated by the regime, even encouraged by military strategists, who favour militarisation of the rural areas to make it more difficult for the Islamist maquis to take root.[17]

The formation of militias fits into a pattern of anti-guerrilla warfare that has become classic since its implementation by General Challe in the Algerian War.[18] The creation of '*haraka*' (army auxiliaries) to fight against the guerrillas of the Front de Libération Nationale served as a model for the armed forces of the apartheid regime in South Africa[19] and also for Peru in the struggle against the Sendero Luminoso, with the creation of '*ronderos*'.[20] The militias in Algeria were entrusted, in this military set-up, with occupying the land so as to prey upon the Islamist guerrillas' supply networks. In contrast to the elite counter-guerrilla units commanded by General Lamari, they remained stationed in the towns and villages where they were born. That meant the army was freed from the need to control all such places. However, recourse to the militias has not failed to create new problems, since because of the war their members have privileges – such as a having a job and money – that complicate any return to civil peace.

The Commune Guard: controlling the town centres. The last link in the counter-guerrilla chain, after the creation of a specialised army corps and militias, was the formation of a Commune Guard. The police, considered not very reliable by the regime in 1992, underwent profound changes from 1994, under the impetus of the Minister of the Interior, Meziane Chérif.[21] In partnership with local community bodies, especially with the DECs (Délégations

---

Algeria, 1954-1962, Harmondsworth: Penguin, 1977, p. 255.

[17] The sponsors of these private militias at the top level, according to *Le Courrier du Maghreb*, were General Betchine (adviser to President Liamine Zéroual) and General Smaïn, and their aim was to said to be to cut down the pretentions of General Lamari's specialised counter-terrorist army corps (newsletter of 7 June 1996).

[18] In 1957, on General Challe's initiative, units of *Harkis* were developed, made up of Muslim Algerians who had chosen, out of conviction, self-interest or fear, the cause of French Algeria. Because of their social proximity to the ALN fighters, they succeeded in weakening their position in the maquis. The strength of the army 'auxiliaries' was estimated at 160,000 men, divided into 'offensive *Harkis*' and village 'self-defence groups' (*Moghazni*). See M. Hamoumou, *Et ils sont devenus harkis*, Paris: Fayard, 1993, p. 46.

[19] S. Ellis, 'Les nouvelles frontières du crime en Afrique du Sud' in J.-F. Bayart, S. Ellis and B. Hibou, *La criminalisation de l'Etat en Afrique*, Brussels: Complexe, 1997.

[20] Yvon Le Bot, *Violence de la modernité en Amérique latine*, Paris: Karthala, 1994, p.179.

[21] Meziane Chérif was replaced on 2 July 1995 by the Wali of Annaba, Mostefa Benmansour; Chérif, considered to be too much of an 'eradicator', was said to have declared at a press conference in Algiers on 14 March 1995, 'Does a gardener talk with weeds? No! He destroys them, that is all. The terrorists are like weeds.' Quoted by A. Taher, 'L'Algérie déchirée', *Politique Internationale* no. 68, summer 1995, p. 19.

Exécutives Communales, temporary appointed local councils) and the Walis (equivalent to prefects in France), the Minister of the Interior gave local authorities the task of fitting into the new counter-guerrilla arrangements. The increase in the regime's revenue from 1994 onwards made it possible for the Ministry of the Interior to take over security in the cities reconquered by the army in 1993-4.[22] The 'pacification' of urban areas by the counter-guerrilla army unit enabled the government to establish control again over the town centres in Algiers, Blida and Jijel, and important communes of the Mitidja such as Boufarik, Larbaa, Khémis el Khechna, etc. Once the militants of the guerrilla factions had been dislodged from those places to join the maquis, the military authorities set up a Commune Guard to control the reconquered urban areas and allow the specialised counter-guerrilla army corps to launch its first attacks on the maquis from 1994. In the suburbs of Algiers where the armed bands declaring allegiance to the GIA were consolidating their positions, the army applied the tactics of letting them rot, pending a reversal of the situation. But in the towns from which the Moudjahidin had had to flee, it was units of the Commune Guard that applied the security policy.

The then Minister of the Interior expected that the strength of the Guard would reach 50,000 men.[23] To achieve this he recruited from the same human reservoir on which the guerrilla factions and the local armed bands were drawing. Young sympathisers with the former FIS joined the Commune Guard, out of political calculation or necessity. In the difficult economic situation endured by young men in Algeria, a security job was a godsend – especially as, unlike the 'militias', members of the Commune Guard did not leave the town centres, they were only operational within them. Even though they sometimes set up roadblocks, if fighting broke out the risks they ran were less than for the operational groups which accompanied the army on 'clean-up' operations. The regime, refloated financially by international bodies, was able to offer many advantages (houses and cars) to those recruits. Thus the Commune Guard was in direct competition with the Islamist neighbourhood armed bands, for it was in a position to provide services that the armed bands could only provide if their warlike business was efficient and lucrative (illicit business dealing, import-export).

However, even within the town centres the Commune Guard still had to face guerrilla commando operations. So it was accompanied in its work by the 'Intervention and Surveillance Group' (Groupe d'Intervention et de Surveillance, GIS), an elite police unit whose men were called 'Ninjas' by

[22] Ali Tounsi, Director-General of National Security, has stated, 'We are in the process of re-establishing police posts also, all over the place, to reinforce certain districts such as Gué in Constantine and Les Eucalyptus...and thus to cover the capital.' *El Watan*, 18-19 Oct. 1996.

[23] Quoted in *Liberté*, 2 Jan. 1995.

the population because of their clothing (they were protected by hoods). The counter-guerrilla struggle was their job, and they had adequate combat equipment (they drove around in four-wheel drive vehicles with communications equipment, etc.) and were permanently mobilised. Lastly, the Commune Guard had the backing of special plainclothes units which patrolled in brand new vehicles of Japanese and French make, putting on an 'American' look with cap back to front and dark glasses. They were seen by people we interviewed, sympathisers with the Islamist guerrillas, as bounty hunters who acted on information received and trailed, hunted down and killed wanted militants. They operated openly and showed self-assurance that even their 'enemy' envied. They were admired by some, as much as the neighbourhood 'Emirs', for their boldness and recklessness which drove them to act without any effort to conceal themselves.

Modernising the apparatus of repression

At the same time as it set up these units taking charge of suppressing resistance, the regime modernised their equipment. Spurred on by the civil war, use of computers became general. From 1994 onwards government departments as a whole (the armed forces, the customs service, ordinary departments) used computers. The barracks were the first to use them; to keep tabs on young men's military status, the army drew up computerised records of persons reaching the age for national service. As those data were available to the customs and police services, the units involved in the anti-terrorist struggle were, informed of the military status of any suspect when identity checks were conducted.

The war against the armed groups was a boost to 'technological innovations'[24] that did not fail to impress sympathisers of the ex-FIS, who were shocked to discover that a regime seen as incompetent and corrupt could make good use of computerised systems:

'*Subhan Allah* [glory to God], it took a war to get them to modernise. They have installed their computers everywhere, at the airports, in the town halls, the barracks, the gendarmerie stations, even in the "Ninjas" vehicles. I swear to you, I would never have thought they would be capable of using a computer.' (Drinks vendor, Algiers suburbs, 1994)

Use of computers in the war effort increased the need for competent staff, so the army opened recruitment offices for trained people. That need did not fail to attract some of the unemployed college graduates, estimated in

---

[24] J.-F. Bayart emphasises that 'war has always been a vehicle of social change. It gives rise to technological innovation, it alters relationships among actors, it redistributes wealth, it propagates new mental outlooks, it is an instrument of protection and economic competition': 'L'invention paradoxale de la modernité économique', p. 40, in J.-F. Bayart (ed.), *La réinvention du capitalisme*, Paris: Karthala, 1994.

1992 to number 74,000,[25] and previously prominent among voters for the FIS. The needs of the apparatus of repression continually increased, especially with respect to modernisation of weapons. For example, in 1994 the Ministry of the Interior placed an order for civilian helicopters of the Ecureuil type, on which counter-guerrilla equipment could be mounted.[26] The army has meanwhile bought from France signals and night fighting equipment capable of being mounted on Soviet-built helicopters.[27]

All this modernisation explains in part the regime's relative success in its capacity to contain the expansion of the Islamist maquis and the local armed bands. The ANP, obliged to adapt to a threat and an enemy not foreseen by the general staff, had to bring the principles of counter-guerrilla warfare into the training of officers and NCOs. Four years after the start of the civil war the first 'special forces' passed out from the Special Forces Training College (Ecole d'Application des Troupes Spéciales) at Biskra; this first group was baptised with 'the name of the martyr [*shahid*] Ali Nemer, one of the heroes of the glorious revolution of 1 November 1954'.[28] The civil war, like the war of liberation, is able to confer revolutionary legitimacy on young military elites.[29]

This disposal of security forces accounts in part for the successful organisation of the presidential election of 16 November 1995. In deploying its 310,000 men under arms over the whole country to provide security for the election process, the regime was responding in its way to speculation about an implosion of the repressive apparatus. In reality that success was due to a great extent to constant backing from its foreign political and economic partners, who were ready to pay the cost of that security apparatus. Once the town centres had been brought under a relative degree of control, offensives then began against the maquis, which were a new threat to the stability and interests of the regime, especially if the armed groups decided to attack strategic resources (gas and oil). In its fight against the guerrillas the army then used the weapon of psychological warfare, in parallel with military assaults by the marine commandos from Cherchell and the paratroopers from Biskra.

[25] Figure cited by A. Benachenhou, 'Inflation et chômage en Algérie', *Maghreb-Machrek*, no. 139, Jan.-Mar. 1993, p.34.

[26] *Très très urgent*, 8 Nov. 1994.

[27] Ibid.

[28] *El Watan*, 7 July 1996.

[29] An editorial in *El Djeich* (October 1997) declared that 'the generation of heroes of the armed Revolution such as Larbi Ben-M'hidi, Didouche Mourad, Ben Boulaïd, Zigout, Colonel Lotfi and others has as its heir a new generation of heroes imbued with the same spirit of sacrifice in the service of building democracy. History will remember the names of these heroes and Algerian children will learn to know them in their school textbooks with plenty of admiration and respect. These heroes are found everywhere today, defending the Algerian state and preserving its unity.'

Psychological warfare and political jobs

With the cities under government control the aura of the district 'Emirs' was tarnished. Because the army refused to confront them and left the communes of the Mitidja to them, they lost what they had been worshipped for – their role as avengers. Their communes sank into terror and boredom; the 'Emir' in the urban setting and his group became a burden, they were a nuisance for the population which no longer saw its interest in supporting them. As for the Islamist sympathisers, they enthused over new heroes, the guerrillas established in the mountains in the interior,[30] who aroused real enthusiasm. We have noted that Abdelkader Chébouti, nicknamed the *liwa* ('general') or 'the lion of the mountains', was a hero for FIS voters and sympathisers in the early period following the halt to the elections in January 1992. Then he was eclipsed in their *imaginaire* by the district 'Emirs'. In Les Eucalyptus it was striking to see how in one year, between 1993 and 1994, the young sympathisers of the ex-FIS transferred their fascination from Abdelkader Chébouti, 'Emir' of the MIA, to Saïd the sheet-metal worker, the local 'Emir'. But 'privatisation' of the armed bands was later to revive fascination for the guerrillas. Active in the mountains, the guerrillas sought to re-enact the liberation war fighters' role of 'rebels'.

In order to demolish this budding myth of the Islamist maquis, from 1995 the regime set about encouraging 'repentant' guerrillas – estimated at 1,000 in 1995 and 2,000 in 1996 – to speak out publicly.[31] Their testimony, broadcast at peak viewing hours on ENTV, described a disillusioned and cruel world. Far from being a source of dignity and pride, they said, the guerrilla campaign was like 'hell'. In January 1995 ENTV broadcast the testimony of two repentant fighters, originally from Bordj Menaiel: 'The terrorists who want to surrender are very numerous, but blackmail, disinformation and death threats practiced by the "Emirs" prevent them.' The new recruits, prisoners of the Islamist guerrillas, were said to be longing only to return to their home districts and obtain pardon from the state. Imam Ali Ayah, kept prisoner for two months by an armed group, declared after his release:

'[in the place of] the pseudo-fraternity of brothers in arms...I experienced horror. They are monsters who have nothing to do with Islam. They are devils; the flames of hell stare out of their eyes. Inhuman, brutish, they refuse any argument based on logic.'

This testimony from repentant guerrillas publicised in the media, or from kidnap victims, concluded with a call to back the regime's war effort: 'Surrender to the forces of order... Help the forces of order in their effort to exterminate the terrorist groups to foil the plot hatched against Algeria and the Algerian people,' one of them declared. According to these repentant people, the guerrillas' recruitment technique was to arouse fear of the

---

[30] Chapter 9 deals with the Islamist guerrillas.
[31] *La Nation*, no. 128, January 1996.

security forces among individuals sympathetic to the ex-FIS: 'I was warned that the gendarmerie was looking for me. I was encouraged to take flight. They made me afraid by telling me that the security forces caused many sorts of misery to those they arrested.' But that man, who later changed sides, became aware of the 'lies' when he realised what the guerrillas were like in practice:

'We were told that the security forces tortured people, but when I saw that innocent civilians carried off to the maquis were flogged, beaten with iron bars, tied up with barbed wire, suffocated, or trampled on and then finished off with knives like sheep, I said to myself that this was the behaviour of devils. They are not Moudjahidin but really and truly terrorists with no *rahma*. I understood that repentance was the best solution, and I thank God for having opened my eyes. Fortunately I understood it in time, when one of those who were supposed to be my companions fired on me to kill me. I was of no use to him, so he wanted to kill me.'[32]

Was this media spotlight on repentant guerrillas effective in putting off potential candidates for the maquis? Official statements are so discredited among young sympathisers with the ex-FIS and supporters of the *jihad* that such a publicity campaign had limited effect – especially as this feeling of suspicion was supported by both groups' experience not only with the Moudjahidin but also with their literature. The use of the term of 'terrorist' indicates a political stance, rarely proclaimed explicitly. Among our research sample former FIS sympathisers remained faithful to the 'Islamist' version of the war. Only the traders parted company with the revolutionary Islamist interpretation of this civil war from 1994, because they were subjected to intensive racketeering by the 'Emirs'. In fact their feeling corresponded with the changes in the armed groups and the transformation of their war tactics, which became less popular because of the increasing use of car bombs. So the media publicity given to guerrillas changing sides was aimed at two groups: people close to the FIS in 1989-91, among whom some doubt was arising about their political choice at that time, and people who had always been opposed to the armed groups, whose existing feelings were confirmed – to them the televised confessions of those 'terrorists' seen as 'criminals' in the Algiers region and 'bandits' in the rural areas was proof that they had been right from the start. The father of one of the people we interviewed thought that those confessions about the armed militants' motivations confirmed that their acts were like criminal behaviour:

'They are just thieves and yobbos, they say so themselves. They raided the bank for money, they kill for money too. They call themselves Moudjahidin but in fact that's untrue. For them it's easier to kill and rob than to work.' (Trader, Algiers suburbs, 1995)

This one-sided and partisan view is representative of the national liberation war generation, but in addition, being abundantly broadcast by the

[32] Quoted by *Algérie Actualité*, no. 1526, January 1995.

state media, it has been seen as a 'true' and 'just' view among senior political and administrative people. The armed opposition can only be shown as a criminal group of covetous layabouts, ready to commit murder in order to take the place of those who condemn them. But the young Islamist sympathisers remain convinced of the 'just cause' of the maquis fighters, and see the official version – of the guerrilla as the devil – as mere lies and propaganda. In any case grievances against the press go back much earlier. 'Hatred' of the local and foreign journalist dates from the coverage of the parliamentary elections of December 1991. Extreme dramatisation of the 'Islamist peril' aroused among the FIS sympathisers a deep-seated bitterness against journalists, accused of caricaturing their party's programme. Karim, a former student of Mohamed Saïd,[33] thought that the reason why the cancelling of the elections and the dissolution of the FIS, the leading political party, did not arouse any reaction from the world community was the 'fear of Islam in the West' – while adding that Algerian journalists were responsible for distorting the ideas of the Islamist leaders. He thought that journalists had fabricated and disseminated a falsified, partisan view and were thus, in reality, agents of the government who deserved their punishment. Accordingly he justified all the murders of journalists and intellectuals, because they were responsible for the failure to set up an Islamic state:

'Mohamed Saïd said one day:, "If there is an Islamic state, Algerians must prepare to change their way of dressing and eating". Journalists took that sentence out of the general context, for he never said Algerians must wear the *djellaba*. What he meant was that in an Islamic state, it would be better to wear the *djellaba* which does not cost much than to buy very expensive clothes manufactured abroad. That is what he meant, that Algerians must not waste money as they do now – they buy just anything and everything at any price because it comes from France. That is what he meant, but journalists twisted everything, they said, "That's it, in an Islamic state they will force us all to wear the *djellaba*". They do that to scare people.' (Karim, student, Algiers suburbs, 1994)

Like Karim, the Islamist sympathisers and activists accuse the media not only of travestying the Islamist programme but of approving, even defending a 'military solution' to the political conflict. The media coverage of the civil war does not escape their criticism. Aware that the image of the *jihad* waged by the armed groups and the Islamist guerrillas has been

---

[33] Mohamed Saïd, whose real name was Lounis Belkacem, was a former lecturer at the Institut des Sciences Islamiques in Algiers and a member of Sheikh Ahmed Sahnoun's Ligue Islamique. He proclaimed himself Chairman of the FIS soon after the arrest of Abassi Madani and Ali Benhadj. In December 1991 he was elected a deputy. Condemned *in absentia* to ten years' imprisonment in April 1992, he joined the maquis and from October 1994 was in charge of the political directorate of the GIA. He was killed in December 1995 in Kabylia, his home region, by the GIA military directorate, consisting of Antar Zouabri and Djamel Zitouni.

'soiled' by journalists concerned to show only certain aspects of the violence, Islamist sympathisers only feel more 'disgust'. The failure of the press to denounce numerous human rights abuses is seen as a deliberate dehumanisation of the Islamists, relegating them to the level of mere criminals without any rights. This view is reflected in practice by refusal to read 'pro-government' newspapers, and by weariness:

'Now we are used to their propaganda, the newspapers say every day that the government is in control of the situation, that they have killed the terrorists, but we know that is untrue, the tension has not ceased, on the contrary it has increased.'
(Wahab, young trader, Algiers suburbs, 1994)

The coverage that cost the media its credibility – its dramatisation of FIS victory in the parliamentary elections and one-sided treatment of the civil war – minimised the impact of the campaign to demolish the maquis in the media. This was especially so as the Islamist guerrillas have since 1993 had considerable propaganda weapons at their disposal: television, radio, communiqués, newspapers. The sympathisers draw on that body of information and reflection, adding their own experience. In their view the repentant guerrillas were merely security agents 'in disguise', or at best 'innocents' forced to talk under threat. The Islamist programme, condemned but rarely debated, has gained in value in their eyes. Mourad, an unemployed man with a higher technical qualification, said:

'Even the so-called intellectuals like Boukhobza cannot – with good reason – manage to explain what is wrong with an Islamic state. He died because the government, so they said later, asked him to alter Algerian society so that it would no longer want an Islamic state. As he was unable to explain why society wanted an Islamic state, he had to change it so that it would refuse such a state. The Moudjahidin killed him first'.[34]
(Mourad, technical college graduate, Algiers suburbs, 1994)

Intellectuals, accused like journalists of distorting 'society', have also been victims of Islamist violence. However, what the regime hoped to get from intellectuals and journalists when they denounced the Islamist programme was not so much elaboration of an alternative programme as demobilisation of the guerrilla sympathisers. For official propaganda has not sought so

[34] M'Hamed Boukhobza, a sociologist and Director of the INESG (Institut National des Etudes de Stratégie Globale), was murdered on 22 June 1993. He was a member of the National Consultative Council and had submitted a report on 'Algeria in 2005', seen by the Islamists as a programme for 'de-Islamisation of society'. The report suggested, among other things, a certain number of conditions for a transition to democracy. It emphasised the risks in universal suffrage in an underdeveloped country, as it favoured the emergence of 'a potentially nihilist populism, fuelled by the structural existence of a numerous population excluded from economic and social progress'. The report therefore recommended 'the necessary revision of the voting age to at least over 21'. To the Islamists this was a means of attacking their electoral following by trying to exclude the youngest members. Quoted in *La Nation*, no. 158, 1996.

much to bring the Moudjahidin back from the 'path of God' (*Sabil Allah*) and towards the way of repentance as to demoralise their potential followers. This propaganda has in fact been accompanied by the establishment of a 'social net' aimed at attracting all those who, for economic and social reasons, would be ready to serve the guerrilla campaign for money. Besides depicting the Islamist guerrillas as diabolical, the regime offered jobs close by, bonuses and assistance for house building, and, above all, contract jobs with the Ministry of Defence. The media operation involving repentant guerrillas sought to make those who could be attracted by the experiment of *jihad* in the maquis change their minds. Instead of the risk of death the regime offered the certainty of housing and a job, for a modest wage certainly, but without risk.

The creation of 'public interest works', like the TUCs (Travaux d'Utilité Collective) in France, made it possible in 1995 to give more than 400,000 people jobs at 21,000 'work sites'.[35] These were devised to check the flow of 'odd jobs' for which the guerrillas paid people, and the priority target for recruitment was the young unemployed people, who were able to earn more than 2,000 dinars per month, half the guaranteed minimum industrial wage. Small as it was, such a wage enabled a family with five or six children to survive. From then on it was not uncommon to see one of the children sacrificing himself by joining the security forces or an armed group. Most numerous, however, were those, while being paid for work on a 'site', continued to do 'odd jobs' for the guerrillas. But in the last resort only joining the security forces made it possible really to escape from material constraints: to obtain a home, buy a car and receive good pay.

The army, the number one state enterprise

The situation of general insecurity, together with the dwindling of secure and risk-free resources, led some young people, ex-FIS sympathisers and others, to join the army. The involvement of the army in the halting of the elections in January 1992 had seemed like a suicidal act, as the Islamist opposition was then seen as too big to handle. Speculation about massive desertion by national servicemen was followed by speculation about an agreement between 'colonels' and Islamist leaders at the expense of 'corrupt' generals. Five years later the paradox of the situation had to be faced: after the speculation about a shortage of men because of pressure from the Islamists, the reality was unceasing enlistment. How could that be explained? Of course the media campaigns to blacken the Islamist guerrillas probably encouraged vocations as 'saviours of the nation'. The early enlistment by 'ex-combatants' was undeniably due to that negative depiction of the Islamists.

[35] *La Tribune*, 11 Oct. 1995.

The People's National Army, spared by the Structural Adjustment Programme.
However, for the youngest men of the towns and villages of the interior,
the chance of a job in the service of a noble and just cause proved decisive, to the great displeasure of the ex-FIS sympathisers, who were eloquent
on the powerful influence of the *'kersh'* (belly):

'It is wretched to see young men in the army, they come from the *douars* [small
villages]. They have been told "The Afghans are destroying Algeria", etc. They have
jumped at the opportunity for that work, because previously the army had not recruited 'illiterates' like them, it was reserved for people with qualifications. For them,
abandoned in their rural homes, this is a stroke of luck. They will be able to fill their
bellies.' (Mourad, jobless technical college graduate, Algiers suburbs, 1994)

The army, with 80,000 conscripts out of a strength of 140,000, had been
running a real risk of seeing national servicemen shirking their duty. That
at any rate was the Islamists' hope: that 'sons of the people', national servicemen with Islamist feelings, would be the armed forces' 'Trojan horse'
or Achilles heel. But paradoxically, the army in this civil war has proved
to be (with the administration) one of the few state enterprises to continue
and even expand recruitment. While the regime privatised state enterprises
to reduce its expenditure and meet the demands of the IMF, the army recruited men, and security-related jobs multiplied, adding to the burden on
the state budget. While some young men in the Algiers area or the Mitidja
opted for enlistment in the armed bands or the Islamist guerrillas, those in
the small and middle-sized towns in the interior chose the army. Undoubtedly
the strong presence of ex-combatants in those regions (Aurès, the Constantine
region, Kabylia) helped keep minds fixed on the war and the importance
of a state. Besides the fear of enduring the fate of post-Communist Afghanistan[36] there was the unexpected possibility of a job and income. The guerrillas'
violence against the 'ex-combatants', and their favourable attitude towards
certain prominent local people, encouraged enlistment in the army by individuals facing unemployment and a precarious existence, subordinated
to local political forces. Their enlistment resembled a sort of emancipation,
unimaginable for them until then.

With an assured supply of new conscripts, the army succeeded also in
persuading national servicemen to stay on at the end of their service. The
threats made against them by the GIA led to the enlistment of some of the
national servicemen of the 1990 and 1992 conscript intakes under contracts of service. Their status, midway between conscripts and enlisted men,
provided for service for a year, renewable. It was some of those soldiers who
were seen parading beside the professional soldiers between 1992 and
1994 in the urban areas of greater Algiers. Being involved in the repressive policy directed against the Islamists, they later had no choice but to

---

[36] A. Akram, *Histoire de la guerre d'Afghanistan,* Paris: Balland, 1996, 636 pp.; see
the chapter 'La guerre civile'.

renew their service contracts, that being their only protection. This practice did not prevent some desertions to the Islamist guerrillas, although the most suspect national servicemen, especially those from the Mitidja, were incorporated in frontier defence units stationed on the borders with Libya and Morocco. In contrast the reservists called up in 1995 to safeguard the holding of the presidential election on 16 November were from Kabylia, and were involved in repression.[37]

Contrary to the remark by the person we quoted above, the army has not been recruiting only 'illiterates'. Recruiting offices have been opened for people with university degrees and higher education diplomas, to enlist those qualified jobseekers who are fed up with the 'system' and sympathetic to the FIS and FFS. The media campaigns to encourage respect for the army, its instruments of war and the status of officers have made it attractive in spite of its role in repression. The unemployed college graduates show understanding of the Islamists' violence, but that has not deterred them at all from joining the army.[38] Their enlistment, decided upon as a gamble with the future, has been experienced as the only way to salvation in a country confronted with civil war.

The new 'green barrage'. Does the challenge of the Islamist guerrilla campaign have something in common with that of the struggle against the advance of the desert? The building of a 'green line' in the 1970s mobilised national servicemen in that labour of Sisyphus. Houari Boumedienne at the time compared this with the previous generation' service in the war of liberation:

'If thousands of young men fought and accepted sacrifices in the past, including the sacrifice of their blood, it is the duty of our youth today and the rising generations to accept the sacrifice of their sweat.'[39]

After the struggle against the advance of the desert and the building of Socialist villages, the ANP put an end to its economic and symbolic activity. As a genuine melting-pot of the technocratic elite, the army was an obligatory stage in the career of future officials, higher and lower, of the state enterprises. The criterion of professional competence was replaced by those of political adherence and regional allegiance. Even so, it was a real instrument of social advancement. At the beginning of the 1980s Tawfiq, about forty years old, a state-employed town planner and private consultant, illustrated that process:

[37] *Algérie confidentiel,* 21 March 1996.

[38] See, in the newspaper *La Croix* (15 July 1995), the portrait of Selim, who after three years of unemployment, joined the army: 'Sometimes I say that the terrorists are right. I myself am capable of becoming one of them, but not for the same reasons as they have. I do not like them because they are Islamists and above all because they terrorise the population. Apart from that, I back all those who want to fight against this regime.'

[39] *El Djeich,* no. 179, April 1979.

'I was doing my national service when the army sent us to Egypt to fight against Israel. We spent months in the desert, nobody asked our opinion. But on my return I obtained a scholarship and studied town planning abroad. With that experience in the army I was able to do things in life.' (Tawfiq, town planner, Hauts-Plateaux, 1994-5)

Finding a place in the economy through the army went together with political socialisation. The view of the ANP as a simple instrument of plunder lies behind many errors of analysis concerning its stability in the civil war. In reality the patronage networks it set up have enabled it to broaden its base. Since independence it has accomplished the training, placement and consolidation of various economic actors, who owe it a debt today. It is possible to see traces of that myth of progress through the ANP in people's criticisms of the Islamist programme:

'I have nothing against the FIS, but I don't understand how they can say that "Islam is the solution" [*El Islam houa el hal*] when women cannot find coils or even basic methods of contraception. They say nothing about the problems of demography, of the economy. An officer friend told me that they (the Islamists) wanted to turn the desert into California, so let them show us what they can do there!' (Tawfiq, 1994-5)

The army's political and economic work programmes came to an end because of its professionalisation, carried out during Chadli Bendjedid's presidency.[40] In order to remove the heirs of Houari Boumedienne, who had come from the army of the borders, as well as the colonels worshipped by the former guerrillas, Chadli Bendjedid opted for modernisation of the military apparatus and the promotion of young officers trained in up-to-date technology, who were to remain loyal to him throughout the 1980s. This 'political withdrawal' of the army was sealed by the promulgation of the Constitution of 23 February 1989. The emergence of a dynamic private sector during the 1980s opened up new prospects for social advancement. Private economic actors saw the army as an obstacle to their expansion and, as we have noted, were to meet again in the Islamist coalition during the elections process.

Islamism in the army's ideology. The ANP's statements and position on the emergence of Islamist tendencies remained constant from 1989 to 1995. The rapid succession of generals at its head did not alter its attitude at all. While homogeneous in its 'eradicator' line, it was nonetheless divided on methods of action and dealing with the 'Islamist phenomenon'. From 1990 clear limits were set to the Islamist opposition's field of action:

---

[40] I.W. Zartman, 'The Military in the Politics of Succession: Algeria' in J.W. Harbeson (ed.), *The Military in African Politics*, op. cit., pp. 21-47.

The ANP considers itself to be assigned the permanent mission of 'the safeguarding of national independence and national defence', as is laid down in Article 24[41] which it is necessary to read in depth and in its entirety, and which cannot be satisfied with an exclusive and purely literary interpretation. Article 24 has to be considered, understood and interpreted as much in the spirit as in the letter. In defending these institutions and their work, in case of threat to them, the ANP will be only carrying out its permanent mission to safeguard national independence; from that point of view, in so doing it will simply be defending the Constitution.[42]

That constitutionalism, rather laughable in view of the grievances expressed against the way oil and gas income has been managed, is nonetheless one of the basic political motivations of the ANP. Does the army, convinced of its superiority over the whole body of society, draw its values from a code derived from forms of authority originating with the 'Janissaries'?[43] The Islamist electorate retained some respect for the army until 1993-4, and only condemned the presence in it of former soldiers of the French army.[44] Farid's reaction to the unsuccessful attempt on the life of Khaled Nezzar on 13 February 1993 underlined this form of selective criticism:

'They just missed him, but his bodyguards were killed; the bomb blew up four cars. They were waiting for him at a speed ramp, it's a pity, *in chah Allah* they'll get him next time. Nezzar, he is "the enemy of Islam", he was a French soldier, he is working for France. He has said there should not be an Islamic state in Algeria.' (Farid, unemployed, Algiers suburbs, 1993)

Those Islamist diatribes against the supposed presence of 'enemies of Islam' within the ANP were extended from 1994 onwards to the army as a whole. The changes at the top levels of the army were not followed by any alteration in the anti-Islamist doctrine. The Islamists of the ex-FIS, intrinsically seen as bringing 'serious dangers for the Nation', were for the ANP a risk for the 'development of Algeria':

[41] Article 24 of the Constitution of 23 February 1989 laid down: 'The consolidation and development of the national defence potential are organised around the National People's Army. The ANP has as its permanent mission the safeguarding of independence and the defence of national sovereignty. It is entrusted with ensuring the defence of the country's unity and territorial integrity, as well as protection of its land space, its air space and the various zones of its maritime waters.'

[42] *El Moudjahid,* 15 May 1990.

[43] It may be recalled that the preamble to the Janissaries' official acts was, 'We, the Pasha and Divan of the Invincible Militia of Algiers'; see R. Mantran (ed.), *Histoire de l'empire ottoman,* Paris: Fayard, 1989, p. 407. A. Yefsah sees in the ANP's reaction to the FIS victory in December 1991 a 'Janissary reflex': A. Yesfah, 'L'armée et le pouvoir en Algérie de 1962 et 1992', op. cit., p. 91.

[44] In *Mots de vérité,* a collection of AIS/FIS texts dated April 1995, those officers were compared with 'Lacoste's corporals': 'The bombing has returned. The destruction is going on now. Firing is everywhere. The SAS are back. The massacres have restarted. Ill-treatment of citizens is a daily routine. In short, all the elements of the colonialist scenario have returned, updated, through the actions of "Lacoste's corporals".' Robert Lacoste was French Governor-General of Algeria from 1956 to 1958.

Politico-religious extremism has been proved in practice to be an insidious means of disintegration of the modern structures of such states [Gulf states] and a factor for immobility and stagnation with respect to development policies. Activist politico-religious movements aim at social destabilisation, the starting of disturbances, a crisis of confidence among the masses and the nationalist elites, deterioration in relations between the army and the nation, and the failure of experiments in development and democratisation.[45]

The ANP was described as responsible for the country's ills, and in 1990 Islamist voters accused it by name of failing to back the cause of Saddam Hussein in Iraq. The energy and power seen in the Iraqi army tarnished the image of the Algerian army, described and perceived as corrupt, incompetent and opposed to the interests of the nation. The Islamist interpretation of the Gulf crisis and war (1990-1)[46] revealed both the Islamist voters' expectations of greatness and power and the deep-seated desire of a certain number of them to go and fight. The radicalisation of Islamist language during that period inevitably clashed with the ANP:

Democracy does not mean anarchy, freedom of expression cannot be synonymous with violence and intimidation. It would be intolerable for men coming to power through democracy to lead us to dictatorship... What have all the achievements of the ANP since independence come to if people come to cast doubt on the authenticity of its roots as well as the respectability of its structures? Does not a holy verse of the Koran proclaim, 'If a depraved man brings you news, get proof together first, for fear of doing people wrong through ignorance and having to regret one fine day what you have done'?[47] (Khaled Nezzar)

Those statements seemed to Islamist voters and FIS leaders like formal ones for internal use. The ANP as purveyor of economic development and guarantor of democracy? That image aroused derision. Did the military themselves believe in what they were saying? The fact had to be faced, five years after the statement of those ideas, that their promises had been kept. The similarity of the language used by Khaled Nezzar and by Liamine Zéroual illustrates a common ideology, fashioned by the spirit of the ANP.[48] The Islamist guerrilla campaign is never mentioned by name, only individuals 'gone astray' are called to order so that they can escape total eradication:

[45] *El Djeich,* editorial, April 1991.

[46] See R. Leveau, *Le Sabre et le Turban* (note 3), p. 144.

[47] *El Moudjahid,* 15 March 1990.

[48] Thus Liamine Zéroual declared in March 1994, 'We shall mobilise all means to fight against the violence and stop the bloodshed, for the use of violence as a form of political expression and as a means of getting access to power will never be tolerated. We shall never accept either fratricidal condlict or anarchy, still less the destruction of the human and material potential of our country, and no religious, political or cultural motive can justify crimes against people and property.' Quoted in *Le Nouvel Afrique Asie,* no. 54, March 1994, p. 20. In fact it was only from November 1994 onwards that Zéroual would show some difference from the other generals, by calling for '*rahma*' (clemency) for the 'people gone astray' (the guerrillas), as we see in Chapter 8.

To those who have soiled their hands with the blood of these defenders of order, I shall say that the most pitiless war will be waged against them until their complete eradication. As for those who are still living underground and who have not yet joined in anything irredeemable, we call on them to cease all activity of that sort and work towards brotherhood. The state will take note if they do.[49] (Khaled Nezzar)

In the aftermath of the halt to the elections the army was convinced that it was in a position to eliminate the ex-FIS from the political scene without running risks. But it was caught unprepared when, a year later, the forces of the police and gendarmerie had still not managed to gain control of the situation. The proliferation of armed groups and the attacks by Chébouti's men forced the ANP to intervene militarily in dealing with violence in the wider suburban areas and towns of the Mitidja. The threat of a 'pitiless war' emerged, and with it the onset of civil war. But very far from putting an end to the violence, the repression aroused among the youth of those communes a real enthusiasm for the guerrilla effort. There followed an increase in the guerrillas' strength and in attacks on the security forces. To various observers an Islamist victory appeared in 1993 to be possible, even inevitable. The speculation about implosion of the ANP under the blows delivered by the Islamist resistance entered into all scenarios, while the press organ of the Ministry of Defence, *El Djeich*, announced:

The army will continue to hold the forces of evil and their treachery and criminal behaviour in check, because it is a solid rampart, an unshakeable shield, firmly determined and ready to pay a heavy price to lead the country along the road to security and peace.[50]

Completely committed from 1993 onwards, the troops of the ANP became the object of constant attacks: military convoys and national servicemen were among the first victims. The army replaced the 'political class' as the Islamists' main enemy. The ANP saw the Islamist phenomenon as a movement for a new society that put the country's future at stake, according to General Touati, adviser at the Ministry of Defence, who thought Algeria was going through a genuine transformation....

....and not an attack of social, cultural and economic fever which can be dealt with by superficial treatment, however violent, or by political analgesics. Algerian society is being seriously confronted about what its future it wishes to have. This is happening in a context of anguish, economic hardship and the questioning of decisions hitherto considered absolute truths...The country is living through reckonings that are a fundamental stage in the consolidation of Algeria's destiny as a modern nation. This dynamic of modernity cannot be seen as opposed, today any more than yesterday, to the values of Islam, which is in the eyes of the Algerian people a source of identity, promotion and progress.[51]

---

[49] *El Moudjahid*, 28 Dec. 1992.

[50] *El Djeich,* April 1993.

[51] *El Djeich,* March 1993.

This sort of language, intended mainly for ANP officers transformed into brokers of modernity, responded to their fear of seeing an alliance struck between the Islamist technocratic elites and ANP generals. There was also the risk of seeming to be, in this civil war, the people mainly responsible for repression in the eyes of public opinion, in view of the fundamental role army officers were in fact playing. Invested with the role of modernist vanguard for Algeria, they appeared to be reconnoitring for an advance on a country preyed upon by 'the forces of evil'. It was as a bearer of that ideology that Liamine Zéroual received his mandate for the presidential election of 16 November 1995. That is to say that, while divergences existed on ways to handle the security challenge of Islamist violence, there was definitely a common outlook among the military leaders, to the greatest regret of the Islamists of the FIS.[52] Probably this common rejection of Islamism, and the mission to safeguard the nation which the ANP assigned to itself, drew strength from the economic capital derived from privatisation and trade liberalisation. This overlapping between the army's political mission and capital formation was probably one explanation for the success of the Biskra Special Forces College.

The army, like other actors in the conflict, has been able to exploit opportunities arising in this civil war. While in 1992 it came near to seeing its authority subjected to FIS elected representatives, in three years of fighting it succeeded in becoming again the hegemonic actor that it had been until the elections. Just like the 'Emirs' and the guerrillas, it benefited from the rescheduling of the debt and the generosity of the IMF. Its relative successes against the Islamists during those three years also provided favourable conditions for increased investment – notably in the oil sector, so far spared – which did not fail to bring in revenue for it. This consolidation of the armed forces, due partly to the unconditional backing of Algeria's international political and economic partners, nonetheless raises questions: does the continuation of the 'eradicating' policy not conceal interests involved in a war economy that ensures a hegemonic role for the army and market openings in the private sector for the army's patronage networks? In short, are the Islamist groups and the military not in the process of becoming 'complementary enemies' finding in the violence of war the way to achieve their aspirations?

---

[52] 'The army must understand that its future – that is to say its status as a modern army, powerful, respecting the Constitution and respected by the people – is guaranteed by the National Contract and by the future National Pact. More than ever, it must take control of itself and stop this fake electoral process which is now plunging the country into chaos', *El Mounqidh,* September 1995, p. 46.

Part III

CONSOLIDATION OF THE WAR

In spite of its illegitimacy immediately after the halting of the elections process in 1992, and its situation of financial bankruptcy in 1993, the regime managed to survive the ordeal of the *jihad*. Refloated financially from the end of 1994, it reversed the balance of forces with the Islamist armed groups to its advantage, and organised a presidential election on 16 November 1995 to give validity to a political situation that had, for a moment, turned in its favour. The election of General Liamine Zéroual as president gave rise to the illusion that the regime had been able to find legitimacy again, having lacked it – a point the Islamist armed groups emphasised – since January 1992.

Helped by its restored financial situation, the government tried to satisfy the social and economic demands of the FIS electorate. For that purpose it undertook a series of reforms in government departments and local government so as to 'restore' citizens' confidence in its institutions. Similarly a construction policy was launched, aimed at overcoming the housing shortage that had grown under Chadli Bendjedid's presidency. Lastly, the regime created service-sector jobs to tackle unemployment, especially among the young. The new local authorities, Walis and Chairmen of DECs (Délégations Exécutives Communales), were made responsible for encouraging initiatives in the domain of job creation. The young, who formed a potential reservoir of guerrilla fighters, became a stake in the regime's economic policy.

The government hoped, with the help of that policy, to erode the support which the guerrilla campaign had among a population descending into pauperisation. However, changes among the guerrillas during seven years of war showed that such an effort was illusory. The Islamist guerrillas, becoming more professional, certainly went through a decline in numbers after the presidential election of 16 November, as the number who changed sides showed. But their successful entry into the trading economy through the creation of import-export companies meant an increase in their financial resources, necessary for modernisation of their arsenal. Now they adapted themselves to the prospect of a long-term struggle, for in contrast to the first years of the *jihad* (1992-4), they no longer counted on a popular uprising to overthrow the regime. However, on that subject divisions appeared in guerrilla ranks over the attitude to adopt towards the 'people'. The revolutionary organisations (the MEI and GIA) thought that only terror was able to induce the people to collaborate; while in the political organisations' (MIA and AIS) view, the war should not be waged against the people, and the guerrillas must try to win its support by trust. Meanwhile, with no end in sight to the civil war, new factions (such as the LIDD formed in July 1996) regularly emerged, and this reduced the guerrillas' chances of forming an armed united front.

Our hypothesis is therefore that the future of the civil war does not lie in the emergence of an improbable Islamic state from a military victory by the guerrillas, still less in the emergence of a democratic state, but in the reinvention of the Beyliks. In the precolonial period the 'Algerian state' constantly assimilated Islamic movements that had turned to dissidence, and that practise was continued in the postcolonial state during successive political crises. Will the present government, imbued with this historical know-how, be able to bring over the Islamist guerrillas?

8

WAR ECONOMY AND
POLITICAL DYNAMICS

After the formation of an army corps specialising in counter-guerrilla war and the modernisation of the apparatus of repression, the regime embarked on administrative reforms and a policy of housing construction and recruitment of young men in marginal situations. To respond to the demands of ex-FIS voters, the local authorities were entrusted with finding solutions to the innumerable local disputes that the FIS municipal councillors had been planning to resolve in 1990-1. It was with some surprise that the population saw the regime applying the former FIS' programme in economic and social matters. Reassured that victory for the Islamist groups was impossible, the government set about reshaping the political field. It made the Hamas-MSI party a key player; representing petty traders and the private sector after the dissolution of the FIS, Hamas, in joining the pro-government coalition, facilitated the assimilation of private economic actors, who were given a major role in Algeria's 'take-off'. This chapter seeks to show the importance of the general context and opportunist arguments in the reforms started by the regime, whose ultimate aim was based on highly political criteria, not having any basis in economic rationality.

Consolidation of the regime

The military leadership, which in the first two years of the conflict had been busy avoiding a collapse of the state, embarked from 1994 onwards on sweeping changes in various government departments. Once the idea of a possible collapse of the ANP in the face of attacks by the armed groups had been put aside, the military leaders developed, in parallel with the anti-guerrilla struggle, a strategy of political reconquest of the nation. One explanation of the regime's consolidation and hence of the relative failure of the Islamist guerrilla campaign lies precisely in that war economic policy, conducted at the same time as the armed struggle. The economic weapon, a card kept up the government's sleeve, came as a surprise to observers who had thought an Islamist victory inevitable in 1993-4. The regime's capacity for reaction and initiative raised a number of questions about its supposed incompetence. More than one sympathiser of the ex-FIS had thought it incapable of rising to the challenge of the war. Surprised by the reorganisation of the apparatus of repression, he was at least equally surprised by the economic policy.

171

The government, fearing possible use of government departments by the Islamist guerrillas, embarked from 1994 on changes both in staffing and in legislative instruments. Besides changes in the customs service and computerisation of departments, there were also transfers of very many senior staff. The appointment of thirty-nine new Walis[1] in June 1994 also formed a part of this restructuring of departments. The restructuring was aimed at restoring the state monopoly over administrative networks built up on the basis of family or regional ties, in which local prominent personalities, suspected of maintaining special relationships with the guerrilla leaders, played an important role. It was also aimed at reviving some confidence among the people in the government's political conduct. Promises to fight against clientelism by reorganising the APCs (Assemblées Populaires Communales) and Daïras (sub-prefectures) – a powerful argument used by the Islamists in the election campaigns of June 1990 and December 1991 – won over a large number of voters then. That was all the more so because such denunciations came not from a few self-proclaimed Imams but from government officials whose minds were open to the ex-FIS programme:

'As the son of a *shahid* [martyr] and an official of Boumerdès Wilaya, I have decided to speak out publicly and make known my anxiety at the total passivity of the country's official institutions in the face of incompetence and dishonesty, the origin of the real difficulties which Algeria is currently going through. To hold the post of overall responsibility for the Wilaya's budget, it is necessary to be a transport inspector and to have a number of foreign currency bank accounts. While the Wilaya decides to sell staff villas to Division Heads, so as to build new villas for them about 800 metres from the first ones, despite the fact that some of those same responsible officials already have seven houses which they use for commercial profit as opportunity arises in this Wilaya, there are still citizens who live in hovels.' (A group of officials)[2]

To deal with these grievances voiced by public opinion and given political expression by the Islamists, the new Walis were from 1994 given responsibility, in coordination with leading officials of the DECs, for developing new forms of local mobilisation, so as to involve the population more. The restructuring of local authorities around the Walis was one expression – according to the Minister of the Interior, Meziane Chérif – of the determination to cure one cause of the discontent 'citizens' discontent and hence of the FIS's success: the absence of official authority in the communes:

'Since the end of the Wilaya Executive Councils in 1986, the Walis have been completely deprived of their prerogatives. They have as a result been isolated in their activity and have lost their power as representatives of the state. This has led to the anarchy in which the citizen lives at present, the lack of trust between the administration and the ordinary people. The new Walis must restore the authority of the state...they must

---

[1] *El Watan*, 27 June 1994.
[2] *El Mounqidh*, Thursday 24 Ramadan, 1410 AH, p. 8.

also be in direct and permanent contact with the population and especially the young, so as to take responsibility for their problems, especially those relating to housing and jobs.'[3]

In reality the subordination of the local authorities to family and professional networks, and to economic actors such as the military entrepreneurs – informal but real figures of power in the communes – began before the dissolution of the Wilaya Executive Councils in 1986. Throughout the 1980s job creation in the communes was also the work of military entrepreneurs, through the organisation of *trabendo*. The local authorities were from 1980 deprived of any influence or authority in policies regarding housing, employment and the creation of urban infrastructure. The people set up their own housing areas illegally, obtaining water from underground supplies through pumps. Although effective, this informal and individualistic organisation of space considerably worsened social tension. In this context the emergence of the FIS and its election victories responded to a need: the need for some way to pacify social relations worsened by the property question in urban areas.

Confronted with the local reorganisation of certain communes subjected to the armed groups, the regime's economic policy then sought above all to deprive the 'Emirs' of their ability to capitalise on the confusion. The object of the Walis' job creation efforts was to get ahead of the 'Emirs' in their recruitment policy, or to reduce the supply of human resources in the Islamist armed bands' urban environment. The creation in 1994 of 'private interdepartmental cooperatives' sought to enlist young unemployed people and place them in economic activity backed by the local authorities. The sorts of job most encouraged were mostly to do with security: watchmen, and security guards for vehicle parks, private cars, buildings and private homes. Although other posts of a more skill-oriented sort were created (glaziers, plumbers etc.), they seem to have been less numerous than the security posts.

This policy did not overlook – far from it – the qualified young people already favoured by the ANP recruiting office, which was looking for technically qualified people able to make the apparatus of repression work as it underwent modernisation. Local initiatives, in zones exposed to violence, were organised to make young people aware of the new job opportunities. In Jijel, a city close to the Chekfa maquis (one of the biggest maquis until 1995),[4] the Wali embarked on a concerted policy of local recruitment of qualified people. Agreements signed with state enterprises were expected to lead to sponsorship of projects for qualified young people. Companies

---

[3] *El Watan*, 26 June 1994.

[4] One of the biggest maquis in the east of Algeria, in 1994-5 it mobilised against it no less than 15,000 troops, including elite units, which did not succeed in putting an end to it.

such as SOTROUJ (road works), DUCHC (town planning and construction), DHW (water works) and EDIED (domestic equipment) were called in to help the fight against unemployment.[5]

The proliferation of job offers in both private and public sectors was one of the key economic events in this war. For sympathisers with the ex-FIS and the armed groups, the new situation was a contrast with the 1990-1 period. Kader, a jobless general practitioner in 1992, an FIS voter who recently became a practicing Muslim, saw his situation definitely improved:

'When I finished my studies in 1989 I wanted to go to France to do specialist training, but studies there were too expensive. So I asked for a posting here. All that they offered me was a job in the Sahara. There, there is a shortage of general practitioners; I refused, I wanted to stay in a big city, Algiers, Oran, Annaba, but not in the desert. I was without work for five years, I was almost ready to join the maquis in 1993, so disgusted was I, because the Moudjahidin need doctors. I didn't go, but now I don't regret that, I've got a job in a hospital (in the Algiers area); for the past year they have been recruiting all nurses and doctors unemployed or, like me, waiting for a posting.[6] It must be said that they need doctors here too, it is equipment that is lacking now, and medicines.' (Kader, France, 1996)

Weary of the civil war, Kader was one of that section of FIS voters about thirty years old, with qualifications, who supported 'Islamist democracy' in 1991 but were disillusioned by the violence that completely marginalised them in comparison with the 'Emirs', their juniors. Having been at the front of the stage during the electoral process (1990-1), they were later confronted with the emergence of the Moudjahidin and their supremacy. Their passions had cooled and they now wanted only to get unharmed through a war whose end they could not see. Doctors, engineers, technicians or teachers, they were a remarkable pool of talent for the FIS in the eventuality of an Islamic state. The regime was able, before the guerrillas, to find occupation for their skills, out of fear that they would join the maquis where they could have improved the fighters' military performance. When many people in senior positions who were threatened by the 'Emirs' fled abroad, the vacant jobs were immediately taken by those unemployed former sympathisers of the FIS.[7]

The restructuring of government departments was also accompanied by the introduction of new professional practices among civil servants. Instructions were given to them to improve the way citizens were received,

---

[5] 'Sotrouj has offered young people with qualifications related to the industry a whole workshop of reaming equipment with plentiful facilities', wrote *La Tribune*, 24 March 1995.

[6] In 1996 ten private clinics were set up in the Algiers area, and the health needs linked to the civil war lead one to expect development of that sector.

[7] According to R. Tlemçani, between 1992 and 1994 over 10,000 people in official and executive jobs left Algeria because of the 'slit throat syndrome'. 'Une approche stratégique', *Les cahiers de l'Orient*, nos 36-37, 1995, p. 28.

and above all to facilitate all applications aimed at obtaining documents. Private traders, up against officials' antipathy since independence, undoubtedly benefited from those new measures which were very favourable to them, following the agreement signed between Algeria and the IMF in April 1994. Thus the conjunction of the reform of the banking system, the devaluation of the dinar whose exchange rate was now close to the unofficial market rate, and the fear of the armed groups' protection rackets was reflected, for the economic actors we interviewed, in an increase in savings. For the private sector this was a break with three decades of hoarding of money and informal loans at interest. In fact private economic actors believe that since 1994 banks have provided the best security for their money. Ali Tounsi, Director General of National Security, has noted that 'today, fortunately, the traders no longer keep their money at home. Since those episodes of protection rackets and theft, there is no longer money circulating outside the banks.'[8] Placing their money in financial institutions spares them the fear of the 'night-time visitors' whose exact identity remains ambiguous.[9]

This process has affected networks based on personal relations, without completely wiping them out. However, it should not be concluded that Max Weber's ideal model of the rational state is being established; these changes in reality affect only the liberation war generation, which has been seeing the people it was accustomed to deal with – those of the same age group – leaving official posts. The 'old men', too inclined to criticise the Islamists (who form a large proportion of the new customers), have been sent into early retirement and their positions have been taken today by former FIS voters, who are establishing new sorts of relationship. Ali, a small-scale grocer in Baraki about sixty years old, leaves his son to negotiate all sorts of requests with officials. When seeking a building permit for a plot of land bought from an individual, and a military 'medical discharge' card, Ali was all at sea in the face of the changes:

'At this time it's difficult, they have changed everything; old men like me, they've given them the boot to bring in young people, that's right, they've got to work too. But in the banks, the customs, the Daïra, all my *maarifa* [acquaintances] have gone. Even in the army, you can't go to see someone if you have a problem any longer; if you talk about your son to someone you know in the army, he tells you, "Your son, you see him only during the day, at night you don't know what he does". They've changed now, they don't trust anyone any more, if you have a problem you can't count on anyone any more.' (Algiers suburbs, 1994-5)

The immediate impact of this restructuring was more on those on people who had spent years building up personal relationships to improve their

[8] *El Watan*, 18-19 Oct. 1996.

[9] Families of traders are sometimes victims of 'night-time visitors' who burgle them at gunpoint. In the view of some these are reprisals by the security forces to punish families suspected of having agreed to pay money to the 'Emirs'.

daily lives. However, it did not work perfectly; it remained possible to 'buy' a military 'unfit for service' card, although it was more difficult to get. Its price rose considerably; in 1980, the price was 5,000 French francs (5,000 dinars at the time), in 1996 it was 300,000 dinars (25,000 francs). The 'Emirs' did not hesitate to help the most underprivileged young men to buy national service exemption cards, in return for logistical help for their guerrilla effort.[10]

The reforms did not extend to all the government departments. The posts and telecommunications department (PTT), although the FIS was well entrenched there, was considered a non-strategic department, staff recruitment not being subject to any previous political screening. This deficient department offered only minor advantages, apart from the informal 'hiring out' of the telephone lines to France. Its staff, at the postman level, was among the most Islamised. Wearing of the beard and *hijab* began in the post office before the formation of the FIS in 1989, and this politico-religious passion was kept up during the civil war. The postman at Les Eucalyptus, despite all the threats he faced, went on wearing his beard and displaying his desire for the creation of an Islamic state. Similarly, from 1993 onwards the armed groups dynamited the main telephone exchanges in the larger suburbs of Algiers, to prevent the installation of a 'Green Number' intended to enable people to telephone district police stations to inform the security forces of the presence of possible 'terrorists' without fear of being overheard. The infiltration of Islamists into the PTT administrative departments was a known fact, which led people to develop codes incomprehensible to the Islamists – who were said to be listening in to individuals' calls – for communication among themselves.

The PTT, brought into line with new forms of communication, introduced terminals for mobile telephones, to the great satisfaction of the better off. A market even developed for Chinese-made mobile phones. The use of that means of communication by the armed groups from 1992 put an end to that experiment. Profoundly affected by the war, because of the widespread destruction of telephone exchanges, the PTT was among the departments least affected by the ongoing restructuring of the civil service; it is true that it was already filled up with young Islamists...

Besides being encouraged to create jobs at the commune level, the new Walis were made responsible for settling local disputes over property rights and building permits. To that was added equitable redistribution of housing and assistance towards ownership of property. Those measures, previously unimaginable, were like a miracle for the population.[11] The

---

[10] According to evidence collected in the suburb of Les Eucalyptus in 1994-5 and among young Algerian 'illegal immigrants' in France, who had national service exemption cards.

[11] According to a study by the Ministry of Housing in 1993, '21 million Algerians are estimated to live in conditions of overcrowding in homes, 12.3 million inhabitants live

local disputes denounced by the FIS municipal councillors in 1990-91 could not be resolved by them, because of the abolition of the APCs' main prerogatives by the government in 1990. After 1994, paradoxically, while state cement works were the object of acts of destruction and sabotage, '180,000 homes were built' according to Ahmed Ouyahia's government, with the help of private entrepreneurs using machinery for cement manufacture set up in the Dellys Ibrahim region. At the same time, a programme to build four new towns was revived during 1995, with the aim of relieving the strain on overpopulated urban areas.

The Walis and heads of the DECs, called upon since 1994 to settle all the local disputes, and striving to 'restore confidence', came up against the authority of the 'Emirs' of the communes of the Algiers area in the course of their work. For example, in Les Eucalyptus the DEC started a concerted policy of regularising illegal building. Villas, business premises and other buildings, built on commune-owned or private land, had never been regularised, but from 1994 this was possible. For that purpose applicants had to pay a local property registration tax, estimated then at 80,000 dinars. Thus what the ex-FIS municipal councillors in 1990-1 had planned to do, the DECs started, to the great relief of the population. However, the 'Emirs' threatened anyone who paid national or local taxes; thus Kassem, a petty trader, who had voted for the ex-FIS – but who, he said, was against the armed groups' *jihad* – wanted to legalise his house, but dared not go against the *diktat*s of the local 'Emir':

'For us it was an unhoped-for opportunity, we had always lived with the fear that they would come to throw us out one day, now today they want to help us, but the way is blocked. If you pay and the others (the armed bands) hear of it, they kill you. They want money for themselves, they accuse you of paying for the army through taxes; so we just wait.' (1994, petty trader, Algiers suburbs)

Clearing the backlog of local disputes by the DECs was part of the economic policy of eroding the FIS' electoral support. The idea was to satisfy those voters' former demands so as to separate them from the armed groups. The duty to pay taxes, although very often evaded, in this case resembled a sign of allegiance to one camp. The struggle for the monopoly of taxation, as Charles Tilly emphasises, foreshadows recognition of the political legitimacy of the authority doing the 'extortion'.[12]

At the same time, the government undertook measures from 1993 to facilitate ownership of property. They concerned people born in villages

---

in homes with an occupancy rate between seven and ten people, 8.9 million live crowded at the rate of more than 12 per house'; 60 per cent of housing in Algeria consists of homes of two to three rooms. See Rabia Bekhar, 'Les habitants bâtisseurs de Tlemcen' in *Les Annales de la recherche urbaine*, no. 66, March 1995.

[12] C. Tilly, 'War Making and State Making as Organized Crime' in P.B. Evans, D. Rueschmeyer and T. Skocpol (eds), *Bringing the State Back In*, Cambridge University Press, 1985, pp. 169-91.

of the interior but living in Algiers or other places and wanting to return to the communes of their birth. Financial assistance of 150,000 to 200,000 dinars was provided by the state for successful applicants.[13] That assistance was intended to encourage the return of migrants from the interior of the 1980s, living in an uncertain situation in the big cities, so as to relieve the pressure on housing. It attracted those who had no capital, who now found this unexpected help from the government. Driss, a day building worker in Algiers, originally from the east, rented a cellar with two other companions in a housing estate. He was married and father of two children; his family lived in his home village. He expressed admiration for the government after that measure. Not interested in politics, he wanted only to arrive unharmed on his monthly bus journey to his home village, as the journey was so full of traps:

'It [the government] helps us now, it's true. They give you money to build your house. The commune where you were born pays you 200,000 dinars, it's unbelievable! As for me, all my family lives in the village. Here in Algiers, I sleep in a cellar or else at the site where I work. Thanks to this assistance I am going to buy a flat and start a small business. What they have been doing is good for us poor people. It's true, it's a law which helps us, I would never have been able to buy it before, I earn 4,000 dinars per month when I work every day. It was impossible without help, thanks to them I am going to get out of here.' (Day worker on a building site, 1994, Algiers suburbs)

The establishment of this procedure for home ownership,[14] and procedures for resolving local disputes, supplemented the job creation measures which, according to Prime Minister Ahmed Ouyahia, made it possible to create 150,000 jobs between 1994 and 1996.[15] Just as the 'Constantine Plan' in 1958 sought to remove the material causes of the uprising,[16] so the government's programme has sought to whittle away the social grievances voiced by the former FIS elected representatives. International financial aid, far from concerning only military employment, has been involved in the elaboration of this economic policy. However, that policy did not follow the logic of production, it had no other purpose than the isolation of the armed groups by challenging them on their own ground. Paradoxically, the people had rarely had so much financial aid offered them, since

[13] Decree no. 93-94 of 23 March 1993.

[14] According to Prime Minister Ahmed Ouyahia 21,000 grants were made by the state for construction of rural homes, equivalent to a financial allocation of 2.6 million dinars; *El Watan*, July 1996.

[15] *El Watan*, 21 May 1996.

[16] The Constantine Plan, writes J.-C. Vatin, a 'technocratic achievement, was a project for Algeria's development formulated during the war of liberation. It aimed to industrialise the country by preparing the ground for heavy industry, and provided for development of agriculture through renovation of the "bled" where the ALN guerrillas found support. The Constantine Plan was a sort of gamble on rapid peace because its political authors thought it could be an instrument for that peace.' J.-C. Vatin, *L'Algérie politique. Histoire et société*, Paris: Presses de la FNSP, 1983, p. 289.

for all the protagonists they were the stake in the contest. Taking part in an economic race against the regime, the 'Emirs' were in an inferior position because their war chest amounted to little in the face of the government's budget. Only large-scale actions of sabotage and destruction against the oil and gas facilities in the 'exclusion zone'[17] would bring the government's budget down to the level of that of the 'Emirs'. Short of that, the social reconquest of the nation seemed to work in the regime's favour, as its resources remained very much greater than those of its rivals.

International aid and redrawing of the political landscape

Financially stifled in 1993, the regime had considerable financial room for manoeuvre again in 1995-6. Debt rescheduling in 1993-4 brought the debt servicing burden down from 90 per cent of exports of goods and services in 1991 to 35 per cent in 1995.[18] That made it possible for Algeria to have available 'until 1998 $7 billion cash from its exports instead of putting them aside to pay its creditors.'[19] To that was added multilateral financial aid estimated at $5 billion in 1994; although this increased the amount of debt in the long term, in the short term it made it possible for the government to pay for its war economic policy. The return of private investment in the oil and gas sector, following the reform of legislation covering that sector in 1991, also facilitated the involvement of private partners in the maintenance of the regime, through investment which increased and in the medium term consolidated the state's revenue. So international financial backing enabled the regime in an initial period, from 1992 to 1994, to develop a security-oriented policy (purchase of arms,[20] recruitment, modernisation of the repressive apparatus), and, in a second period, to establish social and economic arrangements aimed at satisfying the demands of some of those who had voted for the FIS. And did flight of foreign currency in 1994 not reveal the price paid to buy off the former military leadership close to President Chadli Bendjedid, replaced by officers close to General Lamari?[21]

Financial indebtedness: an asset in the consolidation process. The opening up of the oil and gas sector to foreign companies,[22] and the liberalisation

[17] Since 1995 the oil producing regions have been out of bounds to civilians, an official permit is needed to move around there.

[18] Source: Banque d'Algérie, quoted in *La Tribune*, 17 June 1996.

[19] *La Tribune*, 23 July 1995.

[20] Purchase of personnel carriers from Turkey for $200 million: *Très très urgent*, 8 Nov. 1994.

[21] Between 1994 and 1995 financial aid which had vanished into thin air was estimated by the French Nord-Sud Export consultants, in a study of the situation in Algeria, at a billion dollars out of external loans of $7 billion. N. Chevillard (ed.), 'Algérie: l'après-guerre civile', *Nord-Sud Export Conseil*, June 1995, p. 99.

[22] Since the reform of the legislation in 1991, the oil sector has been open to foreign investment.

of trade and privatisation of state enterprises, were responses to economic imperatives linked to implementation of the Structural Adjustment Programme, but also to political considerations. First of all, a sufficient inflow of resources had to be secured to ensure financing of the security policy and the policy of winning over the FIS voters. But at the same time, foreign investors (in oil and gas) have been tying their interests a bit more to the survival of the regime: defence of the profits they are earning means defence of those who make them possible. The multitude of requests for credits and other loans is part of the same logic: they tighten the links between the interests of the international community and the fate of the ruling team. Indebtedness has therefore become a guarantee of creditors' backing for the regime. This international financial backing arouses the bitterness of the Islamists, who are convinced that it is one reason for the guerrillas' relative failure in their efforts to overthrow the regime:

'They should not have given them money directly, they are thieves. I have never seen a country where the leaders think only of placing their money abroad. Those billions they receive, do you think they will come back to Algeria? Never, I swear to you that they will return and immediately go out the other end. Why? Because they don't give a damn for Algeria. In addition, they know the Moudjahidin are going to win, so they are going to place the money in Switzerland or France, as usual.' (GIA sympathiser, Algiers suburbs, 1994)

GIA sympathisers, convinced that international financial aid is diverted for private purposes, discovered in 1996 the other side of the economic weapon. The policy of eroding electoral support for the Islamists and strengthening the apparatus of repression made use of financial aid. This way of seeing international financial aid, a very firmly held one, is part of an outlook which sees the political and military leaders as heirs to the Beylik – that is, to the Turkish occupiers of the Regency of Algiers between the sixteenth and the eighteenth century – and thus as inevitably strangers to Algerian society. It goes together with the 'archaic idea' of the state as an alien structure, whose consequences in practices of theft and embezzlement were deplored by President Boumedienne,[23] and also resembles the 'us' and 'them' of the 'poor man's culture'.[24] That certainly does not mean that there is not real embezzlement in which all the actors are involved.

However, it was only in the aftermath of the presidential election of 16 November 1995 that foreign companies entered into partnership contracts, like that signed by BP, which acquired a stake in gas marketing with an investment of $3.5 billion. An American company has invested $1.3 billion in the Rhourde el Baguel oil field, while Total and Repsol have a joint project, estimated at $700 million, relating to the Tin Fouyé Tabankort site. Those regions, out of bounds to civilians, are under the protection of mercenaries recruited by the oil companies. *Jeune Afrique*, no. 1830, 31 January 1996.

[23] See Houari Boumedienne's speech in *Révolution africaine,* 28 Sept.-4 Oct. 1997.

[24] Richard Hoggart has recorded, in popular culture, escapist and cheating conduct that constitute a form of autonomy: 'Dishonesty towards the others becomes a form

The political prospects opened up by this international financial back-ing have been seen in the reshaping of the system through a coalition of political and economic actors, brought together in support of the regime. The holding of the presidential election on 16 November 1995 was aimed as much at reassuring the international community about the consolida-tion of the government as at restoring a degree of confidence among the various social groups mobilised in the repression. Is the state, having been refloated financially, in a fair way to become the dominant player again?

Formation of new coalitions. The reshaping of the regime's authority from 1994, and its claim to be leader of society again after a phase of loss of legitimacy, were a remarkable demonstration of 'state formation' analysed by B. Berman and J. Lonsdale, in their study of Kenya, as 'an historical process whose outcome is a largely unconscious and contradictory pro-cess of conflicts, negotiations and compromises between diverse groups.'[25] The ability of the actors embodying that authority to form coalitions of interests in spite of varying political commitments ensures their contin-ued tenure of power. The reshaping raises questions, to use J.-F. Bayart's expression, about the 'principle of incompletion which the modern state continues to obey, beyond the illusions of bureaucratic and national cen-tralisation'.[26] These new forms of alliance contracted by the regime since 1992 (with the world community, the private sector, Hamas) are involved in that 'principle of incompletion'. While the three Charters – the Tripoli Charter soon after the Evian agreements, the Algiers Charter of 1964 and the Charter of 27 June 1976 – declared Socialism to be the ideological frame-work, thirty years after independence, with the same conviction, the mar-ket economy is established as the fundamental point of reference for the nation. The nationalisation of oil and gas in 1971 has been answered with the liberalisation of that sector in 1991; in succession to the alliance of the bureaucracy and the FLN with the army has come the creation of new power bases founded on the private sector and Hamas-MSI.

Are such changes in coalitions of interests due to the wider context? While the promotion of the private sector was one demand made by the IMF, the fact remains that that sector includes a large number of 'weighty' Islamist voters whom the regime has been accommodating so as to separate them from the Moudjahidin. In short, the encouragement of the private sector amounts to boosting the finances of Hamas-MSI which has close links with

---

of loyalty to the family or the social group. You don't "pinch" anything from your neighbour, but you "fiddle" what you can out of the firm or the administration.' *La culture du pauvre*, Paris: Minuit, 1970, p. 330.

[25] J. Lonsdale and B. Berman, *Unhappy Valley: Conflict in Kenya and Africa*, London: James Currey, 1992, BK. 1, p. 5.

[26] Jean-François Bayart, 'L'historicité de l'Etat importé', *Les Cahiers du CERI*, no. 15, 1996, p. 17.

entrepreneurs, and this explains why that party has been recently promoted to a role of partnership in power. Has the establishment of a market economy in place of the 'Socialist' development model been aimed at the emergence of a national leadership composed of military officers and Islamist entrepreneurs? In the Mitidja Hamas-MSI had considerable support among traders,[27] like the FIS. The presenting of separate Hamas candidates in the parliamentary elections of December 1991 deprived the FIS leaders of part of their financial sponsorship; the result was deep-seated enmity between the two parties.[28] The 25 per cent share of the vote obtained by Mahfoudh Nahnah in the presidential election of 16 November 1995 showed his capacity to win over not the mass FIS electorate – which was supporting the guerrillas or had joined the security forces – but the expanding Islamist 'bourgeoisie'. The appointment of one of the Hamas leaders, Réda Hamiani, to the post of Minister of Small and Medium Enterprises in the government formed by Ahmed Ouyahia in January 1996 was the direct consequence of that alliance between Mahfoudh Nahnah's party and a private sector with Islamist sentiments.

This political determination to reshape the system of alliances, expressed by the regime in holding the presidential election, forced the ex-FIS leaders to take a position regarding the army and the Islamist guerrillas, and also, more recently, regarding MSI-Hamas also. But can the latter party, which seems to have become very bourgeois – Mahfoudh Nahnah has been nicknamed Sheikh El Paga because of his alpaca suits – take the place of the FIS, whose leaders like to show off their wearing of the *djellaba*?[29] Ideological affiliation to the Muslim Brotherhood of Egypt, and the customary dress code of its militants (suit and tapering beard), set the MSI-Hamas apart from the populist practice of the FIS, inherited directly from the Parti du Peuple Algérien – on which the historian Carlier emphasises the confraternity-type influence of Messali Hadj.[30] So Mahfoudh Nahnah called for that presidential election while the ex-FIS rejected it categorically – while not believing in the possibility of its happening anyway.[31] However, the attitude of the ex-FIS leaders to the redrawing of the political landscape showed clearly the stakes and economic interests behind it:

[27] See A. Kapil, 'Les partis islamistes en Algérie: éléments de présentation', *Maghreb-Machrek*, no. 133, 1991, p. 110.

[28] In the municipal elections of June 1990 the FIS brought together various trends in Islamism; the victory in the municipal elections was therefore the victory of the Islamist camp and not of a single party. But Hamas, less and less inclined to endure the supremacy of the FIS, put forward its own candidates in the parliamentary elections of December 1991. It only got 5 per cent of votes cast then (370,000 votes).

[29] Like Mohamed Saïd, whose statements about wearing of the *djellaba* during the electoral process aroused a storm in the press.

[30] Verbal comment made during a seminar at the CERI in 1996.

[31] In September 1995 the FIS' underground press organ headlined 'the inevitable setback', referring to the holding of the presidential election: 'Now that it is more and

His special adviser Mohamed Betchine, the man who wants to make Zéroual an elected president at any price, is one of the representatives of those interest groups. And behind Betchine, the man of networks who is supposed to protect Zéroual from a new 'Operation Boudiaf', are there not a certain Ketfi and a better known man, Ali Kafi, worthy representatives of the medicines and food and agriculture lobby connected with the Italian market? From that we understand better that Zéroual is now the hostage of a senseless political logic (presidential elections, and ever more eradication) and the insatiable economic appetites of people who would like to operate behind a president created by them.[32]

Apart from the reference to Italy which seeks to compare this system with that of the Mafia, the obstacles to reshaping of the system, far from being shown as political in nature, seem here to be related to economic interests. The hypothesis that can be developed of successful integration of Hamas into the political system is linked with its economic strength. The connection of its commercial networks (jewellery shops, food and agriculture, butchers' shops) with those operating within the regime has facilitated its political integration.[33] That is why the ex-FIS leaders consider it as a 'satellite of the government'.[34] Indeed the overlapping of its political and economic activities has made it a political player that can be controlled, and perhaps the Islamist party most adapted to the political system.

The political extension of international aid is thus not limited to the security policy; aid is a partner in the consolidation of the regime and the reshaping of political alliances. The conditions imposed by the IMF in fact fit marvellously together with the demands of the Islamist 'bourgeoisie', backed by the private sector. The political integration of the Islamists of Hamas (or even of a neo-FIS[35]) is a sort of political consequence of the IMF

---

more obvious that it is impossible to organise the presidential elections within the planned time scale, there remains an honourable solution for the army: to put those elections off to an indefinite date,' *El Mounqidh*, September 1995, p. 46. The AIS embarked on 'a strategy aimed at the fall of the government and the failure of its plan to organise the presidential election', according to a communiqué published in *Al Sharq al-Awsat*, 7 Oct. 1995.

[32] *El Mounqidh*, 5 Sept. 1995, p. 47.

[33] That party's revenue has not come only from donations by traders; since its inclusion in the government it has profited from the 'rent' of the Mecca Pilgrimage (because of the gold jewellery brought in from Saudi Arabia), but above all from the income of the powerful Mosque Foundation (Fondation de la Mosquée) since the appointment of M. Amar Mehdjoubi (close to Hamas) as head of Religious Orientation. The Mosque Foundation is responsible for maintenance of Koranic schools, it receives financial backing from the Ministry of Finance. But in view of the deplorable state of the Koranic schools, the newspaper *La Nation* has asked: 'Where is the Mosque Foundation's money going then?' *La Nation*, no. 176, 3-9 December 1996.

[34] Interview with Anouar Haddam by the newspaper *La Croix l'Evénement*, 16 Nov. 1995.

[35] The hypothesis of the revival of a neo-FIS is based on the attitude of Ahmed Mérani, one of the founders of the FIS. At a press conference held at the Hotel El Djazaïr in

demands. In reality the adoption of a policy favourable to the private sector since 1994 resembles an effort to cure the grievances of that sector, which the Islamists had voiced politically between 1989 and 1991.

The trade economy and assimilation of the Islamists

The liberalisation policy followed since 1994 seeks to increase the private sector's share in the nation's wealth so as to provide indirect backing for the regime's war effort. Although it was started in 1986 the debate on privatisation and on the introduction of a market economy was widened from 1994, when concrete measures were adopted. The support given to the private sector has thus been part of the policy of assimilating economic actors favouring the Islamists.

Assimilation of private economic players. Under these measures a privileged position has been given to private petty traders, one of the few economic success stories in post-colonial Algeria. That sector, despite government hostility since independence, never ceased to prosper during the Boumedienne period, and literally exploded under the presidency of Chadli Bendjedid. Forced to operate informally, it based its operations on secrecy. The fragmentation of private businesses into a multitude of small-scale units, even subdivision of a family's stalls or businesses, were efforts to avoid attracting the authorities' attention. Even so that sector, linked by highly effective networks, never stopped growing. The sociologist M'Hamed Boukhobza noted that despite the halt in licensing during the 1970s, it had 'a particularly vigorous breakthrough'.[36]

Whereas the private sector represented 25 per cent of GDP until 1980, in 1995 it was near 40 per cent, with 33,382 enterprises, and employed nearly 1,200,000 workers. In addition, according to Prime Minister Mokdad Sifi,[37] '5,000 small business were created and provided 160,000 new jobs'[38] in 1994-5. However, while the private sector operated until 1994 on the fringes of the banking system, according to a method of operating described by Liabes,[39] since then it has benefited from the economic reforms and the

---

March 1995, he urged those members of the *Madjless ech Choura* (Representative Council) of the FIS who were still at liberty to 'break their silence and contribute to halting the bloodshed...You cannot stay passive, behind your closed doors, at a time when girls of 15 to 17 years are having their throats cut...What is going on now is anti-Islamic, irrational, inhuman and not politic.' Quoted by *Algérie Actualité*, no. 1536, 1995.

[36] M. Boukhobza, 'Etat de la crise et crise de l'Etat', *El Watan*, 27 June 1994.

[37] Mokdad Sifi was appointed Prime Minister on 11 April 1994; he was replaced in January 1996 by Ahmed Ouyahia.

[38] Quoted by *Liberté*, 8 Sept. 1995.

[39] D. Liabes, *Capital privé et patrons d'industrie en Algérie, 1962-1980*, Algiers: CREA, 1984.

restructuring of government departments as a whole. This favourable context is the counterpart of the policy of assimilating economic elites with Islamist sympathies, close to the FIS or Hamas. The fear of seeing them contribute to the guerrilla campaign has led the regime to satisfy the whole range of their demands – abolition of price controls and liberalisation of access to foreign exchange – although this has not failed to arouse criticisms and bitterness from members of the former single party.[40]

The Algiers authorities were bound to be satisfied with the policy recommended by the IMF, in view of the local political stakes. The abolition of impediments to trade and enrichment corresponded, also, to the 'economic vision' of the Islamist voters of the ex-FIS, especially traders, as we showed in the first chapter of this book. Paradoxically, three years after the halt to the elections in January 1992, the authorities pinned all their hopes for a new economic take-off on private traders. Having been thrust down since independence, the traders have been coddled since the civil war; they no longer have to undergo visits from price control inspectors, previously so quick to penalise them. This economic policy has been expressed in a wider market share for the private sector. Amir, a biscuit manufacturer who runs several small plants around the country, acknowledged a definite improvement since 1994. Appointments with managers in the banks and the customs service have become easier to get than before, when disputes arise. However, he considered that this legal framework favouring a market economy merely legalised a *de facto* situation, as the private sector had not waited for a decree to do well. The serious problem, for him, lay rather in the irresponsibility of the 'Algerians' and their inclination to make the least possible effort, which prevented a real 'development' of the economy:

'Today there is work, that's true, the government has launched work sites for building, roads and especially production of everyday goods. It is inviting private companies to work with it, but it is short of workers. The young here are lazy, they work for three days and then they tell you, "Give me my pay". They go and get drunk, then a week later they come back to ask you if they can work again. Anyone who doesn't work now, it's because he doesn't want to. He says to you, "I'm working for nothing, what you pay me, I can't buy anything with it", and it's true, for them life has become very hard.' (Amir, biscuit manufacturer, Algiers, 1994-5)

The 'insolence' of these employees, too easily described as idlers, should not obscure the share of contempt (*hogra*) which they feel is directed at them. 'Small people' are treated by employers and senior civil servants in a way that colonial paternalism would not repudiate. In many ways they are considered immature and at the mercy of their impulses, incapable of

[40] In *El Moudjahid*, organ of the FLN, an editorial made this comment: 'Very eloquent but also very revealing: it is not enterprises, still less the state that sucks the citizen's blood, it is rather those parasites the traders – obviously not all – who amass considerable sums at the expense of the consumer and the State.' *El Moudjahid*, 13 June 1995.

restraining their desires. Amir's language was typical of the way the economic and political elites regard the 'lower orders'.[41]

Although an FIS voter and supporter of a completely free market, Amir did not for all that become a devotee of the government after the trade liberalisation. His candidate in the presidential election of 16 November 1995 was Mahfoudh Nahnah. However, he condemned without qualification the violence of the armed groups, which he described as 'terrorists'. Although satisfied with the economic measures taken since 1994, he still remained critical of 'Mafioso' practices. In his view they were to be explained by the absence of firm moral standards, which was turning Algerians into 'thieves' and 'profiteers'. He gave the example of a boat loaded with pharmaceutical products which remained alongside the quay for a year because of false invoicing. Internal changes in the customs service, carried out since the liberalisation of trade and impelled by fear of penetration of some departments by the Islamist guerrillas, have led to stricter checks on imported products. In Amir's view this has been disrupting established import networks where fraud has been reigning with the complicity of French companies:

'That boat carrying 800 tons of medicines is an example that the government gives us to tell us that things are going to change now. Those medicines, they are going to end up in the dustbin, and you know why? The civil servant who went to buy them in France, he bought from the bottom of the barrel, the cheapest, that is medicines which are going to become out of date within the year, but the French companies invoiced him for the most expensive, in collusion with him, and at the Customs in Algeria you can no longer get away with that. The goods are overinvoiced, those who bought them have cleared off, the medicines are rotting and we, when we are ill, we find nothing. That's how Algeria is, those who govern us laugh at us, and those who fixed that deal, they have earned millions in foreign exchange and now you don't see them any more.' (Amir, biscuit manufacturer, Algiers, 1994-5)

Private businessmen's bitterness towards France. However, for those private businessmen, responsibility for the difficulties of the Algerian economic situation does not lie with the Algerians alone; Algeria's economic partners, France in particular, have contributed to them.[42] That is why the

---

[41] G. Hidouci, Minister of the Economy in the government of Mouloud Hamrouche, has written, 'I felt considerable pain at the contempt, often unconscious, in which the mass of ordinary people (those we called the base then) was held, and the refusal to listen to them...' *La Libération inachevée*, Paris: La Découverte, 1995, p. 30.

[42] 'French banks which had a big presence, benefiting from the French state's encouragement through an open credit insurance policy, made very substantial profits in Algeria until the end of the 1980s. The biggest French enterprises (Bouygues, Peugeot, Total) have worked in Algeria and are taking part in the organisation by the Nomen- klatura of the rent economy, whether oil and gas, imports or major contracts are involved. Algeria and France are linked by real networks of economic influence.To sum up, Elf has been nationalised but Total is protected...' 'Comprendre l'Algérie', *Note de la Fondation Saint-Simon*, July 1995, p. 28. For a criticism of French policy in Algeria see L. Provost, *La deuxième guerre d'Algérie*, Paris: Flammarion, 1996, 198 pp.

sense of an improvement in the administrative and banking system has been tempered by a rejection of the structural relations linking Algeria with France. Those businessmen consider that the Algerian economy's ills spring from that relationship, and they suggest the alternative of partnership with the United States, supposed to be more efficient.

'Of course it's better to trade with the Americans, they love freedom of trade, they do not give money to the [Algerian] state mindlessly as France does. For us America is better because wheat, sugar, oil, clothes, everything is cheaper there. I went to Saudi Arabia for the *umra* [visit to the Holy Places], the franc is worth nothing there, while the dollar is something. The products came from America, the Saudis are respected by the Americans. We buy everything from France, even toilet soap, and the French treat us as less than zero. They don't like us, why trade with them? The FIS was right, we must learn English to trade with the Americans.' (Petty trader, Algiers, 1994-5)

For that petty trader, the influence of Saudi Arabia was not measured by its religious propaganda (*daawa*) or its position as custodian of the Holy Places of Islam, but by the abundance and diversity of the products offered for sale in its traders' stalls. Certainly he too has been able, since 1994, to get supplies without difficulty and make substantial profits, as the level of prices has risen so much because of the abolition of administrative controls, a measure imposed by the IMF.[43] However, it is from Italy, Spain and Turkey that he has been importing some of his products, those being the only countries that have agreed to give him visas. While state corporations continue to get their supplies on the French market, the private sector traders have since 1992 been building up trade networks with their counterparts in the countries just mentioned. Being unable to go to France, they have been forced to look for new suppliers. In this context Turkey has become the object of boundless admiration. Kaddour, a trader specialising in meat distribution, was 'disgusted' by France's restrictive visa issuing policy; from 1994 he stopped applying for a visa, out of pride. The humiliation felt at the extreme difficulties involved in the process for individuals like him led him to make contacts with Turkey, whose economy has a good image in public opinion. He has a business visa for that country and goes regularly to Istanbul where a community of Algerian private businessmen is beginning to get organised.

In addition that animosity against France and its visa policy has spread to other social groups, such as retired people, former workers in France who turned to petty trade, whose pensions were blocked until 1994. In view of the high cost of living in Algeria, they were angry at not being able to go to France to collect their retirement pensions, which served as a foreign exchange reserve for their small-scale trading activities. The retirement pensions, when exchanged on the unofficial currency market, made considerable gains possible, which were invested in the family business. It was

[43] In July 1995 there was a 50 per cent rise in the prices of food products: *La Tribune*, 23 July 1995.

only in 1994, as a result of the reform of the banking system and an inter-banking agreement, that it became possible to pay the retirement pensions into Algerian banks. Meanwhile the accumulation of criticisms of French policy increased nationalist feeling, already a constant feature of that segment of the population.

Liberalisation of the economy was for the government a political instru-ment for changing public opinion. Steady assimilation of the economic actors from the private sector into money-making networks hitherto reser-ved for the state sector helped to lure them away from the temptation to go into partnerships with the guerrillas. It did not however prevent ties from being formed between the guerrillas and the private sector, although, as we emphasise in the next chapter, those ties were due more to favourable circumstances than to political commitment. In a parallel process, the political opening provided by the Hamas party facilitated the political reintegration of the economic actors after the dissolution of the FIS. The liberalisation of trade thus facilitated the integration of the private trad-ers, it made them respectable actors able to make an economic 'take-off' possible. Those economic actors, considered valuable by the regime and the IMF, were given responsibility in the civil war; for the traders and pri-vate enterpreneurs, the time of contempt and anonymity sees to be gone.

Change of course for the trabendistes. While trade liberalisation had the effect of bring the private sector closer to the interests of the regime, it also allowed the legalisation of *trabendo* for 'petty' operators. The *trabendistes* saw that liberalisation as recognition of their activity, a legalisation of infor-mal trade; permission to import put an end to the 'extra-legal' character of activity that had already been made difficult by the impossibility of trav-elling freely in Europe. The cutback in delivery of visas for France (800,000 in 1991, less than 50,000 in 1994)[44] put an end to the Marseilles trip that people took to buy consumer products for resale in Algeria. Deprived of the means of working, the *trabendistes* placed themselves at the service of the 'Emirs' and the Islamist guerrillas. With their detailed knowledge of the operation of the customs service and informal border crossings, they were a decisive help to the Moudjahidin in the supply of false documents, arms and other necessities for the guerrilla campaign.[45] Those professional traders collaborated with the 'Emirs' when the latter wielded authority over the major suburbs of Algiers in 1992-3, to the detriment of the military entrepre-neurs, their former 'bosses'. The *trabendistes'* dependence on the policy of the 'Emirs' continually grew from then on. It went together with the armed groups' monopoly of management of the main resources of urban districts. Being 'technically unemployed', the *trabendistes* offered the local armed bands and the guerrillas a reserve of dynamic, resourceful and experienced

---

[44] *Le Monde*, 3 Feb. 1995.

[45] According to the evidence of Algerian 'illegal migrants' collected in 1995 in France.

young men, from which they drew some of their logistical staff. Their skill in matters of getting round the state noticeably enhanced the 'professionalism' of the GIA 'Emirs'. However, being by nature ready to 'move on', they anticipated the coming of a trading economy and were later the first to part company with the *jihad*.[46]

From small villages in the interior (such as Barika, a centre of the informal trade) to the big suburbs of Algiers, the *trabendistes'* reputation was by now well established in Algeria. In the 'hit parade' of desirable marriage partners they came just after Raï singers and footballers, well ahead of qualified jobseekers. They were symbols of ambition, daring and the future of a certain generation, lucid and pragmatic about the real possibilities of social advancement. Fascinated by the careers of the *nouveaux riches* in Algeria and elsewhere, they dreamed of imitating them. Their outlook was close to that of the fighters of the armed groups, in which swindling and risk-taking were paths to accumulating wealth; they were however at the opposite pole from the 'militants of Islam' among whom strict and rigorous morality prevailed. Although the latter sometimes envied their skill at adapting to different contexts..

M'hamed the trabendiste. M'hamed, a *trabendiste* by trade, has never done any other sort of work. Coming originally from a small village in the Constantine area, son of a landless peasant who passed half his life in France working in the iron and steel industry before returning at the beginning of the 1980s with the first wave of redundancies and dying two years later, he managed for his family the money orders sent by his father. Like others of his generation he had an ambition to become rich like those who were seen rising up in their Mercedes and Golfs during the 'Chadli years'. His model was Kader, about forty years old, a child of a *douar* like him, today the owner of many businesses. With a Peugeot 505 Kader started his *trabendo* by buying products at Marseilles, when a franc was worth one and a half dinars in 1980. Every weekend, after his work in industrial plants at Sétif where he had got a job thanks to one of his uncles, he crossed the Mediterranean to fill his car with luxury goods (soap, perfume, wedding dresses etc.). His success was so rapid that he employed young men, including M'hamed, who were ready to make such trips with all expenses paid. M'hamed, 'specialising' in the Maghreb, travelled to Algeria's neighbour states:

'I went to Morocco, Tunisia, even Egypt, but never to France. Now I am building my house and I am going to set up a food store downstairs. And, *Inshallah,* I am

[46] 'A good many of [these] applications for registration as trading enterprises are said to come from notorious *trabendistes* who consider that the country's present situation allows them not only to develop trading activity in complete security, but also to make fabulous profits (in the case of the import-export companies) in the absence of strong competition.' *El Watan*, 9 July 1996.

going to get married soon, and we shall go to France for a holiday.' (1993, small village in the interior)

Trade liberalisation greatly assisted his work by legalising *trabendo*. But earlier, 1993 and 1994 had been two difficult years for him; the sudden halt to the automatic issuing of visas by countries bordering Algeria, and the danger involved in smuggling goods because of the risks in illegal border crossings, put a stop to his activity. The state's determination to recover its authority over the territory was reflected in the halt to informal activity, which had been a safety valve for many. The fear that *trabendo* would be converted into a weapon of war used by the guerrillas led to restrictive measures aimed at eradicating it through the closure and increased surveillance of the border with Morocco. This change however caused a real problem for those who, unlike M'hamed, did not have the time to build up capital. Resources that had previously come from *trabendo* were now obtained through war, and they duly sustained the new forms of trade developed in Algeria with the import-export companies.

A *common political* imaginaire

The Wali, the Guerrilla and the Eminent Person: the Bled es Siba *lives again.*

'Here, in the Daïra of Khémis el Khechna and especially in Ouled Moussa, the terrorists are backed by five big families whose children are either in prison or in the maquis. We know them as we know the routes they take when they come down from the mountain which you see facing you. It can happen that you meet them right in the middle of town. We know them and they know us very well.' (A member of the Commune Guard, 1995)[47]

Like the armed bands in the urban areas, the guerrillas of the interior of the country benefit from the complex layout of the local political system. In 1992, while the urban APCs (Assemblées Populaires Communales) headed by ex-FIS elected representatives were dissolved, those of the rural areas, although Islamist, escaped being turned into DECs (Délégations Exécutives Communales). The local elected representatives in rural areas were very close to families of eminent local persons that had emerged through the war of liberation; was that why they experienced less repression than others? In June 1990 their children, FIS activists, took over the APCs, until then controlled by members of their families who were FLN 'activists'. The security measures to deal with the Islamist phenomenon were different in that context from those prevailing in the urban setting.

In fact, on the interior front eminent local personalities, 'Emirs' and Walis are united in a common *imaginaire*, not so much by political or family membership, but by similar personal backgrounds. For example, Si Lakhdar's career arouses fascination among the guerrillas; it fills them with certainty that war leads to social advancement. On his side he acknowledges their capacity for endurance, initiative and cunning which makes them attractive to him to some extent. To him the guerrillas seem like sons worthy of their fathers, looking out for a favourable context for increasing the family's fortune. How many leading families in the interior of the country do not have children in the maquis or in prison? The father's displeasure at seeing one of his sons joining the guerrillas is compensated by the feeling that it shows the son is courageous and enterprising; he feels secret pride at this. In short his son, although mistaken, by acquiring the status of a local 'Emir' enhances the family's name.

The 'Emir' and the prominent local citizen complement each other; the latter is a model for the former. Certainly not all the 'Emirs' have prominent local citizens as fathers; even so, they know the careers of the eminent local persnalities, whom they set forth as an example. Both groups of people are shaped by that war-oriented *imaginaire*; both come up against the state's claim to have a legitimate monopoly of violence. For them the state amounts to families which knew better than theirs how to exploit the war of liberation – in short, an *'asabiya* that has succeeded', according to M. Seurat's expression.[48] The result is hostile coexistence between the prominent local citizen and the 'Emir'. However, with the Wali (prefect) they work tacitly together, despite deep-seated political differences, for the maintenance of civil peace in their commune. The murder of a guerrilla or a politician is the result of a targeted choice, patiently weighed and not supposed to cause any upheaval among the leading people of the village; the victim is very often of humble origin and without any protection. The management of violence thus involves measured doses that are governed by only one imperative: not to set the law of vengeance in motion. Everyone avoids it in the village, which is a rear base for everyone: policeman, Moudjahid and 'Emir' know each other without talking with each other. Outside the village everyone, wearing the dress and title of his function, is free to kill, rape or rob whomever he thinks fit, in accordance with his war tactics. That choice explains the relative calm of many villages in the interior, which in that way avoid the burdensome presence of army units.

Even when the Islamist APCs were dissolved and replaced by DECs in 1992, the Chairmen of the DECs, drawn from the local authorities, only rarely challenged this set-up; this sometimes meant that they were condemned for 'corruption', or even for complicity with the Islamists.[49] Anxious

---

[48] M. Seurat, 'Le quartier de Bâb Tebbâne à Tripoli' in M. Seurat (ed.), *L'Etat de barbarie,* Paris: Seuil, 1989, p. 131.

[49] This sometimes led to dissolution of the DEC; one example was the decision taken against a small town in the east: '...illegal practices by the Chairman of the DEC regarding state property, and his negligence in taking responsibility for citizens' preoccu- pations, as well as his bad management and serious excesses such as favouritism and nepotism, at the expense of the people's interests...', *La Nation,* 7 June 1995.

first and foremost to preserve their communes from the violence experienced by the greater Algiers urban area, they gave priority to political and social compromise. This has sometimes resulted in strange situations where supposed enemies rub shoulders to the great amazement of the population. The violence experienced by the Mitidja has been attributed by those local eminent citizens to an anarchic history reflected in the absence of civic culture among the inhabitants:

'They are thieves settling scores, they take advantage because the state is weak there. They kill women and young people for nothing, they have gone mad, because they are nothing. But it's natural that they kill each other, in that city [Algiers] they are all mingled together: Kabyles, Chaouis...You don't know where they come from, those people, what happens over there is impossible here.' (FLN member, retired, 1993-4)

In 1992 and 1993 Walis and prominent local people were convinced that they had the Islamist phenomenon under control, at least in their own communes. After the banning of the FIS in March 1992, and the flare-up in the Algiers area, they embarked on strict control over their own 'Islamists'. The fear of meeting the same fate as the Mitidja was a powerful incentive. The leading families of eminent people of the FLN, in partnership with other players in the commune, turned the village into a prison:

'Here, every morning the "bearded ones" go to the police station, if they don't go and something happens, it's they who are responsible. One should be without pity for people like that. They are after their own interests, that's all, they can destroy the country just for money.' (FLN member, retired, 1993)

This control became blurred after 1994; the local Islamists joined the maquis and sometimes returned with the title of 'Emir'. For the authorities, from then on it was with the 'Emirs' that negotiations were conducted on the maintenance of civil peace in the commune. Leading citizens and Walis involved them in the running of local affairs, they took part in the life of the village, without any risk to themselves.

In the rural communes the FLN was a much stronger political party than in the suburbs of Algiers. In contrast to the Islamist activists of the Algiers region, those of the small villages had no ambition to reform morals; their social and urban environment was different from that of the large built-up areas of Algiers; and because of the closeness of the Islamist voters to local political personalities, they could not use language too filled with anathemas. Indeed the self-proclaimed Imams had plenty of difficulty in describing the soldiers of the local barracks or the police as '*kuffar*' (impious) when those people often prayed in the mosque. In short, the language developed by the FIS leaders in the urban setting sounded hollow, or at least could not work, in the villages.

Only the meetings organised at the 5 July Stadium in Algiers succeeded in transmitting that passion for Islamism. Before taking seats together on the terraces the rural FIS voters worked themselves up on the bus journey by reciting slogans; by the time they were in the stadium they were noisy 'fans',[50] restless from the tiring journey and eager to see the national leaders of the FIS. After the interruption of the elections in January 1992 they followed, as spectators, the mass arrests of Islamist activists. The absence of a curfew and the local management of the 'political crisis' spared many villages the excesses of the repressive policy. In addition, like M'hamed the *trabendiste*, those sympathisers thought that victory for the 'armed Islamists' was inevitable and the regime's days were numbered. This certainty made it possible for them in 1993 to justify their not joining the maquis, then led by the MIA. As Islamist voters, they expected benefits and privileges from their newly elected representatives whom they thought they could manipulate, but who they hoped, above all, would be allowed the chance to govern:

'Algerians could never live in an Islamic state. We shall see what they do, if they work well, so much the better, but we like to drink, to live, to enjoy ourselves, you see how full the garage [a drinking establishment] is. If you think we can live like in Iran, no, that's impossible.' (M'hamed, small interior village, 1993)

Once the FIS elected representatives were gone, the aim of creating an Islamic state was not a motive for joining the guerrillas. Especially as the DECs were beginning the carry out in part the programme on which the Islamists had got themselves elected.

The 'political bandit'. Once the warring parties had been consolidated and the possibility of victory for one or other of them more or less ruled out, the way in which the war was seen evolved towards a viewpoint in which the protagonists appeared as political bandits thirsting after prestige and power. By the end of 1994 the issues at stake in the war had been reduced to the 'appetite' of the military leaders, desiring to keep the 'cake' for themselves in spite of the 'hunger' of the Islamists.

This loss of interest in victory for one of the camps was due to indifference towards the central government: whether nationalist, Islamist, revolutionary or whatever, its political action boiled down to the local management of the communes, organised according to politically opaque interests. Realising that fact, the Islamist voters in rural areas developed modes of political action in which determination and individualism took precedence over expectations of redistributive policies. Convinced that behind every politician a 'bandit' lay hidden, they observed through the

---

[50] M. Tozy has written: 'The FIS draws its ideas from three registers: political, religious, and football-related...Every indication suggests that we are dealing more with fans than with believers in a religious movement under the control of leaders and acting in accordance with a clear and precise doctrinal line.' 'Les tendances de l'islamisme en Algérie', *Confluences Méditerranée*, no. 12, autumn 1994, p. 58.

prism of local political life the struggle of the 'terrorists' against the 'renegades'. The efforts by the warring parties to distinguish themselves ideologically had few effects on them. The 'culture shock' between Islamists and nationalists was reduced to an everyday struggle for power.

This perception of the conflict was based on that of a deeply-rooted closeness between the opponents on the ground; it was because they aimed at the same jobs and had common desires that they were killing each other; Moudjahidin and military were seen as belonging to the same category, they were among those men who had 'virility' and 'appetite'. They were natural claimants to the wielding of power, the war served only to bring about selection among them. There was no possible doubt that power was taken by force of arms.

Is the figure of the political bandit a consequence of the history of men of power in Algeria? Ferhat Abbas considered that the intrusion of that element was related to the diversion of the 1954 Revolution away from its course: he wrote, 'By his coup d'état, Boumedienne gave the nation a bad example. He opened the door to political banditry.'[51] The usurpation of power by violence and the carving up of the country under his presidency by the interior guerrillas[52] then consecrated the reign of political bandits. They set about pacifying the nation by organising at the local level social control comparable to that exercised by the Caïds and Bachagas during the colonial period. They were political bandits, but even so they became eminent local citizens later.

The itinerary of the political bandit figure spans historical periods. While, in the present civil war, it has led to the positions of Wali, military officer, 'Emir' or prominent local person, at other times banditry was the principal path to political life. We noted in the introduction that, in the view of the Algerian historian M. Kaddache, the 'pillars of the state of Al Djazaïr' in the sixteenth century were none other than the Raïs, the corsairs enthroned as governors of regions: 'The Raïs were the third power in the state of Algiers. Most of the Beylerbeys (governors) had been Raïs, great captains who filled the sixteenth century with their great deeds and their bravery.'[53] As a provider of political jobs, 'bandit' activity is part of Algeria's 'cultural code of social advancement'.[54] The ease with which contending players have been incorporated into the power apparatus illustrates, in a certain way, some degree of skill accumulated by the state in that regard. Does that mean that the ways to reach power (since Algiers no longer has a navy)

[51] F. Abbas, *L'indépendance confisquée,* Paris: Flammarion, 1984, p. 110.

[52] M. Harbi notes that 'predation' has been involved in the process of 'political regulation'. See the chapter 'Régulation politique et prédation' in *L'Algérie et son destin.Croyants ou citoyens?* Paris: Arcantère, 1992, p. 192.

[53] M. Kaddache, *L'Algérie durant la période ottomane,* Paris: OPU, 1992, p. 33.

[54] See J.-F. Bayart, S. Ellis and B. Hibou, *La criminalisation de l'Etat en Afrique,* Brussels: Complexe, 1997, p. 80.

inevitably pass through the maquis? That idea makes it possible to understand better the ties linking a certain number of protagonists.

The political bandit is also a convinced nationalist. In that respect he shares with the Islamists another passion, that of the nation. It may be suggested that the strength of the FIS, between 1989 and 1991, was that it was able to revive that feeling; its weakness, that it tried to monopolise it. For the declining role of Algeria on the regional stage has been accompanied by a conviction that the value of an 'Algerian' has gone down, to the point of being no longer respected. For the youngest people, the contrast between the glory of the old days and present reality was so stark that some registered their names at the Iraqi embassy in Algiers to go to fight alongside a real flesh-and-blood hero, Saddam Hussein. The belated revelation of an Algerian nuclear research programme[55] was not enough to reassure the people that the country still maintained its position. For the youngest people the FIS was well and truly the heir to the nationalists of the war of liberation; they saw proof of this in the way the foreign media depicted their party as the devil.

The regime's internal isolation immediately after the halting of the elections was indeed complete; only the war gave it back a semblance of legitimacy. The reconquest of the nation by the army was reflected in the mobilisation of social groups that had been marginalised until then ('ex-combatants', traders, intellectuals...). In that effort the military benefited from the continuous expansion of the armed groups, which, because of their policy of sabotaging and destroying of the machinery of state, reawakened nationalist feeling among the people. The fear that the *jihad* would lead to the break-up of Algeria into a mass of 'Emirates' was a powerful factor mobilising people to support the regime.

Besides that fear there was, among the 'ex-combatants', bitterness at their useless sacrifice. It was with sadness that they saw how Algeria, far from being peaceful and prosperous, was tearing itself apart. Meziane, a soldier of the ALN for six years during the liberation war, did not understand the young Islamists' impatient longing for power; but above all he was dumbfounded by the pretentions of those who were expecting to lead the nation:

'The Islamists, as they say, are abandoned children, they don't know what is the land, they don't know how their ancestors lost it and how we gave it back to them. It is we who are the leaders of Algeria. Before us, people lived in hovels with animals, they died of hunger. But the young, they know nothing and they want everything, all at once, and we, what is to become of us? They want to throw us overboard as if we

[55] In May 1991 there were revelations in the international press about the purchase from China of a nuclear reactor installed in the Aïn Ousséra region. The fears expressed in those foreign newspapers then aroused an upsurge of indignation in the national press: *Alger Républicain* wrote: 'They want to forbid us research into nuclear science because they want to keep our country, like other developing countries, in a state of technological dependence'; quoted in *Libération*, 2 May 1991.

were nothing; to them we are not Moudjahidin. It's we who waged the real *jihad*, and it's they who call themselves "Moudjahid". But if they don't wait their turn, they'll get nothing. They want what we've got, but it must be earned. They, because they have voted, they think they can take everything from us! For that they will have to kill us all, if not they will never be able to give orders to us.' (Meziane, ex-combatant, small village, 1994-5)

The emergence of 'neo-Moudjahidin' (today's guerrillas) is resented as an aggression against their own history; some 'ex-combatants' see the Islamists only as usurpers capable of destroying what they have built. This realisation has led more than one person to join the Commune Guard and the militias which were formed during the year 1994, to 'defend' the nation.

The consolidation of the regime which is proceeding on the basis of the formation of a new coalition, in which the Islamists of the Hamas party are playing a pivotal role, is not synonymous with civil peace. Certainly the regime, by bringing in the 'petty bourgeoisie' of the ex-FIS electorate in this way – made possible by international financial aid – has been able to confront the guerrilla maquis from a stronger position. The administrative reforms and the policy of recruiting for unproductive work ('works of public interest') have deprived the guerrillas of reinforcements. However, on the interior front such a strategy comes up against special logics of war which allow the guerrillas to stay in their villages without fear of the local authorities. The consolidation of the regime has gone together with the prolonged maintenance of zones of dissidence which benefit various local economic actors.

9

ISLAMIST GUERRILLA IDEOLOGY
AND STRATEGY

After turning the communes under FIS local government in Greater Algiers into Islamist 'ghettoes', inaccessible and unendurable for their inhabitants to live in, from 1994 the regime embarked on a policy of letting the maquis turn into sanctuaries. From 1992 onwards several Islamist factions were formed; besides Abdelkader Chébouti's Mouvement Islamique Armé (MIA) there were the Groupement Islamique Armé (GIA) and the Armée Islamique du Salut (AIS). Apart from the GIA those armed Islamist organisations did not succeed in grabbing media attention; they found difficulty in getting national and international press coverage for their military actions, even more for their political demands. The GIA 'Emirs' drew all the spotlight on themselves and kept those of the MEI and AIS in obscurity. In contrast to the 'Colonels' of the Armée de Libération Nationale during the war of liberation, the guerrillas of the maquis failed to get media attention for their cause; this failure was due to a great extent to the censorship imposed by the regime[1] and to the murders of journalists. Probably the fact that the guerrillas, after five years, had not taken control of any city prevented them from basing their authority on a defined space, as the militiamen in Lebanon[2] and the factions in Mogadishu[3] were able to do. In short, the fact that Algeria has not been dismembered into 'Emirates' has increased the difficulty that the armed movements face in conducting a more effective communication policy and, like other guerrilla movements, making their demands known to the world. Only communiqués, leaflets and eye-witness accounts have made it possible to get information. As control over information has been a weapon of war that remained in government hands, it allowed the government, as we analysed above, to demolish through the media the 'mythology of the maquis'.

The guerrillas, just as much as the regime and the Islamist groups of the communes of Algiers, have undergone changes. Confronted with the

[1] In June 1994 the government drew up a document concerning information related to security, for the national media. The editorial offices of the press are now overseen by a communications cell of the Ministry of the Interior.

[2] E. Picard, 'Le triomphe de la culture milicienne', unpublished text; also G. Corm, 'Hégémonie milicienne et problème du rétablissement de l'Etat', *Maghreb-Machrek*, no. 131, 1991, pp. 13-25.

[3] See R. Marchal, 'Les mooryan de Mogadiscio. Formes de violence dans un espace urbain de guerre', *Cahiers d'Etudes Africaines*, XXXII (2), 1993, pp. 295-320.

consolidation of the regime, and the way in which they have been driven further steadily from the towns under the combined effect of militarisation of the urban areas and the creation of suburban Islamist 'ghettoes', they altered their strategies against the regime. Analysis of the changes among the guerrillas shows that the maquis fighters of the various armed organisations have been forced to alter their ideas about the possibilities of victory.

The political guerrillas

Among the various Islamist factions, two are conducting guerrilla warfare that they portray as an extension of political action: the fighters declare that they are acting because of the interruption of the elections in January 1992 and aim through their military action to force the regime to bring the ex-FIS back into the political field. The AIS in addition defines itself as the 'armed wing' of the FIS and continually emphasises that it owes loyalty to the imprisoned political leaders of that party. The MIA, although autonomous, only went to war against the regime after the interruption of the parliamentary elections. Those two armed movements thus embarked on guerrilla war in the name of political issues, and are distinct from other factions that claim to be acting in the name of the vague general idea of the *jihad*. For the MIA and the AIS the fighting model is the ALN. Both impose a military uniform on their fighters (looted from army barracks – this forced the ANP to change its soldiers' uniform in 1995-6). By that uniform the fighters of those factors distinguish themselves from those of the GIA, who have an 'Islamic look' with shaven heads, beards and ample clothing.

The MIA and AIS are subjected, like the other actors, to the dynamics of the war. So there have been deviations from the primary intention of fighting for the legalisation of the FIS; the factions are driven to fight for their own survival. However, both of those factions are, depending on the situation, ready for political negotiations. As their leaders have through the war become intermediaries who cannot be bypassed either by the politicians of the FIS or by the regime, they hope to make political capital out of their armed struggle. However, to achieve this both the MIA and the AIS need to survive the civil war and the competition from other Islamist factions engaged in non-political guerrilla action.

The MIA. The MIA guerrillas have been visible since 1993, but they have had to endure, at the same time as the attacks of the ANP marine commandos, a lack of media interest, in contrast to the armed groups of the Algiers area. Established in makeshift camps from 1990, the first guerrillas following the Mouvement Islamique Armé anticipated the halting of the elections in January 1992. Convinced that the effort to establish an Islamic state through the ballot box was a dead end, they set up in the Blida Atlas the infrastructure necessary for launching an uprising.[4] By agreement with

---

[4] M. Harbi has noted how, influenced by the model of the war of liberation, the MIA

the FIS elected representatives they did not disrupt the course of the parliamentary elections, but they left the big urban centres after the arrest of Abassi Madani and Ali Benhadj. Estimated by the FIS militants at 2,000 in 1992, the MIA fighters formed, after the interruption of the elections, a pole which people could rally around. The intuition and lucid vision of *liwa* (general) Abdelkader Chébouti, 'Emir' of the MIA in 1992, fascinated the FIS sympathisers.

While the security forces concentrated their repressive activity on the militants of the FIS and the small armed groups, such as the 'Afghans' of the Al Takfir wa-l Hijra group, Chébouti's guerrillas developed their war strategy in the maquis. Well equipped with weapons, they did not feel compelled to attack police stations or barracks, in contrast to the Islamist groups in the Algiers suburbs. Thus they avoided the counter-offensives of the security forces, then under way in Algeria's big urban centres as a whole. The Islamist guerrillas' camps, empty in 1991, were besieged after the halt to the elections by an increasing number of young people wanting to join. The ex-FIS was decapitated and abandoned its voters, although they had followed its short political experience passionately.

That capital of three million voters was the object of all rival attentions, and was a stake that all parties vied for. The regime rapidly started breaking it up by mobilising considerable resources; besides the winning back of 'weighty' Islamist voters (traders and private enterpreneurs) there was the recruitment into economic activity of unemployed college graduates sympathetic to the FIS. The economic and political value of that Islamist capital continued to decline from then on, to the guerrillas' great dismay.

The MIA, the front-runner in the competition for the monopoly of the *jihad*, carried out a rigorous selection of candidates, in spite of very high demand for enlistment in 1992 and 1993. Throughout the 1980s the MIA, set up on the model of the Organisation Secrète,[5] waited expectantly for an event that would catalyse the transformation of the organisation into a centre for resistance. Divided into small watertight groups like the 'activists'[6] of the OS, the MIA did not mobilise much at that time. Its dismantling after 1987 by the security forces provisionally put an end to its strategy of armed struggle against the regime.

That first MIA (1982-7) was to be transformed through the civil war into the advance guard of armed Islamism. For the groups formed from 1992

---

created 'sixteen cells with the armed struggle in view. It divided the territory into ten regions, and after making sure it had significant amounts of arms, it passed to action....' 'Et si l'histoire bégayait', *Jeune Afrique,* September-October 1990.

[5] The OS was a small revolutionary group which, between 1947 and 1950, tried to establish a structure for war against the colonial regime. See M. Harbi, *The FLN, mirage et réalité,* Paris: Jeune Afrique, 1980, p. 72.

[6] O. Carlier, 'La guerre d'Algérie et ses prolégomènes: note pour une anthropologie historique de la violence politique', *Naqd,* no. 4, 1993, pp. 32-44.

onwards, that organisation served as a reference; it made it possible for them to distance themselves from the FIS, which was created in 1989, two years after the end of the failed first experiment in armed struggle. This also made it possible for the guerrillas to base the legitimacy of their struggle not on the halting of the elections in 1991, but on the plan to set up an Islamic state through *jihad* as the only way. In that way they freed themselves completely from the FIS, to which they thought they owed nothing; the ideological autonomy of the MIA guerrilla campaign was then clearly affirmed.

For MIA activists the events of January 1992 and the dissolution of the FIS in March were not only a detonator, they proclaimed the start of the Islamist revolution. This change of perspective explains why the Islamist sympathisers considered that the success of FIS elected representatives was due to the failure of the first MIA (1982-7) during the 1980s. Hence the supremacy of the guerrillas over the politicians in the civil war simply reinstated the proper order of things:

'Madani, who was it who raised him up [to the chairmanship of the FIS]? It was the Moudjahidin, so today, it is they who are bringing him down again. What was he before then? Without them? Nothing, like today, he is becoming once again what he was before, that is, nothing much, like all the FIS people except Ali Benhadj.' (Technically qualified jobseeker, Algiers suburbs, 1994)

However, the MIA, although very well placed to lead the *jihad*, failed to capitalise on its organisation during the civil war. Being a secret military movement, it refused to find places in its ranks for the thousands of individuals seized with a 'desire for dissidence' comparable to that which kept the Mozambique civil war going.[7] Fear of being infiltrated by elements of Military Security explained the closure of all avenues for admission to the status of MIA Moudjahid during the year 1992-3. That refusal to democratise the organisation aroused emotion among the Islamist sympathisers longing to fight the security forces. But the pressure of people wanting to join was such (some districts of Algiers were emptied of their young men in 1993) that the MIA maquis were obliged to take on these apprentice fighters who were escaping from arbitrary arrest. Originally the recruiters, scattered over the whole country in 1992, had to make a prior selection of the candidates, notably by getting information from the local population. Later the tests that they imposed on a candidate made it possible to examine the genuineness of his commitment. Those recruiting procedures, in view of the huge influx of volunteers beginning in 1992-3, aroused frustration among those who wanted to fight straight away and did not find places within the MIA. As demand exceeded supply, Islamist activists such as Saïd Makhloufi, competing for the political leadership of the MIA, seized the ooportunity to set up their own schools of war.

[7] Christian Geffray, *La cause des armes au Mozambique,* Paris: Karthala, 1990, p. 77.

The AIS and the 'militarily correct' jihad. While the MIA drew on the historical example of the Organisation Secrète, the AIS, formed in July 1994, was directly inspired by the model of the ALN: 'There is no shame in being like one's parents', proclaimed one of the 'letters to the Moudjahidin':[8]

Yesterday you liberated the land. Today we are liberating honour and religion. You liberated the plains and the Sahara, we are liberating consciences and minds. You fixed the frontiers within which we are going to apply laws. Our *jihad* is the logical sequel to yours. Our blood that flows is the continuation of yours. Your merit can only be ignored by traitors and Harkis who rush to grab bread soaked in the humiliation imposed by certain French circles. By our *jihad* we release you from your responsibility and the oath you took. Congratulations to every Moudjahid who has fathered a Moudjahid, and a thousand congratulations to a martyr who has planted in his wife's womb the seed of a new martyr. (Letter to former Moudjahidin)

The AIS realised that the guerrilla campaign conducted by the MIA was insufficient and that the armed bands which had sworn allegiance to the GIA were incapable of overthrowing the regime; so it called on its troops to be patient because the war against the regime would be a long one: 'Show patience, because patience is the key to pulling through. Show endurance, because the fight is long and decisive. Show firmness, because the enemy is mischievous.'[9] The MIA's hopes of rapid victory were forgotten. In place of the romanticism of the first Moudjahidin, the AIS called for professionalism from its troops.

So, to retain the confidence of the FIS electorate, demobilised by the 'Emirs' of the armed bands, the AIS set about giving an explicit political content to its violence, giving it the aim of the re-legalisation of the FIS. The increasing autonomy of the armed groups and their reference to the MIA as their model relegated the FIS to a marginal role. In short, the dynamics of the war created their own players, who gradually produced a new meaning for the conflict. In order to control those dynamics the AIS clearly proclaimed its political allegiance to the imprisoned leaders of the party, Abassi Madani and Ali Benhadj, the '*shuyukh*'.[10] People reflected on the MIA's failure to overthrow the regime, in spite of its illegitimacy, and a new

---

[8] Collection of letters of the AIS-FIS, entitled *Mots de vérité à ceux qui se sentent concernés*, edited by the FIS overseas executive, April 1995.

[9] Ibid., p. 23.

[10] The national 'Emir', Madani Mezraq, has written, 'Confirming its loyalty to the historic and legitimate leadership linked to the authentic line of the FIS, and anxious to clear away the ambiguity arising from the choice of a national Emir, the AIS brings the following clarifications to the notice of domestic and international public opinion: The most important positions and decisions are taken by the leadership of the party, represented by (1) the *shuyukh* Abassi Madani and Ali Benhadj – may Allah facilitate their release; (2) the AIS, represented by its national Emir, Sheikh M. Mezeraq; (3) the *shuyukh* who have been released; (4) the FIS overseas executive, represented by Sheikh Rabah Kébir': Communiqué no. 3, in *El Mounqidh* June 1995, no. 6.

strategy of struggle emerged. Similarly, the aura surrounding the GIA, and its omnipresence in the national and international media, obliged the fighters of rival groups to respond in kind.

However, the AIS, created in 1994, no longer benefited from the great waves of enlistment in the maquis typical of the years 1992-3. The GIA rallied to its cause all those who wanted to make careers in the *jihad*, notably the district armed bands which claimed to be fighting in its name. The theory that the prisoners in the camps in the South,[11] released from 1993-4 onwards, provided the essential part of the AIS' troops is the most probable. Outside Algeria the AIS in 1994 had human resources at its disposal among Algerian students; it took over all the external networks of the FIS without difficulty. In 1995 its strength increased and was estimated to have reached '40,000 men'[12] before declining in the course of 1996, as will be shown later. It attracted a large proportion of the military deserters who came together in the Conseil du Front Islamique et du Djihad Armé (CFIDA). That structure, sponsored by the AIS, sought to subvert the soldiers of the ANP to its advantage. Paradoxically, the fact of starting two years late in the *jihad* race allowed the AIS to benefit from the misdirections of two years of civil war:

The *jihad* in Algeria has entered its fourth year. The first three years saw the natural emergence of a popular movement of resistance to the generals' dictatorship. It should be said that the interruption of the electoral process in January 1992 and the repression that followed precipitated the movement...The AIS, one of the biggest groups resisting oppression, is established in the four corners of the country. It leads its movement within the strict bounds of the Islamic *Shari'a* which forbids killing of the innocent, mutilation of victims and attacks on those who are not concerned in the conflict, whether they are men or women, children or adults, Muslims or non-Muslims, Algerians or foreigners.[13]

Besides the initial problems there was the question of geographical location, a fundamental one for capitalising on the war economy. For the GIA, established in the Mitidja (the Blida Atlas and Kabylia), used from 1994 the territory previously controlled by the MIA, by then considerably weakened by the security forces. So in the centre and the east, the GIA dominated the strategic main roads (Route de la Corniche, 'Shari'a Express', etc.). There remained for the AIS only the west, the Sidi bel Abbès region in the Ouarsénis, where its first 'companies' set up their maquis. Their lack of income was compensated for by the Islamist pro-FIS diaspora; while the GIA was first able to exploit the resources available in Algeria to the maximum (bank

[11] Soon after the halting of the elections process, between 7,000 and 20,000 activists and militants of the FIS were arrested and held in camps in the Sahara. They were gradually released from later in 1992.

[12] According to *Al Sharq al Awsat*, quoted in *Courrier International*, no. 276, 1996.

[13] *Mots de vérité* (note 8), p. 1.

robberies, protection rackets, hijacking of goods in transit), the AIS benefited from external networks possessing foreign exchange and able to supply arms all the more easily as the GIA networks dominated the attention of the media. The GIA, on the other hand, was only able to convert its stocks of dinars in 1994, after the installation of a trading economy and the partial liberalisation of the foreign exchange market under IMF auspices.

Since its creation the AIS has made a point of distinguishing its struggle from that waged by the other Islamist organisations. It has rejected the GIA's ideology and war strategy because it sees is struggle as political, and military operations remain within strict limits:

The apostate regime today attributes to the *jihad* certain abominable operations of which the defenceless people have been victims...These untruths lead the Armée Islamique du Salut to reply that it is innocent of all those acts and has never given an order to attack a woman, to burn a school or a hospital, or for any other operation contrary to our religion.[14]

Aware that the total war waged by the GIA risks eventually exasperating the people, including those who were favourable to the FIS between 1989 and 1991, the AIS has aimed to rehabilitate the meaning of the *jihad*, distorted by the armed groups. That view of the civil war aims also to win back fighters disappointed by their Moudjahid experience and ready to join the security forces. Humanising the guerrilla campaign seems to have been the aim of the AIS in 1994; this concern responds to the anxiety of all the symapthisers who have witnessed the atrocities committed in the name of the *jihad* in the communes and areas previously supporting the FIS. That political decision is the result of a better understanding of the balance of forces, for in 1994, when the AIS emerged, the flights of lyrical and romantic language on the part of the first Islamist militants had come up against the solidity of the regime.

Drawing lessons from the way in which certain armed groups had evolved, the AIS warned its fighters against the deadly ideology of the GIA which equated the state with 'Taghoût' and the people with 'idolaters'.[15] The AIS considered that the suburban 'Emirs' who had given allegiance to the GIA had squandered the electoral capital of the ex-FIS by their policy, to the benefit of clients linked to its war economy. That was why the AIS, in tandem with its armed struggle, embarked on ideological criticism of the GIA:

They [the GIA fighters] also spread the idea that the people are idolatrous and sometimes Taghoût. They ceaselessly keep count of its simple sins and minor errors which can be corrected by a good word, wisdom, good preaching and good example. This

---

[14] *El Fath el Moubine,* no. 2, 1994.

[15] 'Tâghout' in the Islamic lexicon means the Tyrant, the oppressive state; 'idolaters', those who worship other gods than Allah.

people which has been submissive to God for centuries, which has proved its allegiance to God, its attachment to His religion and its rejection of evildoers on many occasions through glorious revolutions...After all that, it is ignoble to want to treat this people as Tâghout, and yet that is what certain 'Moudjahidin' have reserved for this people which has given them trust and allegiance.[16]

The AIS' analysis has been based on the idea that the GIA is harming the cause (the installation of an Islamic state) more than it serves it. The application of ideologies imported from the Middle East irritates the people and turns Islamist sympathisers away from the *jihad*. Similarly the not very creditable motives of certain 'Emirs' (self-enrichment, hatred, madness etc.) tarnish the general image of the Moudjahidin. Because the AIS was formed two years after the launching of the *jihad*, its activists have the benefit of hindsight to analyse the reasons for the failure of the rebellion. They conclude:

Jihad is not suicide which those in dead end situations take as a solution, those are wretched characters; nor is it vengeance for the benefit of those who want to settle scores, those are motivated by hatred; nor is it an adventure with an uncertain outcome, started by adventurers and outlaws; nor an anarchist movement recruiting all the fugitives and hotheads without standards or rules of life; nor is it a matter of blind honour such as is practiced by the ignorant; nor a leap forward with closed eyes, which would mean a lack of vision and programme.[17]

For the AIS the *jihad* is not that which was waged until 1994 by the 'Emirs' of the GIA, whose motivations are denounced in the text just quoted. This courageous realisation has been all the more urgent for the AIS because in 1994-5 'the adventurers of the *jihad*' drained the reservoir of sympathy among the population formerly supporting the FIS.[18] Popular support for the cause weakened, to the benefit of networks of clients paid by the 'Emirs' to maintain their armed groups. The *jihad*, deprived of political sense, was then seen as a convenient and useful means of appropriating resources. Has the effort made by the AIS to rehabilitate the *jihad* not come too late? For the effort to win back the FIS's Islamist voters is coming up against the effects of consolidation of the civil war.

Indeed, instead of the rapid victory for which ex-FIS militants had such hopes in 1992, there is a daily routine of violence. Having held hegemony between 1989 and 1991, the ex-FIS became just one actor among others after the halt to the elections. While the Greater Algiers communes under the influence of that party were ravaged by the formation of Islamist armed bands and groups of criminals acting with complete impunity, the idea of

[16] Letters to the Moudjahidin, in *Mots de vérité* (note 8), p. 1.

[17] Ibid., p. 20.

[18] The GIA, says a founder member of the FIS in exile, Kamr Eddine Kharbane, 'does nothing but carry out orders from the secret services, and it carries out brutalities in the name of Islam with the aim of befouling the image of the *jihad* and the Moudjahidin'. *Al Hayat,* quoted in *Courrier International*, May 1996.

an Islamic state ceased to mobilise support, and the population took refuge in survival strategies. The issue at stake for the FIS from then on became not only successfully imposing its position within the guerrilla campaign, but giving the use of violence a clear political aim again.

But, being a prisoner of the logic of war imposed by the 'Emirs' of the GIA, it had to react even on ground that it did not choose, such as the internationalising of the conflict, which secured an assured audience for the 'Emirs'. The diatribes of the 'Emirs' against France obliged the AIS to outdo them. Thus France became for the *kata'ib* (companies) an indispensable enemy for a strategy of mobilisation. The 'Brigade of the Oath', affiliated to the AIS, declared, 'The war against France has become a legal duty'.[19] To compete with the GIA's radical rhetoric, the AIS also developed its criticisms; the failure of the rebellion was thus explained by Paris' unconditional backing for the regime:

Crusader France and some of the leaders of unbelief and atheism are working to encircle the FIS leaders who are abroad to impose a political blockade on the voices calling for the right to the Umma and the building of an Islamic state on Algerian soil...Atheist France is not content with its support for the unjust junta, it has even gone so far as supplying it with sophisticated military material such as night combat helicopters and chemical bombs which exterminate living things without destroying buildings.[20]

The determination not to leave the GIA with the monopoly of criticisms of France forced the AIS to keep up its position in the verbal competition. However, it could not allow itself all the excesses like attacks on French soil, for that would mean putting its external support networks in danger, like those of the GIA, which were partially dismantled after the attacks committed in the summer and autumn of 1995.[21] That was why it intensified its efforts principally in the interior of the country, where it tried to bring morality into the *jihad*. As a political guerrilla force, it sought to create 'partisans' totally devoted to the cause of an Islamic state and capable of serving as a model for the population backing it. It called on people not to do what the GIA fighters were doing:

The *jihad* is conscious persistence in principle, great patience in renunciation, strong perseverance in the face of difficulty, sincerity in fighting, contentment with one's fate, humane treatment of the enemy, struggling against aggressors and their puppets, presence at times of sacrifice, restraint in the face of booty, abstinence in the face of pleasure, and renunciation in the face of whisperings from the heart and from Satan.[22]

---

[19] *El Fath el Moubine*, no. 25, 30 Dec. 1994.

[20] Ibid.

[21] Between 25 July and 17 October 1995, three armed groups, in France, carried out a series of bomb attacks in Paris and other parts of France. Those networks were broken up during 1996. *Le Monde*, 17 Jan. 1996.

[22] Letter to the Moudjahidin, in *Mots de vérité* (note 8), p. 22.

These ideological divergences, while they gave rise to disputes among rival 'Emirs', degenerated into armed conflict when one group tried to take over the territory of another. For in doing so such a group placed the very resources of the organisation, and hence its assets in the struggle for the monopoly of the *jihad*, in danger.

The revolutionary guerrillas

The Mouvement pour l'Etat Islamique (MEI). Because there were so few places for candidates for the *jihad* in the ranks of the MIA at the beginning of the civil war, numerous autonomous armed groups were formed. The arrest of ex-FIS cadres initially made it possible for the MIA to have a monopoly of the *jihad*, but rivals were to emerge rapidly: the MEI and GIA. The result was competition for the leadership of the *jihad*, but above all the birth of new forms of war. In place of the elitist vanguard model of the MIA there arose armed groups open to all candidates. The creation of the MEI by Saïd Makhloufi fitted in with this determination to alter profoundly the strategy of the *jihad*. In a pamphlet calling in January 1991 for 'civil disobedience', he turned to an uprising of the population against the regime, as the only chance of overthrowing it:

Injustice is arising and persisting mainly because of the docility and silence of the majority. The government in power has no authority outside that which society willingly gives it through its silence, submission and cooperation. Without our consent and our silence, the regime cannot control more than twenty million people with four hundred thousand soldiers and police...So it is a question of struggling against the unjust and corrupt government by withdrawing confidence from it in order to change it. If the people shows its determination and remains united, the regime in power will fall, despite all the means at its disposal.[23]

Being in favour of an Islamist people's army, the MEI opposed the MIA's strategy based on a war of attrition carried on by professionals. The MIA's refusal to accept the apprentice Moudjahidin into its ranks facilitated the creation of the MEI. The very strong demand for admission into the maquis, because of the repression in the big urban centres, allowed it to hope for a major role in armed resistance. Convinced that it was impossible for the government to maintain itself in power by the use of violence alone, Saïd Makhloufi laid down as his organisation's duty not a struggle against the Algerian army – in view of the imbalance of forces – but politicisation of the 'people' in favour of Islamist ideas, that being, in his view, the only way to overthrow the government. It set about working on the 'people' so as to isolate the regime, because without the 'people' the regime could not survive. In that way he altered the stakes in the war and clearly parted company with the MIA. While the MIA confined itself to a strictly military logic, Makhloufi's armed organisation took upon itself to teach the

---

[23] S. Makhloufi, *Traité de la désobéissance civile,* 1991 (clandestine publication).

'people' the way to follow. The resort to violence was not directed against the security forces alone, but considered reactionary civilians, among the 'people', to be targets:

A people which supports, out of fear or ambition, a regime that tyrannises over it and oppresses it becomes its ally. In fact not only does the struggle become a duty, but ceasing to collaborate with the regime in power and the corrupt oppressors becomes an imperative.[24]

Between 1991 and 1993 appeals for 'civil disobedience' aroused no response; the universities, government departments and factories continued working more or less. One could wonder whether the 'oppressed people' preferred the tyranny of Tâghout or the adventure of the *jihad*.[25] The MEI concluded that only its organisation could show the 'people' the right way to act, because the people, under the combined effect of fear and state terror, could not be properly free to choose its destiny. Thus the MEI tried to apply counter-terror, which alone was able to shake civilians out of their indifference and force them to choose sides. Aware that war is a fertile ground for 'ambitious' people, the MEI saw itself as an organisation able to satisfy even the most material aspirations of its members, so as to keep hold of thousands of people wanting to join the *jihad*, who might otherwise go over to the regime's side to get a better position.

Because the MEI refused to recognise the autonomy of the state and the capacity of its repressive apparatus to reproduce itself, it ended up seeing the 'people' as the sole cause of the regime's remaining in power. The revolutionary principle of the 'Emir' of the MEI – that the attitude of the people is the guarantee of success for the rebellion – expressed the error of revolutionary romanticism. The illegitimacy of a regime does not necessarily lead to its defeat, especially when it is ready to bear the cost, which in any case was in this case met in the short term by the international community through the IMF. The opposition to apartheid, although it was in the 'majority', did not succeed in overthrowing the illegitimate South African regime by violence. The strategic choice of the MEI, which concentrated more on the 'people' than on the security forces, probably contributed greatly to the choice made by the GIA.

The ideology of the GIA and its strategy of 'total war'. From 1993 the ideological influence of the MEI is perceptible behind the actions of the GIA armed groups. The analysis of the situation by the 'thinkers' of the GIA was based on the realisation that a deep-seated 'longing for dissidence' existed among the young. That longing would, in a war of professionals of the MIA

[24] Ibid., p. 3.

[25] An expression that has grown up during the war expresses this dilemma: 'We have a choice between those who are strangling and starving us [the regime] and those who want to cut our throats [the Islamist revolutionaries].'

type, die away very quickly, in view of the mastery of behaviour to be acquired and the meticulous preparation of military operations. The GIA, attracted by Saïd Makhloufi's analysis of the importance of the 'people's' attitude in the armed struggle, classified all individuals as either 'enemies of Islam' or 'supporters of the *jihad*'. Hence civilians were called upon to choose sides under pain of death. The GIA, decreeing the principle of 'total war', considered not only that the regime was illegitimate, but that it should be destroyed as the incarnation of Tâghout. Transferring from the political register to the religious turned the struggle into a conflict of values. In doing this the GIA combined Saïd Makhloufi's revolutionary principle (combating the people's fear through terror) and the theory of the state as '*jahiliy*', derived from Sayyid Qutb.[26] Thus, far from confining its attention to the security forces, the GIA went to war against all the social groups which, involuntarily or deliberately, ensured that the regime continued in power. Hence government departments, the educational system and foreigners became 'legitimate' targets, no less than agents of the security forces.

To that end the GIA left its armed groups complete autonomy, and every suburban 'Emir' had the right to claim to represent it in his commune. While the MIA and MEI attracted the more competent elements (students, qualified jobseekers, deserters, former FIS militants), the GIA gathered only 'fanatics', impelled by hatred of the regime, rather than trained Islamist militants. It encouraged applicants for the *jihad* not to hesitate to go ahead without parental authorisation if it was refused: 'As for the consent of one's family, seek it, but if it is not given to you, go ahead anyway, *jihad – fi sabil lilah* – is above ties of blood.'[27] The struggle against the regime went with the formation of new loyalties and the family, until then considered sacred by all the Islamist movements, was thrust aside.

This radicalism, attacking both the political and the family order, was the strength of that faction which, unlike the AIS, did not at all aim to show 'respect' for the elders and their principles in its action. The war tactics of the GIA seemed unstoppable; its spectacular coups, highlighted in the media, combined with a rapidly expanding war economy, attracted a large proportion of the suburban Islamist armed bands towards it in 1994, and from then on they bore its standard. The GIA label attracted Islamist sympathisers desiring to fight the security forces because they were fascinated by the prestige of the 'Emirs'. Their epic outshone the 'stars' of the ex-FIS and

[26] That term, in the Islamist vocabulary, denotes the period of 'ignorance' before the coming of Islam. It was used by Sayyid Qutb to describe twentieth-century societies. G. Kepel notes that, according to this theory, 'the true Muslim must break with the Jahiliyya, then struggle to destroy it and build up an Islamic state over its ruins'. See G. Kepel, *La revanche de Dieu,* Paris: Seuil, 1991, p. 39; and O. Carré, *Mystique et politique. Lecture révolutionnaire du Coran par Sayyid Qutb, Frère musulman radical,* Paris: Presses de la FNSP/Ed. du Cerf, 1984, 248 pp.

[27] Excerpt from a cassette circulating in Algeria in 1994, later in France.

relegated the *liwa* Chébouti to a bygone age. Intoxication with violence placed the names of successive 'Emirs'[28] firmly in the *imaginaire* of the *jihad* sympathisers, alongside the heroes of American television series. The extreme freedom granted to the GIA armed groups made every district a space for that organisation, leaving an impression of hegemony.

The GIA, which was in a sort of osmosis with the general feeling of some of the least politicised – but at the same time most anti-regime – of the young people, embarked in 1993 on internal ideological purification. It was a military and religious movement, whose aim went beyond the strictly limited one of reintegration of the ex-FIS into the political system. The political view of the conflict was based on the GIA's motto, 'No dialogue, no reconciliation, no truce'.[29] The radicalism of that approach led to the temporary marginalisation of the other armed Islamist organisations. Its spectacular 'communications' policy (killings of foreigners and well-known intellectuals[30]) secured a wide audience for its claim to be at the head of the *jihad* in Algeria. Its initial establishment in the Algiers area favoured media coverage of the GIA, at the expense of the MIA, MEI and AIS, established in mountainous areas too far from Algeria, where the echo of their struggle was limited to the villagers who were witnesses.

The GIA's mobilisation strategy was also based on remarkable use of the feeling, very strong in Algeria, of being persecuted by the world community. Far from confining its struggle within the bounds of Algeria, it set about building up a highly effective image of an external enemy: France, the 'Jew' and the 'apostate', were the parties mainly responsible for Algeria's sufferings. While the MEI put forward the idea that only a change of attitude among the people could create conditions for victory for the guerrillas, the GIA included in its analysis of the conflict the major role played by the international community. From that viewpoint the regime now appeared as a mere transplant, and its agents were mere 'renegades' in the service of the 'Jews' and France. In contrast, Saïd Makhloufi's criticism of the world community related to the economic aspect:

The regime in power will fall despite all the means at its disposal, that regime which was and still is the cause of the unbelievable oppression and corruption that will intensify as the liberal economy is opened up to the enemies of Islam, Christians and Jews which have all the wealth of the country at their disposal.[31]

[28] Allal Mohammed alias Moh Leveilly, the first 'Emir' (killed 31 August 1992); A. Layada (imprisoned at Serkadji); Dja'afar el Afghani (Mourad si Ahmed, killed in February 1994); Abou Abdalla Ahmed (Cherif Gousmi, killed in September 1994); Abou Abderrahman Amîn (Djamel Zitouni, killed in July 1996); Antar Zouabri...

[29] Slogan attributed to Qari Saïd, one of the ideologues of the GIA.

[30] On the relationship between the media and terrorism see R. Dufour, 'Les ressorts psychologiques de l'efficacité publicitaire du terrorisme', *Etudes polémologiques,* 1986, no. 1.

[31] Ibid., p. 3.

The GIA complements this way of looking at the situation by adding political and religious aspects; the meaning which that movement gives to the word *jihad* sums up its principle for the war: 'The *jihad* in Algeria is an absolute religious obligation which is imposed on everyone, like fasting, prayer, the almsgiving required by law and the Pilgrimage, and the killing of foreigners forms part of this major obligation.'[32] This interpretation, which incidentally conceals the media-oriented function of killing foreigners in the GIA's strategy, truly derives from the principle of 'total war'. The GIA's *jihad* accordingly sees itself as a war 'on all fronts, within and outside Algeria'. This generalisation of the idea of the enemy favours every type of action and thus leaves wide room for manoeuvre to all the armed groups claiming to follow it. Through that subterfuge the GIA has appropriated to itself all the forms of violence in the country and is credited with an almost national representative character. However, it understood better than its rivals that the economic factor was decisive for the permanence of the regime. The creation in 1993 of an 'economic destruction and sabotage' section clearly proclaimed that its struggle involved the weakening of the government's resources. Aware that the main obstacle to success for the guerrilla campaign came from the maintenance of the economic machinery (especially the oil and gas sector), the GIA, following the MIA, MEI and FIS, redefined the space of the *jihad*. Hence the destruction of the economic structure was justified because it was 'an artificial economy, totally dependent on the Crusader countries'.[33] But there remains an enigma, because even up to 1997 the only state enterprises destroyed were unproductive ones which the IMF was in any case encouraging the state to stop subsidising. The oil and gas sector has, despite verbal attacks by the GIA, experienced a dynamism which has not failed to grieve the sympathisers of that faction.

Far from being an organisation gone adrift, the GIA represents the most advanced form of eradication policy, Islamist version. The raising of stakes by the regime has been answered with the 'total war' of the Emirs who, not being able to overthrow the regime, are at least working to destroy its resources.[34] The Emirs' *jihad*, led by military rather than religious leaders, has become a permanent part of the scene.

On the symbolic level the 'Emirs' have been trying to appropriate for themselves the prestige of the historical figures scattered throughout the social history of Algeria: Raïs, rebel, rural lord, Moudjahid. They drew from those past examples their model of a fighter forged by violence, and proclaim the primacy of warrior skills over religious and political abilities. Chérif Gousmi, head of the GIA in 1994, Chairman of its 'Commission for Political

---

[32] *El Ansar,* July 1994.

[33] *El Ansar,* no. 46, May 1994.

[34] We emphasised in Chapter 6 that between that strategy and actual practice there have been ambiguities, especially in the economic targets chosen (transport etc.).

Affairs and Religious Legislation', mentioned in a press interview the criteria for choosing 'personalities for leadership':

'Besides certain qualities of command, the person in question must have taken part in the *jihad* through military operations, and he must also have killed a sufficient number of the enemies of God.'[35]

According high status to the warrior in this way has led to real competition to obtain the political and military leadership among the local 'Emirs' claiming the title of national 'Emir'. Inexplicable acts of violence correspond most often to a gain in status for the 'Emir' of a local group who aims to rise higher. The use of the international media (when a victim with a world reputation is selected, for example) is also related to that competition for the job of 'national Emir', in which the local 'Emirs' of the Algiers region have a special advantage because they are close to strategic and high-profile places (embassies, airports, foreign communities, etc.). The logic of this struggle for hegemony explains why, when several 'Emirs' live together in the same commune or region, that area becomes, to the great regret of its people, a 'battlefield' because the 'Emirs' must redouble their activity in order to stand out from their rivals. The institutionalisation of violence as a means of access to political leadership accordingly incites people to crime.

The GIA proclaims explicitly that 'the installation of the Khalifa's state will come only through the *jihad*'.[36] Resolutely rooted in a logic of war, it has thus weakened all the Islamist political actors who practice violence as a means of political negotiation. Thus, by its intransigence, it has made itself the political ally of the regime, which has found in that armed Islamist organisation proof that only an eradication policy is capable of restoring civil peace. In addition, by its war strategy it prevents the AIS 'companies' from taking root in areas which had supported the FIS between 1989 and 1991. Thus it plays the same useful role for the regime that was played previously in South Africa by Inkatha, which hampered the establishment of the ANC in the townships.[37] The ideological training of the guerrilla campaign has been developed in accordance with the concrete situations faced by the fighters. Certainly it draws on the 'world views' produced by the classical Islamic ideologues (Sayyid Qutb), but it borrows a great deal from local revolutionary myths. Mohamed Saïd, an ideologue who was for a moment the supreme 'Emir' of the GIA in 1994, uses the pseudonym of a famous ALN officer, like him a native of Kabylia.[38] The use of the term 'Moudjahid'

---

[35] Interview with Chérif Gousmi, *El Wasat*, 29 Jan. 1994.

[36] GIA communiqué published in *Al Hayat*, 18 Jan. 1995.

[37] S. Ellis, 'Les nouvelles frontières du crime en Afrique du Sud' in J.-F. Bayart, S. Ellis and B. Hibou, *La criminalisation de l'Etat en Afrique*, Brussels: Complexe, 1997.

[38] Mohammedi Saïd was the head of Wilaya III in the war of liberation: 'He was one of the ruthless advocates of strong methods. And he sought at independence to make

(fighter for the Faith) recalls the use of that term by the ALN soldiers during the liberation war. These ideological references should not conceal the guerrillas' constant adaptation to their enemy: in accordance with each 'Emir's' war tactics, certain targets can be legitimate or not – an inconsistency that can only be highly unsettling to the population. This difficulty in understanding the *jihad*'s space favours the regime, for it reveals the nihilism of the Islamist groups. Conversely, it is possible to see in the diversity of action among the Islamist factions a flawless organisation where a clearly established division of labour operates – the AIS and MIA dealing with the army, the MEI with the 'people' and the GIA with the economic and media sector. However, that appearance of a division of labour among armed organisations should not conceal their struggle for monopoly of the *jihad*.

The struggle for monopoly of the jihad

The GIA armed groups and AIS companies, present until 1995 in all the big mountain massifs – the Blida Atlas, the Ouarsenis, the Aurès, the Hauts-Plateaux of the Constantine region and the Edough Massif – set up a series of 'fake roadblocks' on the strategic or secondary main roads, to mark off their respective spaces and control movement of commercial vehicles. However, not all those regions experienced the same intensity of violence as the Algiers region, where fierce competition reigned among the groups for control of the urban areas. The absence of endemic violence in a large portion of Algeria's territory did not mean that the guerrillas were absent from those areas. Paradoxically, it was in the 'calmest' regions (Greater Kabylia, Ouarsenis, the Constantine region) that the guerrillas' war infrastructure was located (the Chekfa and Azazga maquis for example). It was in those regions that the pro-government militias were formed and became, from 1994-5 onwards, formidable obstacles to the consolidation of the maquis. Ex-combatants 'took to the maquis for a second time', but this time to dislodge the new Moudjahidin from there.

Those regions offered all the necessary 'facilities' for guerrilla war: a complex topography, closeness to major urban centres, access to the sea, natural hiding places, and a population that had grown familiar with war. From Jugurtha's revolt against Rome to the modern guerrillas, they have been the favoured places, constantly re-used throughout history. Their value is very great, and they are coveted and fought over by guerrillas.

In 1992 the MIA began to establish itself in the zones stretching from the Chréa Massif in the Blida Atlas, where it was encamped, to the Constantine region. When the fighters left Algiers and its suburbs, the scenes of intense repression, they established themselves solidly in those maquis. However, the emergence of the GIA and its rapid establishment in the Mitidja reduced

---

praying obligatory,' writes G. Meynier in 'Emigration, armée, culture et démocratie en Algérie', *Confluences Méditerranée*, no. 3, spring 1992.

the MIA's field of action considerably. In 1993 and 1994 the GIA recruited widely and established its first maquis in the mountains near to the town of Lakhdaria and the Constantine region, despite the presence of the MIA and MEI in those zones sought after by the 'Emirs' coming from the Algiers suburbs. The MIA was, according to what its sympathisers were saying in July 1994, weakened because army units had launched a real war against it. Sometimes bombed with napalm as at Meftah, the MIA maquis were from 1994 unable to function, which led to the dispersal of the MIA fighters. The GIA, taking advantage of the weakening of the MIA, occupied successively the positions abandoned by the maquis subjected to the bombing. Later on, army units set about eliminating the MEI. The MEI maquis located between Boumerdès and Jijel were broken up and the GIA, the only guerrilla group relatively spared in 1994, announced the merger of all those bodies,[39] in order to incorporate the MIA and MEI fighters into its own ranks. Some of the fighters refused to join the GIA and preferred to merge with the new organisation which arose then, the AIS. The 'favourable treatment' given by the army to the GIA aroused questions among survivors of the MIA and MEI groups about a rival which had then succeeded in acquiring a monopoly of the *jihad*.

While the MIA attacked units of the army or certain 'strategic' government departments, the GIA undertook the systematic destruction of railways, bridges, telephone lines and state enterprises. These acts of economic sabotage won it objective allies in the private sector, which ended up being almost the sole supplier of consumer goods and products to the cities of the interior. Meanwhile, in the Algiers and Constantine regions and Kabylia, control of highways became a stake in the rivalry between the AIS and GIA. The Route de la Corniche passed from MIA to GIA control as soon as the former organisation became weakened. Similarly the main Algiers-Constantine road, initially controlled by the MIA as far as Lakhdaria (70 km. from Algiers) and by the MEI between Sétif and Constantine, came under the control of the GIA 'Emirs' for the whole of its length in 1994. The volume of commercial vehicle traffic on that road linking the small towns of the interior gave the GIA, through the 'fake roadblocks' that it set up, an assured regular income which made its lightning rise possible. The management of that flow of money involved counting the vehicles using that road, to maximise the extortion of goods:

'They stop cars, lorries, buses...They ask for your papers. If you don't work for the state, you have nothing to fear. Otherwise, for state-employed drivers, they seize your

---

[39] 'On 13 May 1994 the GIA issued the Communiqué of the Union and the Jihad and Respect for the Book and the Sunna. It was signed, for the attention of the Djamma Emir, Abou Abdallah Ahmed (alias Chérif Gousmi), by Sheikh Rajjam in the name of the FIS and Sheikh S. Makhloufi in the name of the MEI', wrote *Al Wasat*, no. 173, 22 May 1995; see also F. Burgat, 'Algérie: l'AIS et le GIA, itinéraires de constitution et de relations', *Maghreb-Machrek*, no. 149, July-Sept.1995, p. 105.

lorry and if they let you live, you can say, *"Hamdou lillah"* [thank God]. But that depends on the region also: at the roadblocks near Jijel they destroy car radios, they say music is *haram* [unlawful], they machine-gun your radio set if they see it; but otherwise, there too, they are dressed like gendarmes, with the *klash,* the cap, you don't know from far off that they are fake. They never touch privately-owned lorries, they ask you who you are working for, where you are coming from, who you are delivering to. But they take the goods from you sometimes and say, "We'll tell your boss that it's we who took them, you have nothing to fear". They do that calmly; the first time I thought I was going to die, but now it's better, when I see them on the road, I'm easy.' (Driver of privately-owned commercial vehicle, 1994, Algiers)

Control over that road was exerted at the expense of the MIA and MEI maquis. In 1995 the GIA succeeded in holding the monopoly of extortion there, which partly explains its success. Well established in the Mitidja and in the East, the GIA has sought since then to extend its influence and control over the regions of the west bordering the Algiers-Mascara highway where the towns of Miliana, Aïn Defla and Chlef are situated. Those regions, however, are places where the AIS maquis is established. So to avoid a direct confrontation which would weaken both, the GIA and AIS have been using the security forces – without their knowledge – to fight each other by proxy, each directing those forces to where the other's maquis stands in its way. At the time of the Aïn Defla ambush in March 1995, in which leading members of the GIA were defeated by an army operation in a zone controlled by the AIS, rumour accused the latter of having reported the GIA fighters' meeting place to the army.[40]

That struggle for monopoly of the *jihad*, however, remained confined within the military and political domains, for the guerrillas of both the GIA and the AIS made efforts – unlike the small self-proclaimed 'Islamist' armed groups of the Algiers suburbs – to conserve the resources of their environment. Established in the mountainous regions of the interior of Algeria, the guerrillas latched onto local private economic activity without, however, destroying or ruining it. Quite the reverse – the destruction of state economic activity was for the private sector, especially in transport and distribution, compensation for losses due to extortion. The presence of the maquis helped to bring about a reorganisation of the control of resources among the economic actors. Far from being passive and submissive, they exploited to their own advantage the insecurity hanging over the state corporations. For the guerrillas, what mattered above all was to avoid causing the economic bankruptcy of those actors, who willingly or not gave them an assured supply of resources to keep them going.

---

[40] In March 1995, in the Beni Bouateb forest, 160 leading members of the GIA, at a meeting, were reported to have fallen victim to a surprise offensive by the army. *El Watan,* 25 March 1995.

The development of the guerrilla campaign

Impact of the regime's war economic policy: Dwindling Numbers of Recruits? The guerrilla forces, estimated in 1992 at 2,000 men (mainly with the MIA), grew in 1993 to a strength of 22,000 men[41] with the formation of the GIA, and reached a peak of 40,000 men, including logistical support, in 1994[42] with the emergence of the AIS. After the presidential election of 16 November 1995, did their strength decline? The GIA, for which only the 'hard core' is counted, is estimated at 2-3,000 fighters;[43] the AIS is believed to have seen its forces decline to 4,000 men, including 2,500 in the east and 1,500 in the west, while the MEI and MIA are thought only to comprise some small groups in the Mitidja now. In all the guerrillas' strength was believed to be around 10,000 fighters, all factions included, in 1996. Although unverifiable, these figures cannot conceal one essential fact: the value of a guerrilla war effort does not lie so much in that of its fighters, still less in their number, as in the reliability of its logistics and its 'political infrastructure',[44] which includes both support networks in the big cities and partners abroad who facilitate financial dealings. So a decline in manpower in the Islamist guerrilla campaign should not necessarily lead to the conclusion that the factions are growing weaker; quite the contrary, the dwindling in the numbers of fighters has been accompanied by professionalisation of the maquis: manufacture of mortars, protection of the maquis by 'carpets' of anti-personnel mines, etc.[45] With replenishment of their troops assured from the reservoir of young men, the factions' strength has been stabilised since 1994. To establish a war economy capable of sustaining their troops, they are obliged to find funds and sustain their clientage networks, necessary for the urban guerrilla campaign.

The relative weakness of the guerrillas' manpower in relation to a theoretical reservoir of three million Islamist voters is explained by the steady integration of that human capital into the state system. Analysis of the development of the guerrilla campaign over four years of war reveals the systematic elimination of the political guerrilla fighters (MIA militants), to the benefit of the revolutionaries (the GIA). The formation of the AIS in 1994 resulted from a realisation of that phenomenon by the ex-FIS activists, who feared that the regime would favour the 'out of control' elements of the *jihad* so as to make sympathisers with the ex-FIS recoil from

---

[41] *Algérie-Actualité*, 1-7 Nov. 1993.

[42] Quoted in the newspaper *Al Sharq al Awsat*, cited in *Courrier International* no. 276, 1996.

[43] *Al Hayat*, 2 June 1995.

[44] G. Chaliand has written: 'The most important thing in a guerrilla campaign is its political infrastructure among the population...', *Stratégie de la guérilla*, Paris: Gallimard, 1984, p. 37.

[45] *Algérie Confidentiel*, 10 Feb. 1997.

joining the armed struggle. By going easy on the GIA, the military leaders hoped to induce the AIS to surrender by causing it to lose its base of support as a result of the impact of GIA violence.

Once the work of demoralising the Islamist sympathisers had been completed, the government hoped to encourage the diversion of the 'hard core' groups towards the trading economy, in the hope of hastening their 'abandonment' of the *jihad*. The economic reforms were a weapon of war, they led to partial demobilisation of candidates for the *jihad*;[46] however, the spread of poverty was accompanied by the appearance of new armed groups.[47] Trade liberalisation put an end to replenishment at the grass roots, as the local 'Emirs' in urban areas had facilities for switching to 'trade'. But paradoxically it increased the pauperisation of the population, and made it partially dependant on the Islamist armed groups, enriched by guerrilla war and trading.

Increased resources for the guerrilla campaign. The regime's economic policy had profound effects on the guerrilla campaign's human resources. The erosion of the ex-FIS electoral capital partly achieved the desired result: 'disgust' and 'nausea' seem to have replaced the Islamist passion of the first period. For those demobilised and demoralised voters, the temporary alternative of the maquis gave way to a disillusioned view of life, to which the AIS sought to respond by its professional guerrilla warfare, 'militarily correct' and without 'excesses' or flagrant injustices. The corollary to this shift in the replenishment of the fighters was professionalisation of the guerrilla war effort. The GIA and AIS, adapted to rural conditions, developed maquis well away from the urban zones which they could not occupy. On any assumption, trade liberalisation and the reform of the banking system made it possible for the guerrillas to build up the best possible financial resources, which compensated for the decline in their strength.

The guerrillas: a state within a state? The overlapping between guerrillas' military and economic activities brought their business into partnership with the regime's; by latching on to the trading economy from 1994 onwards they were able, thanks to the financial facilities available as a result, to exert invisible control over new territories. For as military victory over the regime gradually receded, new strategies became necessary: instead of head-on confrontation with the security forces (1993-4) there came the creation of a state within a state. The GIA, failing to overthrow

---

[46] The use of economic reforms against guerrillas has been tried out in Latin America also: 'Edwin Corr, in July 1988, stated that without the reforms "there would have been not 12,000 but 60,000 guerrillas".' A. Rouquié, *Guerre et paix en Amérique latine*, Paris: Seuil, 1982, p. 295.

[47] In July 1996 a new faction emerged in the Mitidja, the LIDD (Ligue Islamique pour la Da'wa et le Djihâd).

the regime, adopted a policy of substitution for state institutions, like other political-criminal organisations such as the Italian Mafia. Although it did not occupy any city militarily, it still remained present through a whole network of surveillance and control in urban areas. In the southern suburbs of Algiers, 'pacified' by the security forces in 1993 and 1994, the GIA, through the district 'Emirs' claiming to act in its name, maintained its war logistics. As a leading GIA figure told a Turkish journalist,

'We have patrols in all the districts, who go around day and night, except in the central district. We have own own cars followed to make sure of them.'[48]

This presence of GIA elements 'in plain clothes', without beard or *djellaba* or *kamis*, in contact with numerable social groups, was one of that organisation's adjustments to the failure of its policy of military occupation of urban areas. Not counted among the guerrilla's supposed manpower, described by the security forces as 'criminals' or 'delinquents' which they sometimes are, they are the 'hidden' part of the guerrilla war effort, of which the fighters in the maquis are only the most visible part. The GIA's cooperation with the district armed bands has led it to exercise greater vigilance. Progressive integration of some partners of the GIA into Mafioso activities has been one aspect of the counter-guerrilla struggle waged by the regime. In answer to the Turkish journalist's observation that 'It is said that the Mafia has taken root among the Islamist movements!', the suburban GIA leader said:

'Those are organisations set up by the state to disturb the population. Last week we laid hands on two people in El Harrach. They confessed and we gave them the punishment they deserved. Hydar and Rachid, two agents who inflitrated the Moudjahidin at Serkadji prison, were also punished.'

Besides infiltration by agents of the state, the GIA has also feared being indirectly used as a hit squad in the service of persons or social groups behind the scenes. After four years of war the GIA's record aroused doubts among the population about the organisation's real intentions. The systematic destruction of the state sector, besides putting thousands of workers out of a job, made things easier for the government policy, recommended by the IMF, of ending subsidies to loss-making enterprises. This halt to subsidies spared the regime from industrial conflicts and diverted the workers' anger towards the disastrous policy of the Islamist groups. In addition, while the regime's main resources come from the sale of oil and gas, there have only been rare attacks on oil and gas installations, to the great regret of the social strata in which the 'Emirs' have their base, and which are convinced that such attacks would not upset their daily existence. So might the GIA not be the hidden face of a military regime faced with the need to rearrange

---

[48] '*Hürriyet* interviews the GIA', *Hürriyet*, 5 March 1996.

its economic resources? From that point of view a comparison with 'narco-states', in which guerrillas' economic interests overlap with the governments', leads one to take a new look at the consolidation of the war.[49]

The illusion of re-enacting the War of Liberation

The consolidation of the regime, as we have noted, has fitted in very well with the violence of some guerrilla factions, such as the GIA; but is it leading, even so, to the final defeat of the guerrillas? Nothing is less certain. In fact the reconquest of the country by the military has come up against the limitations of their war economy, which has left intact the economic, social and political conditions that gave legitimacy to the Islamist mobilisation. While the military have succeeded in eroding Islamist electoral support, the basic issues in the conflict remain. Will they suffer the fate of Third World revolutionary ideologies that have become outdated? The growth of the Islamist guerrilla campaign is based on a misunderstanding, because those basic issues, probably fitting the real situation in a colonial war context, as in Algeria's liberation war, are less so in a civil war context. Abdelhamid Brahimi, Prime Minister of Algeria from 1984 to 1988, has written:

> Some French leaders declare, as the Algerian regime has done since the coup d'état of 1992, that the problem in Algeria is not political but essentially economic. Both have been saying for more than three years that it is unemployment that has caused the swelling of the FIS ranks. The cure, they think, consists of reviving the economy and proceeding to economic reforms to undermine the base of support for the FIS from the Algerian youth. The Algerians heard the same ideas during the war of liberation between 1954 and 1962. Just as the nationalist ideal was obscured in 1954 by the colonial power, placing its hopes in the Constantine Plan and the revival of investment, so the nationalist ideal is obscured today by the dictatorial and repressive Algerian regime in its recourse to IMF treatment.[50]

Will the regime meet the same fate as the colonial regime? For the guerrilla factions there is no doubt that in spite of the regime's consolidation, victory for them remains probable. Thus the regime's war strategy against Islamist violence, although it has weakened the guerrilla campaign's human resources, remains ineffective against the doctrine that has brought it about. While the purifying ideology of the GIA has within it the seeds of self-destruction, the Third Worldist ideology of the AIS retains its capacity to mobilise:

> They want to destroy the Islamist model so that oppressed peoples have no example to serve them. Thus victory for the Algerian people in the Islamic battle will be good

---

[49] Compare the changes of occupation among the Angolan military during the civil war. M.E. Ferreira, 'La reconversion économique de la nomenklatura pétrolière', *Politique Africaine*, March 1995, pp. 11-27.

[50] Abdelhamid Brahimi, 'La faillite de l'économie algérienne: causes et perspectives', *El Mounqidh*, no. 6, June 1996.

news for the world's peoples, and its defeat – may Allah not permit it – will have profound psychological consequences for condemned peoples longing for justice, truth and freedom. That is why we are bound to succeed whatever the sacrifices required may be.[51]

This determination to return to an Algeria in the vanguard of the 'oppressed peoples' reveals the populist and nationalist influences on the thinking of the ex-FIS and its military wing the AIS. Is the Islamist guerrilla campaign therefore bringing Algeria's 'second liberation',[52] as F. Burgat suggests? Undoubtedly it considers its *jihad* as a continuation of past actions:

Here is a warning for all the organisations or persons who have chosen to oppose the people in its *jihad* against the forces of robbery and Westernisation driven by a gang of France-obsessed military people. Know that they have put their money on a limping horse, because the movement of history is always in tune with the oppressed peoples.[53]

Convinced that they are 'on the side of history', the Islamist guerrillas revive for their own use the myths of 'sacrifice' and 'liberation'. The ambivalence of the relationship between the guerrilla campaign and the regime comes from their complementary nature: their war logics reinforce and consolidate each other. The civil war, despite the language used by the guerrillas, is therefore not a 'second war of liberation'; the Islamist factions, unable to form a united front, risk becoming victims of the 'Turkish technique' which, as J.-C. Vatin explains, has been fatal for many religious insurgent movements: 'Particularly violent movements almost brought the regime down before 1830. For several years, from 1804 onwards, Algeria in the east and the west, in the north and the south, was shaken under the onslaught of the biggest confraternities and marabouts. At one moment everyone seemed to be ready to take up arms at the same time. But every group pursued the struggle on its side, in the name of its own saint, depriving the religious forces of a spectacular victory. In 1817 order was finally restored. The confraternities came to their senses, one after the other. Once again, the Turkish technique had borne fruit.'[54] In the next chapter we shall put forward, as an alternative to the hypothesis of victory for one of the two warring parties, one suggesting that the civil war is capable of ending up with the merger of the warrior elites rising from the ranks of both the army and the guerrillas.

---

[51] Letters to the Moudjahidin, in *Mots de vérité...*, p. 2.

[52] F. Burgat, *L'islamisme en face,* Paris: La Découverte, 1996, 285 pp.

[53] Letters to the Moudjahidin, in *Mots de vérité...* , p. 6.

[54] J.-C. Vatin, *L'Algérie. Politique, histoire et société,* Paris: Presses de la FNSP, 1983, p. 104.

10

BACK TO THE BEYLIKS

The consolidation of both the regime and the Islamist guerrilla campaign, inherent in the impossibility of one destroying the other, makes them seem in many respects like complementary enemies. Just as the Taïfa of the Raïs (the corsairs' corporation) under the Regency of Algiers, between the sixteenth and eighteenth centuries, prospered in the shadow of the 'Military Republic',[1] the 'Emirs' and the guerrillas found favourable conditions for their development in the economic liberalisation policy. Similarly, just as the Janissaries left local governors (Beys) to deal with the dissidence of tribal confederations, the current government leaves it to prominent local citizens and their militias to contain the Islamist guerrillas' violence. Thus the warring parties are unconsciously reinventing a form of political organisation, the Beylicate, which had ensured a certain stability to the Regency of Algiers despite internal dissidence. J.-C. Vatin writes of that period: 'A military oligarchy controlled Algiers closely and the hinterland from afar...The provinces tended to organise themselves in their own way and the Turkish officials at their head left enough autonomy to the local chiefs for the whole to appear, in retrospect, particularly stable, compared with the palace conflicts, assassinations and revolts which occurred so frequently in Algiers. What distinguished the eighteenth century was the government's determination no longer to extend itself and impose itself on everyone, not to assimilate or associate the population to its leadership, nor to make any switch to economic activity, but to try to keep things as they were, to survive on a balance that had been finally struck. From the outside, the dominant feature seemed to be stagnation. Neither economic progress, nor struggles against foreigners.'[2]

The comparison with the Beylicate does not mean there are not major differences between the Beyliks of the sixteenth or the eighteenth century and the Algerian state. The analogy with that pre-colonial political organisation merely makes it possible to emphasise the survival of some of those practices, more specifically that of management of armed dissidence, without losing sight of the warning of Michel Camau: 'Reference to "classical" or "traditional" political models, adorned with the prefix "neo" (patrimonial or Mamluk, or Khaldunian or segmentary), has the merit of marking the limits of the process of transformation of the social structures underlying

[1] An expression used by M. Kaddache, *L'Algérie durant la période ottomane,* Paris: OPU, 1992, p. 76.

[2] J.-C. Vatin, *L'Algérie. Politique, histoire et société*, Paris: Presses de la FNSP, 1983, p. 89.

those models. However, it has the disadvantage of opening up problems of transposition based on analogies between old and new forms, whereas the problem in fact is that of their interconnection.'[3]

In this chapter we intend to emphasise how the heritage of the Beylicate in dealing with dissidence is connected with contemporary political practise of the Algerian state. From that perspective, the aim is to show how different forms of opposition constitute ways of negotiating with the government, which in fact have assisted the consolidation of the regime – like the 'Kabyle rising' in 1963 or even the reappearance of 'bandits of honour' in the Aurès in 1964.[4] Similarly Karen Barkey has stressed how the 'Celali bandits' under the Ottoman Empire favoured state centralisation: she wrote, 'Their "rebellions" were therefore maneuvers for mobility within the system, not opposition to the system. Accordingly, the Ottoman state made use of these bandits for consolidation, reinforcing its hold over its servitors, eliminating potential contenders, and appointing trusted and powerful men to positions of importance in the provinces.'[5]

Continuation of the guerrilla war in the interior, besides allowing the regime to maintain greater cohesion in its repressive apparatus, has also facilitated changes in the political field and the creation of a new rent derived from exploitation of the Islamist threat.

The Politics of 'Depoliticisation': the Authoritarian Illusion

War settling down to routine: is the 'longing for dissidence' exhausted?

'They shouldn't have done that democracy. You see now what shit we're in. We aren't ready for democracy. The people are barely emerging from savagery and you give them democracy.' (Young delivery man, Algiers suburbs, 1993)

Although he abstained in the parliamentary elections in December 1991, Lahcen was an FIS sympathiser. Living in an Algiers commune impassioned by the dynamics of that party, he, like his friends, went through a euphoric revolutionary period where they felt that the 'FLN-state' was ended and saw the dawn of democracy coming. For him FIS victory did not mean the prelude to introduction of an Islamic state, of whose possible character he knew nothing, except that it could not be an imitation of the Islamic Republic of Iran, even of the Sudan, still less of the Kingdom of Saudi Arabia, despised since the Gulf War (1990-1). The FIS offered an exciting political adventure through the risks lying ahead, the new political personalities

---

[3] Michel Camau, 'Politique dans le passé, politique aujourd'hui au Maghreb' in J.-F. Bayart, *La greffe de l'Etat,* Paris: Karthala, 1996, p. 87.

[4] Jeanne Favret, 'Le traditionalisme par excès de modernité', *Archives européennes de sociologie,* 7 (1), 1967, pp. 71-93.

[5] Karen Barkey, *Bandits and Bureaucrats: The Ottoman Route to State Centralization,* Ithaca, NY: Cornell University Press, 1994, p. 195.

it comprised, its declarations and its methods of communication, which marked a break from the self-assurance and monotony of the FLN.

The civil war, accompanied by the shrinking of the political field to the benefit of the warriors, used up that passion without, however, causing it to vanish altogether. The result for some ex-FIS sympathisers was a feeling of disillusion and vulnerability, for the power which everyone drew from the party's strength had been eclipsed. Loneliness and fear led the youngest to flee into the maquis, where life expectancy was low. Others, like people we interviewed, 'counted the blows' in the hope of a rapid victory for their new heroes. But as the conflict became routine, and the 'Islamist violence' was politically unintelligible while the regime – above all – retained its power, that hope faded away. In place of the Islamist passion there then came first of all fear, then withdrawal into oneself, for daily coexistence with death led to a desire, quite simply, to go on living.

This adaptation to war was accompanied by new interpretation of the causes of the violence. While the interruption of the elections in January 1992, and the subsequent banning of the FIS in March, had been considered the main reasons for the outbreak of the war, now other causes were seen, such as 'the savagery of the people' and its 'warlike madness'. The political immaturity of a people unprepared for war could, in Lahcen's view, only lead to civil war. For him war, far from being a political instrument for settling of conflicts, sharpened 'appetites' and caused divisions among the people who did not want it. Exhausted by the ordeal of civil war, he longed only for peace and quiet and more security for his close kin. After four years of violence did that feeling, shared by a number of people, indicate that the 'longing for dissidence' clearly displayed in 1992 was exhausting itself? The Islamist passion, widespread during the electoral process and at the origin of many conversions to Islamism, seemed to fade as the war became routine. Certainly, while that change only had a mild effect on those engaged in the armed struggle (only 2,000 'repentant fighters' were counted[6]), it was observable among the political class which, as many of its members returned little by little to a space marked out by the government, gave up its radical criticisms of the nature of the regime.

From the 'Rejection Front' to 'Open Dialogue': the political parties return to the fold. After meeting in November 1994, under the auspices of the Catholic Community of Sant' Egidio in Rome, in a 'Rejection Front' formed principally by the FFS, the FLN and the FIS[7] with a view to setting up a

[6] *La Nation,* no. 128, 1996.

[7] In November 1994 a first meeting of representatives of the FLN, the FIS and the FFS, as well as other personalities, was held in Rome, under the auspices of the Catholic Community of Sant'Egidio. The participants wanted to bring an end to the civil war. In January 1995 the main opposition parties met again and agreed on a 'Platform for a political and peaceful solution to the Algerian crisis'. That initiative clashed with the strategy of the military

'platform for peace', the political parties took the road back to Algiers after the presidential election of 16 November 1995, which they had urged voters to boycott. The surprisingly high turnout (officially 71 per cent)[8] and the successes of General Liamine Zéroual and Mahfoudh Nahnah showed that the government had to a great extent achieved what it had been setting out to get – the political parties that had won the first round of parliamentary elections in December 1991 had now lost legitimacy.[9] The choice of civil war strengthened the military in their political and economic choices. After its relative military victory against the Islamist guerrillas and the financial success of its liberalisation policy, the government, in successfully holding presidential elections, wanted to add a process of bringing the political class back on board.

The FLN was the first to end its period of dissidence, and set about regaining the confidence of the regime; this was illustrated by the removal of Abdelhamid Mehri and the choice as his successor of Boualek Benhamouda, who had been a minister continuously from 1965 to 1986. The 'open dialogue' organised in April 1996 by the Presidency and the legal opposition symbolised, through the participation of all the political parties, their recognition of the government's hegemony. Their participation in the

---

authorities who set a timetable for elections in motion (holding of a presidential election on 16 November 1995, then parliamentary and municipal elections in 1997) to show that the FIS was no longer the central player on the political stage. It can be presumed that the failure of the Community of Sant'Egidio initiative was due to the absence of the army, a major player on the Algerian political stage, and to failure to understand the motives behind the strategy of the actors involved in the *jihad*, for whom any political solution to the war would put an end to the ways in which they had been accumulating wealth and prestige. That initiative was the last resort for political actors marginalised by the dynamics of the civil war.

[8] Four candidates stood; General Liamine Zéroual was elected with 61 per cent of votes cast, Mahfoudh Nahnah (Hamas-MSI) won 25.58 per cent, Saïd Sadi (RCD, Rassemblement Culturel pour la Démocratie) 9.6 per cent and Noureddine Boukrouh 3.8 per cent. Those results were followed by a call for dialogue by Rabah Kébir, Chairman of the FIS Overseas Executive. In an 'open letter' to President Liamine Zéroual, he wrote: 'Following your election to the Presidency of the Republic in a vote on which we do not wish to dwell since you have the details of its operation and results, the message of the Algerian people, both through its boycott and through its participation in the election, is a desire for peace, democracy and freedom from restrictions and poverty...We think that the popular backing which you have received can be, for the government and the opposition, a great opportunity that could overcome the obstacles until now preventing the national dialogue from achieving its objectives of restoring peace, freedoms and understanding...Lastly we confirm our permanent readiness for dialogue, consultation and mutual assistance with the government and the opposition...' (Open Letter, 21 Nov. 1995)

[9] In the first round of parliamentary elections in December 1991, the FIS won 47.27 per cent of votes cast (3,260,222 votes), the FLN 23.8 per cent (1,612,947), the FFS 7.4 per cent (510,000), Hamas 5.35 per cent (368,000) and the RCD 2.9 per cent (200,267). On 16 November 1995 the RCD won 1,115,796 votes and Hamas 2,971,974; so those two parties benefited from switching of votes from the FFS and FIS, which had called for a boycott. See J. Fontaine, 'Algérie: les résultats de l'élection présidentielle', *Maghreb-Machrek*, no. 151, January-March 1996, pp. 107-17.

National Conference,[10] in July 1996, to draw up an election timetable including the organisation of municipal and parliamentary elections during 1997, resembled what Paul Veyne called the fiction of 'Augustan de-politicisation', beloved of 'dictatorships':[11]

A long period of civil wars had just ended; taking advantage of general weariness, an authoritarian monarchy took power. It succeeded in driving the masses out of the political arena and reduced public opinion to subjection; everyone felt that it was now useless not to stay in the ranks, and that the government intended to make policy alone.

Although the civil war has not ended in Algeria, the war economic policy, whose 'de-politicisation' is a part of the programme, indicates the exhaustion of political resistance, or even submission. The regime has been aiming, once the legal opposition has been brought under control, to replace the FIS with an Islamist party respecting the prevailing political norms. For that purpose it has been facilitating the entry of Hamas-MSI, led by Mahfoudh Nahnah, into the political system. Hamas, since 1991 a rival of the FIS for the symbolic management of dissident Islamist ideas, has found in the civil war an opportunity to increase the marginalisation of the FIS. The 25 per cent of votes cast in the presidential election for Mahfoudh Nahnah roughly corresponds to the votes for the FIS in the parliamentary elections in December 1991. However, the contrast is obvious between the leaders of the FIS, who promised to 'turn the Sahara into California', and the programme of Hamas-MSI, based on steady Islamisation of society, following the model of the Muslim Brotherhood of Egypt.[12] For the former FIS voters, recent converts, the Islamist passion has been losing all its excitement. The political meetings organised by Nahnah, dressed in a three-piece suit,

[10] In July 1996 the Presidency invited all the political parties (except the FIS) and 'forces in society' to 'discuss' a political agenda including the organisation of a referendum on the Constitution and parliamentary elections.

[11] Paul Veyne, *Le Pain et le Cirque*, Paris: Seuil, 1976, p. 95.

[12] According to Gema Martin-Muñoz, 'Mahfoudh Nahnah represents the Egyptian tradition of the Muslim Brotherhood in Algeria, with which the Brotherhood has always had close ties. But while that convergence is undeniable on the ideological level, M. Nahnah's political role has always been that of constructive fundamentalist opposition to the government, and even involvement with it; he drew nearer to it after his release in 1981, distancing himself gradually from the dissident line of his companions A. Madani, A. Sahnoun and A. Benhadj, going so far as to refuse to join the FIS at the time of its formation. Tensions between M. Nahnah and the FIS were constant from 1989 onwards, and were heightened when M. Nahnah refused to back the FIS in the municipal elections of 1990. At the doctrinal level...in M. Nahnah's line of argument there are two types of Ulema (doctors of the Faith): those who, following the traditional line, set themselves up as the conscience of the Muslim community in the face of the government, without giving priority to the question of political power; and those who call for direct exercise of power. Hamas has aligned itself with the first, the FIS with the second.' 'Le régime algérien face aux islamistes' in B. Kodmani-Darwish and M. Chartouni-Dubarry (ed.), *Les Etats arabes faces à la contestation islamiste*, Paris: A. Colin, 1997, p. 55.

resemble those of other political parties. Hamas-MSI's serious and monotonous character symbolises the process of 'freezing' of passion which, for those who had been involved in the glorious period of the FIS, has been shown in a decline in fervour.

First fruits of de-politicisation of daily life. Ostentatious signs of political commitment like the *hijab*, the beard and the *kamis* were gradually dropped in 1994-5. In reality the meaning of those signs had been considerably altered; the significance of the beard and the *kamis*, symbols of membership of the FIS during the election process, was distorted in the civil war. As policemen disguised as Islamists with flowing beards sowed confusion, the GIA was able to find a way to hit back: its supporters shaved their heads to prevent any misunderstanding. The politicisation of religious signs during the war altered some practices. Collective Friday prayers at the mosque represented in some communes and mosques a message of support for the Islamist guerrillas. Did the abandonment of that ritual by ex-FIS sympathisers indicate de-politicisation of religious practise?

Kader: how a convert to Islamism lost his fervour. Carried along by the conversion of his friends to Islamism in 1989-90, Kader, a medical student in 1991, was fascinated by the dynamics of the FIS, and said he was ready to join the MIA maquis after the halting of the election process: 'Up there, in the mountains, there is work,' a friend told him. An Islamist 'in his heart', he prayed at the mosque on Fridays in the company of his friends, sympathisers of the FIS and the guerrillas. However, he did not go so far as to wear the *kamis*, he merely let a wisp of beard emphasise his belonging to the Islamist camp. Between 1992 and 1994 he did not miss any of the meetings that his friends organised after Friday prayers, in the drawing room of a house, where followers met and drank a glass of milk together and ate pastry. Everyone discussed there the news of the *jihad*, set out in leaflets stuck up stealthily by children paid to help the cause. Kader, because of his intellectual level, was respected in the group; his support for the Islamist idea reassured those who had enlisted out of simple contempt for the regime. But in 1995 he refused for the first time to go to the mosque on Friday, shaved off his wispy beard and, after a two-year halt, went again to the Riad al Fateh (Galeries Marchandes, shopping mall), which he had been calling 'Houbal' since 1989.

His behaviour inevitably aroused criticism from his closest friends, who reproached him for his lack of resolution. One of them saw it as treachery and did not hesitate to call him a *munafiq* (hypocrite). Kader's departure from his group happened as suddenly as his conversion to Islamism. The settling down of the war to a routine, and his employment in 1995 in a hospital service, partially weakened his religious fervour. Without at all disowning his former passion for the FIS, he looked on the war in quite another way;

having disagreed with his father over recent years, he had recently come round to his way of thinking, and had adopted the analysis of the 'ex-combatants', who saw all that hatred and violence as due only to hunger for *kursi* (power). Abandoning Islamism did not mean that he became a sympathiser of the regime, and he retained profound respect for the ex-FIS for having made him dream for the first time of a better future for Algeria. However, by voting for Nahnah in the presidential election of 16 November 1995 and spending some time in France a few months later, he ceased to structure his life around the orders of the Islamists.

Was 'de-politicisation' of daily life a prelude to political submission? The way in which the conflict became routine was probably one of the reasons for the failure of the Islamisation of the FIS voters, in whom the guerrilla organisations had seen a reservoir of fighters for an Islamic state. The non-involvement of those voters in the *jihad*, as well as their participation in the presidential election of 16 November 1995 despite the calls for a boycott by the ex-FIS, cruelly demonstrated to the leaders of that party the fluid-ity of its electorate, which is imbued even so with what the historian Mohamed Harbi calls the 'individualist anarchism'[13] characteristic of the 'Algerian people'. But does this political disavowal not relate more to ra-tional considerations by voters, aware that the regime was consolidating itself, than to local cultural characteristics? Kader's support for Hamas-MSI in 1995 was a way of backing at the lowest cost a possible alternative to the regime. However, it also showed rejection of a 'clergy' brought forth by the armed struggle; the determination that the FLN had shown in its day to order people around[14] now put people off new claimants to command.

Rejection of clergy thrown up by the war. Kader's abandonment of Islam-ism from 1995 was due to the extreme politicisation of Islam; this led some ex-FIS sympathisers to cease to identify with the ideology of factions like the GIA. The all-out struggle against the *'jahiliy'* society and the Tâghout-state led to demobilisation of voters like Kader and, above all, of the weightier electoral supporters of the FIS, such as the traders who had enabled that party's mobilisation strategy to succeed in 1990 and 1991:

'They say that we are no longer Muslims, but that is false, we have not become pagans (*ma jahlunash*). That is a pretext for stealing and killing. Since when are we suppo-sed to be no longer Muslims? We observe Ramadan, the *haj*, the prayers...everything! What we have less than other people, I don't see. It's incredible that they accuse us of that, they don't know anything about Islam and they judge us, but we, we fear only God.' (Petty trader working in Morocco and Algeria, 1995)

---

[13] Mohamed Harbi, 'La tragédie d'une démocratie sans démocrates', *Le Monde*, 1 April 1994.

[14] In July 1968 the Wali of Algiers wanted to force taxi drivers to 'cut their hair and wear moustaches'. Quoted by André Nouschi, *L'Algérie amère, 1914-1994*, Paris, Ed. de la MSH,1995, p. 273.

The perverse effect of the determination of the GIA 'Emirs' to set themselves up as exclusive managers of the word of God was to provoke the rejection, in the name of Islam, of clergy emerging as a result of the war. The Islamists' real capacity for political mobilisation came up, in their hegemonic ambitions, against the existence of numerous interpretations of Islam. When the armed groups stuck to the defence of those oppressed and tortured by the regime, they had the full support of sympathisers of the ex-FIS. From the moment that their struggle became exclusively religious, it aroused suspicion, even a certain demobilisation. It can be suggested that those ideas had something in common with the earlier political methods of the FLN in its ambition to rule over the people in the name of Islam and the nation. The resemblance of the GIA's methods to those of some leaders of the FLN during the liberation war caused the GIA's ideas to lose their initial strength.[15] The two parties, considered together, were reduced to normalcy in a common space in which the figure of the political bandit was dominant. As the conflict became routine there was disarray among the sympathisers convinced of the 'just cause' of the Moudjahidin, frightened by the idea that their heroes might go into partnership with the regime so as to govern the country:

'There will be no agreement with the army, it's impossible. The army holds on to the economy and the oil and gives the Moudjahidin education, culture and the commune police, that's not an agreement, I say that's just the "Beylicate", nothing more.' (Mourad, Algiers suburbs, 1994)

After five years of conflict the fear of seeing their movement absorbed by the regime caused some of the 'converts' to bring forward their abandonment of Islamism. On the other hand, the continuation of guerrilla violence allowed the regime to enjoy international financial backing.

Exploitation of the civil war

As the prospect of establishing an Islamic state by force of arms became increasingly remote, bitterness developed among its advocates, and the regime, which had been facing a collapse of the state apparatus in 1992 and 1993, was able in clever ways to exploit the threat of that happening. Over five years of civil war it developed networks of support for its cause, both with international monetary institutions and with foreign governments (particularly the French one) and even private international companies. In parallel with the rebuilding of its internal social and political base of support, it tapped international sources for the essential part of the financing needed

[15] The methods of certain 'Emirs' recall those of an FLN leader like 'Amrouche the Terrible', head of Wilaya IV (Kabylia) in 1958. Accused of causing the deaths of at least 'possibly as many as 3,000, women as well as men', he held his Wilaya 'in an iron grip' to guard against the counter-revolutionary war waged by the French army's security services. A. Horne, *A Savage War of Peace: Algeria, 1954-1962,* Harmondsworth: Penguin, 1977, pp. 322-4.

for its war political economy. Five years after the outbreak of the civil war, it was able to make the best use of a highly unfavourable internal situation and get the world community to bear the cost of the operations.

The IMF: a new Sublime Porte? The international financial institutions, and in particular the IMF, have played a fundamental role in keeping the regime going. The establishment of a market economy from 1994 onwards earned Algeria the IMF's seal of approval at a crucial moment in the exponential growth of the armed groups. Just as the Regency of Algiers drew its resources from piracy and the Sublime Porte, the Algerian government has been able to make the IMF the treasurer for its security policy. It obtained 40 billion francs from the international community in 1994 in the form of loans, credits, gifts and other financial arrangements, to back the policy of economic liberalisation carried out under the structural adjustment plan provided for by the agreement with the IMF in April. This did not deceive all the private Algerian economic players – not Si Lakhdar, for example:

> 'They brought the war to Algeria, and now they are making foreigners pay for it! Our political chiefs are very cunning: even when everything is going wrong, they manage to earn money, and in addition they would like people to make sacrifices for them again. They didn't have education in France in fact but they have it in their brains.' (Si Lakhdar, prominent personality and entrepreneur, small village, 1994)

This financial backing denounced by the Islamists did not only pay for modernisation of the machinery of repression. It also paid for the regime's economic policy, through the construction of homes and the creation of jobs in 'public interest worksites'. Thus, besides the revenues from the sale of oil and gas, the regime was able to add a form of rent based on the threat of an Islamic state led by the local 'Emirs' and the guerrillas. Looking at the help from international financial bodies, the debt repayment facilities negotiated in 1994 and renegotiated in 1995, one cannot fail to see that the IMF is filling the role of a new Sublime Porte.[16] However, the bilateral relations with Algeria's privileged partners have a share in that rent; France is exemplary in that respect.

France: the price of the Islamist threat. Is France's financial backing for the Algerian government since 1992, expressed in a financial package worth

---

[16] J.-C. Vatin emphasises that the Regency's main resources came from piracy: 'The Corsairs' fortune made the Regency's... The essential part of the resources for long came from outside, and those resources were such, at certain times, that taxes raised within the country could seem like topping-up or a surplus.' The Sublime Porte's contribution consisted mainly of 'payment of a portion of the pay of the militia' of the Janissaries, writes M. Gaïd. Thus the IMF and the Sublime Porte participated in the budget to some extent, but the essential portion of the resources came from piracy for the Regency and from oil for the Algerian Republic. On the historical aspect of the Regency's finances see J.-C. Vatin, op. cit., p. 107, and M. Gaïd, *L'Algérie sous les Turcs,* Algiers: Mimouni, 1991, p. 94.

6 billion francs,[17] to be explained by fear of an Islamic state in Algeria? The thousand speculations of the press about the consequences that would follow such an event (massive emigration to France, loss of economic interests to the United States, risks of the export of terrorism, etc.)[18] explain the violence of the Islamist guerrillas against journalists, who are accused of frightening Algeria's privileged partners by dramatising the idea of an Islamic state. The lucrative theme of the menace of an Islamic state seems, like the ideas of the market economy, to have been perfectly mastered by the new Algerian political leaders. Thus President Liamine Zeroual, in terms borrowed from Samuel Huntington,[19] spoke at Copenhagen in March 1995 of the new challenges to be faced,

'The threat of a generalised conflict has now been averted, but many local conflicts still continue...in which spiritual values and civilisation are placed at stake to serve hegemonistic schemes...Universal détente should not divert our attention from new threats which are more insidious, but already very dangerous.'[20]

Will the Islamist threat be for Algeria what the Communist threat was for the pro-Western regimes of South-East Asia, a geopolitical rent? The fear of an Islamist state in Algeria, expansionist and capable of destabilising the neighbouring states, explains in part France's support for the Algerian regime. On their side the leaders of the ex-FIS, so as not to become the new world threat after the Communists, have been actively trying to distance themselves from the role which they are supposed to be playing. Thus Rabah Kébir declared:

'It is absolutely necessary to avoid treating the other person as the devil. God has willed the world in its diversity. The responsibility of men of religion is to explain the faith, peacefully. The Koran lays it down: he who wants to believe, he can, he who does not want to, that is his business. It is good that the Rome platform was worked out under the auspices of the Catholic Community of Sant'Egidio. That encourages coexistence between Christians and Muslims.'[21]

The GIA, with which the FIS has recalled 'that it has no connection',[22] has greatly contributed to French backing for the Algerian regime; its criticisms

---

[17] C. Ardouin, 'Economie algérienne: quelles perspectives?', *Maghreb-Machrek,* no. 149, 1995, p. 20.

[18] Abdelhamid Brahimi, the former Prime Minister from 1984 to 1988 who is close to the FIS, has written, 'Their fallacious argument, repeated and amplified by some French leaders to their European partners, consists of declaring that if the FIS came to power democratically, there would be two to three million Algerians fleeing their country by emigrating to France, from which they could infiltrate their way into any European country', *El Mounqidh,* no. 6, June 1995.

[19] S. Huntington, 'The Clash of Civilizations?', *Foreign Affairs,* 72, 3, 1993, pp. 23-49 (he developed his ideas in the book *The Clash of Civilizations and the Remaking of World Order,* New York: Simon and Schuster, 1996).

[20] AFP despatch, March 1995.

[21] *La Croix l'Evénement,* 21 Jan. 1995.

[22] 'As for certain acts of violence and atrocities attributed to the GIA against women and

of 'Crusaders', its call on Jacques Chirac to convert to Islam,[23] and its claim of responsibility for outrages committed in France in 1995 made it the enemy of the Algerian government and of France,[24] but also of the FIS. And many doubts remain about the 'Emirs' of the GIA armed bands, as they have so weakened the cause they are supposed to be serving.

Private international companies. The amendment in 1991 of the legislation on investment in the oil and gas sector has made it possible for the government to involve international companies in its defence, because of the profits it has been offering them. However, it was only after the presidential election of November 1995 that contracts were signed. Reassured as to the continuation of the regime, British Petroleum did not hesitate to commit investment estimated at three and a half million dollars, followed by other companies like Exxon, Repsol, Agip, Total etc.[25] Some of the Saharan regions have been declared 'exclusion zones' and closed since 1995 to civilians without authorisation. Besides this measure, aimed at reassuring the staff of those foreign companies in the face of GIA threats, the companies were offered the possibility of ensuring their own security by recruiting 'mercenaries'.[26] This investment, besides restoring Algeria's financial credibility and hence the possibility of obtaining new loans, has also ensured substantial profits due to setup fees paid by investors.[27] The discovery of new oil fields and the completion on schedule of oil and gas pipelines to Morocco and Tunisia have allowed the military to consolidate the revenue from oil and gas. The international oil companies are involved in the same way as the international financial institutions and favoured economic partners such as France, and through their investment in Algeria are partners in the restoration of state authority. The civil war, far from putting an end to foreign investment, has despite repeated threats from the

---

civilians, the FIS cannot be responsible for obvious reasons, that there is no link between the FIS and the GIA', *El Mounqidh*, September 1995, p. 38.

[23] GIA communiqué, *Al Hayat*, 8 Oct. 1995.

[24] 'France has well and truly increased its financial and logistical aid to the putschists and has above all used, since the month of June, all its means to persuade its partners to facilitate access by the putschists of Algiers to the facilities of the international financial institutions...In behaving in that way, the French government is putting the medium and long term interests of its people and its country at risk. It is certain that Algerian women and men, suffering today from the repression imposed by the putschists supported and encouraged by Chirac and his government, will know how to recognise their friends and...the others when the time comes'. 'Chirac backs the junta', *El Ribat,* October 1995.

[25] *Jeune Afrique,* no. 1830, 31 January 1996.

[26] 'In 1995 the authorities set up in the Sahara four exclusion zones guarded by the army, and companies now send practically no Westerners to work in Algeria – except for mercenaries in charge of security'. *Le Monde,* 16 Feb. 1996.

[27] According to *Algérie Confidentiel,* no. 72, 1996, Arco was said to have paid 230 million francs to win the contract for marketing of gas in partnership with Sonatrach.

guerrillas considerably increased it.[28] It is true that in this matter the oil companies have experience, and that in Angola, for example,[29] the civil war did not alter their investment strategy at all: private companies of mercenaries such as Executive Outcomes, staffed by former South African military personnel, have contributed to the stability of oil exploitation zones in Africa.

The Algerian government, against all expectations, has succeeded in exploiting the civil war. After being viewed as militarily beaten at the outset, it has succeeded in creating a form of rent derived from the Islamist threat. That threat was publicly denounced at the Barcelona Euro-Mediterranean Conference[30] in November 1995, and was actually given the status of 'enemy' at the Sharm el Sheikh summit in Egypt in March 1996. The struggle against 'Islamist terrorism' is the common denominator of certain states, among which Algeria plans to be fully included, extracting some advantages in the process. It is with some bitterness that some Islamists of the ex-FIS realise that the 'just cause' is not treated favourably by the international community.[31]

Military and guerrillas in the pursuit of war

Self-interested pursuit of the war. After five years the military leaders seem to have made the 'right choice' between the risk of being swept away by the democratic process and that of halting the parliamentary elections and setting off a civil war. The war has in many respects restored their authority and ensured profits for them. Having been in a politically weak position *vis-à-vis* the FIS in 1991, they have succeeded in marginalising the FIS in the war. But the military, like the Islamists, have gone through changes

---

[28] 'Sonatrach has signed thirty-four prospection agreements of the production sharing type with more than twenty companies. The results are more than convincing. The success rate for wells completed is over 50%. In 1994 Algeria was ranked as the first "discoverer" with eight oil wells found.' *La Nation*, no. 128, 2-8 Jan. 1996.

[29] On Angola see M.E. Ferreira, 'La reconversion économique de la nomenklatura pétrolière', *Politique Africaine*, March 1995, pp. 11-27.

[30] On 27-28 November 1995 the 15 states of the European Union and the 12 southern and eastern Mediterranean states met at Barcelona to establish the bases for an overall Euro-Mediterranean partnership. This project had three aspects: political, economic and social. The political and security partnership envisages 'intensifying the political dialogue on the basis of a certain number of values and principles: respect for territorial integrity; non-interference; respect for human rights; the rule of law; democracy; non-resort to force and peaceful settlement of disputes; control of armaments, disarmament and non-proliferation; the struggle against drugs, terrorism and organised crime.' See *Ramsès 97*, IFRI, 1996, p. 72; also B. Hibou and L. Martinez, *L'Afrique du Nord et le partenariat euroméditerranéen. Les ambivalences d'une intégration régionale*, study prepared for the Commissariat Général du Plan, Paris: Karthala (forthcoming).

[31] Anouar Haddam regrets that 'unfortunately, the just cause and the armed struggle are not recognised as a legal and legitimate action by the international community', *La Croix l'Evénement*, 21 Jan. 1995.

brought about by the civil war. The army special forces, whose first class graduated in 1996, illustrate that process. They were tempted to keep up the war indefinitely against Islamic groups which, after all, have been securing them an inflow of funds and facilitating 'de-politicisation' – that being, as P. Veyne emphasises, only a 'natural apoliticism' – among voters considered as 'under-developed' and therefore tempted by 'radical populism'.[32] Once the government was capable of installing a controlled political system, with actors obedient to the military leadership at the outset, the latter rejected any negotiation with the leaders of the ex-FIS: that would put at risk the resounding and staggering profits derived from the Islamist 'peril'.

The determination of the military to keep the war going is seen in different ways by the various Islamist factions. While it does not surprise the groups affiliated to the GIA, it arouses incomprehension in the AIS, even though that faction is ready to negotiate with the regime:

The way you have become mixed up in this filthy mission has caused the military profession to lose its message and lose respect, to be relegated to a collaborationist and mercenary role. We do not understand how you bring yourselves to kill your fathers, your sons and your brothers for the pleasure of a minority of unbelieving Communists! We do not understand how you have been able to accept collective suicide to serve 'Lacoste's corporals'.[33]

But that 'collective suicide' affected the local population more than the warrior elites, both Islamist and military, which found in it opportunities for accumulation of wealth and prestige. As the war has settled down to a routine, will the leaders of armed groups become indispensable intermediaries if there are negotiations with the government? The steady marginalisation of the FIS has strengthened their authority, and has also confirmed how entrenched the belief in war as a means of making money has become.

Reproduction of elites by the war. Thanks to the war, more than one leader of an armed group has become the equal of an elected political representative or a local eminent personality. For them, as for the new army elite emerging from the special forces of the Biskra college, the end of hostilities would mean the end of privileges. The 'Emirs' have become political actors whose presence is of prime importance in a negotiation process, as Anouar Haddam has said:

[32] See the report 'Algérie 2005' prepared by experts who maintain that the democratic transition process, in countries in a state of under-development, faces an obstacle in a 'potentially nihilist populism, fuelled by the structural existence of a numerous population excluded from economic and social progress...a population in a permanent situation of breach with the state and the institutions embodying it.' Quoted by *La Nation*, no. 158, 1996.

[33] 'Lacoste's corporals' were the Algerian officers trained by the French army who joined the FLN during the war of liberation, like General Khaled Nezzar. *Lettre à l'ANP et aux forces de l'ordre*, p. 15, in collection of letters of the AIS-FIS entitled *Mots de vérité à ceux qui se sentent concernés*, edited by the FIS overseas executive, April 1995.

We say that if the government in power accepts the principle that we should meet, we the FIS leaders, with all the leaders of the underground armed fighters, the Moudjahidin without exception, at that moment, as they will be part of the decision making process – we shall then be ready to call a cease-fire before starting negotiations properly.[34]

If this were to happen, it would show that an Algerian war *imaginaire* remains operative; following the success of local prominent personalities through the war of liberation, the 'Emirs' would be continuing their elders' tradition. In reality that would only be a form of recognition and legalisation of a *de facto* situation, for the 'Emirs' are already partners in local decisions, as is shown by their relations with the Walis and the local eminent personalities. So, like the chiefs of the maquis during the national liberation war, the local 'Emirs' have been able to make themselves indispensable to the politicians of the ex-FIS. Will they succeed in doing the same where the regime is concerned? The steady weakening of the ex-FIS has been to the benefit of the local 'Emirs', and the GIA leaders have at present nothing to gain from a compromise between the regime and the leaders of the ex-FIS. Such an agreement would restore primacy to the gaoled Islamists, including activists and elected representatives of the ex-FIS, who would invoke their political legitimacy derived from the December 1991 elections, and their academic competence, against the ambitions of 'Moudjahidin by trade' spawned by the civil war.

The 'Emirs', influenced by the models of their elders and knowledge of the local eminent personalities' careers, know that their future lies in the continuation of the *jihad*, which alone can bring maximum returns on their initial investment. Masters of the terrain, integrated into the eminent personalities' local systems, sometimes intermediaries with lieutenants of the army on operations, they have raised themselves to a position which fascinates the children of their home suburbs. What neither emigration, nor *trabendo,* nor crime ever did, the *jihad* has achieved. Djamel Zitouni, 'Emir' of the GIA until July 1996, achieved that status of 'star' which until then only sportsmen like Noureddine Morceli and Raï singers like Cheb Khaled had succeeded in reaching. Their 'zone' in the interior of the country, with control of highways and the '*ghazias*' that they launch against 'rebel' villages, has made them political intermediaries who cannot be bypassed, known to the world press.

In that case, can the 'Emirs'' continue their *jihad* independently of the political will of the ex-FIS? The latter is probably capable, if there are direct talks with the regime, of guaranteeing a credible ceasefire, on condition that it is accompanied by recognition of the position of the 'Emirs'', as Haddam has emphasised. This would amount to recognition of their status as new eminent personalities, legitimate candidates for the jobs of

[34] *La Croix l'Evénement,* 13 Jan. 1995.

mayor and deputy, even for the acquisition of state enterprises being privatised. Prolonging the conflict, while it favours that process, removes all
hope of benefiting from it legitimately, that is by victory. Only the legitimising
of their wealth within the framework of a return to a political process
would make it possible for them to move out of the *jihad*. The local capital of the 'Emirs', acquired at the risk of their lives, is – like the wealth of
military leaders in charge of the repression – not about to be disposed of
without something in return. Everyone has an interest in the continuation
of the war. Far from being 'collective suicide', the war is for them much
more like a school for power. 'Emirs', guerrillas and military, all influenced
by a common war-oriented world view, know that it was through the use
of violence that the big names and big families of old Algiers – 'city of
upstarts and peasants' as F. Braudel put it – emerged. For the Islamist politicians marginalised by the dynamics of the conflict, there remains only
finding a place in the assimilation procedures set up by the regime.

From war economy to peace economy

Development of the Islamist political elites. Having obtained the results
expected, the war economic policies and the campaigns of de-politicisation
have been replaced, since the presidential election of 16 November 1995,
by creation of procedures for assimilation of the Islamist elites and 'laundering' of the guerrilla campaign. In fact the winning over of the ex-FIS
electoral base after the imprisonment of the party's national leaders and
local cadres has been accompanied by a break-up of its monopoly of symbolic management of the Islamist resistance. That break-up is illustrated
by Hamas' political success and the continuation of an assortment of armed
groups (MIA, MEI, GIA, AIS, FIDA, LIDD). Numerous fighters independent
of the FIS have arisen and imposed their presence, able to negotiate
with the government without the agreement of the leading elites of that
party. Those elites, members of the *Majliss ech Choura*,[35] have been the
object of a strategy of assimilation on the part of the regime. Consisting of
Islamist academics, lawyers and engineers, mostly trained abroad, they
come from well-off families. Although spared during the civil war, like the
leading families, they are frightened even so by the increasing autonomy
of the Islamist fighters and by the loss of their hold over the Islamist movement in general.

The Islamist elite, the main producer of resistance rhetoric during the
electoral process, has since the start of the civil war – which has increased
its marginalisation – been paradoxically hoping for a restoration of state

---

[35] According to A. Mérani, out of 35 members of the supreme first organ of the *Majliss ech
Choura*, 25 were still in Algeria at liberty in early 1995. Of the other ten, three were in prison,
two overseas, two had died and two were on the run. AFP despatch, March 1995.

authority. Is its assimilation into the state apparatus the prelude to restoration of the hegemony of the regime? The Islamist elite's non-participation in the armed struggle against the regime is for the latter a guarantee of its seriousness; it has instead followed the alternative courses of exile, imprisonment or political submission. Aware that time is not on its side and that the rising power of the suburban 'Emirs' and guerrillas risks making those rivals in due course the regime's privileged partners in talks, the Islamist political elite has found in the regime's survival a guarantee of its own existence. Thus Rabah Kébir, chairman of the FIS executive in exile, has stated:

The people still has confidence in the FIS and there is no other alternative to the regime. But a dictatorship, even an Islamist one, would still be a dictatorship and we want none of it...Neither the army nor the Islamic opposition are today in a position to win a military victory. We want to preserve what remains, human lives, infrastructure...if not, tomorrow will be a disaster for the people and for whoever will want to govern.[36]

The fear among the Islamist political elite – represented by a portion of the FIS activists – of an Islamic dictatorship taking over recalls the fear expressed in 1961 by the FLN political cadres, represented by Ferhat Abbas, at the time of the seizure of power by the army of the borders. The GPRA (Gouvernement Provisoire de la République Algérienne), headed by Ferhat Abbas, replaced in September 1958 the FLN's Comité de Coordination et d'Exécution (CCE); it rapidly came into conflict with the general staff set up in December 1959 under the leadership of Houari Boumedienne with responsibility over the army of the borders stationed in Tunisia and Morocco. In 1961 and 1962 the general staff's strategy, Mohamed Harbi notes, aimed at establishing 'the primacy of the military over the political'.[37] On 28 June 1962 Boumedienne ordered the army of the borders (21,000 men in Tunisia and 15,000 in Morocco) to 'prepare themselves to enter Algeria', the GPRA having decided to abolish the staff and dismiss Colonel Boumedienne. The final phase of the war of liberation removed political leaders like Ferhat Abbas and, by the same process, put an end to the installation of democracy, to the advantage of the military.

That precedent explains the ex-FIS politicians' fear of seeing the Islamist military ('Emirs', guerrillas, district Moudjahidin) coming to power through violence. Such an eventuality would undermine their own political legitimacy based on the parliamentary elections of December 1991, to the advantage of Moudjahidin with the aura of 'revolutionary legitimacy' acquired in the exercise of violence, like their elders thirty years earlier. The breach appearing between the former FIS elected representatives in exile or on conditional release and the armed Islamist elite ('Emirs' and guerrillas) was a boon for the regime in its strategy of assimilation. The various

---

[36] *La Croix l'Evénement*, 21 Jan. 1996.

[37] M. Harbi, *Le FLN, mirage et réalité*, Paris: Jeune Afrique, 1980, p. 325.

informal meetings between the government and imprisoned FIS leaders were aimed precisely at compromising those leaders, with a view to inducing them to dissociate themselves explicitly from the armed factions and especially from the AIS, which had declared allegiance to the FIS.[38] That process would not fail to weaken the AIS, which from then on would lose its political legitimacy and thus its original aspect compared with the GIA. So, faced with such a prospect, the AIS leaders did not fail to issue a warning:

Know that the people and its fighting vanguard – the Front Islamique du Salut – will never accept a truce contrary to religion, nor corruption in fundamental choices, whatever the massive scale of terrorism imposed by the junta. They will continue to walk in the way of the *jihad* until the installation of an Islamic state following the example of the Prophet.[39]

The way in which the guerrillas took root, and their determination to take over the legitimacy held by the ex-FIS elected representatives, created a threatening situation for the latter who, deprived of a political space, found that they were dependent on the guerrillas. The AIS was summoned to respond to the challenges of the GIA which declared that there would be 'no truce, no negotiation'. The Islamist elected representatives had two options: either to join the armed organisations like Mohamed Saïd and many other militants – at the risk of death – or to act as guerrilla reserves. The second choice involved the risk that a guerrilla victory would make them suffer the dismal fate of the FLN political leaders in 1961-2, forced to submit to the ALN guerrillas; while if the guerrillas failed, they would enter on a process of steady marginalisation in which some could experience the same indefinite exile as Aït Ahmed, Boudiaf and others. It can be conjectured that those elected representatives, faced with such prospects, and now convinced of the solidity of the regime, will prudently find their way back into the political system, starting with the world of business, in particular, where the Islamist elites rub shoulders with political actors of various tendencies.

[38] In May 1995 there were direct negotiations between the Presidency and Abassi Madani. They broke down over the fact that the FIS leaders rejected the government's programme which made the following demands: '(1) He must issue an appeal for a halt to acts of violence. That would be followed by the release of all the leaders of the banned party who agreed to support this solution. (2) Once that phase was completed, a deadline would be given to the elements of the armed groups for them to lay down their arms. (3) Once that second phase was completed, the leaders of the banned party could return to political life through a new organisation with a new name...(4) Within the framework of national reconciliation to be consolidated, elements that had been involved in the violence would be the object of legal provisions for *rahma* (clemency) and a gradual policy of clemency.' Madani, meeting with other leaders of the FIS, issued counter-proposals, among them the following: '(1) Placing the institution of the ANP outside political affairs...(2) Non-resort to force as a means of remaining in power or attaining power, and the right of the people to defend its choice by legitimate means. (3) Compensating all the victims and stricken people of the crisis', etc. The talks came to a halt in June 1995. *La Tribune,* 12 July 1995.

[39] *Lettre à l'ANP et aux forces de l'ordre* (note 33), p. 16.

'Merger of Elites'. Few Islamist political leaders – apart from Ahmed Mérani, member of the FIS *Majliss ech Choura* and then of Ahmed Ghozali's government in 1990 and Ahmed Ouyahia's in 1996 – dissociated themselves from the movement in the early stages, for they were convinced that the regime's days were numbered and that time was on their party's side. But after the presidential election of 16 November 1995, a group of ex-FIS elected representatives set up in Turkey an 'offficial bureau of the Front Islamique overseas',[40] joined by members of the former *Majliss ech Choura* and some elected representatives. Encouraged by the government, this bureau aimed to replace the FIS in the political system, and therefore to break with the opposition led by Rabah Kébir, Chairman of the FIS overseas executive. In that way the regime encouraged other leaders to seize their chance, after the failure of the direct negotiations with leaders of the party in June 1995, which had covered among other subjects the creation of a new Islamist party. That initiative aroused the anger of the Islamist leaders, who described it as treachery:

From a reliable source we learn that a plot against the progress of the Algerian people and its just cause is being organised by Ibn Azouz Zoubda...We learn also that that group consists of about thirty people, including parliamentarians and members of the previous *Majliss ech Choura*. It should be recalled that the leader of this clique, the man named Zoubda, has lived in Turkey for some time, and has become a businessman there, living in the elegant ambassadors' district. Is what he did to his brothers before not enough for him?[41]

The steady assimilation of the ex-FIS political elites is inherent in their enrichment. Ben Azouz Zoubda's desire to lead the new Islamist party which the military are encouraging was shared by other former leaders of the FIS and members of the *Majliss ech Choura* living in Algeria on conditional release (25 out of 35 members). By that initiative the government increased its pressure on those of the leaders who were still imprisoned, to bring them to accept its conditions.

However, as J.-F. Bayart stresses, the merger of elites 'occurs also in the world of business' and 'is located first and foremost in the private sector'.[42] The personal experiences of the political leaders of the ex-FIS, far from making them alien to the military-nationalist elites, bring them closer to those elites. Besides belonging to the same land, they also have experiences and close relations which, even in time of war, transcend ideological alignments. The life story of Othmane Aïssani, presented as a 'negotiator of the armed wing of the FIS (AIS)', illustrates this process:

[40] *Al Tabsira,* no. 188, February 1996.

[41] According to rumour Ben Azouz Zebda, who was living in Libya before going to Turkey, was said to be responsible for the disappearance of ex-FIS militants who had taken refuge in Libya in 1995. *Al Tabsira,* no. 188, February 1996.

[42] J.-F. Bayart, *L'Etat en Afrique,* Paris: Fayard, 1989, 439 pp., p. 205.

Othmane Aïssani, 47 years old, for long played in a Constantine region Chaabi [popular songs of the east] band, before becoming a travelling Imam in Abdallah Djaballah's Islamist movement, 'En Nahda' (the Rebirth), a rival party to the FIS. Othmane Aïssani, coming from a very poor devout family, is today a prosperous man. His clothes shop and his ready-to-wear clothing workshop mean that he does not go short. His elder brother Moussa was the personal secretary of Colonel Chaabani, executed by the Ben Bella-Boumedienne team in 1965. The Aïssani family is close to Moudjahidin circles (the Organisation Nationale des Moudjahidin), the ministry for Moudjahidin having been for long headed by Mohamed Djeghaba, Colonel Chaabani's former right-hand man. Aïssani, who comes from Jijel, has already exercised his talents as a negotiator in the past, obtaining the readmission of ten dissident members of the FIS out of seventeen expelled after the stormy Batna Congress,[43] on 26 August 1991.[44]

This man's story illustrates well the links between the Islamist political elites and the state elites. In popular parlance the term 'Beard-FLN' is given to those eminent personalities, politicians and military people with Islamist convictions, who have today turned into negotiators and managers of the procedures for co-opting of the Islamist political elites. That is why the Presidency did not fail to call back the caciques of the Boumedienne period at the time of the 'open dialogue' in April 1996,[45] so as to make use of their experience in the area of co-optation and assimilation of the Islamist elected representatives, even of the guerrillas.

Co-opting the guerrillas? The experience of the former members of the Conseil de la Révolution in that area was a winning card for the regime. Former guerrillas or soldiers of the army of the borders, during the 1970s they assimilated or eliminated all political forms of opposition.[46] Serving as models for the Islamist guerrillas, they share with them a pronounced taste for violence and power; that is to say that there are numerous points

---

[43] After the arrest of Abassi Madani and Ali Benhadj, Abdelkader Hachani, 'promoted head of the Political Affairs Commission, decided at the beginning of July 1991 to call a national conference for the purpose of giving the FIS a provisional leadership.' The Congress at Batna ended with the formation of a new political bureau favouring the so-called '*djaz-ara*' tendency. See S. Labat, *Les islamistes algériens. Entre les urnes et le maquis*, Paris: Seuil, 1995, p. 119.

[44] *Algérie Confidentiel*, 8 April 1996.

[45] While General Liamine Zéroual's election campaign concentrated on breaking with the past, the national press noted with surprise that in the 'open dialogue' political leaders active under the Boumedienne regime rose up: people like A. Benouada, A. Habbachi, M. Mechati, *et al.,* all former members of the 'Committee of 22' (22 militants who in 1954 opposed the line of the 'Centralists' of the MTLD on the armed struggle strategy to follow): *La Nation,* no. 146, 7-13 May 1996.

[46] Ghazi Hidouci has written, 'The historic leaders who had become too much of a burden were therefore to be physically hunted down; others, and their clients, would be offered economic rewards in proportion to the political sacrifices imposed on them', in *Algérie. La libération inachevée,* Paris: La Découverte, 1995, p. 42.

of convergence. The integration of local 'Emirs' into the state institutions is thus a plausible hypothesis, in view of the government's practice in dealing with the most challenging opposition. For qualified jobseekers, army deserters and reformed criminals, access to responsible positions in the apparatus of repression, owing to their experience in the *jihad*, is a priceless opportunity.

On the other hand, just like the military, the 'Emirs' are afraid of the political legitimacy of the activists of the ex-FIS, and have begun to eliminate some of them physically.[47] For these adolescents of the civil war, any return to peace means, if the FIS is legalised again, a return to their precarious situation as *hittistes*, or at best to jobs as policemen in the future Islamist local authorities headed by elected representatives of Nahnah's party. The *rahma* (clemency) granted to 'terrorists' by President Liamine Zéroual,[48] as a preliminary to their recruitment into the security forces, has only attracted a limited number of fighters: 2,000 are said to have given themselves up since 1994. Co-optation of the 'Emirs' requires, like the assimilation of ex-FIS parliamentarians and members of the *Majliss ech Choura*, an accompanying financial policy. But 'laundering' the financial resources of the local 'Emirs' remains a slow process. Their investments in real estate, trade or import-export are tokens for the regime of their intention to move out of the *jihad*, but the fear of being murdered or denounced by the guerrilla organisations that they have been supposed to serve holds back that process. Here again the comparison between the leaders of the interior maquis during the war of liberation and the local 'Emirs' remains pertinent: the maquis chiefs had to wait for the consolidation of Houari Boumedienne's regime to prosper in peace.[49]

Such a process is a part of 'state formation': the integration of guerrillas means for the regime recruitment of younger men to its ranks, rather than a break in the political system. The empathy of the local 'Emirs' with the population confronted with pauperisation has made them the best

---

[47] According to Karam Eddine Kherbane, a founding member of the FIS in exile in London, the GIA is considered responsible for the murder 'of a certain number of our brothers'. *Al Hayat,* quoted in *Courrier International,* May 1996.

[48] In one of his speeches Zéroual emphasised that 'Algeria is the homeland of all Algerians without any being excluded. Repentance is an Islamic virtue. *Rahma* (clemency) is a noble principle of Islam. National legislation is a guarantor of that *rahma* towards the children of Algeria who will know how to regain self-control....Algeria must also heal the whole of its wound, Algeria must reject the culture of hatred and division among the children of a united nation...' Quoted in *La Nation,* no. 124, week of 5-11 Dec. 1995.

[49] On this period see J. Leca and J.-C. Vatin: 'The alliance of 1965 with the former heads of Wilayas (in the Council of the Revolution but also through certain advantages granted to possible opponents among former guerrilla officers) allowed the "external" leaders to obtain acceptance by the "internal" ones. This alliance allowed the demobilised "troops" to prosper under the protection of their leaders, integrated into the organs of the state.' *L'Algérie politique, institutions et régime,* Paris: Presses de la FNSP, 1975, p. 395.

agents of social control, while their aura as well as their wealth indicate new forms of patronage. From such a viewpoint the political advantages for the government are guaranteed: the 'Emirs', who have become subcontractors, are to be the 'Caïds' of modern times, responsible for order and security according to the principles of the *shari'a*. Although their activity, in some communes of the Algiers region, already comes within the category of that sort of work, the 'Emirs' are waiting for political recognition of their status.

What ways out of the civil war?

War as a way of life. Against the theory of 'political bandits' becoming government servants are the facts of privatisation of violence, rejection of the state and the continuation of guerrilla warfare for its own sake. Like Renamo in Mozambique, the Algerian guerrillas could become a social body.[50] They would then develop, in connection with other war-oriented enterprises or political organisations, a whole infrastructure capable of providing services, forming a state within a state. The refusal to find a place in the state is compensated by the status and pay that they offer the fighters, for as the guerrilla campaign has become a sanctuary, it is in a position to guarantee its territorial fiefs. Such a guerrilla campaign does not threaten the consolidation of the regime and can be a cause of profit for it through the 'Islamist rent' – that is, external financing of the struggle against the 'terrorist threat' in the Maghreb. That hypothesis, however, can only be borne out on condition that the Islamist political elites dissociate themselves from the guerrillas and find a place in the system again – in fact, the FIS and its armed wing the AIS must move out of the *jihad* and leave the GIA to wage its 'total war'.

Complementary enemies. The steady closing of exits from Algeria, following the restrictive visa policy towards its people, has favoured a limited number of military enterpreneurs (about 25,000) who have alone been able to leave the country for business reasons. Thanks to their contacts they enjoy the right to negotiate to their best advantage on the imports which can now be afforded because of the debt rescheduling. Perpetual continuation of the civil war therefore guarantees substantial profits for the warring parties' middlemen. This alliance of interests has led more than one economic actor who has suffered from the violence to express the wish that the warring parties will destroy each other:

[50] C. Geffray writes: 'Declarations thus fulfil an almost technical function, subordinate to the war-oriented social programme which is its real purpose. In that sense Renamo is a social body: an institution with no other purpose than its own reproduction. Its members, precisely because they enjoy and benefit from the social effects of the war, are essentially occupied with new supplies of the oxygen that allows them to survive: war'. *La cause des armes au Mozambique,* Paris: Karthala, 1990, p. 167.

'They are similar, the two camps resemble each other like brothers, they want power by force and they only give it up out of weakness. The FIS is like the FLN in the war, it is ready with its Moudjahidin to kill us all to achieve success. But we, *hamdou lillah*, we have nothing more to do with them, we watch them slaughter themselves, and as for me I hope that both of them (army and Islamists) will kill each other, that way we'll have peace and quiet.' (Chemist, father of a family, 40 years old, Morocco, 1995)

After five years of conflict guerrillas and military have found that they are very close. They are complementary enemies, they share the same perception of power and the means of taking it. While the regime has improved its base of support by bringing the bourgeois of the ex-FIS on board, the guerrillas have taken on the subsidising of a part of the population heading for pauperisation.[51] This division of labour ensures, after a fashion, performance of a task of regulation which restrains social demands longing for expression.[52] The Islamist guerrillas, complementary with the government, raise revenue in the place of the official tax authorities by demanding a protection levy from private economic actors – the government being unable to raise taxes because it is anxious to accommodate the leading figures in the private sector backed by the IMF, who are in practice exempt from taxes.[53] Together with this redistribution activity through the 'Emirs' there has been social control which saves the regime from facing a social crisis.

From the FFS maquis in 1963 to the Islamist guerrilla campaign. The hypothesis of co-optation of the Islamist political elites and the 'laundering' of the guerrillas' funds must inevitably have implications for the political system. Is the gradual but continuous integration of ex-FIS voters into the administrative machine (recruitment of skilled jobseekers), into money-making networks (dealers in the trading economy), and into the forces of order (the commune police and militias for the local 'Moudjahidin' of the armed bands) capable of altering the nature of the regime? Is the winning over of FIS voters by the government since the dissolution of the party in March 1992 leading to an 'Islamisation' of the regime? While the political leaders of the ex-FIS hesitated over the strategy to follow against

[51] In the fortnightly *La Cause,* mouthpiece of the former FIS elected representatives, they explain: 'The Moudjahidin are proceeding to distribute food supplies, clothing, educational materials and money to the most deprived, ever more numerous, to those whom the agreement with the IMF and the war have cast into ghettoes of more and more blatant destitution'; no. 18, 5 May 1995, p. 6.

[52] There were only 225 strikes in Algeria during the year 1995.

[53] In 1995, out of '12,000 persons subject to income tax, only 2,000 presented their returns. That was revealed, during a tour of the west of the country, by Prime Minister Ahmed Ouyahia, summoning officials of the region: "Love of one's country – where does it lie? It does not lie in the Kalashnikov alone, gentlemen, but in application of the law!"' Quoted by *La Nation,* no. 142, 9-15 April 1996.

the army after the halting of the elections, their voters undoubtedly anticipated the possibility of a political compromise. Satisfying the demands
of the Islamist electorate – installation of a minimum state, settling of land
disputes, a jobs and housing policy – led to its demobilisation. Those voters' political fluidity foiled the FIS' strategy of struggle; the Front has been
deprived of its social base, which has become a hostage to the 'Emirs'; it
faces competition from the trading bourgeoisie which has rallied behind
Hamas-MSI, and has at the same been torn by personal disagreements.

The party has caused cracks in the political system which its voters have
been able to exploit. Is that intrusion the harbinger of political change? Have
the voters renounced the Islamist programme for a job? The regime, convinced that the cure for resistance is to be found in political integration and
enrichment for the 'ringleaders', has deliberately instigated this process of
winning people over. In thirty years of handling opposition, its methods
in that business have continually been perfected. It has notably made
profitable use of its experience of the FFS dissidence in 1963, whose cause
and treatment were in many respects similar. When it took to the maquis
in 1963 the Front des Forces Socialistes wanted to denounce the conditions
in which the referendum on the Constitution in September 1963, which
established the one-party system, was being organised:

'To put an end to dictatorial power and the personal regime which is trying to impose itself on our country...to start from today the decisive fight, with discipline
and strict obedience to directives...We are counting', said Aït Ahmed, 'on a revolutionary contagion, that is, we think that the deep-seated discontent of the people,
which exists all over Algeria, will not fail to reveal itself.'[54]

Amrane Ahdjouj has written: 'To defuse the discontent, the government
announced a series of measures, including an emergency plan for Greater
Kabylia providing for replacement of agricultural credit in that region by
state subsidies, implementation of a plan to construct 2,700 rural dwellings,
bringing of water and electricity supplies to the villages, establishment of
industrial workshops and reopening of all those which had been closed
after the departure of the settlers...That response was coupled on the
ground with military action. With thirteen battalions mobilised, the army
riposted by covering and systematically combing Kabylia. The blow was
hard, the population was to remain affected for several years by the shock
of a repression recalling in many ways the sad colonial period.' That author attributes the failure of the FFS' armed struggle to the faith in 'spontaneity'
and 'voluntarism' that inspired that party at the time: 'Taking to the maquis
is not enough for the people's energies to be released and for the vast majority of the people to organise and mobilise against the regime...The
Algeria of 1962 was not the Algeria of 1954.'[55]

---

[54] Quoted by A. Ahdjouj, *Etat, pouvoir et société,1962-65,* Paris: Armand Colin, 1997,
p. 112.
[55] Ibid., p. 115.

Certainly the militants of the FIS, in contrast to those of the FFS in 1963, had the advantage of a highly favourable revolutionary context. For the 'revolutionary contagion' on which Aït Ahmed had counted had been limited then because of the exhaustion of a society emerging from seven years of war against the French army. In 1992, when the Islamists launched the *jihad*, this was in tune with the 'longing for dissidence' analysed by C. Geffray in Mozambican society.[56] Yet although the conditions were favourable, the Islamists' revolutionary dynamic came up against the 'power' and 'resistance' of the Algerian state, studied by J.-C. Vatin.[57] In addition, just as the regime of Ben Bella did its utmost to integrate people from Greater Kabylia into the security forces,[58] Liamine Zéroual's regime strove to contain Islamist dissidence through a combined military and economic policy.

Can what succeeded with the FFS succeed with the ex-FIS? The extent of the Islamist resistance and the duration of the conflict show the limits of the comparison. In addition, the cost of dealing with the FFS dissidence was well below the current cost of the Islamist dissidence. Certainly the regime, with the help of international assistance, remains less affected than in 1963, when its resources were far more limited. However, analysis of the five years of war shows that such a hypothesis is plausible. The fact remains that prolonging the war, although lucrative, has weighty political consequences for those managing it. The conflict, in becoming endless, confers a new legitimacy on those who are in charge of the repression; it can challenge the revolutionary legitimacy of the '54 generation' still in power. Thus one cannot exclude the hypothesis of a coup d'état on the initiative of the '92 generation' composed of young officers responsible for the repression. They know better than anyone their enemy, young 'Emirs' thrown up by the war like them. If the '54 generation' does not succeed in assimilating them, it can be supposed that the officers of the '92 generation' will take the initiative of establishing direct connections with them. If the opposite happens, a merger of the protagonists is the most probable outcome of this civil war.

To carry out fully the de-politicisation and assimilation of the Islamist elites, the regime needs the violence of the guerrilla factions. The government's retention of power goes hand in hand with the endless continuation

---

[56] Geffray, op. cit., p. 77.

[57] See J.-C. Vatin's analysis, already quoted, on the inability of Islamic movements in the contemporary history of Algeria to take power: 'Puissance d'Etat et résistance islamique en Algérie. Approche mécanique, XIXe-XXe siècles' in J.-C. Vatin and E. Gellner (eds), *Islam et politique au Maghreb*, Paris: Ed. du CNRS, 1981, p. 267.

[58] Following the 'Kabyle dissidence', an agreement was signed between President Ben Bella and Colonel Mohand el Hadj, the ally of Aït Ahmed. This agreement included a guarantee of the integration of former leaders of the home Wilaya of Aït Ahmed and Mohand el Hadj into 'more important posts in the ANP'. See J. Leca and J.-C. Vatin, op. cit., p. 338.

of violence by the Islamist guerrillas who, unintentionally, produce new wealth for the military. The fear of an Islamic state headed by autonomous 'Emirs' is leading ex-FIS leaders in exile to hope for negotiation with the government rather than the success of the most radical guerrilla factions like the GIA. Hence the Islamist groups engaged in 'total war' serve the interests of their adversary, the army. Guerrillas and soldiers are becoming complementary enemies whose war logic is unfavourable to the political actors engaged in dissidence until the presidential election of 16 November 1995. The existence of the guerrillas makes it possible for the Presidency to subject the political parties to its authority and to choose its new partners from among them. Five years after the interruption of the parliamentary elections, the regime had succeeded in turning the imminent risk of being swept away into a financial asset, in the form of foreign aid for the struggle against the 'Islamist threat'.

11

CONCLUSION

We hope we have shown that war is, to the protagonists, a virtuous way of accumulating wealth and prestige and that, in that sense, the consolidation of violence is the result of the opportunities for social advancement which it creates. Far from being enemies with irreconcilable values, the military and the Islamist guerrillas are driven by a common war-oriented *imaginaire*. This analysis of the civil war makes it possible for us to suggest a certain number of conclusions and to put forward new hypotheses on the effects of continuation of the war.

Neither side can win

It has to be accepted that five years after the outbreak of the civil war, neither of the warring parties has succeeded in winning. The Islamists of the ex-FIS, although they initially had considerable capital at their disposal (three million voters, political legitimacy and influence over traders of the private sector), did not succeed in capitalising on those assets. Quite the contrary – several autonomous military-Islamist organisations (MIA, MEI, GIA, FIDA, LIDD) emerged, breaking the FIS monopoly of those assets and even taking over the essential portion of them. However, it would be a mistake to declare that the FIS has lost its popularity during the war. And the Hamas-MSI party's share of votes in the presidential election of 16 November 1995 shows that an Islamist political alternative remains relevant.

On the other hand, the military regime has managed to survive the test of the *jihad* in an unexpected fashion. By liberalising the oil and gas economy and implementing a Structural Adjustment Plan under the direction of the IMF, it has been able to obtain new financial contributions which have been partially invested in the security policy. Having been in a weak position in 1992, the regime has been able to take advantage of the civil war better than its adversary the FIS. However, while it has succeeded over these years in reducing the chances of the FIS leaders coming to power, it is confronted even so by the emergence of a new actor thrown up by the war, whose ambition to overthrow the regime has not lost its edge – the new Moudjahid, now an Islamist guerrilla. He too has been able to profit from the war, as a means of acquiring wealth and prestige. The Islamist guerrillas, influenced by the model of success of the Moudjahidin of the liberation war, believe in the virtues of violence as a way to social progress.

Many of the Islamist armed groups established in the outskirts of Algiers have through the *jihad* accumulated funds that they have ploughed back into trade.

The military and the guerrillas, having succeeded in setting up an effective war economy, are settling down to a long-term struggle. So we do not think it wrong to say that the period we have been studying is no more than the preface to a conflict whose end is constantly receding into the distance. It is not a struggle for independence; in contrast to 1954-62, therefore, possible losers have no place of asylum waiting for them. That is why it is an illusion to imagine that if one of the protagonists gains supremacy, peace can return. The military, despite their capacity to keep going, remain confronted by permanent replenishment of the Islamist armed bands; as for those bands, when they achieve control over a suburb or a village they produce a reaction in the formation of self-defence groups or militias. So one effect of the situation in which neither side can win is the development of insecurity, which in turn is part of the dynamics of the war. And endless continuation of the war is accompanied at the social level by numerous effects which foreshadow new redrawing of the political landscape.

The revival of the regime's fortunes has not been accompanied by a return to civil peace. Certainly the violence is no longer on the massive scale typical between 1993 and 1995, when there were sometimes more than 500 victims per week.[1] Since 1997 most estimates are of less than 500 dead per month. Those figures back the regime's contention that the 'security situation' has improved. With this change in the war has come a change in the nature of the violence. From being political, violence has become 'general', following its own dynamics because it is freed from the initial causes of its outbreak.

Daniel Pécaut explains how 'generalised violence' in Colombia has followed its own logic, 'cutting across both social relations and those among individuals, affecting both the functioning of institutions and social values'; that violence 'no longer has to deal with any context external to it, and does not accept intervention by any third party...It appears as an everyday process, offering opportunities, encouraging accommodation, having its own norms and rules.'[2] In Algeria, with the increased number of actors the violence has steadily become unintelligible. The emergence of numerous paramilitary groups (militias, 'death squads', special units, etc.), and the constant splits among the Islamist armed groups, have changed the character of the war through imposition of other war logics. Paradoxically the risk of 'generalised violence', illustrated by the series of

---

[1] Rémy Leveau (ed.), *L'Algérie dans la guerre,* Brussels: Presses de Sciences-Po, 1995.

[2] Daniel Pécaut, 'De la banalité de la violence à la terreur. Le cas colombien', *Cultures et Conflits,* 24/25, p. 154.

massacres during the summer of 1997, brought about conditions for reconciliation within the army and among the AIS-FIS Islamists. That theme was at the heart of the campaign for the presidential election of 15 April 1999. The civil war has destroyed the political machinery of social control, and changes over the last seven years have consolidated the dynamics of violence.

War and social change

The consolidation of the civil war, due to the impossibility of victory for one side or the other, has been accompanied by social change. For those at the lower end of the scale, the war seems to have completely replaced *trabendo* (informal trade) as a means of making money. The development of the profession of arms, as practiced in state organisations (army, police, gendarmerie, special units) and parastatal ones (militias) and in private structures (armed Islamist groups, criminals, protection and security agencies), was in 1997 one of the major economic activities. The expansion of that profession from 1994 onwards has been due to a great extent to the profits and prestige that it brings. It has been able to attract a section of the youth, especially those confronted with joblessness and poverty, but the motives for enlisting, as we have shown, also include a desire for revenge and the general feeling of insecurity. In addition the demand for fighters by the military organisations, both state and Islamist ones, presents an opportunity to get a job and enjoy, thanks to the prestige of the '*klach*' (Kalashnikov), a certain respect.

If at that lower end the civil war represents an opportunity for social advancement, at the upper end of the social scale it has been a time of reallocation of privileges and increase in wealth.[3] While the *jihad* has made it possible for some young people with no resources to acquire some, the elites for their part have installed an 'economy of plunder' through economic liberalisation. Does the civil war represent for its 'shareholders' a period of transition from the Democratic and Popular Republic to the 'Containers Republic', to use the derogatory term employed (to indicate the preoccupation with profitable dealing in imported consumer goods) by some local organisations?[4] The civil war is a social war for the most deprived who have taken the road to the maquis or to the barracks in the hope of social advancement; but it is also, for some well-off people, an exceptional period for making fortunes.

[3] A process comparable to that of redefining of roles among merchants during the civil war in Somalia. See R. Marchal, *The Post Civil War Somali Business Class,* European Commission/ Somali Unit, September 1996.

[4] The Association des Amis de l'Initiative pour la Résistance Sociale (AIRS) states: 'Considering the *nouveaux riches,* senior civil servants and other men of straw, front companies have amassed very big fortunes.' Quoted by *La Nation,* no. 146, May 1996.

The profits from the war explain why the protagonists reject a political settlement. It is pertinent to note that, five years after the outbreak of the conflict, the three major parties that won the parliamentary elections of December 1991 (the FIS, FLN and FFS) backed the 'Appeal for Peace' launched in November 1996;[5] a fear of being marginalised to the benefit of war-oriented organisations 'addicted' to the dynamics of civil war no doubt explains that understanding among them. In fact the way the war has settled down into a routine suggests increasingly a style of life that continually reinforces the supremacy of the warrior over the political actor.

The warriors are characterised by a large number of 'looks' that have emerged during the conflict; they provide a structure for the protagonists' portrayals of themselves, and identify them. On the Islamist fighters' side the Gulbuddin Hekmatyar style, with Afghan outfit and flowing beard, is characteristic of the GIA guerrillas, while the AIS wear the clothing of the Cuban-type guerrilla: faded military uniform and beard. As for the 'fighters' of the autonomous armed bands in the outskirts of Algiers, they shave their heads, put on head-bands and do not necessarily wear beards. The same diversity exists among the the security forces. Besides the classical distinctions among soldier, gendarme and policeman there are those among 'Ninjas'; elite soldiers of the Groupe d'Intervention et de Surveillance (GIS) with black uniform and hood; policemen specialising in the anti-Islamist struggle who wear dark glasses, jeans and trainers, with caps back to front, and drive brand new vehicles; and plainclothes militiamen. Each of these types of fighter has a respected position in this war, and we have sought to show that the choice of one or the other has resulted more from the local context than from political motivation. These types of 'warrior', however varied, are inspired by a common war-oriented *imaginaire*, in which violence has the virtues of an instrument for advancement. In that sense the civil war has been accompanied by a reconstitution of social hierarchies, it takes the place of a means of redistributing wealth.

The figure of the 'Emir' illustrates the central hypothesis of this book. Like their predecessors, the 'Raïs', the 'Caïds' and the 'Colonels', the guerrilla 'Emirs' have achieved social promotion through *jihad*. Will they succeed in definitively replacing the military leaders and taking over political power for themselves? That is not certain, and as we have emphasised several times, one of the most probable outcomes of the civil war involves not the military victory of one of the warring parties, but their possible merger. However, this would be a long-term process, and we recalled in the introduction how the 'Chaouchs' only succeeded in supplanting the 'Djouads' (the warrior nobility of the east) in acquiring the status of Caïd (native official under the French) at the beginning of the twentieth century, through the long duration of the war of colonial

[5] On 9 November 1996 an 'Appeal for Peace' was launched by Algerian personalities of various political tendencies.

occupation (1832-71). Will the 'Emirs' be in a position to follow the example of the 'Chaouchs' and eventually occupy senior military positions and become the new managers of the Algerian state? It has emerged from this study that there is historical continuity linking them with earlier figures of social achievement in Algeria, those whom we have called 'political bandits' to emphasise their progress from outlaw to representative of the state. It is not, then, the collapse of the state that we are observing in the civil war, so much as its reconstruction, carried out by specific social actors.

A long war ahead?

Several factors suggest that the civil war is settling in for a long stay. In the first place, it generates wealth and prestige for the warring parties, despite the human tragedies which it causes. In addition, all the fighters are today prisoners of their war, because on both sides the brutalities that have been committed arouse fears of reprisals in case of defeat. Neither of the adversaries considers itself as being in a position of weakness. The military and political leaders of the regime have been declaring – wrongly – that the Islamist threat has been reduced to 'residual terrorism'. Accordingly they have considered that the problem to be resolved is that of the political conditions that led to the emergence of the Islamist parties. So they set about revising by referendum[6] – on 28 November 1996 – the Constitution of February 1989, so as to outlaw, among others, parties professing religious allegiance. It is not necessary to dwell on the political illusion lying behind that move. Obviously the Islamist guerillas, by declaring the *jihad* and settling down to a long struggle, are no longer following a logic of participation in the political system. What is worse, that process led the armed groups that had declared allegiance to the FIS to redouble their military efforts, as the chances of 're-legalisation' of their party receded to such a distance.

The redrawing of the political landscape which the regime carried out in 1996 through the revision of the Constitution, and its commitment to the holding of municipal and parliamentary elections in 1997, did not follow a logic of peace, but rather one of institutional consolidation of its hegemony. Despite that electoral agenda the guerrilla war continued to govern the daily life of the population – especially as the Islamist guerrillas, far from exhausting their tactics for overthrowing the government, had only just started them. We have emphasised at length the changes in the different guerrilla factions' war strategies, the contradiction between proclaimed intentions and practice. From those observations it has followed since

[6] On 28 November 1996 a draft revision of the Constitution was put to a referendum; it provided for creation of a second chamber (Conseil de la Nation) and banned political parties from basing themselves on a region or religion. The draft was accepted after voting whose results were contested by political parties as a whole.

1994 that none of the factions will be able to set up an Islamic state through the *jihad*. However, it would be wrong to conclude, as the Algerian military do, that the defeat of the guerrillas is assured. For until now the regime's strategic resources – oil and gas – have been partially spared by the Islamist guerrillas. As we have emphasised, that target seems to have held no interest for the district armed bands, but equally it has come to be seen by the 'Emirs' of the national guerrilla campaign as the 'sinews of war' for their enemy. With the completion of the project for export of natural gas to Morocco and on to Europe at the end of 1996, the military leaders are in a position to count on extra financial income[7] and thus to increase the capacity for repression. Should one then consider that the time factor, which at the beginning of the conflict was a winning card for the guerrillas in a strategy of exhausting the regime, has definitely shifted in the regime's favour in the course of the war? Probably, but on condition that the oil and gas sector continues to enjoy the relative security which it has had since the start of the *jihad*.

The fact must be faced that few factors are working towards ending the civil war. The social changes in progress are in the direction of expansion of the profession of arms, bringing with it increased privatisation of violence. The redrawing of the political landscape under way is part of a process of consolidation of the government's power, not national reconciliation. Assuming that no major change occurs – such as 're-legalisation' of the FIS or sabotage of the oil and gas sector – Algeria seems to be well and truly stuck in a 'war of attrition'. On that assumption, the war can be expected to end in the merger of the warring parties, perpetuating the model of reproduction of elites through violence and in violence. However, it is also possible that this conflict will show glimpses of the first signs of a democratic *imaginaire*.

From a war-oriented to a democratic imaginaire

Could the civil war give birth to a new model of reproduction of the political elites, or will it serve only to enrich a war-oriented *imaginaire* peopled with historical figures for whom violence was the way to social advancement? It goes without saying that a victory for the Islamist guerrillas would inevitably reinforce that *imaginaire*. Success for the 'Emirs' would definitely confirm the belief in the virtues of violence. And, far from breaking with the military regime born of independence, the 'Emirs' would only be its extension. Thus a future Islamic state would in its exercise of power inevitably resemble the 'Socialist state', that is, a political system governed by experience of the maquis, where shared friendships, wounds and

---

[7] To this structural increase in financial resources was added another, more dependent on circumstances, which was linked to the price of oil, in the region of $19 per barrel in 1996 ($16 in 1994), and the rising value of the dollar.

suffering would take the place of political competence. For through its violence the civil war – in the absence of political experience – has revealed the emptiness of Islamism as an original ideological movement; *jihad* has simply been poured into moulds already used by the nationalists during the war of liberation. In addition the conduct of the war between the Islamist guerrillas and the military has already aroused, among the political leaders of the FIS, a reaction of 'moderation'. That party no longer claims a monopoly of the religious field, and is committed to respecting the possibility of changing a government through elections; its demands, of a maximalist nature during the elections process, have been watered down in the course of the war.

This change applies just as much to the armed forces, guardians of the memory of the 'heroes' of the war of liberation – which seems three decades later like a war of appropriation, personal appropriation of the colonial heritage by some fighters. The fact must be noted that a myth is crumbling in the present civil war: the myth of national liberation. For whether it likes it or not, the Algerian army is taking on the role of the soldiers of the former colonial power. However, unlike the latter, it is not accused of maintaining a certain order – specifically, the colonial order – by violence, but of defending its interests alone. Could the double revelation of the emptiness of the utopias of Islamism as an original political alternative, and of the myth of the armed forces as the guarantors of the nation, lead to the beginnings of political modernity? Could the civil war be the foundation stone of a state based not on the ideology of a reified war of liberation, but on the acceptance of difference? In short, is the present confrontation capable of producing an *imaginaire* oriented towards democracy?

Among the factors capable of explaining Algeria's descent into civil war after the short experiment in multi-party democracy in 1990-1, that of the war-oriented *imaginaire* seems to us to be central. Our study has tried to show that the failure of Algeria's 'democratic transition' can be explained by belief in the virtues of violence as a means for keeping the ranks of the elites filled. Soldiers and Islamist guerrillas saw the rise of new political elements, emerging no longer from the maquis but from the legitimacy of election victory, as a big change in the process of producing leaders. At the gates of power in 1991, the FIS elected representatives became, through the civil war, real victims of the Islamist guerrillas[8] who see them as dangerous rivals. Violence is far from being limited to the struggle between the armed groups and the regime; within each coalition another war is going on, its aim being exclusive control over operations.

---

[8] The newspaper *La Nation* wrote: 'The FIS is showing that it is seriously committed to following the path of a political solution, which perhaps explains the physical liquidations carried out within the armed groups against activists suspected of loyalty to the banned party. Once again, the "warriors" are suspicious of the politicians and are making them pay dearly.' *La Nation*, 26 Dec.-1 Jan. 1996.

Obviously a definitive victory for the guerrilla Moudjahidin over the ex-FIS elected representatives would reinforce the war-oriented *imaginaire* at the expense of the democratic one. We have tried to show how such a process, if confirmed, would turn the adversaries – the regime and the Islamist guerrillas – into complementary enemies whose sole objective would be to continue the war until the complete marginalisation of the FIS political leaders.[9] The outcome of that process would then be the gradual assimilation of the Islamist guerrillas into the machinery of state, according to the model of revival of the Beylicate.

[9] The FIS overseas executive has written: 'Some may believe that the outcome of the war is its continuation until one of the two protagonists wins total victory, whereas the only outcome to the war is peace. The Front Islamique du Salut has, for its part, chosen the strategy of a peaceful political outcome, and is proposing solutions making possible rapid progress from war to peace.' *Pour une stratégie de sortie de crise en Algérie,* May 1997

BIBLIOGRAPHY

BOOKS

Addi, Lahouari, *L'Algérie et la démocratie. Pouvoir et crise du politique dans l'Algérie contemporaine,* Paris: La Découverte.

Ageron, Charles-Robert, *Politiques coloniales au Maghreb,* Paris: Presses Universitaves de France (PUF), 1973.

—(ed.), *La guerre d'Algérie et les Algeriens, 1954-1962,* Paris: Armand Colin, 1997.

Ahdjouj, Amrane, *Algérie: Etat, pouvoir et société: 1962-1965,* Paris: Arcantère, 1991.

Al-Ahnaf, Moustapha, Bernard Botiveau and Franck Frégosi, *L'Algérie par ses islamistes,* Paris: Karthala, 1991.

Al-Ashmawy, Saïd Muhammad, *L'islamisme contre l'islam,* Paris: La Découverte, 1989.

Amin, Samir, *Les enjeux stratégiques en Méditerranée,* Paris: L'Harmattan, 1992.

Amrane, Djamila, *Les femmes algériennes dans la guerre,* Paris: Plon, 1991.

Arkoun, Mohamed, *L'Islam, morale et politique,* Paris: Desclée de Brouwer, 1986.

Ayyachi, H., *The Algerian Islamists between Power and Arms* [in Arabic], Algiers Dar el Hikma, 1991.

—, *The Islamic Movement in Algeria* [in Arabic], Casablanca: 'Uyun, 1993.

Badie, Bertrand, *Les deux Etats. Pouvoir et société en Occident et en terre d'Islam,* Paris; Fayard, 1987.

—, *L'Etat importé essai sur l'occidentalisation de l'ordre politique,* Paris: Fayard, 1992.

Balandier, Georges, *Anthropologie politique,* Paris: PUF, 1978.

Barkey, Karen, *Bandits and Bureaucrats: The Ottoman Route to State Centralization,* Ithaca, NY: Cornell University Press, 1994.

Bayart, Jean-François, *L'Etat en Afrique. La politique du ventre,* Paris: Fayard, 1989.

—(ed.), *La réinvention du capitalisme,* Paris: Karthala, 1994.

—(ed.), *Religion et modernité politique en Afrique Noire. Dieu pour tous et chacun pour soi,* Paris: Karthala, 1993.

—, *L'illusion identitaire,* Paris: Fayard, 1996.

—, Achille Mbembe and Comi Toulabor, *Le politique par le bas en Afrique Noire. Contribution à une problématique de la démocratie,* Paris: Karthala, 1992.

—, Stephen Ellis and Béatrice Hibou, *La Criminalisation de l'Etat en Afrique,* Brussels: Complexe, 1997.

Benissad, Hocine, *Algérie. Restructurations et réformes économiques (1979-1993),* Algiers: OPU, 1994.

Bennoune, Mahfoud, *The Making of Contemporary Algeria, 1830-1987: Colonial Upheavals and Post-Independence Development,* Cambridge University Press, 1990.

253

Bernard, Chantal (ed.), *Nouvelles logiques marchandes au Maghreb*, Paris: Ed. du CNRS, 1991.

Berque, Augustin, *Ecrits sur l'Algérie*, Paris: Edisud, 1986.

Berque, Jacques, *Ulémas, fondateurs, insurgés du Maghreb. 17ᵉ siècle*, Paris: Sindbad, 1982.

—, *Le maghreb entre deux guerres*, Paris: Seuil, 1969.

—, *L'intérieur du Maghreb: XVᵉ-XIXᵉ siècle*, Paris: Gallimard, 1978.

Beydoun, Ahmad, *Le Liban: itinéraires dans une guerre incivile*, Paris: Karthala, 1993.

Botiveau, Bernard, *Loi islamique et droit dans les sociétés arabes. mutations des systèmes juridiques du Moyen-Orient*, Paris: Karthala, 1994.

Boudon, Raymond, *La place du désordre*, Paris: PUF, 1984.

Brahimi, Brahim, *Le pouvoir, la presse et les intellectuels en Algérie*, Paris: L'Harmattan, 1990.

Braudel, Fernand, *Autour de la Méditerranée*, Paris: Ed. de Fallois, 1996.

—, *La Méditerranée et le monde méditerranéen à l'époque de Philippe II*, Paris: A. Colin, vols 2 and 3, new edn 1990.

—, *Civilisation matérielle, économie et capitalisme, XVᵉ-XVIIIᵉ siècle*, Paris: A. Colin, new edn 1990, vols 2 and 3.

Burgat, François, *L'islamisme au Maghreb*, Paris: Payot, new edn 1995.

—, *L'islamisme en face*, Paris: La Découverte, 1995.

Burke, Edmund, and Ira M. Lapidus (eds), *Islam, Politics and Social Movements*, London: I.B. Tauris, 1988.

Cahen, Claude, *L'Islam des origines au début de l'Empire ottoman*, Paris: Hachette, 1995.

Camau, Michel (ed.), *Changements politiques au Maghreb*, Paris: Ed. du CNRS, 1991.

Carlier, Omar, *Entre nation et jihad. Histoire sociale des radicalismes algériens*, Paris: Presses de la FNSP, 1995.

Carré, Olivier, *L'utopie islamique dans l'Orient arabe*, Paris: La Découverte, 1991.

—, *L'Islam laïque. Le retour à la Grande Tradition*, Paris: A. Colin, 1993.

Chalabi, El-Hadi, *L'Algérie, l'Etat et le droit: 1979-1988*, Paris: Arcantère, 1992.

Chaliand, Gérard and Julie Minces, *L'Algérie, bilan d'une révolution nationale*, Paris: Maspéro, 1972.

Charef, Abed, *Algérie, le grand dérapage*, Paris: La Tour d'Aigres, 1994.

Clancy-Smith, J.A., *Rebel and Saint: Muslim Notables, Populist Protest, Colonial Encounters: Algeria and Tunisia, 1800-1904*, Berkeley, CA: University of California Press, 1994.

Claverie, Pierre, *Lettres et messages d'Algérie*, Paris: Karthala, 1996.

Colonna, Fanny, *Les versets de l'invincibilité. Permanence et changements religieux dans l'Algérie contemporaine*, Paris: Presses de Sciences Po, 1995.

— and Zakya Daoud, *Etre marginal au Maghreb*, Paris: Ed. du CNRS, 1993.

Corvisier, André, *La guerre, essais historiques*, Paris: PUF, 1995.

Cote, Marc, *L'Algérie ou l'espace retourné*, Paris: Flammarion, 1988.

—, *L'Algérie,* Paris: Masson/Armand Colin, 1996.

Crépon, Pierre, *Les religions et la guerre,* Paris: A. Michel, 1991.

Décobert, Christian, *Le mendiant et le combattant. L'institution de l'islam,* Paris: Seuil, 1991.

Deheuvels, Luc-Willy, *Islam et pensée contemporaine en Algérie. La revue Al-Asâla 1971-1981,* Paris: Ed. du CNRS, 1992.

Delmas, Philippe, *Le bel avenir de la guerre,* Paris: Gallimard, 1995.

Djaït, Hichem, *La grande discorde. Religion et politique dans l'Islam des origines,* Paris: Gallimard, 1989.

Djedjiga, Imache and Inès Nour, *Algériennes entre islam et islamisme,* Aix-en-Provence: Edisud, 1994.

Dobry, Michel, *Sociologie des crises politiques. La dynamique des mobilisations multisectorielles,* Paris: Presses de la FNSP, 1992.

Entelis, John-Paul, and Ph.C. Naylor, *State and Society in Algeria,* Boulder, CO: Westview Press, 1992.

El Kenz, Ali, *L'Algérie et la modernité,* Dakar: Codesria, 1988.

Establet, Colette, *Etre caïd dans l'Algérie coloniale: tribus des Nemenchas, 1851-1912,* Paris: Ed. du CNRS, 1992.

Etienne, Bruno, *Abdelkader. Isthme des isthmes,* Paris: Hachette, 1994.

Fisher, Godfrey, *Barbary Legend: War, Trade and Piracy in North Africa (1415-1830),* Oxford University Press, 1957.

Frémeaux, Jacques, *Les bureaux arabes dans l'Algérie de la conquête,* Paris: Denoël, 1993.

Freund, Julien, *Utopie et violence,* Paris: Rivière, 1978.

Furley, Oliver (ed.), *Conflict in Africa,* London: I.B. Tauris, 1995.

Gadant, Monique, *Le nationalisme algérien et les femmes,* Paris: L'Harmattan, 1995.

Gaïd, Mouloud, *L'Algérie sous les Turcs,* Algiers: MTE, 1974.

Geffray, Christian, *La cause des armes au Mozambique,* Paris: Karthala, 1990.

Gellner, Ernest, *Muslim Society,* Cambridge University Press, 1981.

John Waterbury (eds), *Patrons and Clients in Mediterranean Societies,* London: Duckworth, Centre for Mediterranean Studies, 1977.

Ghalioun, Burhan, *Le malaise arabe. L'Etat contre la nation,* Paris: La Découverte, 1991.

Goumeziane, Smaïl, *Le mal algérien. Économie politique d'une transition inachevée,* Paris: Fayard, 1994.

Grandguillaume, Gilbert, *Arabisation et politique culturelle au Maghreb,* Paris: Maisonneuve et Larose, 1983.

Grimaud, Nicole, *La politique extérieure de l'Algérie: 1962-78,* Paris: Karthala, 1984.

Guillard, Pierre, *Ce fleuve qui nous sépare. Lettre à l'imam Ali Benhadj,* Paris: Loysel, 1994.

Gurr, Ted Robert, *Why Men Rebel,* Princeton University Press, 1970.

Hachemi, Fawzi Oussedik, *Sheikh Mahfuz Nahnah* [in Arabic], Algiers: Dar al intifida li-l-nashr wa-l-tawzi, 1991.

Hamoumou, Mohand, *Et ils sont devenus harkis,* Paris: Fayard, 1993.

Harbi, Mohammed, *Le FLN, mirage et réalité. Des origines à la prise du pouvoir (1945-1962)*, Paris: Jeune Afrique, 1980.

—, *1954. La guerre commence en Algérie*, Brussels: Complexe, 1984.

—, *L'islamisme dans tous ses états*, Paris: Arcantère, 1991.

—, *L'Algérie et son destin. Croyants ou citoyens*, Paris: Arcantère, 1992.

Hassan, *Algérie. Histoire d'un naufrage*, Paris: Seuil, 1996.

Hibou, Béatrice, *L'Afrique est-elle protectionniste? Les chemins buissonniers de la libéralisation extérieure*, Paris: Karthala, 1996.

Hidouci, Ghazi, *Algérie, la libération inachevée*, Paris: La Découverte, 1995.

Hobsbawm, Eric, *Primitive Rebels: Studies in Archaic Forms of Social Movement in the 19th and 20th Centuries*, Manchester University Press, 1959.

—, *Bandits*, London: Weidenfeld and Nicolson, 1969.

Horne, Alistair, *A Savage War of Peace: Algeria, 1954-1962*, Harmondsworth: Penguin, 1977.

Hourani, Albert, *Histoire des peuples arabes*, Paris: Seuil, 1993.

Howard, M., *La guerre dans l'histoire de l'Occident*, Paris: Fayard, 1976.

Hussein, Djamel ed Din, *Algeria over the Volcano* (in Arabic), Cairo: Mawalif, 1992.

Julien, Charles-André, *Histoire de l'Algérie contemporaine. La conquête et les débuts de la colonisation (1827-1871)*, Paris: PUF, vol. 1, new edn 1986.

Julien, Charles-André, *Histoire de l'Algérie contemporaine (1871-1954)*, Paris: PUF, vol. 2, 1979.

Kadache, Mohamed, *L'Algérie durant la période ottomane*, Algiers: OPU, 1992.

Kepel, Gilles *Le Prophète et Pharaon. Aux sources des mouvements islamistes*, Paris: Seuil, new edn 1993.

—, (ed.), *Les politiques de Dieu*, Paris: Seuil, 1993.

—, (ed.), *Exils et royaumes. Les appartenances au monde arabo-musulman aujourd'hui*, Paris: Presses de la FNSP, 1994.

—, *A l'Ouest d'Allah*, Paris: Seuil, 1995.

Khelladi, Aïssa, *Les islamistes algériens face au pouvoir*, Algiers: Alfa, 1992.

Khosrokhavar, Farhad, *L'islamisme et la mort. Le martyre révolutionnaire en Iran*, Paris: L'Harmattan, 1995.

Labat, Séverine, *Les islamistes algériens. Entre les urnes et le maquis*, Paris: Seuil, 1995.

Labter, Lazhari, *Journalistes algériens. Entre le bâillon et les balles*, Paris: L'Harmattan, 1995.

Lacoste, Yves, André Prenant and André Nouschi, *L'Algérie passé et présent*, Paris: Souida, 1980.

Lamchichi, Abderrahim, *L'islamisme en Algérie*, Paris: L'Harmattan, 1992.

Lavenue, Jean-Jacques, *Algérie: la démocratie interdite*, Paris: L'Harmattan, 1993.

Le Bot, Yvon, *Violence de la modernité en Amérique Latine. Indianité, société et pouvoir*, Paris: Karthala, 1994.

Leca, Jean and Jean-Claude Vatin, *L'Algérie politique. Institutions et régimes*, Paris: Presses de Sciences Po, 1975.

Leveau, Rémy, *Le Sabre et le turban*, Paris: F. Bourin, 1993.

— (ed.), *L'Algérie dans la guerre*, Brussels: Complexe, 1995.

Lewis, Bernard, *Le retour de l'islam. Essais traduits de l'Anglais par Tina Jolas et Denise Paulme*, Paris: Gallimard, 1985.

Luciani, Giacomo and Hazem Beblawi, *The Rentier State*, London: Croom Helm, 1987.

Luciani, Giacomo, *The Arab State*, London: Routledge, 1990.

Mahfoudh, Amine, *Algeria between the Military and the Fundamentalists* (in Arabic), Cairo, no publisher, 1992.

Malek, Redha, *Tradition et révolution. L'enjeu de la modernité en Algérie et dans L'Islam*, Paris: Sindbad, 1993.

Maupassant, Guy de, *Ecrits sur le Maghreb*, Paris: Minerve, new edn 1991.

Merad, Ali, *Le réformisme musulman en Algérie de 1925 à 1940. Essai d'histoire religieuse et sociale*, Paris: Mouton, 1967.

Morizot, Jean, *L'Aurès ou le mythe de la montagne rebelle*, Paris: L'Harmattan, 1991.

Nouschi, André, *L'Algérie amère, 1914-1994*, Paris: Ed. de la MSH, 1995.

Provost, Lucile, *La seconde guerre d'Algérie. Le quiproquo franco-algérien*, Paris: Flammarion, 1996.

Rarrbo, Kamel, *L'Algérie et sa jeunesse. Marginalisation et désarroi culturel*, Paris: L'Harmattan, 1995.

Raymond, André, *Les grandes villes arabes à l'époque ottomane*, Paris: Sindbad, 1985.

Redjala, Ramdane, *L'opposition en Algérie depuis 1962*, Paris: L'Harmattan, 1988.

Rodinson, Maxime, *L'islam. Politique et croyance*, Paris: Fayard, 1995.

—, *Islam et capitalisme*, Paris: Seuil, 1966.

Rouadjia, Ahmed, *Les frères et la mosquée, enquête sur le mouvement islamiste en Algérie*, Paris: Karthala, 1990.

—, *Grandeur et décadence de l'état algérien*, Paris: Karthala, 1994.

Rouquié, Alain, *Guerre et paix en Amérique Latine*, Paris: Seuil, 1982.

Roy, Olivier, *L'Afghanistan: Islam et modernité politique*, Paris: Seuil, 1985.

—, *L'échec de l'islam politique*, Paris: Esprit/Seuil, 1992.

Saadi, Saïd, *Algérie, l'heure de la vérité*, Paris: Flammarion, 1996.

Salamé, Ghassan (ed.), *Démocraties sans démocrates. Politiques d'ouverture dans le mode arabe*, Paris: Fayard, 1994.

Santucci, Jean-Claude, and Habib El Malki (eds), *Etat et développement dans le monde arabe. Crises et mutations au Maghreb*, Paris: Ed. du CNRS, 1990.

Sivan, Emmanuel, *Mythes politiques arabes*, Paris: Fayard, 1995.

—, *Radical Islam, Medieval Theology and Modern Politics*, New Haven, CT: Yale University Press, 1985.

Skocpol, Theda, *Etats et révolutions sociales*, Paris: Fayard, 1985.

Spencer, William, *Algiers in the Age of the Corsairs*, Norman: University of Oklahoma Press, 1976.

Stora, Benjamin, *Histoire de l'Algérie depuis l'indépendance*, Paris: La Découverte, 1994.

Tilly, Charles, *From Mobilization to Revolution*, Reading, MA: Addison Wesley, 1978.

Touati, Amine, *Algérie. Les islamistes à l'assaut du pouvoir*, Paris: L'Harmattan, 1995.

Tridi, Rachid, *L'Algérie en quelques maux ou l'autopsie d'une anomie*, Paris: L'Harmattan, 1992.

Valensi, Lucette, *Le Maghreb avant la prise d'Alger*, Paris: Flammarion, 1969.

Vatin, Jean-Claude and Philippe Lucas, *L'Algérie des anthropologues*, Paris: Maspéro, 1975.

—, *L'Algérie politique. Histoire et société*, Paris: Presses de la FNSP, 1983.

Weber, Max, *General Economic History,* tr. Frank H. Knight, New York: Collier Books, 1961.

—, *The Sociology of Religion,* tr. Ephraim Dischoff, London: Methuen, 1966.

—, *Economy and Society*, 2 vols, ed. G. Roth and C. Wittich, Berkeley: University of California Press, 1978.

Wievorka, Michel, *Sociétés et terrorisme*, Paris: Fayard, 1988.

Yefsah, Abdelkader, *Le processus de légitimation du poivoir militaire et la construction de l'Etat en Algérie,* Paris: Anthropos, 1982.

Zartman, William, *Collapsed State: the Disintegration and Restoration of Legitimate Authority*, Boulder, CO: Lynne Rienner, 1995.

— (ed.), *Polity and Society in Contemporary North Africa*, Boulder, CO: Westview Press, 1993.

Zimmermann, Ekkart, *Political Violence, Crises and Revolutions: Theories and Research,* Cambridge: Schenkman, 1983.

ARTICLES

Arkoun, Mohamed, 'Pour une islamologie appliquée', published by collective Le Mal de Voir, Paris, 1976, pp. 167-87.

Bayart, Jean-François, 'Le politique par le bas en Afrique Noire. Questions de méthode', *Politique africaine*, January 1981, pp. 53-82.

Belhimer, Ammar, 'Les groupes armés de l'opposition islamique', *Les Cahiers de l'Orient*, 1st quarter 1995, no. 36-37, pp. 61-92.

Benkheira, Hocine, 'Ivrognerie, religiosité et sport dans une ville algérienne (Oran), 1962-1983', *Archives de sciences sociales des religions,* Jan.-March 1985, no. 59/1, pp. 131-51.

Berque, Augustin, 'Esquisse d'une histoire de la seigneurie algérienne', *Revue de la Méditerranée*, 1949, no. 7, pp. 18-34.

Bigo, Didier, 'Les conflits post-bipolaires. Dynamiques et caractéristiques', *Cultures et conflits,* 1992-93, no. 8, pp. 3-14.

Bourdieu, Pierre, 'Une interprétation de la théorie de la religion selon M. Weber', *Archives européenes de sociologie*, 1971, no. 12 (1), pp. 3-21.

Braud, Philippe, 'La violence politique. Repères et problèmes', *Cultures et conflits,* 1993, no. 9-10, pp. 13-42.

Braudel, Fernand, 'Faillite de l'aristocratie indigène en Algérie (1830-1900)' in
F. Braudel, *Autour de la Méditerranée*, Paris: De Fallois, 1996, pp. 151-4.

Carlier, Omar, 'De l'islahisme à l'islamisme: la thérapie politico-religieuse du FIS',
Cahiers d'étude africaines, 1993, vol. XXXII (2), no. 126, pp. 185-219.

Chazel, François, 'Les ruptures révolutionnaires' in M. Grawitz and J. Leca (eds),
Traité de science politique, Paris: PUF, vol. 2, pp. 635-86.

Corm, Georges, 'La réforme économique algérienne: une réforme mal aimée',
Maghreb-Machrek, 1993, no. 139, pp. 9-27.

Cresti, François, 'Alger à la période turque: observation et hypothèses sur sa population', *Revue de l'Occident musulman et de la Méditerranée*, 1987, no. 44, pp.
77-109.

Derradji, A., 'The Algerian Traditional Guerrilla Resistance', *Arab Review*, vol. 3
no. 2, autumn 1994, pp. 13-21.

Fardeheb, Abderrahmane, 'Crise, contradictions et économie de marché en Algérie',
Issue, 1993, no. 44, pp. 77-109.

Frégosi, Franck, 'Fondamentalisme islamique et relations internationales. Le cas
du FIS', *Trimestre du Monde*, 1st quarter 1994, pp. 29-40.

Harbi, Mohammed, 'L'interruption du processes électoral. Respect ou déni de la
constitution?', *Maghreb-Machrek*, Jan.-March 1992, no. 135, pp. 145-54.

Khiari, Farid, 'Les modes de domination et leur reproduction. Approche des mécani-
smes de pouvoir dans le pachalik d'Alger de 1570 à 1670', *Annuaire de l'Afrique
du Nord, 1992*, no. 31, 1994, pp. 347-88.

Leca, Jean, 'Etat et société en Algérie' in Bassma Kodmani-Darwish (ed.), *Maghreb:
les années de transition*, Paris, Masson, 1990, pp. 17-58.

—, 'La démocratisation dans le monde arabe. Incertitude, vulnérabilité et légitimité.
Un essai de conceptualisation et quelques hypothèses' in Ghassan Salamé (ed.),
Démocraties sans démocrates, Paris: Fayard, 1994, pp. 35-95.

—and Rémy Leveau, 'Démocratie, politiques économiques et demandes sociales',
Maghreb-Machrek, Jan.-March 1993, no. 139, pp. 3-8.

Leveau, Rémy, 'Anatomie d'un coup d'état', *Esprit*, March-April 1992, pp. 90-4.

Marchal, Roland, 'Les temps de la violence et de l'identité' in D.-C. Martin (ed.),
Cartes d'identité. Comment dit-on 'nous' en politique? Paris: Presses de la FNSP,
1994, pp. 185-205.

Mbembe, Achille, 'Pouvoir, violence et accumulation', *Politique africaine*, 1990,
no. 39, pp. 7-24.

Moussaoui, Abderrahmane, 'De la violence au djihâd', *Annales, ESC*, no. 6, 1994,
pp. 1315-33.

Pfeirer, Karen, 'Economic Liberalization in the 1980's in Comparative Pers
pective' in John Entelis and Philip Neylor (eds.), *State and Society in Algeria*,
Boulder, CO: Westview Press, 1992, pp. 97-116.

Prochaska, David, 'Fire on the Mountain: Resisting Colonialism in Algeria' in Donald
Crummey (ed.), *Banditry, Rebellion and Social Protest in Africa*, London: James
Currey, 1986, pp. 229-52.

Roberts, Hugh, 'Doctrinaire Economics and Political Opportunism in the Strategy
of Algerian Islamism' in J. Ruedy (ed.), *Islamism and Secularism in North Africa*, Basingstoke: Macmillan, 1994, pp. 123-47.

—, 'The Islamists, the Democratic Opposition and the Search for a Political Solution in Algeria', *Review of African Political Economy*, 1995, vol. 22, no. 64, pp. 237-44.

Taïbouni, Abdelkader, 'Réformes économiques et ajustement structurel en Algérie', *Les Cahiers Alternatives Sud*, 1995, vol. II no. 3, pp. 81-133.

Tilly, Charles, 'War Making and State Making as Organized Crime' in Peter B. Evans, D. Rueschmeyer and T. Skocpol (eds), *Bringing the State Back In*, Cambridge University Press, 1984, pp. 169-91.

Vatin, Jean-Claude, 'Religion et Etat. Puissance d'Etat et résistance islamique en Algérie', XIXᵉ-XXᵉ siècles. Approche mécanique' in E. Gellner and J.-C. Vatin (eds), *Islam et politique au Maghreb*, Paris: Ed. du CNRS, 1981, pp. 243-69.

Von Sivers, Peter, 'Rural Uprisings as Political Movements in Colonial Algeria, 1851-1914' in E. Burke and I. Lapidus (eds), *Islam, Politics and Social Movements*, London, I.B. Tauris, 1988, pp. 35-59.

JOURNAL SPECIAL ISSUES

Confluences: 'Maghreb, la démocratie entre parenthèses', 1992, no. 3.

Peuples méditerranéens: 'Algérie: vers l'Etat islamique', 1991, no. 52-53.

Confluences Méditerranée: 'Comprendre l'Algérie', 1994, no. 11.

Esprit: 'Avec l'Algérie', January 1995.

Revue du monde musulman et de la Méditerranée: 'Algérie incertaine', 1993, no. 65.

Les Temps Modernes: 'Algérie: la guerre des frères', Jan.-Feb. 1995.

NEWSPAPERS AND PERIODICALS

El Alem el Siyasi (The Political World, independent fortnightly newspaper in Arabic).

El Mounqidh ('The Saviour', fortnightly FIS newspaper, in Arabic, 1989-91).

La Nation (weekly in French, independent).

El Masaa (weekly newspaper of Hamas-MSI, in Arabic).

El Watan (daily in French, independent).

El Moudjahid (government daily, in French).

La Tribune (daily tending to the government side, in French).

Liberté (daily in French, close to the RCD).

El Djeich (monthly of the Ministry of Defence, in French and Arabic).

Algérie Confidentiel (fortnightly in French).

GUERRILLA PUBLICATIONS

GIA

Leaflets placarded on the mosques of Algeria.

Al Raya islamiya ('The Islamic Standard'), weekly (?) in Arabic.

En Ansar (printed in Europe), weekly in Arabic which publishes GIA communiqués as well as 'news of the *jihad*' (military operations).

El Djihad (printed in Pakistan), weekly or fortnightly which publishes GIA communiqués. Communiqués are published on the Internet and in *Al Hayat*.

Videocassettes on life in the maquis, distributed in Algeria and Europe.

AIS/FIS

A collection of letters from the AIS/FIS entitled *Mots de vérité: à ceux qui se sentent concernés*, April 1995.

El Mounqidh, fortnightly in Arabic and French; assumed the title of the FIS newspaper banned in 1992.

El Tabsira, weekly in Arabic.

El Ribat, weekly in Arabic.

The Enlightenment, weekly in English.

La Cause, weekly in French and Arabic.

El Fath el moubine, weekly (?) in Arabic.

MEI

Traité de la désobéissance civile, produced in 1991 by S. Makhloufi, 'Emir' of the MEI.

INDEX